Love Your Neighbor
and Yourself

ELLIOT N. DORFF

Love Your Neighbor and Yourself

A JEWISH APPROACH TO MODERN PERSONAL ETHICS

5763   2003
The Jewish Publication Society
Philadelphia

The Jewish Publication Society
2100 Arch Street, 2nd floor
Philadelphia, PA 19103

Composition by Book Design Studio

Manufactured in the United States of America

03 04 05 06 07 08 09 10   10 9 8 7 6 5 4 3 2 1

Library of Congress Cataloging-in-Publication Data

Dorff, Elliot N.
  Love your neighbor and yourself : a Jewish approach to modern personal ethics / Elliot N. Dorff.— 1st ed.
    p. cm.
  ISBN 0-8276-0759-8
  1. Ethics, Jewish. 2. Conduct of life. 3. Jewish way of life. 4. Philosophy, Jewish. I. Title.
  BJ1285.D67 2003
  296.3'6—dc21
                              2003004773

In gratitude to our extended family,
Close friends, near and far,
Models of morality and caring,
Whose love enriches our lives.

"Love your neighbor as yourself."

Leviticus 19:18

Contents

Preface

I HAVE BEEN MOST FORTUNATE IN FINDING THE JEWISH PUBLICATION Society to publish three of my books on Jewish ethics. The first was *Matters of Life and Death: A Jewish Approach to Modern Medical Ethics* (1998). The second was *To Do the Right and the Good: A Jewish Approach to Jewish Social Ethics* (2002). And now, with this book, I explore the import of the Jewish tradition for matters of personal behavior. I only hope that readers of these books will find our collaboration as productive and happy as we have!

Why a book on *personal* ethics? In some ways, I suppose, the answer is obvious. We are, after all, individuals, with deep concerns for our own welfare and serious questions about our interactions with others. Therefore, in addition to our interest in the welfare of our body (the book on medical ethics) and our society (the book on social ethics), we want to know how we should conceive of ourselves and others and how we should conduct ourselves in our private lives and in our interactions with others. Only those who would deny that the realm of ethics has anything to do with their private behavior and their relationships with other individuals would doubt the need for thinking seriously about the matters addressed in this book.

Why a book on *Jewish* personal ethics? As I explain in the first chapter, one of the things that religions do is to provide us with a picture of who we are and who we ought to be. Secular philosophies like Western liberalism, Marxism, and existentialism do that too, but religions are more often connected with a specific community of people who try to live by their religion's view of the world through rituals and moral rules, stories, and ideals. The various religions and secular philosophies of the world may overlap in some respects, but they each present ideas of who we are and who we should strive to be that are *different* in degree or kind from other views. Specific moral norms, then, are rooted in these larger pictures. Thus it makes sense to look at a Jewish view of personal ethics because Judaism has a distinctive way of understanding our nature, our role in life, and what we should strive to be, both as individuals and as members of a community.

In fact, it is more complicated than that, for one cannot reasonably speak about only one Jewish way of looking at almost anything. If we Jews are anything, we are obstreperous. One of our distinctive traits—dating back to Abraham questioning God about the justice of destroying all of Sodom and Gemorrah if there were any righteous people living there to all the arguments on virtually every page of the Talmud—is our urge to question anyone and anything. This is so ingrained in us that we Jews find it hard to imagine that most other religious traditions expect adherents to be much more passive in their acceptance of the religion's doctrines. But all that questioning inevitably means that there are multiple approaches that Jews have taken to many issues—so much so that sometimes we cannot accurately speak of *a* Jewish approach to a given issue at all and must just say that Jews disagree about it.

In many cases, though, Jewish questioning does not rise to the level of making the tradition incoherent, and in the first chapter I describe some of the main features of at least many Jewish perspectives on life. Readers need to be forewarned, however, that throughout the book I present what I take to be an authentic reading and application of the Jewish tradition but surely not the only one. I therefore take care to use *judgment* in assessing how the tradition should be best applied to modern circumstances, by providing arguments from the tradition and from modern sources and circumstances to *justify* my reading of the tradition and by arguing against alternative readings of the tradition when they are common ("The best defense is a good offense"). Thus, although my presentation of Judaism's personal ethics in these pages is definitely not the only possible way of understanding Judaism's import for individuals in modern times, I provide a serious, deeply Jewish, and, I hope, wise application of the Jewish tradition to these matters.

The first chapter in this book, then, describes some of the distinctive ways in which Judaism approaches matters of ethics. In the opening chapters of my previous two books, I delineated the fundamental convictions of Judaism that shape medical ethics and social ethics, with some comparisons to American secular ethics and Christianity to illustrate that Judaism's view is not obvious or even entirely shared by other intelligent, moral people who follow other systems of thought and action. In this book the first chapter approaches the distinctiveness of Judaism's worldview by describing some of the primary features of a Jewish approach to ethics (in the first part of the chapter) and morals (in the second part). I return to such philosophical matters in the Appendix; but because many readers of this book are primarily interested in addressing specific moral issues that affect their lives, I deliberately made the first chapter as concrete as possible and left the more abstract issues of how Judaism goes about defining morals and inculcating them into us for the Appendix.

In Chapter Two, I begin with the individual as such. Our first concern is to retain our own individual identity and integrity, and to do that we need privacy. This chapter, then, first describes the practical, moral, and theological reasons why we do and should value privacy, and then it considers two threats to privacy: namely, intrusion and disclosure. These dangers have become ever more worrisome in our time, as the Internet and other technological devices have invaded our space, both literally and figuratively, more pervasively than ever before. Big Brother is watching us in ways that George Orwell's *1984* never imagined. At the same time, employers have a right to ensure that employees are doing their work, and the government has not only the right but also the duty to ensure our safety. How, then, should we balance our concern with privacy with these conflicting rights and duties?

Once having looked at the individual as such, I consider in Chapter Three our most intimate relationships with others. This chapter grew out of discussions on sexual activity that I first conducted with teenagers at Camp Ramah in California, during the sixteen years that I was Rabbi-in-Residence there; then it took a major leap forward when I was embroiled, with the rest of the members of the Conservative Movement's Committee on Jewish Law and Standards, in the heated discussions in 1991 and 1992 about homosexuality. During those discussions, I pointed out that whatever we rabbis said about homosexuality would rightly fall on deaf ears, because gays and lesbians could justly say that heterosexuals should first figure out the Jewish norms that govern them before pontificating about what gays and lesbians should do. I suggested that we form a Commission on Human Sexuality, which the Rabbinical Assembly ultimately did. One product of that committee, which met from 1992 to 1994, was the *Rabbinic Letter on Human Intimacy,* which I wrote together with the other members of the commission. Most of Chapter Three is based on that letter, but while that was the joint position of the commission and while my own opinion closely allies with it, the chapter is completely my own reading of the tradition. This point is especially important in the sections on sex outside of marriage and on homosexuality, where I take a somewhat different approach from the one officially adopted by the commission.

Sex sometimes produces children, and so Chapter Four treats the interactions between parents and children. In addition to presenting the primary Jewish sources on those relationships, this chapter focuses on two serious issues that modern Jews face more commonly than our ancestors did: namely, caring for elderly parents who live into their eighties, nineties, and beyond and, second, paying for the Jewish education of one's children.

While most families have those problems, some families have considerably worse ones, because one or more members of the family are the perpetrators or victims of some form of abuse. Chapter Five, then, deals with family violence of all sorts: physical abuse, sexual abuse, verbal abuse. It discusses how this manifests itself in the beating of spouses, parents, and children; in unwanted and unhealthy sexual advances; and in demeaning verbal attacks. After describing classical Jewish views on these matters, the chapter deals with two hard questions: How can and should victims and those who witness abuse respond to it? How do we determine that abuse has occurred while still maintaining Judaism's presumption of innocence? The chapter closes with some suggestions for preventing abuse in the first place.

Chapter Six speaks of forgiveness. In *To Do the Right and the Good*, I addressed the question of how communities might assess a request for forgiveness and then act on it; here, I focus on individuals who have wronged others or have been wronged themselves. Unlike many forms of Christianity, the Jewish tradition does *not* assume that we are automatically and immediately forgiven whenever we do something wrong. On the contrary, as Judaism presents it, forgiveness must be *earned*. This chapter describes why we are reticent to forgive when we have been wronged, why we want forgiveness when we have wronged others, and the steps people should take to warrant forgiveness. It also talks about when forgiveness should not be granted and the differences between forgiveness and reconciliation.

Chapter Seven speaks of hope. For all its insistence on justice and earning forgiveness, Judaism is ultimately a very positive religion. The anthem of the State of Israel is *Hatikvah*, "The Hope," and the Jewish tradition embodies many forms of hope for a better future. The chapters of this book on concrete moral issues, then, closes with a chapter on hope—on what we can and should hope for and how we should live in order to realize our hopes.

Finally, the Appendix discusses some very important issues in Jewish moral theory. It describes the features of religion that encourage *immorality* to make it clear that the relationship between religion and ethics is not always positive. Then it discusses the other side of the coin—that is, how do features of Judaism contribute to morality. After describing a number of elements of Judaism that do that, the chapter focuses on two distinctive ways in which Judaism fosters morality: namely, through study and law. Although the subject matter of the Appendix is theoretical, I have done my best to make sure that nonphilosophers can understand it. I strongly urge readers to try their hand at it, because it discusses some vital matters.

And now for some appropriate expressions of gratitude. Many of these chapters were first drafted for other contexts, and I thank those who provided the settings for my creativity in the first notes of those chapters. Like everyone else, I grow immensely from what I learn from others, and much of what is good in this volume is a product of that. All those involved in the projects that led to my writing have my deepest appreciation. They include the Rabbinical Assembly and its Committee on Jewish Law and Standards and its Commission on Human Sexuality; the Georgetown University Department of Political Science; the Templeton Foundation's project on forgiveness; the Blackwell books on Judaism edited by Jacob Neusner and Alan J. Avery-Peck; and the project on suffering and faith organized by Margaret Mohrmann of the University of Virginia and Mark Hanson of the Hastings Center.

Rae and Jack Gindi and Bruce and Shelly Whizin have been good friends for several decades. I feel honored to have them sponsor the publishing of this book. Indeed, it feels like a big hug, and they have my sincere thanks.

Friends who have stimulated me throughout the years and provided camaraderie, comfort, and joy are the ones to whom this book is dedicated. Marlynn and I have had the wonderful gift of close friends from Camp Ramah, the Jewish Theological Seminary of America, the University of Judaism Temple Beth Am in Los Angeles and its Library Minyan, the University of California at Los Angeles, the Bureau of Jewish Education of Los Angeles, and the general and Jewish Los Angeles community— all of whom we think of as our extended family. I have dedicated books in the past to the members of my family—my beloved Marlynn and our children, Tammy, Michael, Havi, and Jonathan. Now our family is blessed with Michael's wife, Tanya; Havi's husband, Adam; Jonathan's wife, Mara; and our first grandchildren, Noa and Zachary—may there be many more! Since I have already honored my family in this way, Marlynn and I both feel that a book on personal ethics can be dedicated to nobody more appropriate than the friends we consider to be our extended family. May they know only joy, and may they continue to contribute to our lives and to those of everyone around them as they have done so generously in the past for many, many years to come.

Elliot N. Dorff
Los Angeles, California
April 6, 2003

Acknowledgments

THIS WORK GROWS OUT OF MANY PROJECTS OVER THE YEARS. While I have revised many of the chapters from the way they originally appeared, I would like to thank the following publishers for permission to use materials that they originally published and for providing me with the opportunity to publish and test my ideas.

The original version of Chapter One was published as "Doing the Right and the Good: Fundamental Convictions and Methods of Jewish Ethics," in *Ethics in the World Religions,* ed. Joseph Runzo and Nancy M. Martin (Oxford: Oneworld, 2001), 89–114.

Chapter Two is an expanded version of the responsum Rabbi Elie Spitz and I wrote in 2001 for the Conservative Movement's Committee on Jewish Law and Standards (CJLS) titled "Privacy on the Internet." I would like to thank Rabbi Spitz and the Rabbinical Assembly for permission to reprint that here.

Chapter Three is a revised version of the Rabbinic Letter I wrote for and with the Rabbinical Assembly's Commission on Human Sexuality and published as *"This Is My Beloved, This Is My Friend": A Rabbinic Letter on Intimate Relations* (New York: Rabbinical Assembly, 1996).

Chapter Four is based on a responsum I wrote for the CJLS titled "Family Violence" and published in *Responsa 1991–2000:*

The Committee on Jewish Law and Standards of the Conservative Movement, ed. Kassel Abelson and David Fine (New York: Rabbinical Assembly, 2002), 773–816.

Chapter Six was originally published as "The Elements of Forgiveness: A Jewish Approach," in *Dimensions of Forgiveness: Psychological Research and Theological Perspectives,* ed. Everett L. Worthington Jr. (Philadelphia: Templeton Foundation Press, 1998), 29–55 [reprinted by Templeton in paperback in 2001 as *Forgiveness: Theory, Research, and Practice.*]

Chapter Seven is based, in part, on my article " 'Heal Us, Lord, and We Shall Be Healed': The Role of Hope and Destiny in Jewish Bioethics," *Judaism* 48, no. 2 (spring 1999), 149–164.

The Appendix is based, in part, on two previously published articles: "Study Leads to Action," *Religious Education* 75, no. 2 (March–April 1980), 171–192 and "The Interaction of Jewish Law with Morality," *Judaism* 26, no. 4 (fall 1977), 455–466.

CHAPTER ONE

Judaism and Ethics

A LL THE OTHER CHAPTERS OF THIS BOOK ADDRESS A NUMBER of concrete moral questions of personal ethics. A perusal of the table of contents reveals that the topics include privacy, sex, parent–child relations, family violence, forgiveness, and hope. All of those discussions are down-to-earth and practically oriented, and I ask: What would the Jewish tradition have us *do* in a particular situation and why?

This chapter and the appendix, though, are somewhat more theoretical. I say that not to scare people off. On the contrary, I have deliberately tried my best to make the material of this chapter and the appendix as clear and as jargon-free as possible. Nevertheless, some readers may prefer to skip the part of this chapter where I describe the most prominent theories of ethics to show how Jewish ethics fits among them. Readers who do this should read the next brief section, which defines the difference between ethics and morals, and then proceed directly to the section titled "Jewish Morals." Again, I would encourage readers to give it all a try; but, on the other hand, the rest of this chapter and the rest of this book stand on their own for those who want to delve immediately into the concrete issues.

ETHICS VERSUS MORALS

While the terms "ethical" and "moral" are often used interchangeably in common parlance—or even to reinforce each

other, as in "He is unquestionably a moral and ethical person"—
in philosophy, the two terms denote different things. "Morals"
refers to the concrete norms of what is good or bad, right or
wrong, in a given situation. Thus the extent to which life-support mechanisms should be used for dying patients, the degree to
which an employee's privacy must be maintained, and the
norms that should govern sexual relations between unmarried
people are all moral questions. "Ethics," in contrast, refers to the
theory of morals. Ethics, in other words, is one level of abstrac-
tion higher than moral discussions. That does not mean that ethical questions are more important than moral ones; they just
occupy a different level of thought. Thus in a university course
in ethics one would examine *questions of meaning, knowledge,
justification,* and *comparison,* such as these:

- How should you define the terms "good" and "bad," "right"
  and "wrong," and why?
- How are judgments of "good" different from judgments of
  "right"?
- Are there universal, absolute standards of moral norms, or do
  they extend only to given societies (or perhaps only to
  individuals)?
- Whatever the scope of moral norms, how do you know what
  is right or wrong, good or bad? (Do you, for example, take a
  vote, ask an authority figure, decide what pleases you, use
  your conscience, seek God's will in some way, or do something else?)
- How do you know that that is the proper method to determine
  what is moral?
- To what factors do you appeal in justifying your moral judgments? (Some possible answers: The act designated as good
  provides the most happiness for the greatest number of people; it fits the requirements of conscience; it follows from
  some previously justified principles or decisions; it obeys an
  authority figure, whether divine or human; it is what most
  people in my community think is right; it is what the law requires; or it is what pleases me personally.)
- How is morality related to law? to religion? to custom? to pol-
  itics? to police or military power? to economics? to art? to
  education?

THE VARIETY OF ETHICAL THEORIES

Although one can certainly study Jewish ethical and moral discussions on their own, it is helpful to place such discussions in the broader rubric of how ethics has been approached in non-Jewish settings. The summary I give below may offend professional philosophers, for I paint these theories in much too broad sweeps and pay little attention to proper nuance. Still, I try to give a reasonably accurate picture of at least some of the most important approaches to ethics in the general philosophical literature, so that readers of this book can understand where Jewish ethics fits in.

What I present next has all the advantages and disadvantages of a survey course in college and of a first trip to a place that you do not know. Like them, this survey does not stop for the intriguing diversions and byways that one might want to explore if one had the time. Sometimes that may mean that those being exposed to such a survey lose not only some of the flavor of a given theory and some of its motivation but even some of its meaning and implications. At the same time, I hope I provide an accurate depiction of the essentials, just as survey courses and good tours do. The advantage of this approach is that one can see the broad picture, and that helps place any piece of it in its context and thereby helps explain it. Moreover, a survey of some of the most prominent ethical theories reveals the choices that Judaism did *not* make in both content and method so that we can see the importance of what it did choose.

This is especially important because Jews tend to believe that everyone else in the world thinks and acts just as Jews do. In *To Do the Right and the Good*, I demonstrated how Jewish moral values and methods are often different from those in secular America and in Christianity. Here, I want to bring to bear the larger world of philosophical ethics so that we can place Judaism in that context.

When describing the major theories of ethics, I follow Table 1.1, which gives a visual picture of the lay of the land. As the table indicates, the major theories of ethics can be divided into three major categories: consequentialism, deontology, and virtue or character ethics.

TABLE 1.1
THEORIES OF ETHICS IN THE GENERAL LITERATURE

Theory	Moral Claim	Major Theorist	Explanation
Consequentialism (whether an act is good is defined by its consequences)			
Ethical egoism	Good is that which serves one's self-interests; sometimes helping others serves this purpose	Thomas Hobbes	Although they are related, egoism as a philosophical viewpoint should not be confused with egotistical (meaning conceited)
Act utilitarianism	Good is that which is useful for the person or people in a particular situation, without taking into consideration all such situations	Jeremy Bentham	Bentham particularly focused on physical pleasure (i.e., hedonism), although the theory may be applied to other circumstances (e.g., the true story portrayed in the movie *Alive*, in which people who were stranded in the Andes ate dead humans to stay alive)
Rule utilitarianism	Good is that act which produces the most usefulness for the greatest number of people as a general rule—that is, when considering all similar situations	John Stuart Mill	Mill thought that the good must be able to be generalized to all situations and people; psychological and intellectual pleasures are just as important as physical
Deontology (there are moral principles in the very nature of things that govern us, regardless of their consequences)			
Natural law	Like physical rules (e.g., gravity), moral rules are built into the structure of nature	Thomas Aquinas	The lists of such moral rules vary in accordance with each natural law theorist
Kantian ethics	Moral rules can be generated from the mind because the mind has a logical structure	Immanuel Kant	Kant has two versions of his categorical imperative: Do only that which can be generalized to others, and never treat people merely as a means

Ross's theory of ethics	There are seven moral principles that all people have the duty to fulfill (e.g., keeping promises and being truthful)	W. D. Ross	Ross claims that moral situations are complex and that people have intuitive moral duties to one another; thus, when moral duties conflict, one must balance the fulfillment of those duties
Theological ethics	God defines what is good and bad	Western religious theorists	God's will is usually derived from the literature that the theorist deems to be a true revelation or prophesy

Virtue or character ethics (a person deemed moral or worthy of setting values defines what is good)

Moral perfection	The moral champion, who strives for moral perfection, is the ideal	Prophets, Book of Psalms	
Wisdom; success in life	The person who succeeds in life because of vast life experience is the moral authority	Books of Proverbs, Ecclesiastes	
Combining the ideal and real	The person who embodies moral qualities or virtues in concrete life situations is the moral authority	Aristotle; the Rabbis	
The powerful noble man	The noble person (one who creates his or her own values as opposed to being subservient to others' values) is the moral authority	Friedrich Nietzsche	
Feminist ethics	The morally ideal person thinks of men and women as equals	Betty Friedan, Gloria Steinam, Judith Plaskow	Traditionally, women have had ideas and solutions for moral issues that were ignored; therefore, ethics must be rethought with a view to correcting whatever male bias it may contain

Source: Created by Paul Steinberg, my rabbinical student and the author of the study guide for this book.

CONSEQUENTIALISM
Consequentialism measures the morality of an action in terms of its consequences. There are three major types of consequentialist theories: ethical egoism, act utilitarianism, and rule utilitarianism.

ETHICAL EGOISM
Ethical egoism maintains that what is good is whatever serves one's own interests. Ethical egoists need not be short-sighted in thinking only of themselves; they may recognize that what serves their own interests may coincide with helping others. So, for example, ethical egoists may support honest payment of taxes because they want the various things that government provides with tax money. Similarly, ethical egoists may aid the poor, because they may not want a society with beggars on the streets and potential rebellion always lurking in the background. One of the first and chief exponents of ethical egoism was Thomas Hobbes, a seventeenth-century British philosopher, who claimed that everyone acts only for his or her own interests and that what everyone wants is power. Nevertheless, John Aubrey, in his sketch of Hobbes in his book *Brief Lives*, reports an exchange between Hobbes and a clergyman who had just seen Hobbes give alms to a beggar. The clergyman inquired whether Hobbes would have given alms if Jesus had not commanded it. Hobbes's reply was that by giving alms to the beggar, he not only relieved the man's distress but also relieved his own distress at seeing the beggar's woeful state.[1] This is a clear example of the fact that what defines an ethical egoist is that whatever is done for others is good only if it benefits the doer.

ACT UTILITARIANISM
Act utilitarianism measures the morality of an act on the basis of whether it provides the greatest good for the greatest number of people involved. The person usually associated with this theory is Jeremy Bentham (1748–1832, England), who, like many of his nineteenth-century contemporaries, was very much impressed with the power of science and technology to explain things and enhance life, and so he sought to put ethics on a

scientific basis as well. He was a hedonist—that is, he measured good results in terms of pleasure and pain. He then created a "utilitarian calculus," according to which acts would be evaluated in terms of the intensity and duration of the pleasures they provided to those involved as against the intensity and duration of the pain they entailed. The act that provided the greatest pleasure and the least pain for the greatest number of people involved he defined as best. Act utilitarians need not be hedonists, and there are real problems in measuring one person's level of pleasure or pain against another's; but act utilitarians are attracted to the theory because if some form of utilitarian calculus works, this theory has the advantage of defining good and evil, right and wrong, in objective terms.

RULE UTILITARIANISM
This theory of rule utilitarianism is usually associated with John Stuart Mill (1806–1873, England), who was also impressed with the power of science and technology. Mill expanded the utilitarian calculus from attention to a particular act to more general cases. That is, in evaluating the morality of a particular act, I must, according to his theory, take into consideration not only the balance of utilitarian benefits and harms of that act but also the benefits and harms that acts of this type *as a rule* produce. So, for example, if I decide to follow Bentham when deciding whether I should obey a stop sign at 3:00 A.M., when nobody else seems to be around, I need only consider the advantages and disadvantages of stopping for me and anyone else involved at that moment. According to Mill, on the other hand, I need to consider the benefits and harms in stopping or not in such situations *as a general policy*. It may be the case that in a particular instance no harm would be done and I would gain the advantage of saving the time and gas involved in stopping, and so Bentham would recommend going through the stop sign. However, Mill might say that, as a general policy, not stopping is a bad idea, since the stop sign was put there in the first place because the traffic or obstructions at that corner require that I stop for everyone's safety.

Unlike Bentham, Mill was not a hedonist. That is, he recognized that in measuring utilitarian value, we must take into consideration the various types of benefits and harms involved, because

> if the sources of pleasure were precisely the same to human beings and to swine, the rule of life which is good enough for the one would be good enough for the other. . . . Human beings have faculties more elevated than the animal appetites and, when once made conscious of them, do not regard anything as happiness which does not include their gratification. . . . But there is no known Epicurean theory of life which does not assign to the pleasures of the intellect, of the feelings and imagination, and of the moral sentiments a much higher value as pleasures than to those of mere sensation. . . . It is better to be a human being dissatisfied than a pig satisfied; better to be Socrates dissatisfied than a fool satisfied. And if the fool, or the pig, are of a different opinion, it is because they only know their own side of the question. The other party to the comparison knows both sides.[2]

DEONTOLOGY

Deontology—from the root "de," meaning "from," and "ontology," meaning "the study of being or existence"—maintains that the moral measure of an act depends on principles that are embedded in nature. The question then is, Exactly what part or aspect of existence produces moral norms? I discuss below four major deontological theories, each of which focuses on a different aspect of being as the root of moral norms.

NATURAL LAW THEORIES

Advocates of natural law theories maintain that just as there are physical laws built into nature, such as gravity, so too there are moral laws built into nature. Thomas Aquinas (1225–1274, Italy) is probably the most well-known proponent of this view, but its adherents include both ancient and modern figures as well. The great advantages of this view are that moral norms are universally binding on all of humanity and their authority is as strong as nature itself. That is, just as the laws of gravity are potent and inescapable, so too, according to this approach, are moral laws such as prohibitions against murder and theft and duties such as honoring parents and civil authorities. The major disadvantage of this approach is epistemological: Once you get beyond a few fairly obvious moral norms, like the ones just mentioned, just how do we know what nature requires of us? This approach is also very conservative, for usually the advocates see nature as fixed and static. That, in fact, is what gives moral norms their authority. Such an understanding of nature, however, leaves little room for changing moral norms in, for example, the view of women, sexual orientation, or other races.

A SINGLE PRINCIPLE (MONISTIC DEONTOLOGY)

Immanuel Kant (1724–1804, Germany) is arguably, along with Plato and Aristotle, one of the three most important philosophers that the West has produced. In ethics, he is known for rooting moral norms in the structure of the human mind; in particular, its ability to generalize. This leads him to his famous "categorical imperative"—that is, the foundational norm that has no exceptions. As he said, this norm "is not concerned with the matter of the action and its intended result, but rather with the form of the action and the principle from which it follows; what is essentially good in the action consists in the mental disposition, let the consequences be what they may."[3] Thus the categorical imperative is not about a specific issue ("a matter of action") but rather is a general form of imperative that distinguishes all truly moral norms from pragmatic ones. Pragmatic imperatives (such as "If you want to be healthy, lose weight") carry a duty to comply if, and only if, you have the goal described in the "if" clause. Moral duties, by contrast, apply to us with no ifs, ands, or buts. They are, therefore, unexceptionable and universal (categorical).

Kant provided two formulations of the categorical imperative, and scholars suggest that the two do not really amount to the same thing, as Kant claimed. The first formulation is "Act only according to that maxim whereby you can at the same time will that it should become universal law."[4] That is, act only in such a way that you would wish everyone else to act as you do. Putting it another way, act only in such a way that you would will your action to be generalized among all human beings. It is this *form* of imperative that Kant called categorical and that he thought was rooted in the very nature of human minds.

Kant's second formulation of the categorical imperative is this: "Act in such a way that you treat humanity, whether in your own person or in the person of another, always at the same time as an end and never simply as a means."[5] Kant tried to prove that all concrete moral norms could be generated from the human mind using his categorical imperative, and he was probably most successful in his example of the duty to keep promises and possibly also in his example of the duty to tell the truth; but generating most other moral norms from his generalizing use of the mind is much more problematic. Thus Kant could not accommodate the varying ways in which societies understand sexual or commercial norms, for example; on the contrary, one of the attractions of his theory for those who affirm it is that all human beings would recognize the same moral principles if they only knew how to use their minds correctly.

MULTIPLE PRINCIPLES (PLURALISTIC DEONTOLOGY)
In his book *The Right and the Good*, William David Ross (1877–1971, United Kingdom) maintained that, like Aristotle, "The moral convictions of thoughtful and well-educated people are the data of ethics, just as sense-perceptions are the data of natural science."[6] These duties, the "convictions of thoughtful and well-educated people," are known by intuition and are thus built into our very nature as human beings. He identifies seven such "*prima facie* duties"—that is, duties that one must fulfill unless, in a given situation, there is a conflicting duty. They are nonmaleficence (not harming anyone else who does not deserve it), beneficence (seeking to benefit others), fidelity (keeping promises and being truthful), reparation (making up to someone for an injury one has done to that person), gratitude (repaying a benefit or kindness), self-improvement, and justice (making sure good things go to those who merit them). The advantage of this approach is that, unlike Kant, Ross does not depend on just one duty and can therefore take account of moral conflict. The disadvantage of this theory is that Ross maintains that these duties are built into us, so that we simply intuit them; but, at the same time, he knows these duties from the fact that cultured people hold them. However, this means that the duties are

themselves a product of a specific (British) culture rather than the nature of humanity.

Another form of deontological ethics roots moral norms not in nature as we know it, but in God, the creator of everything. Western religious theories—Jewish, Christian, and Muslim—are typically of this sort, although some thinkers in each of the traditions maintain that God's will is also manifest in nature. Because Judaism is one example of this type of ethics, I spell out some of the implications of this theory, specifically as they are articulated in Judaism, in the latter part of this chapter and in the Appendix. Here, however, suffice it to say that the great advantage of this theory is that moral norms gain their authority and universality from God Himself, who is presumed to be both moral and powerful. The problem with this approach, though, is that even if we seek to do what God wants of us—and there are some questions among Jews after the Holocaust about whether we should—how do we know what that is? I return to this question later in the chapter.

VIRTUE OR CHARACTER ETHICS
The point of virtue or character ethics is that in understanding morality, one should not focus on particular qualities of a specific act but rather on the character of a person, because the good act is one that is done by the good person. What, then, characterizes the good person?

THE MORAL CHAMPION
One vision of character ethics emerges out of the biblical prophets and the Book of Psalms. The prophets demand not only that we do what God's law demands of us but also that we go further in trying to make this an ideal society. In Abraham Joshua Heschel's apt phrase, the prophets are "an octave too high"[7] in that they envision a moral world that is much purer than human beings can actually achieve. It is good to have such people around to prompt us to aspire to do more than we otherwise would do in helping others and in making this a better world, but there is something unreal about the prophets' demands, and so one tires

of them and avoids them after a while. The Psalms describe the moral person in somewhat more realistic terms, as in the following:

Happy is the man who has not followed the counsel of the wicked,
or taken the path of sinners,
or joined the company of the insolent;
rather, the teaching of the Lord is his delight,
and he studies that teaching day and night.[8]

Who is the man who is eager for life,
who desires years of good fortune?
Guard your tongue from evil,
your lips from deceitful speech.
Shun evil and do good,
seek integrity and pursue it.[9]

THE ONE WHO SUCCEEDS AT LIFE

The biblical Wisdom literature in books like Proverbs and Ecclesiastes depicts a very different model of who the ideal person is. The model here is to learn what to do and say from experience (biblical *hokhmah*, "wisdom," or *savoir faire*, "street smarts") so that one can live one's life *successfully*. Thus the person who takes the safe and sane approach is the ideal, and the Book of Proverbs articulates a series of rules by which an upper-class young man should live in order to succeed in life. The author of Ecclesiastes (*Kohelet*), who takes on the guise of Solomon, experiments with the knowledge and wealth for which Solomon was famous and finds them both wanting, because knowledge only informs you of painful events that you would otherwise not know and wealth only makes you vulnerable to theft and extortion, especially since you cannot take knowledge or wealth with you to the grave and nobody remembers your good reputation long after you die. Moreover, nothing changes in life, despite the best of human efforts, for God has appointed a season for everything under heaven. As a result, there is no point in striving to improve the world.

Only this, I have found, is a real good: that one should eat and drink and get pleasure with all the gains he makes under the sun, during the numbered days of life that God has given him; for that is his portion. . . . Don't overdo goodness and don't act the wise man to excess, or you may be dumbfounded. Don't overdo wickedness and don't be a fool, or you may die before your time. It is best that you grasp the one without letting go of the other, for one who fears God will do his duty by both. . . . Go, eat your bread in gladness, and drink your wine in joy; for your action was long ago approved by God. Let your clothes always be freshly washed, and your head never lack ointment. Enjoy happiness with a woman you love all the fleeting days of life that have been granted to you under the sun—all your fleeting days. For that alone is what you can get out of life and out of the means you acquire under the sun. Whatever is in your power to do, do with all your might. For there is no action, no reasoning, no learning, no wisdom in Sheol [the grave], where you are going.[10]

THE GOOD PERSON

Another picture of the ideal person comes out of Aristotle and the Rabbis. Coming from very different cultures with very different visions of what is and what ought to be, both Aristotle and the Rabbis tried to create the good person through a combination of the ideal and the real. Aristotle responded to Plato's ideas with a heavy dose of realism, just as the Rabbis responded to the idealism of the Prophets with the realism that came out of their experience as judges. The Rabbis, of course, grounded their morality in the commandments of God, which Aristotle did not do. But for both, the exemplar of morality was the good person, who managed in his or her life to combine the ideal with the real.

THE NOBLE MAN

Friedrich Nietzsche (1844–1900, Germany) scorned the ideal of the good person as the product of slave morality, where the goal is to create "the *safe* man: he is good-natured, easily deceived, perhaps a little stupid, *un bonhomme.*"[11] In contrast, Nietzsche espoused master morality, where the goal is the noble man:

> The noble type of man regards *himself* as a determiner of values; he does not require to be approved of; he passes judgment: "What is injurious to me is injurious in itself"; he knows that it is he himself only who confers honor on things; he is a *creator of values.* He honors whatever he recognizes in himself: such morality is self-glorification. In the foreground there is the feeling of plenitude, of power, which seeks to overflow, the happiness of high tension, the consciousness of a wealth which would fain give and

13

bestow:—the noble man also helps the unfortunate, but not—or scarcely—out of pity, but rather from an impulse generated by the superabundance of power. The noble man honors in himself the powerful one, him also who has power over himself, who knows how to speak and how to keep silence, who takes pleasure in subjecting himself to severity and hardness, and has reverence for all that is severe and hard.[12]

Some maintain that Nietzsche's overturning of Western values— the soft, compassionate values of "slave morality" that he attributes primarily to Jews—is the forerunner of Nazi ideology, and the Nazis used Nietzsche to justify their doctrines of national and racial superiority and to despise political democracy and equality. Most scholars, though, regard that as a perversion of Nietzsche's thought, pointing to his strong individualism and his contempt for the state, especially the German state. Still, his writings propose an ideal human being who is extremely different from those lauded in most other theories, one who is downright dangerous, as the Nazi use of his work all too graphically illustrates.

FEMINISM

Yet another kind of character ethics emerged in the last half of the twentieth century. Early feminist writers in the 1960s and 1970s declared that any dissimilarity between men and women was the result of long conditioning by patriarchal societies and that equality between the sexes entailed that (except for their genitals) they were the same. However, feminist writers in the 1980s and beyond, while asserting gender equality, have pointed out the distinctions between men and women. Much of this research was done by women—for example, Carol Gilligan, Nel Noddings, and Deborah Tannen. One avenue of research used magnetic resonance imaging (MRI) of the brain activity of men and women and noted that the sexes used different parts of their brains when answering the same questions. In any case, Gilligan, Noddings, and Virginia Held in particular advanced the thesis that boys and men tend to interact with each other according to rules of the game; but for girls and women, the personal relationship—especially caring—takes precedence over rules.[13] That theory is probably overstated; after all, men care about other people and women care about moral rules. Still, it may be that the ideal moral person that men imagine is defined more by the rules of the moral game than the ideal in women's minds and, conversely, the women's ideal may be marked by more personal caring than is the case for men. To determine whether this idea is true or not requires further research and refining.

JEWISH ETHICS

While Jews have addressed all of the standard questions of ethics concerning meaning, knowledge, justification, and comparison from a distinctly Jewish point of view, two particular issues have occupied Jewish thinkers most: Why should one carry out Judaism's moral demands, and how can one define and know what is moral?

The variety of rationales to obey God's commandments that have been suggested may be surprising to some contemporary readers who, motivated perhaps by the biblical depiction of the Revelation of the Torah at Mount Sinai amid thunder, lightning, and earthquakes, are used to thinking that there is really only one reason to obey: God will punish you if you do not and reward you if you do. A mere forty days after that revelation, though, the very people who experienced it were worshiping the Golden Calf; and so it became clear early on that divine reward and punishment alone would not suffice as reasons for obedience. As a result, the Torah itself provides an immensely sophisticated list beyond reward or punishment at the hands of God or human beings of why people should obey laws and act morally. That list includes the inherent wisdom of doing so; the Covenant, with its implicit morality of promise keeping and the duties of the relationship between God and the People Israel that it established; gratitude toward God; the responsibility we have to preserve and enhance God's reputation and our own; the aspiration for holiness; and, ultimately, the love between us and God.[14] Rabbinic literature adds a few more rationales, including, for example, that the commandments create a separate, national identity, have aesthetic value, and make us more humane. Medieval Jewish literature specifies additional rationales, in particular the rationalist philosophers' insistence that the commandments accord with, and are demanded by, reason, and the mystics' affirmation that Jewish norms bridge the gap between us and God, enabling us to know God—not just intellectually, but intimately—and, in some later versions of Jewish mysticism, actually to become part of God. Modern Jewish thought adds yet further rationales such as, for example, Franz Rosenzweig's assertion that the commandments create a personal relationship between each of us as individuals and God.[15]

Even if we are convinced that we should adhere to Jewish moral norms, how do we know what they are? Classical Judaism defines the moral in terms of God's will as articulated in God's commandments. Some modern theorists, however, have challenged the nexus between God's will and Jewish law, and some humanistic Jews have even denied that we should look to God's will in any form to define the right and the good. Even those who believe that Jewish moral norms are to be defined in terms of God's will and that Jewish law is the proper vehicle for knowing what God wants of us cannot rest with Jewish law alone, for the Talmud itself declares that the law is not fully sufficient to define morality, that there are morals "beyond the letter of the law" (lifnim m'shurat ha-din).[16] Beginning, then, with Abraham's challenge to God, "Shall the Judge of all the earth not do justice?"[17] one ethical question addressed throughout Jewish history has been the relationship between moral norms and God's word.

Another, more modern question, is this: If we assume that God's will defines that which is morally right and good, how shall we discern what God wants us to do now? Reform theories, such as that of Eugene Borowitz,[18] maintain that individual Jews should make that decision. They should inform themselves as much as possible about the relevant factors in the case and about the Jewish sources that apply, but ultimately individual Jews, rather than rabbis, should determine what God wants of us on the basis of their knowledge and conscience.

This Reform methodology raises major questions about how to identify any Jew's decision as being recognizably Jewish. Indeed, it makes it possible and even likely that there will be multiple, conflicting moral decisions, all claiming to be Jewish, because each and every Jew has the right to articulate a "Jewish" position on a given issue. This challenges the coherence and intelligibility of the Jewish moral message. Moreover, Borowitz's methodology depends crucially on the assumption that individual Jews know enough about the Jewish tradition and about how to apply it to carry out this task, an assumption that regrettably does not comply with reality.

Positively, though, Reform methodology empowers individual Jews to wrestle with the Jewish tradition themselves, and it encourages—even demands—that Jews learn more about their tradition in order to carry out this task. By making the decision depend on a specifically *Jewish* self, rather than an isolated, undifferentiated self, Borowitz also goes some way in the direction of explaining how such choices can be identified as specifically Jewish: Jewish choices come from self-identified and self-consciously Jewish people.

At the other end of the spectrum, most Orthodox theorists claim that Jewish law as it has come down to us should serve as our authoritative source for knowing God's will, and the more straightforwardly and literally we can read those sources, the more assured we can be that we have discovered God's will. No change is necessary or possible, for God has proclaimed these moral norms through the Written Torah (the Five Books of Moses) and the Oral Torah that, Orthodox Jews believe, was given to Moses at Mount Sinai simultaneously with the Written Torah.

For those who affirm these beliefs, this methodology imparts a sense of assuredness that one knows how to identify God's will and why one should obey it: God demands that of you. On the other hand, this methodology rests, first, on the assumption that God's will is literally expressed in the Torah and later rabbinic literature; that is a conviction of faith that one either affirms or denies. Beyond that, to adopt the Orthodox approach one must believe that we have the exact expression of the divine will in hand in the texts that have come down to us. That assertion is largely undermined by the overwhelming evidence that biblical and rabbinic literature—including the Torah itself—were written at a variety of times and places. Moreover, even if one believes in the literal, divine authority of the Torah and rabbinic literature, one still needs to interpret and apply those sources, and that leaves plenty of room for human controversy and error. Thus this methodology does not deliver the certainty it promises to inform us what God demands. Finally, as some left-wing Orthodox rabbis have themselves noted,[19] we still have to ask whether the law defines the entirety of our moral duty—and, I would add, whether the law might actually conflict with what morality demands.

Conservative theorists and rabbis (and a few Orthodox ones) use Jewish law as much as possible to know God's will (and hence the right and the good), and they pay attention also to Jewish theological convictions and Jewish stories.[20] They combine this broader use of Jewish sources with a historical understanding of them. Thus, when it comes time to apply them to contemporary circumstances, Conservative theorists look carefully at the ways in which a given contemporary setting is similar to or different from the historical one in which a given source was written, in order to be able to judge the degree to which it should guide us today. They also look to the sources not so much for specific directions as for the principles that underlie past applications of Jewish law so that we can intelligently apply them to the modern context. For that matter, a historical understanding of the Jewish tradition requires that even past ethical principles themselves be subject to recurrent evaluation. Both past principles and past applications of them, however, are assessed with a bias toward conserving the tradition (and hence the name "Conservative"), such that the burden of proof rests on the one who wants to change a particular moral or ethical stance rather than on the one who wants to maintain what has come down to us.

This Conservative approach does not present a neat, clearly identifiable lesson on all moral matters in our day; on the contrary, it invites discussion and controversy. Moreover, it requires *judgment;* no source may be taken at face value, none is immune from evaluation. This is clearly not a methodology for the anal compulsive! Unlike the Reform approach, though, the Conservative methodology requires that such evaluation be done not just by individuals but by the community, thus preserving a greater degree of coherence and Jewish identity. It makes such decisions primarily through its rabbinic leaders, because they are the ones most likely to know what the tradition says and how to apply it to modern circumstances. Thus this way of discerning what God wants does not depend on knowledge and skills that most Jews lack. In contrast to the Orthodox approach, the Conservative one has the distinct advantage of historical awareness and authenticity, for it interprets sources in their historical context and, like generations past, combines received Jewish law with an openness to the moral sensitivities and needs of the time. It thus has a greater balance of the traditional with the modern, greater openness to learning from others, and greater flexibility.

Yet a fourth way of discerning God's will is that pioneered by Martin Buber, developed further by Emanuel Levinas, and articulated in a contemporary feminist version by Laurie Zoloth-Dorfman.[21] In this approach we discover Jewish moral norms through our encounters with other human beings in one-to-one, direct interactions.

This approach, sometimes called "personalist" or even "feminist," suffers from the same problems that Reform individualism has: It is weak on Jewish identity, continuity, coherence, and authority. At the same time, it locates moral decisions where they in fact lie, in the interaction among human beings. Moreover, it invokes the inherent authority another human being has over us simply by virtue of being another human being who faces us directly.

JEWISH MORALS

Why should Jews use any of these methodologies to determine what is moral? Why, in other words, should we expect that Judaism has anything to teach us about morality?

The reason is inherent in the word "religion," which comes from the Latin root meaning "bonds" or "linkages," the same root from which we get the word "ligament," which is connective tissue. Religions describe the ties that we have to our families, our community, the rest of humanity, the environment, and the transcendent. In so doing, religions give us conceptual eyeglasses, as it were, through which we look at the world. Secular philosophies like liberalism, Marxism, and existentialism do that too, but philosophies, *qua* philosophies, are purely intellectual. Religions, on the other hand, by their very nature embody their views of life in myths and rituals and thereby form communities of people connected to each other and to their shared vision of what is and what ought to be. Such religious communities provide camaraderie, strength, and meaning in the ongoing aspects of life—the life cycle, the seasonal cycle, and, indeed, the progress of each day and week; they furnish moral education in a variety of formats; and they also work together toward realizing their ideals. Religions, then, are related to morality because they depict the way the world is, offer visions of what it ought to be, and define communities to teach morality and work toward moral goals.

Religions do not all present the same moral view, however. Some norms, of course, are virtually universal—prohibitions against murder and theft, for example, and demands to help others. Even widespread norms, though, vary in definition; so, for example, for some pacifist religions, all killing of human beings constitutes murder, whereas for most religions killing an enemy in war or in self-defense is not only permissible but mandatory. Furthermore, even when a norm is defined in the same way by two religions, each of them may give it a different degree of emphasis. Finally, some positive duties or prohibitions are affirmed by some religions and not by others.

As a result of these variations, each religion presents a picture of reality and of the ideal that is distinctive in degree or kind. Each religion also, in its own way, inculcates its version of morality in its youth and adults. To understand Jewish morality, then, I shall describe some important elements of Judaism's vision of the real and the ideal. Because Jews often think that the entire world thinks as Jews do, it will be helpful along the way to compare the Jewish norm with Christian norms and with Western norms as embodied in secular culture.

THE HUMAN BEING

I begin with several Jewish convictions about the individual. Since I have spoken at some length about Judaism's view of the body and of the person in *Matters of Life and Death* and *To Do the Right and the Good*, here I will only summarize the fundamental elements of the classical Jewish view of the individual.

20

The body belongs to God. For Judaism, God, as creator of the world, owns everything in it, including our bodies.[22] God loans our bodies to us for the duration of our lives, and we return them to God when we die. Consequently, neither men nor women have the right to govern their bodies as they will; God, as creator and owner, asserts the right to restrict how we use our bodies in ways articulated in Jewish law.

Some of God's rules require us to take reasonable care of our bodies, just as we would be obliged to protect and clean an apartment that we rent. Rules of good hygiene, sleep, exercise, and diet in Jewish sources are, therefore, not just words to the wise designed for our comfort and longevity, as they are in American thinking; they are, rather, commanded acts that we owe God.[23] So, for example, American ideology and law would permit me to eat a half gallon of ice cream every night of the week; I might be stupid to do so because I will look and feel terrible and endanger my life, but that is my choice. In Jewish law, though, I do not have that right, because I have a fiduciary duty to take care of my body since it belongs to God.

Just as we are commanded to maintain good health, so we are obligated to avoid danger and injury.[24] Indeed, Jewish law views endangering one's health as worse than violating a ritual prohibition.[25] Conservative, Reform, and some Orthodox authorities have thus prohibited smoking as an unacceptable risk to our God-owned bodies.[26] Judaism also teaches that human beings do not have the right to commit suicide, for doing so obliterates something that belongs not to us but to God.[27] In contrast, the laws of most American states permit suicide (although most prohibit aiding and abetting a suicide).[28]

Being created in God's image imparts value to human life, regardless of the individual's level of capacity or incapacity. The American way of thinking is thoroughly pragmatic: A person's value is a function of what that person can *do* for others. That view, so deeply ingrained in American culture, prompts Americans to value those who have unusual abilities, who *succeed*— and, conversely, to devalue those who are disabled in some way.

In sharp contrast, the Torah declares that God created each of us in the divine image: "God created the human being in His image, in the image of God He created him; male and female

21

God created them."[29] Exactly which feature of the human being reflects this divine image is a matter of debate within the tradition. The Torah itself seems to tie it to humanity's ability to make moral judgments—that is, to distinguish good from bad and right from wrong, to behave accordingly, and to judge one's own actions and those of others on the basis of this moral knowledge.[30] Another human faculty connected by the Torah and by the later tradition to divinity is the ability to speak.[31] Maimonides claims that the divine image resides in our capacity to think, especially discursively.[32] Locating the divine image within us may also be the Torah's way of acknowledging that we can love, just as God does,[33] or that we are at least partially spiritual and thus share God's spiritual nature.[34]

Not only does this doctrine *describe* aspects of our nature but it also *prescribes* behavior founded on moral imperatives. Specifically, because human beings are created in God's image, we affront God when we insult another person.[35] More broadly, we must treat people with respect, recognizing each individual's uniqueness and divine worth, because all human beings embody the image of God.[36] Perhaps the most graphic articulation of this doctrine is the traditional blessing to be recited when seeing someone with a disability: "Praised are you, Lord our God, *meshaneh ha-briyyot,* who makes different creatures," or "who created us with differences." Precisely when we might recoil from a deformed or incapacitated person, or thank God for not making us like that, the tradition instead bids us to embrace the divine image in such people—indeed, to bless God for creating some of us so.[37] Moreover, the Torah demands that the body of a person who was executed for a capital crime be removed from the place of hanging by morning out of respect for the divine image inherent in even such a human being.[38] Ultimately, disrespect of others amounts to disrespect of God:

> Rabbi Akiva said: "You shall love your neighbor as yourself" (Leviticus 19:18) [implies that] you should not say that inasmuch as I am despised, let my fellow-man be despised with me, inasmuch as I am cursed, let my fellow-man be cursed with me. Rabbi Tanchuma said: If you act in this manner, know Who it is you despise, for "in the image of God made He man" (Genesis 1:27).[39]

The human being is an integrated whole, combining all aspects of our being. Western philosophical thought and Christianity have been heavily influenced by the Greek and Gnostic bifurcation of body and mind (or soul). In these systems of thought, the body is seen as the inferior part of human beings, either because it is what we share with animals, in contrast to the mind, which is distinctively human (Aristotle), or because the body is the seat of our passions and hence our sins (Paul in Romans and Galatians[40]). Even though the Greeks glorified the body in their art and sculpture, it was only because developing the body was seen as a means to an end, a necessary prerequisite to cultivating the mind (as, for example, in Plato's pedagogic program in *The Republic*). Similarly, Paul regarded the body as "the temple of the Holy Spirit,"[41] but only because it serves to sustain the soul so that it can accept faith in Jesus; the body per se "makes me a prisoner of that law of sin which lives inside my body."[42]

Such classical views have shaped Western and Christian traditions from ancient times to our own. In Christianity, Augustine, Luther, and Calvin followed the lead of Paul and maintained that the body's needs are to be suppressed as much as possible; indeed, asceticism and monasticism have been important themes in Christian ideology and history. In secular philosophic thought, the "mind–body problem" continues to be a stock issue in philosophic literature, which asks how the two, presumed to be so different and separate, are related in some ways to each other.

While some Jews (in particular, Philo and Maimonides[43]) were heavily influenced by the doctrines of the people living around them, biblical and talmudic literature does not share in this understanding of the human being as divided into parts. In the Talmud and Midrash, our soul is, in some senses, separable from our body. For example, when the Torah describes God as breathing life into Adam's body, rabbinic sources understand that to mean not only physical life but consciousness. God repeats that process each day by taking our souls away during sleep and returning them to us again when we awake. Moreover, at death, the soul leaves the body only to be united with it again at the time of resurrection.[44] Rabbinic sources conflict, however, as to whether the soul can exist apart from the body, and even those who say it can exist separately depict the soul in physical terms, capable of performing many of the functions of the body.[45]

In any case, in sharp contrast to the Greek and Christian traditions, classical rabbinic sources maintain that the soul is definitely not superior to the body. Indeed, one rabbinic source speaks of the soul as a guest in the body here on earth: One's host must accordingly be respected and well treated.[46] Moreover, since the Rabbis regarded the human being as an integrated whole, the body and the soul are to be judged as one.[47] Furthermore, the Rabbis' recipe for life and their method for moral education reflect this integration of body and soul. Thus, although the Rabbis emphasized the importance of studying and following the Torah, even placing it on a par with all of the rest of the commandments,[48] they nonetheless believed that the life of the soul or mind by itself is not good, that it can, indeed, be the source of sin:

> An excellent thing is the study of Torah combined with some worldly occupation, for the labor demanded by both of them causes sinful inclinations to be forgotten. All study of Torah without work must, in the end, be futile and become the cause of sin.[49]

Thus, while the Rabbis considered it a privilege to be able to study Torah, they themselves—or at least most of them—earned their livelihood through bodily work, and they also valued the hard labor of the field worker who spent little time in the study of Torah.[50]

The body is morally neutral and potentially good. The body is neither bad nor good. Rather, its energies, like those of our mind, will, and emotions, are morally neutral. All our faculties can and should be used for divine purposes as defined by Jewish law and tradition. Within these constraints, the body's pleasures are God-given and are not to be shunned, for to do so would be an act of ingratitude toward our Creator. The body, in other words, can and should give us pleasure to the extent that such pleasure enables us to live a life of holiness. As I explained in *To Do the Right and the Good*, in these matters Judaism differs markedly from both the American secular view of the body, on the one hand, and from Christianity, on the other.

Because of its view of the body and its central story of Jesus dying on the cross, pain plays a positive role in much Christian thought. The closest Judaism comes to that attitude are the rules governing Yom Kippur and historical fast days like Tisha be Av, on which we are to "afflict our souls" through fasting, sexual abstinence, and other forms of physical self-denial. But in each case, such abstinence is restricted to that day alone and is designed to call attention to the spiritual theme of the day; deprivation itself is not expected to effect atonement or historical memory. In fact, if a person's life is medically endangered on Yom Kippur, the law not only permits but actually requires him or her to refrain from fasting and to take appropriate measures to ensure life and health.[51]

The Jewish mode for attaining holiness is thus not to endure pain but rather to use all of our faculties, including our bodily energies, to perform God's commandments. For example, although we eat as all animals do, our eating takes on a divine dimension when we observe Jewish dietary restrictions and surround our meals with the appropriate blessings.

Some bodily pleasures are even commanded. Thus, with the exception of Yom Kippur, we may not fast on the Sabbath and we must eat three meals to celebrate it. We should also bathe and wear clean clothes in honor of the day.[52] Furthermore, as I amplify later, the ideal in Judaism is marriage, where sex can bring not only children but also physical pleasure, joy, and companionship. In fact, according to the Rabbis, it is an outright sin to deny ourselves the pleasures that God's law allows. Just as the Torah demands that the Nazirite bring a sin offering after denying himself the permitted delight of wine, so we will be called to account in the world to come for the ingratitude and haughtiness involved in denying ourselves the pleasures that God has provided.[53]

According to Maimonides, bodily pleasures are most appropriately enjoyed when we have the specific intent to enhance our ability to do God's will:

> He who regulates his life in accordance with the laws of medicine with the sole motive of maintaining a sound and vigorous physique and begetting children to do his work and labor for his benefit is not following the right course. A man should aim to

25

maintain physical health and vigor in order that his soul may be upright, in a condition to know God. . . . Whoever throughout his life follows this course will be continually serving God, even while engaged in business and even during cohabitation, because his purpose in all that he does will be to satisfy his needs so as to have a sound body with which to serve God. Even when he sleeps and seeks repose to calm his mind and rest his body so as not to fall sick and be incapacitated from serving God, his sleep is service of the Almighty.[54]

THE FAMILY

The family is a critical unit in Jewish ideology and practice, for it serves several purposes.

The family provides for adult needs. Ever since the Torah's story about the creation of Eve out of Adam's side, the Jewish tradition has considered it to be God's plan that "a man leaves his father and mother and clings to his wife and they become one flesh."[55] They do not "become one flesh" in the ontological way of becoming one being, never to be rent asunder through divorce; for divorce, while often sad, both is permissible, as Deuteronomy 24 makes clear, and is sometimes the right thing to do. They instead become one flesh in several other important ways.

Physically, they become one flesh when they have sexual relations together; marriage and family are designed, in part, to satisfy the sexual needs of both spouses. Most other traditions in both the Occident and the Orient—and in American law as well, until recently—assume that men have sexual drives and women do not, but women acquiesce to the sexual advances of their husbands because they want economic security and children. Judaism, by contrast, from its earliest sources, assumes that women have sexual needs just as much as men do. Thus Exodus 21:10 stipulates that even a man who marries a slave "must not withhold from her her food, her clothing, or her conjugal rights," and the Rabbis reasoned that this holds even more obviously for a man marrying a free woman. Thus, while a husband may never force himself upon his wife, the Mishnah stipulates the number of times each week he must offer to have sexual relations with her, which depends on how often his job enables him to be home. Conversely, he has rights to sex within marriage, too, and if his wife consistently refuses to have sex with him, he may gradually reduce the amount of money he would have to pay her in a divorce settlement until he does not have to pay her anything.[56] Both parties may agree to have sexual relations according to a different schedule, but these provisions in Jewish law establish clearly that both partners to a marriage are entitled to have their sexual needs satisfied.

The spouses become one flesh psychologically as well. Thus the Rabbis declare that "although a man may have many children, he must not remain without a wife," for, as God declares in the Garden of Eden story, "it is not good for a person to live alone."[57] Moreover, the Rabbis affirm, "a man without a wife lives without blessing, without life, without joy, without help, and without peace."[58] Conversely, the Rabbis denigrate bachelorhood[59]—a far cry from the ideal of asceticism in other cultures. Marriage, in the Jewish view, is thus the optimal context for human development and for meeting adult needs.

Because a major objective of marriage and family is mutual love and support, spousal, parental, or child abuse—aside from being violations of Judaism's laws prohibiting assault and battery—is a total undermining of what family relations should be. Abuse is also a desecration of the divine image inherent in each of us and a failure to respect those so created. Such acts are, therefore, condemned and punished in Jewish law.

The family creates, educates, and supports the next generation. Sex within marriage has two distinct purposes: companionship and procreation. Thus, on the one hand, sexual relations are valued as a form of human love even when the couple cannot or is not planning to have children. On the other hand, procreation is an important activity, so important, in fact, that it is the very first commandment mentioned in the Torah: "God blessed them [the first man and woman] and God said to them: 'Be fruitful and multiply.' "[60] The Rabbis later define that obligation as the duty to produce minimally one boy and one girl—although this does not apply to those who cannot comply because of problems of infertility—and the ideal is to have as many children as one can.[61]

Marriage not only provides the venue for having children but is also, in the Jewish view, the context in which children are educated. Parents have the duty to educate their children in

Judaism, including its moral components.[62] Parents may use schools to help them fulfill that duty, but they must periodically check to make sure that their children are in fact learning what they should, because ultimately the duty to educate children remains theirs. Moreover, much of the Jewish tradition can be taught only at home, for this is a tradition that is not restricted to the synagogue or school: It intends to influence virtually every detail of life.

EDUCATION

Education is not only for children but is a lifelong activity in Judaism. Thus already in the Torah "Moses summoned all the Israelites and said to them: Hear, O Israel, the laws and rules that I proclaim to you this day! Study them and observe them faithfully!"[63] Moreover, the Torah requires that once every seven years all the Israelites—"men, women, and children"—gather to hear the entire Torah read.[64] Later Jewish tradition would make this instead a weekly reading from the Torah on each Sabbath, with smaller sections read on Mondays and Thursdays, the market days, as well. From the very beginning, then, this was not to be an esoteric tradition, kept a secret by the few privileged to know; it was, rather, to be an open, public tradition, studied and interpreted by Jews of both genders and all ages. One striking indication of the depth of this Jewish value is that while the Bible calls Moses a "prophet" and describes him as a military leader and an intermediary between God and the Israelites, the Rabbis call him "Moses, our teacher."[65]

For generations, Jews identified this commandment with studying the Jewish tradition, convinced that one should "turn it over, and turn it over again, for everything is included in it."[66] As Jews interacted with other cultures that were making progress in science, medicine, law, and other fields, however, a number of Jewish scholars learned those lessons and integrated their new knowledge into their practice and understanding of Judaism. This became considerably more pronounced after the Enlightenment, so much so that even a nineteenth-century Orthodox thinker like Samson Raphael Hirsch could affirm that Jews should learn other fields, for God's revelation is contained not only in traditional Jewish literature but also in the world that God created. One's study of the world in fields like science and philosophy must, in his view, be evaluated by what one learns in the Torah, for that was given by God, while the topics taught in universities were developed by fallible human beings; but one must study the results of human inquiry nevertheless.[67] Not all Orthodox Jews then or now agree with this approach, but many do; and certainly the vast majority of Jews, who are not Orthodox, take general education seriously.

THE COMMUNITY

If the family is the primary unit in Jewish life, the community follows close behind. Communities are necessary, in part, for practical purposes, for only through living in a community can one have what one needs to live life as a Jew—synagogues, schools, kosher food, a person skilled in circumcision, a cemetery, and more. Furthermore, only in a community can all the duties of Judaism be fulfilled, because justice, care for the poor, education, and many other Jewish demands require other people. Thus Jewish life is organized around the community.

The community is not only important for practical purposes, though; it also has theological import. Israel stood at Sinai as a community, and it is as a group that they made the covenant with God. From then on, each Jew, as the Passover ritual powerfully states, is to see himself or herself "as if he himself left Egypt" and stood at Sinai, thereby sharing in God's work of liberation and God's covenant with all other Jews in all generations. Judaism, contrary to Enlightenment ideology, does not see us as isolated individuals with rights; it sees us rather as members of a community, with duties to each other and to God.

This sense of community is much stronger than the kinds of communities we are used to in modern, post-Enlightenment societies. In the United States, for example, all communities are voluntary: I may choose to join a group or to leave it at any time. I may even choose to give up my citizenship as an American. In Jewish law, though, once I am Jewish by either being born to a Jewish woman or converting to Judaism, I am Jewish for life. If I convert to another religion, I am an apostate, and I lose the privileges of being Jewish (such as being married or buried as a Jew and being counted as part of the prayer quorum), but I retain all the obligations of being Jewish! This is, then, not a thin, voluntary sense of community, but a thick, corporate sense, in which I am literally part of the body of the Jewish community and cannot be severed from it.[68]

This thick sense of community in covenant with God is symbolized by the *minyan*, the prayer quorum consisting of ten Jewish adults. Jews may pray or study individually, but some parts of the liturgy can be recited and the official Torah reading can be accomplished only in the presence of ten Jewish adults, the minimum number deemed a community. Only in that setting can we bless and sanctify God fully, and only in a group can we hear and study God's word adequately.

The following talmudic list of facilities and people that are to be part of any Jewish community fit for a rabbi to reside there reveals the nature of what a community is understood to be within the Jewish tradition:

> It has been taught: A scholar should not reside in a city where [any] of the following ten things is missing: (1) a court of justice that can impose flagellation and monetary penalties; (2) a charity fund, collected by two people and distributed by three [to ensure honesty and wise policies of distribution]; (3) a synagogue; (4) public baths; (5) toilet facilities; (6) a circumciser; (7) a doctor; (8) a notary [for writing official documents]; (9) a slaughterer [of kosher meat]; and (10) a schoolmaster. Rabbi Akiva is quoted [as including] also several kinds of fruit [in the list] because they are beneficial for eyesight.[69]

The community must thus provide facilities and people necessary for justice (a court and notary); Jewish religious life (a synagogue, a circumciser, and a kosher slaughterer); Jewish education (a rabbi and schoolmaster); charity and other social services; and health care, including public baths and toilets (remember that this was written before the advent of indoor plumbing), a doctor, and—according to Rabbi Akiva—even the foods necessary for health.

If the Jewish community of talmudic times did not live under foreign rule, this list would undoubtedly also include other things that the rulers supplied—such as defense, roads, and bridges. Still, in many times and places, Jewish communities had semiautonomy, with the powers of taxation and policing thus implied. The Jewish court would, for example, appoint inspectors of the weights and measures used by merchants to ensure honesty in business.[70]

SOCIAL ACTION AND THE MESSIANIC FUTURE

All of these elements of Jewish life—the individual, the family, education, and the community—are necessary for the ongoing life of Jews, but they are also intended to enable Jews to carry out the Jewish mission. Jews believe that the Messiah has not yet come, that the world is still broken and fragmented by war, disease, poverty, meanness, and the like. Only God can ultimately bring the Messiah; the *Aleinu,* the prayer that ends every Jewish service, expresses the hope that God will "utterly destroy false gods and fix the world through the reign of the Almighty."[71] Nevertheless, we human beings are to help God in that task as God's agents and partners in the ongoing repair of the world. This includes research into preventing or curing disease, political steps to avoid war and reinforce peace, political and economic measures to stop hunger and provide the other elements of substantive justice, legal methods to ensure procedural justice, and educational efforts to teach morality and understanding. Jews have been and continue to be heavily involved in social action; indeed, they overwhelmingly see that as the most important factor in their Jewish identity.[72] This commitment to repair the world stems from the convictions that the world is not now redeemed and that we must act to help God bring about the messianic hope for the future.

NOT IN THE HEAVENS

In the end, both Jewish ethics and Jewish morality shape the Jew. Jewish theoretical convictions about the divine source of morality and the ways to discern God's will give Jews a sense of why they should be moral and how, even in the radically changed world of today. Jewish moral beliefs about the nature of the human being, the family, education, the community, and the future define what is important in life and motivate Jews to try to achieve those moral goals. Together, they pose a distinct challenge to Jews to know God's will and to do it, just as it was in the time of the Torah:

Surely, this Instruction which I enjoin upon you this day is not too baffling for you, nor is it beyond reach. It is not in the heavens, that you should say, "Who among us can go up to the heavens and get it for us and impart it to us, that we may observe it?" Neither is it beyond the sea, that you should say, "Who among us can cross to the other side of the sea and get it for us and impart it to us, that we may observe it?" No, the thing is very close to you, in your mouth and in your heart, to observe it.[73]

CHAPTER TWO

Privacy

I BEGIN OUR DISCUSSION OF JEWISH PERSONAL ETHICS WITH PERHAPS the most personal issue possible—the ability to safeguard one's own privacy. Specifically, in this chapter I explore the individual's right to privacy within the community, balanced against the community's right to set standards of behavior. Although practical considerations inevitably and properly play a role in this chapter, much of the discussion focuses on the theological and moral foundations of privacy and the grounds to invade it in specific circumstances.

THE INTERNET AND PRIVACY

The wide availability of personal information available on-line undeniably and thankfully benefits us all. Heartwarming stories abound of long-lost relatives and friends reunited through on-line, national directories of residences and businesses. Medical costs have decreased as a result of computerized record keeping, not only because it is faster and clearer than paper records but also because it can eliminate duplicate testing procedures. Moreover, electronic records make medical care safer and more efficient by alerting medical personnel to the other medications that their patients are taking (thus avoiding harmful drug interactions) and to the allergies and other conditions that might suggest or contraindicate certain drugs or therapies. The lawyer trying to locate critical witnesses or parties to a lawsuit finds the Internet a major boon, and businesses learn how to target their markets to those most likely to buy. We also value the sheer convenience, as well as the savings, in buying airline tickets and a host of other things through the World Wide Web, and we take for granted the ability to use our credit cards worldwide and quickly. Federal, state, and local governments use personal information to collect taxes, allocate government benefits, and enforce the law.

As with most things in life, though, electronic sharing of information has both advantages and disadvantages. Society must now delicately balance the rights of potential employers and insurers against protections for the individuals they are thinking of hiring or insuring. Now, or in the not-too-distant future, the information at issue might include not only people's own medical histories and those of their families, but their genetic predispositions as well. Easy access to everyone's financial information helps thieves use people's credit card or bank information to steal from them or defraud them. Knowledge of people's buying habits might be used by telemarketers to bombard them with unwanted phone calls. In the wake of the confirmation hearings of Judge Bork, in which his video-renting habits were revealed, legislation has already been adopted to keep such records off limits to anyone lacking a court order, to prevent snooping and possible embarrassment, and more such legislation has been, and will be, enacted to protect people from knowing what they have no right to know about others.

The government's increased access to information about its citizens also poses problems. Although the confidentiality of Americans' tax, social welfare, and criminal history is protected by law, available only to authorized government employees, records of a person's birth, marriage, death, property, court cases, motor vehicle history, and voter registration are open to the public in many states,[1] and the information in such records may be used by enforcement agencies against that individual. Furthermore, some governmental agencies, such as the Federal Bureau of Investigation, keep records about people unbeknownst to them. How shall we balance the need for government to carry out its legitimate functions, including security, with the rights of individuals to be free from unwarranted tracking, intrusion, or harassment? Moreover, how can the accuracy of such records be ensured, and who has the right to see them? Without carefully constructed safeguards, government records might be used to harm an individual in ways the government itself never intended.

These problems with everyone's enhanced ability to know about everyone else have generated immense concern. Part of our anxiety stems from pragmatic concerns, but part of it comes out of a sense that much information about us is not anybody else's business. So, for example, we do not want to be barred from employment or medical or life insurance on the basis of parts of our medical history that we did not disclose; even when we have nothing to hide, we want our medical condition to be known only by those to whom we choose to disclose it. Similarly, people should not only be barred from using our credit cards or stealing from our bank accounts but should not even know what our assets are unless we choose to tell them. We do not want our buying habits to be widely known, not only for fear of losing money but also, and more broadly, because others do not have a blanket right to know our assets and liabilities, our likes and dislikes.

For good, pragmatic reasons, we want to know the content of the records about us that various arms of the government and credit agencies have, we want to be guaranteed the right to correct such records when they are inaccurate, and we want to ensure the security of these databases. But, on moral grounds, we also want the government or credit agency to have the burden of proof to show why it needs a particular type of record about us in the first place, so that we do not have the constant feeling that "Big Brother" is watching us.

THE VALUES AND CONCEPTS MOTIVATING A CONCERN FOR PRIVACY

We value privacy, then, not only for pragmatic reasons but for other reasons as well, reasons that are moral and religious in character. Let us examine some of the more important ones.

The right to privacy is at the core of human dignity. The more our privacy is invaded, the more we lose two central components of our dignity—namely, our individuality and the respect we command from others. When our innermost selves become the subject for the knowledge and criticism of others, the resulting social pressure quickly wears away our individuality. According to a deservedly famous passage from the Mishnah,[2] God created each of us as a unique person, a factor that differentiates divine creation from human creation and contributes to our individual significance and value. An original Picasso painting is much more rare and expensive than the several hundred prints of it, and the prints are more dear than the myriad photographs of it. Similarly, the more distinctive we are, the more worth we have in our own eyes and in the eyes of others.

If, however, many of the details of our lives are open to the public, many of us will be afraid to veer from whatever is socially endorsed, lest we be subject to criticism or even attack. That is, we will relinquish our individuality so as to be able to survive within the group. Some such social constraints are necessary for any society to function, and some limitations imposed by society actually benefit the individual by teaching and enforcing important social norms. But when people can know the most personal of things about everyone else, individual identity and uniqueness become hard to sustain. That is social pressure run amuck. The investigations and confessions typical of commune meetings in Communist China are good examples of how making everything public scares everyone into blending into the one, accepted model of how one should act and even feel. Add modern technology to the methods of intimidation used there, and none of us will dare break out of our socially determined mold. Privacy is thus essential to each person's individuality and the self-worth that accompanies it.

But it is not only how we think of ourselves that is at stake. Privacy is also necessary to protect our reputation among others. We all think or do things that others disapprove of. To the extent that that is known publicly, we lose their respect. The community does have a right and, indeed, a duty to establish and enforce some norms, but if the community can know and scrutinize absolutely every one of our thoughts and actions, we will inevitably displease the majority in some ways and lose their esteem in the process. Conversely, the very requirement to honor and protect a person's privacy both stems from and engenders an inherent regard for that person. Thus by preserving human individuality and honor, privacy contributes to human dignity.

Privacy is at the heart of mutual trust and friendship, tolerance and creativity. If you reveal things I tell you in confidence, I will think twice before trusting you as a business partner, a colleague, or a friend.[3] Privacy also enables creativity to flourish, for it protects nonconformist people from interference by others.[4] Along the same lines, privacy is a prerequisite for a free and tolerant society, for each person has secrets that "concern weaknesses that we dare not reveal to a competitive world, dreams that others may ridicule, past deeds that bear no relevance to present conduct, or desires that a judgmental and hypocritical public may condemn."[5]

These moral concerns justify the protection of privacy in any society, but a religious tradition like Judaism adds yet other rationales for safeguarding an individual's privacy. First, since human beings, according to the Torah, are created in God's image, honoring them is a way to honor God and, conversely, degrading them is tantamount to dishonoring God.[6] One way we respect others is to safeguard their confidences. On the other hand, revealing people's secrets shows disrespect for them—and often downright shames them. But the Jewish tradition teaches us that when we reveal a person's secrets we not only defame that person but also we dishonor the image of God within that person and thus God Himself.

Moreover, God intends that the Israelites be "a kingdom of priests and a holy people."[7] Among other things that the Torah requires of Jews so that they might become a holy people, it states that a lender may not intrude on a borrower's home to collect on a loan and people may not be talebearers within the community.[8] Thus a holy people must protect a person's home, reputation, and communication by forbidding both *intrusion* and *disclosure.* I discuss both of these aspects of privacy in some detail in this chapter.

Just as the Jewish religious mission mandates privacy, so too does Jewish theology. "You shall be holy, for I, the Lord your

God, am holy"; "Walk in all His ways"; and "Follow the Lord your God."[9] The Rabbis understood these biblical verses as establishing the principle of *imitatio dei*, of modeling ourselves after God: "As God is gracious and compassionate, you too must be gracious and compassionate; . . . as the Holy One is righteous, you too must be righteous; as the Holy One is loving, you too must be loving."[10] But God, as understood in the Jewish tradition, is in part known and in part hidden. God is made known to human beings through revelation and through divine acts in history, but no human being, even Moses, can comprehend God's essence.[11] Furthermore, the Mishnah declares that one who probes God's essence beyond what God has chosen to reveal to human beings should not have been born, for, as the Jerusalem Talmud explains, to know more about God than the Holy One chooses to reveal is an affront to His dignity.[12] If God is to be a model for us, then, we, like God, must take steps to preserve our own privacy. We, then, out of respect for God's commands as articulated in the biblical passages just cited, must also respect the privacy of others.[13] Thus these demands are deeply rooted not only in morality but in Jewish theology.

CONTRASTING AMERICAN AND JEWISH INTERESTS IN PRIVACY

While the American and Jewish traditions both seek to protect people from invasions of privacy, the grounds for that effort differ markedly, and so do the limits of the protection. In Jewish law, as we have seen, the claim to privacy is grounded in Jewish theology: The nature of each human being as someone created in the image of God, the nature of the Jewish community as "a kingdom of priests and a holy nation," the commands of God to respect other people's privacy by refraining from intrusion into their physical and psychological space and by avoiding disclosure of what others have no need or right to know, and the nature of God as One who is partly revealed and partly hidden.

In the American tradition, by contrast, privacy is rooted in the "unalienable rights . . . to life, liberty, and the pursuit of happiness." Although the U.S. Supreme Court in 1973 admitted that "the Constitution does not explicitly mention any right of privacy," it maintained that in a line of decisions going back as far as 1891 the court has recognized the right itself or at least the roots of that right

> in the First Amendment, . . . in the Fourth and Fifth Amendments, . . . in the penumbras of the Bill of Rights, . . . in the Ninth Amendment, . . . or in the concept of liberty guaranteed by the first section of the Fourteenth Amendment. . . . These decisions make it clear that only personal rights that can be deemed "fundamental" or "implicit in the concept of ordered liberty" . . . are included in the guarantee of personal privacy. They also make it clear that the right has some extension to activities relating to marriage, . . . procreation, . . . contraception, . . . family relationships, . . . and child rearing and education.[14]

The court itself in that decision favored the Fourteenth Amendment's liberty clause as the basis for this right, together with the amendment's restrictions on state governments as well as on the federal government to infringe on the right to privacy.

These dissimilarities in rationale lead to differences in application. The very Supreme Court case that established an American right to privacy illustrates this, for the court invoked it to justify a woman's right to abortion on demand, at least during the first two trimesters of pregnancy.

The Jewish tradition mandates protection against intrusion and disclosure, but it clearly does not extend those protections to permitting abortion on demand. On the contrary, the woman's body, of which the fetus is a part, belongs to God and, therefore, may not be injured through abortion unless the woman's physical or mental health or her life is at stake. According to some modern authorities, that would include, on the basis of the mother's mental health, permission to abort if she has been raped or subjected to incest or if the fetus will suffer from a fatal disease or be grossly malformed. Even with these expansions of the sanction to abort, however, Jewish law begins with a presumption against abortion as an act of self-injury and therefore demands a justification beyond the will of the mother.[15]

As another example, since the 1973 *Roe v. Wade* decision of the U.S. Supreme Court, American legislatures and courts have moved to expand considerations of privacy into permitting consensual sex among adults, regardless of their marital status. Moreover, even though the Supreme Court decided (5 to 4) in 1985 that the constitutional right to privacy does not extend to private, consensual homosexual sex,[16] state legislatures and courts have increasingly seen that as protected by their own laws governing privacy and the U.S. Supreme Court itself is now reviewing that decision. The classical Jewish tradition does not permit either of these things. Moreover, those trying to mount an argument for changing Jewish law on these matters would not find Jewish conceptions of privacy to be much help, for the theological and communitarian elements of Jewish law are too strong to permit an individual's privacy to be a defense against a divine or communal prohibition or duty. Instead, those like me who would argue for a more liberal Jewish approach to nonmarital or homosexual sex must base their arguments on other grounds.[17]

The American approach to privacy, in sum, seeks to stop interferences of some people (employers, insurance agents, etc.) or the government in the life of individuals in the continual conflict of all against all. In this meaning, the right to privacy is akin to, or rooted in, the right to liberty. American sources also seek to protect privacy in the narrower sense of making certain information about a person inaccessible to others—again, to secure the individual against others and against the government. The Jewish approach to privacy instead sees it as an integral part of the mission to build an ideal community that aspires to follow God's dictates and to model itself after God. The American conception of protection against intrusion and disclosure leads to a discussion of individual liberties; the Jewish understanding of why intrusion and disclosure must be prevented instead leads to considerations of how to safeguard the image of God within us and the holiness of the community.

INTRUSION

In a 1928 dissenting opinion, Justice Louis B. Brandeis worried prophetically about increasing governmental intrusion in our private lives. In that opinion he defined privacy as "the right to be let alone—the most comprehensive of rights and the right most valued by civilized men."[18] Our concern about intrusion today applies equally to nongovernmental agencies—to credit card companies, health insurance agents, financial institutions, employers, and even individuals—any of whom might do us harm.

THE JEWISH PRINCIPLES GOVERNING INTRUSION

The Torah bans intrusion for the purpose of collecting a debt: "When you make a loan of any sort to your countryman, you must not enter his house to seize his pledge. You must remain outside, while the man to whom you made the loan brings the pledge out to you."[19] Later Jewish law restricted the debtor's right against intrusion. Because Jewish law does not permit creditors to charge interest on a loan to fellow Jews, the Rabbis worried that if collecting the loan became an onerous process, people would no longer be willing to lend money to those who needed it, thus in the Talmud's phrase, "locking the door in the face of [future] borrowers." The Rabbis also wanted to prevent debtors from using their homes to hide items that could be used to repay the loan.[20]

Even with these later restrictions, the Torah's law prohibiting intrusions was taken very seriously. Creditors, after all, are justified in trying to recover the property owed to them in pledge, and even so the Torah limits their access to the debtor's home. Those who lack such grounds for entry, then, are all the more required to respect the privacy of those who dwell within. Thus, in general, people may not enter someone else's home without permission; and, if they do, the landlord may eject them even by force, if necessary.[21] Furthermore, the Rabbis advised people not to enter even their own home without warning, lest they surprise and embarrass someone inside.[22] In one passage, they use God as the model: Before God revealed Himself to Adam, He first called out to him, "Where are you?" to warn him that He was coming—and we should learn such good manners from God.[23]

In interpreting the biblical law prohibiting intrusion for collecting loans, the Rabbis maintained that this law bars not only physical trespass but also visual penetration of a person's domain (*hezek re'iyah*; literally, "injury done through seeing"). They thus insisted that two joint landowners contribute equally to erect a wall between their respective halves of the property to serve as a deterrent to visual intrusion, and they prohibited making a hole in the wall opposite the neighbor's window. Along these lines, they interpreted Balaam's praise of the tents of the Israelites—"How fair are your tents, O Jacob, your dwelling places, O Israel"—as arising from his observation that the

Israelite tents were so situated that the tent openings did not face each other, thus preventing people from seeing into the tents of their neighbors.[24] Even if landowners tolerated such intrusion for a period of time, they may take steps to prevent spying on their property in the future. Indeed, they should do so, because while they may waive their own interest, the general interests of decency and public peace are at stake.[25]

In the Middle Ages, when the mail system expanded, Rabbenu Gershom (c. 960–1028, Germany) issued a decree prohibiting mail carriers and others from reading other people's mail lest they learn trade secrets or spread gossip, thus violating the prohibition of talebearing.[26] According to the decree, violators would be subject to excommunication, even if they did not publicize the improperly read letter. He thus recognized privacy as an important value in its own right, apart from its importance in protecting people from harm.[27]

Rabbi Norman Lamm, president of Yeshiva University in New York, has argued that, in modern circumstances, this can and should be applied not only to visual incursions but to aural ones as well. Eavesdropping, in other words, is just as heinous an invasion of privacy as spying is. Rabbi Menahem Meiri (1249–1316, France) ruled that the biblical law interdicts only visual surveillance and not aural snooping; hence the wall that talmudic law demands between neighbors needs to be high but not thick. As Rabbi Lamm points out, however, Rabbi Meiri assumed that people normally speak softly when they think they can be overheard; therefore, the wall did not have to protect them. That reasoning, though, clearly does not apply to wiretapping and other forms of electronic bugging, and so, for Rabbi Lamm, "all forms of surveillance—natural, mechanical, and electronic, visual and aural—should be prohibited under Jewish law's strictures on *hezek re'iyah*."[28]

U.S. law has gone through a similar evolution. In the 1928 *Olmstead* case, the majority decided that the Fourth Amendment protected individuals only against "physical invasions" by law enforcement officers; therefore, wiretapping by government officials was permissible. Justice Brandeis at that time dissented, arguing for an expanded notion of the nature of privacy to accommodate new technology. In 1967, the Supreme Court overturned *Olmstead* in *Katz v. United States,* holding that instead of the original physical trespass requirement, the threshold question is whether there is a "reasonable expectation of privacy," because "the Fourth Amendment protects people, not places. What a person knowingly exposes to the public, even in his own home or office, is not a subject of Fourth Amendment protection. . . . But what he seeks to preserve as private, even in an area accessible to the public, may be constitutionally protected."[29]

There are, though, several ways in which Jewish practices specifically promote intrusion.[30] For example, Jewish law demands that as many friends and family as possible attend a funeral, comfort the mourners in their home, and join them there in prayer for a full seven days after the burial. Similarly, friends and family are expected to celebrate the *brit milah* (ritual circumcision) of a newborn boy with his parents, even though that is surgery on his most private parts. Here social needs to express appropriate emotions and to articulate traditional Jewish understandings of a life-cycle event, as well as the needs of the people themselves for communal support on such occasions of great joy or sorrow, outweigh the needs for privacy.[31] These are exceptions, though, to the general rules that prohibit spying on others and that require people to erect walls to protect their own privacy.

WORK: SPYING ON EMPLOYEES
Some specific applications of these principles of privacy to modern circumstances will make their import clear. One place where new technology has indeed increased the ability of people to intrude on others is at work. The practice common in many businesses today in which employers "spy" on their employees presents an interesting case for applying the Jewish principles described above.

In a survey of five hundred executives by the Society for Human Resources Management, 36 percent said that they looked at employee E-mail, and a similar study conducted by *MacWorld* magazine showed that nearly two-thirds of the employers who monitored their employees' E-mail, electronic work files, network messages, or voice mail did so without warning their employees.[32] Even if airlines, for example, announce to callers that their call "may be monitored for training purposes and to ensure better service," does that make the intrusion on both the employee and the caller legitimate? Is it proper for employers to download employees' computer data or check their office telephone records to see how much time they are spending on business and how much on personal matters or to evaluate their efficiency and effectiveness for purposes of determining their future job status?

Employers monitor employee E-mail, telephone calls, and other electronic records for a number of reasons. Some businesses, as the notice commonly used suggests, have supervisors listen in on calls as part of their training of new employees, and others want to ensure quality of service overall. Still others oversee electronic transmissions in an attempt to avoid, or at least, discover employee misdeeds, such as transmission and misappropriation of trade secrets, infringement of copyrights, defamation or harassment, or fraud.[33] Until now courts have generally held that employers have this right because employees do not have a reasonable expectation of privacy in their workplace E–mail and computers and thus fail to meet the standard announced in *Katz v. United States*.[34]

What must be balanced in these cases is the right of the employer to ensure that employees are doing their job well as against the right of employees to privacy. Historically, employers certainly have had the right in Jewish law to supervise their employees and to determine their job status and compensation on the basis of performance. Moreover, while E-mail and on-line commerce have been a major boon to worker productivity, they also provide those working at a computer with an incredible opportunity to slough off. One recent study, in fact, found that of forty thousand people randomly chosen, 30 percent viewed pornographic Web sites from work, spending an average of forty-six minutes a month at such sites; and other studies have shown heavy use of the Internet for games, shopping, and stock trading for oneself during work hours.[35] At the same time, it is clear that employees do not give up their rights to privacy altogether just because they have entered the workplace.

To balance these conflicting principles, employers need to establish clear ground rules for the good of everyone concerned.

Specifically, if the employer intends to monitor employee performance by examining computer files and telephone communications, he or she must announce that policy to employees when they first apply for a job so they know the policy is one of the conditions of employment; they can then choose to accept or reject employment on those terms. Similarly, employers must announce their policy on private use of office telephones and computers clearly, whether they forbid all such use or permit some such use, restricted by time and/or purpose. These policies must then be reiterated in periodic training sessions or bulletins.

With that amount of fair warning, employers would have the right to supervise their employees electronically. On the other hand, without such warning, employees have the right to assume that their computer and telephone records will remain private, even those within the employer's office. The right to privacy, in other words, is the default assumption in employment as well as in other arenas of life, an assumption that is rebuttable only when clear and complete warning is given ahead of time and repeatedly as to the conditions of using the machines belonging to the business. In the absence of those conditions, employers may not survey employees' electronic communications, just as they may not open mail specifically addressed to employees as personal.

VIDEOTAPING AND PHOTOGRAPHING

We are regularly videotaped every time we step into a bank, the room housing automated teller machines, most stores, and even many apartment buildings. California has increasingly been using photograph machines to catch those who drive through a red light at busy intersections. We generally acquiesce to, or even approve of, these uses of Big Brother technology to deter crime and to aid in law enforcement, thus affording us greater safety and security.

Like all technology, though, videotapes and cameras can be used for immoral purposes. A 1999 case in Louisiana illustrates an egregious breach of the Jewish principles we have been considering. A man entrusted with a key to his neighbors' house in case of emergencies used his access to the house to install videocameras hidden in several places in the house so that he could

45

spy on his neighbors' most intimate moments. Jewish law's prohibition of "injury through seeing" (*hezek re'iyah*) would clearly
forbid such videotaping. The Peeping Tom laws of Louisiana,
however, covered only older technology, like telephone lines and
telescopes, and even those types of spying were classified as mis-
demeanors with minimum penalties. The family understandably
felt "raped," and they are now fighting for new state and possibly
federal legislation to make such activities a felony.[36] We clearly
have to be alert to the continual need to update our laws to respond appropriately to the illegitimate uses of new technology,
much as we employ it and appreciate the ways it aids our lives.

OVERRIDING PRIVACY IN THE NAME OF NATIONAL SECURITY

National security concerns may trump the Jewish demand for
privacy. In regard to individuals, saving a life takes precedence
over all the other commandments except for three—the prohibitions against murder, adultery/incest, and idolatry. That is, except for engaging in one of those three activities, a Jew is
actually commanded to violate any other laws necessary to save
a life.[37] Jewish law has a similar provision on a social level: While
Jewish evidentiary rules for proving a capital offense are extremely rigorous, a number of the stringencies are waived in
proving a case against a person who leads others to idolatry
(*masit*), presumably because that crime puts at stake the very
existence of the community as "a kingdom of priests and a holy
nation" under God's aegis.[38] To the extent necessary, then, the
effort to protect the life of the community justifies breaching its
normal rules, including those prohibiting invasion of an individual's privacy. It is this line of reasoning that would provide
the Jewish justification for government wiretapping, for example, of suspected spies or drug dealers.

Clearly this exception must not be abused to give the government warrant to spy on everyone at all times. The case against
the one leading others to idolatry, after all, had to be demonstrated
to the court, albeit under diminished evidentiary protections.

Similar judicial procedures have been enacted in the United
States and in many other Western countries to protect citizens
from an overzealous government using wiretapping and other

means of spying for other purposes. Governments, of course, dislike such restraints on their power. Moreover, particular breaches of security engender calls by citizens themselves, let alone government officials, for looser constraints on governmental spying. So, for example, in the wake of the discovery in 1999 of Chinese espionage at American nuclear laboratories, allegedly extending from the 1960s, several proposals to tighten the 1978 Foreign Intelligence Surveillance Act (FISA) through extended polygraph testing of employees and through cutting the budget for declassifying documents have been discussed in Congress. Steven Aftergood, director of the Project on Government Secrecy at the Federation of American Scientists, persuasively maintains that such measures are knee-jerk reactions to what has not yet proven to be a serious breach of American security and, in any case, "could infringe upon the constitutional rights of Americans, divert security resources into a mindless spy hunt, and leave government increasingly unaccountable to its citizens."[39] As he says,

> In the past, the 1978 surveillance act had been criticized for making it too easy for government agencies to violate the privacy rights of Americans. Specifically, critics pointed to the seemingly automatic approval of applications—796 in 1998—for clandestine search and surveillance. But with the media's virtual "conviction" of [Wen Ho] Lee [despite the Justice Department's claim that it had no "probable cause" to violate Lee's constitutional rights], the dominant criticism today is that the law makes it too difficult to spy on Americans suspected of espionage.[40]

If that was true after the Lee case, it has been even more true after the destruction of the World Trade Center and a wing of the Pentagon on September 11, 2001, by Muslim terrorists. Thus whether Aftergood's warnings about unwarranted governmental spying were warranted in the Lee case, after the terrorist attacks of September 11, his words have become critical: While we clearly need the government to be able to apprehend criminals and terrorists, we must also be alert to the need for vigilance to protect individuals' privacy so that national security does not become simply an excuse for eviscerating our rights to privacy.

From a Jewish perspective, the principle, at any rate, is clear: The burden of proof always rests with the government to show why it must invade people's privacy at this time and in this way to protect the body politic. When it meets that burden, it has the right and the responsibility to intrude on people's privacy for that purpose, but only after an independent judiciary has determined that that considerable burden has been met.

PRIVACY AND DIVERSITY VERSUS SAFETY

In recent years, determining when the government has demonstrated the need to override privacy has become increasingly difficult, for the government's claim has extended beyond dramatic cases of espionage and terrorism. New waves of immigration to the United States from Africa, Latin America, and East Asia have yielded the largest number of immigrants per year since the 1880–1920 era. These new residents have brought with them cultural practices that are sometimes at odds with middle-class American values. In Maine, for example, a refugee from Afghanistan was seen kissing the penis of his baby boy, a traditional expression of love by his father. To his neighbors, the police, and the district court, however, that constituted child abuse, and the child was taken away by the social welfare authorities. Ultimately, on appeal, the Maine Supreme Court researched the family's cultural heritage and restored the child to his father, but the court's decision made it clear that this was an exceptional case, not a precedent.[41]

"American laws and welfare services have often left immigrants terrified of the intrusive power of government," a 1999 *New York Times* article noted.[42] The author went on to say:

> Among the ethnic minority activities at risk of being dubbed 'un-American' are the use of disciplinary techniques such as shaming and physical punishment, parent/child co-sleeping arrangements, rituals of group identity and ceremonies of initiation involving scarification, piercing and genital alterations, arranged marriage, polygamy, the segregation of gender roles, bilingualism and foreign language use, and many more."[43]

Other traditional practices that have put immigrants into trouble with the law include spanking, puberty rites, animal sacrifices, enforced dress codes, leaving children unattended at home, and the use of narcotics in specific rituals. The issue is complicated yet further by the fact that some immigrants have fled their home countries precisely to escape one or more of their homeland's cultural practices.

The new immigrants to the United States, then, poignantly pose one of the most trenchant dilemmas in moral philosophy: Are moral norms objective, transcending all cultural barriers (moral absolutism), so that some cultural practices can and should be universally condemned; or are moral norms relative to specific societies (moral relativism), so that Americans should learn to stretch their understandings of what is acceptable and tolerate differing practices in the name of freedom, pluralism, and privacy?

I explore that question in my book *To Do the Right and the Good.* I devoted two chapters of that book to the grounds and limits of pluralism within the Jewish community and in interfaith relations, and in an appendix, I explored how we determine moral norms in the first place. Here, though, I want simply to note the important link between the issues of privacy and pluralism: The right to privacy and its corollary, freedom from intrusion, depend in large part on the degree to which people have the right to follow practices different from those of the majority—that is, the degree to which pluralism is accepted and supported within a given society. Only if a given society protects its members from intrusion on at least some issues can there be pluralism within that society, for a lack of privacy will all too readily produce a totalitarian state, where the social norms are enforced on everyone on all matters. Conversely, only if a society values pluralism and takes steps to guarantee it does it make sense to protect people from others intruding on their turf to see if they are following the social norm, for if only those in power are right, why should individuals be allowed to hide their deviant behavior?

Furthermore, even those societies that value pluralism and privacy must set limits to both. To take an extreme example, may you murder your own child and claim on grounds of pluralism that the society has no right to intrude? Jews, Christians, Muslims, and secular Americans would all say: "Clearly not!" At the same time, as the plethora of new immigrants to the United States should remind us, we must not presume that only the middle-class American values of our time are correct. Thus the discussion in *To Do the Right and the Good* on pluralism and its limits, both within a society and among groups, is tightly linked with the present topic of the degree to which we should all be protected from intrusion.

DISCLOSURE

THE JEWISH PRINCIPLES GOVERNING DISCLOSURE

The classical Rabbis also sought to ensure privacy of communication. They forbade a judge to reveal his vote lest the privacy of the other judges on the panel be compromised. The Talmud actually records that someone was ejected from the academy when he revealed such information a full twenty-two years after the trial![44]

The demand to protect confidential matters applies not only to public authorities like judges but to private individuals as well. The Torah prohibits spreading not only falsehoods about other people (*sheker*, "lying") but also true facts about someone else that the hearer has no need to know—in other words, *rekhilut* (gossip).[45] The Talmud takes this further, insisting that even if there is no harm intended or anticipated, a person may not reveal a private conversation to an outside party, unless the original speaker gives explicit permission to do so.[46]

This rule restricts the information shared even with a spouse. Indeed, in marriage one may and should keep some of one's own thoughts or actions to oneself, for despite the physical and emotional intimacy of the relationship, married people continue to need and deserve a degree of privacy. People clearly have the duty to inform their spouses about anything that will have an impact on their lives in the present or future, but when there are no such practical implications, spouses should not be told or reminded of past actions or of present or past thoughts that will only upset them.[47] For that matter, as a general rule, spouses have no obligation to tell each other everything they have done or thought and, conversely, they do have the right to be downright uninterested in some aspects of the other's life. Some things, even in marriage, may and should remain private with the individual.[48]

AMERICAN LEGISLATION BANNING DISCLOSURE

In American law, the first federal statutes regarding privacy (in addition, of course, to the Fourth Amendment) were the Privacy

Act of 1974, governing the federal government's acquisition and use of federal agency records containing personal information, and, in that same year, the Federal Educational Rights and Privacy Act, which protects the confidentiality of student records and allows access of students to their own records. The right to informational privacy was first addressed by the U.S. Supreme Court in *Whalen v. Roe* (1977), wherein the court upheld a New York State statute requiring physicians to submit copies of prescriptions for abused drugs to authorities for inclusion in a centralized computer file but specifically stated that while government functions require collecting data "much of which is personal in character and potentially harmful if disclosed," "the right to collect and use such data for public purposes is typically accompanied by a concomitant statutory or regulatory duty to avoid unwarranted disclosure."[49]

This was followed by a series of federal statutes that seek in a piecemeal fashion to address specific privacy concerns, including unauthorized access, interception, or disclosure of private electronic communications by the government as well as by individuals and third parties; government record keeping and disclosure of certain personal information; the acquisition and disclosure of information by the credit-reporting industry; the unauthorized use of computers to access national security information, financial information of institutions, credit card users, financial reporting agencies, or passwords; the use of government computers in a way that damages them or prevents their normal functioning; videotape rental records; motor vehicle records; cable television subscriber information; the practices of, and information held by, telemarketers; and taxpayer records. The Privacy Protection Act of 1994 limits, among other things, governmental seizure of publishers' work product materials, a provision that may be far reaching since anyone posting messages on-line or on the Internet may be considered a "publisher."[50] In addition, some courts have interpreted their state's constitution or statutes to provide more privacy protection than that afforded by federal law or judicial rulings.[51]

In 1890, Samuel D. Warren and Louis D. Brandeis first suggested that the common law ought to recognize a right to privacy, lest technological inventions decrease the personal dignity of the individual. Such protections did not enter the common law, though, until 1977, when four such rights were included in the Restatement (Second) of Torts—namely, protections against unreasonable intrusion on the seclusion of another, unreasonable publicity given to another's private life, publicity that unreasonably places another in a false light before the public, and appropriation of another's name or likeness.[52]

EXCEPTIONS TO THE BAN AGAINST DISCLOSURE

The general Jewish ban against disclosure has an important exception—namely, when someone has a legitimate, pragmatic need to know the information—with special application in our own time to adoptions and to the relationships between some professionals (clergy, healthcare personnel, and lawyers) and the people they serve. In the next three sections, I explore each of these items in turn.

THE PRAGMATIC EXCEPTION IN JEWISH LAW TO PROTECTION FROM DISCLOSURE

The claim to privacy is set aside when it is necessary to protect an individual, family, or group. So, for example, the Torah imposes a duty to testify in court when one knows of relevant facts, even though they may be incriminating.[53] In private settings as well, Jewish law insists on breaking confidentiality when keeping the secret would harm someone. This is based, in part, on the balance that the tradition strikes between the Torah's command, "Do not stand idly by the blood of your neighbor"[54] with its prohibition of *lashon ha-ra*, "speaking of the bad," or "evil speech." Under the first law, we have a positive duty to come to the rescue of another person's life or property, and that would argue for divulging whatever is necessary to accomplish those aims.[55] Under the second law, though, one may not slander someone else—that is, tell truths about someone that will cast a negative light on that person.[56] That would apparently argue for never saying anything negative about anyone else.

The tradition balances these two rules by limiting the latter rule. Specifically, the prohibition of defamation is not violated, according to the Rabbis, when there is a practical need for the hearer to know the negative truth. So, for example, under the

Torah's rule, "Reprove your kinsman," later Jewish sources specify that leaders' sins should be revealed when that is necessary to dissuade people from following their example in committing those sins.[57]

Not only should leaders be criticized when practical needs require it but private individuals should be, too. Two sources in the Talmud make that clear. First, the Talmud records that Rabbi Yoḥanan ben Zakkai publicly denounced the devious business practices of some merchants, despite the defamation involved, so that potential buyers would be forewarned and the merchants themselves might change their ways.[58] Moreover, the Talmud asserts that one must (not just may) publicize illegal land acquisition to protect the lawful owners.[59] Thus if people need to know something negative about someone else in order to avoid physical or even monetary harm, the information may, and indeed should, be made available to the potential victims.

Even so, another passage in the Talmud warns us not to take the prohibition against slander lightly. It interprets the Torah's command not to hold a grudge but rather to rebuke your neighbor as permitting reproof only if it does not involve insult. If, however, you make the neighbor blush or turn pale from shame or fury, then you have violated the ban against slander.[60] Thus these two commandments together require rebuke when there is a practical need, but only in a way that will avoid embarrassment.

For example, if a person asks someone to write a letter of recommendation as part of a job application, the recommender must be forthcoming and honest about the person's strengths and weaknesses in tackling that job, for the potential employer can be harmed by not being told. My friend and colleague on a federal commission, Dr. Robert Levine of the Yale School of Medicine, suggested to me a kind way of handling such situations: Have applicants write a letter that they think that you can sign and then discuss the claims made in such letters with them. This makes clear to them their own assets and liabilities for the job as well as whether you should be the one writing the letter. Clearly, those who have little good to say about a person may suggest that the job seeker ask someone else to write a recommendation for him or her; the duty to come forward with evidence applies only to official court cases and not to other contexts.

Note how this contrasts with American practice. In Enlightenment ideology, the right to privacy trumps the potential employer's right to know. Indeed, after the Buckley Amendment and other legislation established the right of an applicant to read letters of evaluation, people are wary of writing anything negative about a person lest they be sued. In fact, for fear of lawsuit, some companies and nonprofit agencies will verify only the dates that an employee worked for the firm and will say nothing good or bad about the employee's performance. This is an example of the effects of the differing fundamental principles of Jewish and American ideology: Judaism's demand to tell negative truths about a person when necessary for practical reasons is evidence of its communitarianism, whereas American individualism instead led Congress to protect individuals against negative information about them, even when that information is true and significant for other people's future plans.

Rabbi Israel Meir Ha-Kohen (1838–1933, Poland), the Ḥafetz Ḥayyim, provided another example of this pragmatic exception to privacy in Jewish law. The situation he addressed is that of a potential business partnership between B and C, where A knows that it may well work to B's disadvantage. In such circumstances, according to the Ḥafetz Ḥayyim, A *must* warn B *if* six conditions apply:

1. A does not rely exclusively on his own assessment, let alone his snap judgment, but instead thoroughly examines the extent to which B will be harmed by the business deal. On the one hand, this condition precludes A from interfering if others evaluate the situation differently, for then A must assume that however unwise he personally thinks the deal is, B sees the situation as others do, and so there is no warrant to spoil the deal for C. B, after all, has the right to assume his own risks. At the same time, A's information need not be firsthand, and so some sources permit and even require warning B of rumors whose substance would be significantly damaging if they were true.[61]
2. A must not exaggerate the extent of the potential harm.
3. A must be motivated solely by the desire to protect B, not by dislike of C, the desire to pass along a juicy rumor, or by A's own financial gain. This condition permits A to pass along

the information only if he is convinced that *B* might change his mind as a result of it; otherwise *A* would not be protecting *B* by sharing the information, and thus *A* would be besmirching *C*'s reputation as a business partner with no pragmatic justification.

4. The information is not such that *B* could easily discover it himself if he were to bother to investigate. That is, *A* has neither the right nor the responsibility to make up for *B*'s negligence when *A*'s doing so comes at the expense of *C*.

5. *A* cannot think of a way for *B* to learn the information without telling him himself.[62]

6. *A* only harms *C* to the extent of thwarting the partnership and does not tell *B* anything that will cause *C* to be personally and publicly embarrassed. The one exception to this condition is if *C* had been convicted of a crime, such as fraud, that calls his reliability into question in this undertaking; then *B* has the right to know this and to assess on his own whether *C* has changed his ways sufficiently to trust him now.[63]

Rabbi Alfred S. Cohen, a contemporary scholar, applied a similar analysis to a more personal situation: *A* knows that *B* has diabetes and knows that *B* has not disclosed that fact to his girlfriend. Although Rabbi Cohen indicates that the point in the relationship when the woman should be told is not clear, *A* must, according to the rabbi, tell her at some point before she marries *B* so that she can decide for herself whether to marry him under that condition.[64] That, though, is not the best solution; it would be better if *A* could persuade *B* to tell her himself.

ADOPTIONS

Until recent years, when a mother gave her baby up for adoption, she expected never to hear from, or of, the baby again. State laws uniformly protected her identity from disclosure to both the social parents and the child. Several concerns produced these laws: the need to avoid shaming the woman who gave up the child; the desire to encourage the woman to carry through with the pregnancy rather than seek what was until 1973 most often an illegal and treacherous abortion; and the ability of the social parents (that is, those who adopted and are raising the child) to be secure in their role as parents, both in their own eyes and in the estimation of the child. Only necessary factors in the child's medical history were shared with the social parents, and then only sparsely.

This had the effect, though, of leaving adopted children without a ready source of information about their full medical history. At least as important, adopted children lacked the psychological sense of identity that comes from knowing your biological relatives. When children know the way they are like, and unlike, the people whose genes created them, they understand why they have certain talents and traits and not others. We all crave this sense of rootedness and self-understanding throughout our lives, but especially in our teens and twenties. These same concerns, in recent years, have affected children born through the new assisted-reproductive technologies that use donor eggs or sperm, for there, too, at least half of the child's biological parentage is kept secret.[65]

In response to adopted children seeking their biological parents and, to a lesser degree, to parents seeking their children given up for adoption, recent legislation in many states has opened adoption records to adoptees when they reach their eighteenth or twenty-first birthday. Sometimes, the records are insufficient to find either of the biological parents, and then adoptees remain unsatisfied in their search for their own roots. Sometimes, though, the information is enough of a clue to track down one or both of the parents. That may turn out to be a pleasant experience for both parent and child, but it also may be a disappointment or, worse, a threat to a person's life. If a woman has been raped, for example, and her testimony has sent the father to prison, she may well want to remain in hiding from the rapist; a child seeking out both her and the father may well reveal the mother's whereabouts, putting her in danger.[66] Furthermore, the social parents often have real fears that the biological parents will someday reappear and undermine their status as the child's "real" parents.

Balancing the need that both the biological and the social parents usually have for keeping the identity of the biological parents confidential with the child's need for disclosure of his or her identity requires some creative thinking. Neither full secrecy nor full disclosure is the answer. Instead, the biological parents of adoptees and of children born through donor insemination or egg donation may remain anonymous, but they must provide sufficient information about their medical history, their character traits, and their talents so as to give the child as much personal information as possible without compromising the confidentiality of the biological parent. The biological parents gave the child the gift of life, and even though they have passed on to others the parental tasks of supporting and raising the child, often for the good of the child, they nevertheless still must do what they can to enable the child to grow up both physically and psychologically healthy.[67]

These factors also impinge on specifically Jewish obligations. Children have a variety of duties toward their parents in Jewish law. These include honor, which the Talmud defines as specific positive duties of caring for the parent in old age, and respect, which the Talmud defines as negative duties of refraining from insulting the parent. In addition, children must bury their parents and fulfill the mourning rites in their honor, and children are known in Jewish rituals by their first name and then son or daughter of their parents' names.[68] The child clearly owes these things to his or her social parents, for the Talmud states that children must honor and respect their stepfather and stepmother.[69] But if the child discovers the identity of his or her biological parents, does he or she owe these duties to them as well? And which parents should be named when the child is called up to the Torah or identified in a wedding contract? Disclosure of the biological parents certainly complicates things!

Let's begin with the one clear aspect of this: Only the biological child of a *kohen* (priest) or a *levi* (levite) inherits that status. Thus, unless it is known that a child's biological father was a member of one or the other of these family trees, the child is to be known as a *yisrael* (Israelite), the default option that characterizes the vast majority of Jews.

The other matters, though, are not nearly as clear in established Jewish law. As I discuss in Chapter Five, when parents have abused their children or otherwise violated the law, Ashkenazic sources (Rashi, Rabbenu Tam, Rabbi Moses Isserles) maintain that the Torah's commands of honor and respect for them no longer apply, whereas Sephardic sources (Rabbi Alfas, Maimonides, Rabbi Karo) assert that they do.[70] When parents give up their children for adoption, though, they are not violating Jewish law: They are rather delegating their parental responsibilities to other people. It is one thing if they abandon the child on a street corner, with no assurance that the child will be cared for; it is quite another when they work through legal authorities to make sure that the child will grow up with caring parents. Moreover, biological parents who give up their children for adoption usually do so because they are unable to care for the child, and they are thus acting in the child's best interests; that clearly is not a violation of Jewish law or a dereliction of parental duty. At the same time, the biological parents did renounce their duties by transferring them to others with no intention of ever resuming them, and adopted children often feel that their biological parents rejected and abandoned them, however insensitive that may be to the circumstances that warranted giving them up for adoption. Moreover, the biological parents presumed that they would never be known by the adopted child, let alone be the beneficiaries of filial duties of honor and respect.

Thus, although filial duties do not usually depend on how good a parent the person was, except in the extreme case of abuse, in this murky area of emerging Jewish law, when an adopted child does in fact discover his or her biological parents, the relationship that develops between them may be an appropriate factor in determining the scope of the child's duties to them. So, for example, if the biological parents and child become close, the child might fulfill the filial duties of honor and respect for them and observe mourning rites for them when they die, including the recitation of *Kaddish* for eleven months thereafter and on the anniversary of their deaths. If, on the other hand, the biological parents and child do not become close, the child may do none of these things. In any case, the child would continue to identify herself or himself in Jewish rituals and legal documents as the daughter or son of the social parents and would be obliged to fulfill all normal filial duties toward them.

BANS AGAINST DISCLOSURE IN THE PROFESSIONS
Professional ethics raises yet another complication. Doctors, lawyers, mental health professionals, and members of the clergy

must operate under rules of confidentiality, for only then will current and potential clients seek their services, trust them, and be helped by them. So, for example, a survey conducted in November and December 1998 by the nonprofit California Health-Care Foundation found "that a significant percentage of people in this country are afraid to talk to their doctors, are afraid to be honest with their doctors and in some cases are afraid to seek care." One in six Americans, according to that survey, takes precautions in their medical care to protect their privacy, such as paying out of pocket for care otherwise covered by insurance, lying to a doctor about their medical history, or staying away from the medical establishment altogether. They do this to avoid losing benefits or their job and to avoid being embarrassed.[71]

To make it possible for society to have effective medical, psychological, legal, and religious services, the privacy of interactions between the professionals who provide such services and their clients has been protected by law in most jurisdictions. First known as the "priest-penitent privilege," stemming from the unique theology of the Catholic confessional process, it has been extended in our time to lawyers, physicians, mental health professionals, and clergy who are not Catholic. Therefore, even if some individuals, hospitals, or insurance companies would benefit from knowing something about particular congregants, clients, or patients, the professional standards of ethics of clergy, attorneys, and health care workers bar them from divulging such secrets. Moreover, in many states the law protects such professionals from being forced by courts, police, or other parties to reveal their clients' secrets and imposes legal liability for a breach of that confidence.[72]

One important limit on this guarantee of privacy was articulated in the landmark *Tarasoff* case, in which the California Supreme Court maintained that a psychologist had not only the right but also the duty to break a patient's right to privacy if the client indicated an intention to endanger others—in that case, to kill someone.[73] It is not clear whether the court would have extended this exception to cover the client's intention to commit nonviolent felonies, such as damaging a person's reputation or property; it ruled that "the public policy favoring protection of the confidential character of patient-psychotherapist

59

communications must yield to the extent to which disclosure is essential to avert danger to others. The protective privilege ends where the public peril begins."[74]

The fact that the court specifically said "danger *to others*," though, would mean that the *Tarasoff* limit on privacy does not apply to clients who announce that they plan to harm themselves, except in the extreme. Thus most states permit and even require measures to prevent a person from committing suicide; but short of that, people have the right to hurt themselves. So, for example, a doctor would neither be permitted under the medical profession's ethics of confidentiality nor required under *Tarasoff* to divulge a wife's drug habits to her husband. The predominant rationale for protecting the wife's privacy is to preserve her own confidence and that of others in telling doctors things that patients do not want shared with others. Without assurance of such confidentiality, people would be wary of seeking the help of doctors—and clergy and lawyers—altogether, and that would impoverish the community in vital services. The doctor may, and probably should, urge her to talk to her husband about her drug habit so that he can aid in her rehabilitation, and it would be good for the physician to volunteer to help her have that conversation; but her permission is necessary for the husband to be informed.

Even minors are protected to some degree by these privileges. In California, for example, for those health care services for which the minor has the legal capacity to consent, the minor is entitled to see the portions of his or her medical record that pertain to such services, and the minor's representative (for example, parent or guardian) does not have a right to look at those records without the minor's authorization.[75] Even when a minor does not have the legal capacity to consent to a particular treatment, the minor's representative is not entitled to inspect the minor's health records if the provider determines, in good faith, that access to the records requested by the representative would have a detrimental effect on the provider's professional relationship with the minor patient or on the minor's physical safety or psychological well-being.[76]

Both state and federal law have taken special care to protect minors' privacy in regard to substance abuse and HIV testing.

Federal regulations provide that if state law permits a minor patient to apply for and obtain substance abuse treatment, then only the minor may authorize disclosure of information and records that are maintained in conjunction with those services.[77] California law, for example, permits minors twelve years of age or older to consent to medical care and counseling relating to the treatment of problems stemming from alcohol or drug abuse and exposure to HIV.[78] Therefore, for minors twelve years of age or older, only the individual being treated may authorize disclosure of information about such treatments to parents or others.[79] For an individual younger than twelve, providers must gain permission of the child's parents, guardian, or other person lawfully authorized to make such health care decisions before they can receive or release test results on the minor.[80] Even for those older than twelve years of age, however, California law stipulates that "The treatment plan of a minor authorized by this section shall include the involvement of the minor's parent or guardian, if appropriate, as determined by the professional person or treatment facility treating the minor."[81] Thus, while it would be good practice to involve related adults in the treatment of an adult, for minors it is a legal requirement.

On the other hand, California law does not authorize minors to receive methadone treatment without consent of a parent or guardian, and forty-two states have enacted laws that require the notification and, in some cases, consent of one or both parents before a minor may have an abortion.[82] When state law does not permit a minor to consent to a specific mode of treatment, federal regulations require that written consent for disclosure of the medical record to anyone must be given by both the minor and his or her parent, guardian, or other person authorized by law to act on his or her behalf.[83] Moreover, when state law requires parental consent for substance-abuse treatment, the fact that a minor has applied for treatment may be communicated to the parent or guardian only if the minor has given written consent to disclosure or lacks capacity to make a rational choice regarding consent because of extreme youth or a specific mental or physical condition.[84] Finally, in drug or alcohol treatment or in any other situation, facts relevant to reducing a threat to the life or physical well-being of a minor who has applied for treatment or any other person threatened by the minor may be disclosed to the parent, guardian, or other person legally authorized to act on behalf of the minor *if* the program director judges that the minor lacks capacity to make a rational decision on whether to consent to the disclosure and if the threat to the minor or other individual may be reduced by communicating the relevant facts to the parent or guardian.[85]

These complex legal limits to protect the privacy of interactions between professionals and their clients buttress the willingness of people to consult professionals in the first place. Those are clear benefits for the individuals involved and for society in general. Other factors, though, argue against such protections, especially in regard to medical confidentiality. Patients could die if emergency doctors cannot gain quick access to reliable medical information through computerized records. Even in routine care, the multiple physicians that a typical patient sees need to know what the others are prescribing to avoid harming patients through adverse drug interactions or incompatible therapies. Health plans need information on patients to ensure and improve standards of care. Researchers need to have accurate information about their subjects if they are to succeed in their efforts to discover or invent new therapies. How, then, do we provide such information to those who have a legitimate need to know it without compromising the privacy of patients through their computerized records?

In 1996, Congress imposed a deadline on itself, requiring the secretary of Health and Human Services to issue privacy rules if lawmakers failed to pass health privacy legislation by August 21, 1999. That deadline came and went, and so on October 27, 1999, the Clinton administration proposed rules to protect medical privacy, and those rules became final after public comment on February 21, 2000, because Congress did not act. Under the rules, health care providers and health maintenance organizations do not have to get a patient's consent before disclosing information needed for medical treatment or the payment of claims, but they must get the patient's consent if the information is to be used for marketing or certain types of research. Furthermore, the rules forbid the wholesale release of entire records when a small part would suffice for the medical purpose for which the record was requested. Finally, the rules give patients the right to see, correct, and supplement their medical records and to obtain a copy of them at a nominal copying fee.

Medical administrators objected to the proposed rules because of the cost of implementing them, and police officers wanted access to medical records without obtaining a search warrant in emergency situations; for these and other reasons, the Bush administration is in the process of proposing changes, and the shape and fate of these rules are not clear as of this writing. What is clear is that the privacy of electronic medical records is a national concern.[86]

Jewish sources do not speak directly about whether professionals have special duties to keep their clients' physical, mental, legal, financial, or moral condition confidential. That is probably because our society educates and relies on professionals far more than any community did in the past, and so the special issues involved in the professional–client relationship did not arise then to the same degree of urgency and complexity. This is one area among many, in other words, where we cannot look to the tradition for specific instructions; we instead must identify the tradition's principles and legal precedents that can guide us in this matter and then apply them to current realities.

Why, then, does American law extend these protections and responsibilities to professionals? It is because American society has determined that the services of clergy, attorneys, and health professionals are critical to society, that people will not avail themselves of those services if their confidentiality can be breached, and that the social interest in maintaining these services generally outweighs the social or individual interest in knowing someone's secrets. The question, then, is whether Jewish law similarly privileges one social interest over another and over the interests of an individual.

The answer is yes on both scores, but only with careful assessment and judgment. Jewish law provides some clear examples of choosing one social good over another. So, for example, in a ruling that I discuss at some length in *To Do the Right and the Good*, the Shulchan Arukh specifies that in conditions of scarcity, the community must feed the hungry before they clothe the naked, that women are to be given such social support before men are, and that redeeming captives takes precedence over sustaining the poor and clothing them.[87]

Communal needs also can take precedence over the interests of individuals, although only within limits. One such limit is life itself. So, for example, according to another Jewish legal precedent that I discuss at length in *Matters of Life and Death*, all of the inhabitants of a city under siege must give up their lives rather than sacrifice an innocent person's life.[88]

When individuals would pay a price less than their lives, though, social needs can trump their interests and even their rights. So, for example, the Talmud relaxes its normal qualifications for judges in cases of collecting loans "so as not to lock the door before [potential] borrowers"—that is, to make it reasonably easy for creditors to convene a court to regain the money or objects that a borrower is refusing to return. Since Jewish law forbids taking interest on loans to fellow Jews, creditors do not have a self-interest in granting loans in the first place. They would be sorely tempted to ignore the Torah's commandment that they nevertheless lend money to the poor if it were also onerous to convene a court to get their principal back from borrowers. Therefore, even though the judges chosen through the relaxed requirements may not be as qualified as those appointed through normal channels—thus infringing on the rights of the borrower to competent judgment—the talmudic Rabbis created this looser standard to ensure that money will be available for those who need to borrow it in the future, an important component of the economic welfare of the community.[89] They enacted other revisions in the law "for the fixing of the world" (*mipnei tikkun ha-olam*), including a number of aspects of Jewish commercial and family law that limit the former rights of specific parties.[90] These examples demonstrate that in some circumstances, at least, the social good can outweigh the individual's good.

Thus, even though the historical contexts of traditional Jewish law did not raise the question of special privacy requirements for professionals, in our day we may apply its concern for the general welfare to protect professional–client confidentiality. So, for example, if a lawyer knows that a client has a criminal record of fraud, Leviticus 19:16 ("Do not stand idly by the blood of your neighbor") would seem to require the lawyer to warn any of the client's potential business partners of the extra risks involved in doing business with him or her. Because society needs legal services, though, and because people will seek the aid of an attorney only if they can be assured of confidentiality, we may interpret Jewish law as permitting—or even insisting—that the lawyer keep quiet about the client's past. That clearly impinges on the potential partners' welfare, for they may be taking on a larger level of risk than they realize or want; but the need of the community for legal help and for confidentiality in attaining that help may outweigh the partners' individual or collective well-being. In interpreting Jewish law in this way, I am narrowing the domain of Leviticus 19:16 to exclude professionals who are keeping confidences made known to them in their professional roles.[91]

On the other hand, if there is no practical need to reveal negative facts about a person, disclosing them is itself a sin. Thus, even though the Torah says cryptically that Zelophehad had "died for his own sin"[92] without identifying it, Rabbi Akiva asserted that Zelophehad was the unnamed man in Numbers 15:32–36 who chopped wood on the Sabbath and suffered the death penalty for thus desecrating the Sabbath. Rabbi Judah ben Betaira then said to Rabbi Akiva: "Akiva, one way or another, you will have to answer for what you said: If you are right [that Zelophehad is the one who desecrated the Sabbath], the Torah shielded him [by not spelling out his sin] while you divulged it; and if not, you have maligned a righteous person."[93] Even if Zelophehad had desecrated the Sabbath, by Rabbi Akiva's time Zelophehad had long been dead, and so there was no practical reason that anyone had to know that. Without such a pragmatic justification for divulging the sin, Rabbi Akiva was at fault for violating the strictures against "speaking of the bad" (lashon ha-ra). Thus, if I am interpreting Jewish law to allow professionals to keep confidences that reflect badly on the client and may even cause harm to third parties, I would surely insist that professionals keep their clients' confidences when nobody else has a practical reason to know those facts.

PROPOSALS FOR PROTECTING AGAINST INTRUSION
AND DISCLOSURE

As we have seen, to protect individuals' privacy and the dignity that comes with it, Jewish law from the Torah to our own day forbids both intrusion and disclosure. These prohibitions become acutely needed in a society like ours in which more and more intrusion and disclosure invade our lives each day. Indeed, in a 1994 Harris poll, 82 percent of respondents stated that they were concerned about threats to their personal privacy, and 78 percent believed that consumers have lost all control over how businesses circulate and use personal information.[94] Those concerns have become even greater in the wake of Congress's 1999 revisions of the Depression-era banking legislation so that commercial institutions of all sorts may provide integrated financial services. Now, "financial institutions will be able to share not only information on their customers' incomes, investments, possessions, and credit ratings, but also detailed summations about where they go for dinner, where they buy their lovers' presents, and what medical expenses they have paid."[95]

Government commissions, congressional hearings, academic conferences, and extensive news coverage have all warned us of the threats to our privacy posed by our use of the Internet. Despite popular impressions, though, most invasion of our privacy in contemporary times does not come from the Internet. A June 1999 study by Georgetown University indicated that nearly two-thirds of the most popular commercial sites voluntarily post privacy policies (in contrast to only 14 percent that did so in June 1998). Moreover, data-driven industries from direct marketing to private investigating "remain overwhelmingly dependent on courthouse records, credit card transactions, product warranty cards and other mundane sources. These rivers of offline data keep rising, largely beyond consumers' radar or control."[96] As a result, consumer privacy may ironically be more secure on-line than off.

Especially as more people begin to use the Internet for commercial transactions, though, the threats to privacy in that medium will increase, and, in any case, we already have cause for concern, both on- and off-line. The sale of information generates annual revenues for private companies and for state and federal governments in the billions of dollars. Moreover, the money available to suppliers of information has been growing dramatically each year, with no signs of slowing down.

The need for further American regulation becomes especially evident when comparing American protections of consumer data to the level maintained in Europe. Because of the Nazi history of misusing personal records to identify "undesirables," Germans, in particular, are more wary than Americans of assaults on their privacy. As a result, Germany has some of the most stringent privacy-protection laws in the world, and they served as the model for the European Union standards adopted in October 1998.

According to European law, recording any conversation without participants' permission is illegal, a ban that is strictly enforced; privacy laws block unsolicited marketing phone calls; no record may appear on telephone bills of citizen contacts with counseling services, abortion counselors, sexual assault hot lines, or AIDS testing services; and client profiles, including credit card records, may not be shared via the Internet. Moreover, Europeans can also examine computer files of their credit ratings, personal history, and health records. Finally, the European Union bans electronic transfer of personal data to countries—including the United States—with less stringent controls on use of that information. As one might imagine, that has become a matter of considerable dispute, for the United States claims that that ban constricts free markets.

The United States is not likely to win, though, for Europeans insist on a higher degree of consumer protection: "For many years, the fear was that Big Brother could be watching our behavior too closely, but now people have to be more worried about misuse of their data by private entities, like businesses," says Thilo Weichert, a Kiel, Germany, resident who heads the Data Security Association, which works with German agencies to propose privacy legislation.[97] Moreover, Europeans prefer laws whereas Americans favor self-regulation.

The Jewish tradition also trusts law more than self-regulation, as the vast number of laws and rabbinic rulings within Judaism testify. This, in fact, is one example of the difference between American ideology and Judaism discussed in Chapter One—

namely, the American way of seeing the world as filled with individuals with rights, but the Jewish way of seeing the world as filled with communal duties. Thus the Jewish side of American Jews would prefer the European mode of ensuring privacy. Moreover, in light of the fact that the Torah already seeks to protect us from intrusion and that the Rabbis throughout the ages added further protections, the Jewish tradition would clearly embrace the European understanding of not only the method for guaranteeing privacy but also the bigger picture of what privacy should mean in our technological age.

In line with the Jewish preference for encasing moral norms in law as much as possible, Elie Spitz, rabbi of Congregation B'nai Israel in Tustin, California, and a member of the Conservative Movement's Committee on Jewish Law and Standards, suggested in 1986 that the Jewish tradition should impel Jews to lobby for four changes in civil society and law that pertain to confidentiality.

CONFIDENTIALITY AS A VALUE

Like Rabbenu Gershom's insistence that a letter's confidentiality must not be breached by reading it, let alone by divulging its contents to others, so too American law should not demand a showing of damages to enforce confidentiality. Instead, businesses should be permitted to gather from potential clients only that information that is directly relevant to the product or service they are providing and then only with the person's explicit consent, and the law should ban the sharing of information among businesses without the individual's explicit permission.

The need for such measures was dramatically illustrated during the summer of 1999. Throughout that summer, there were no comprehensive federal laws protecting patients' health information from being shared with anyone else. Worse, a bill overwhelmingly passed by the U.S. House of Representatives (343–86) on July 1, 1999, included a provision that would allow medical information held by insurance companies to be released to a variety of entities to determine charges for premiums and for research projects of any kind—medical and nonmedical. The parties that could review individual medical data, according to the bill, included credit card companies and banks, and there was no restriction in the bill as to how the information could be used. Since the Senate did not act on the bill, however, and since Congress thus failed to meet its deadline to pass legislation on medical privacy by the end of that summer, the Clinton administration, in accordance with previously enacted legislation, published a first draft of its proposed rules in August 1999; and after considering some fifty-two thousand comments, it published the final version in its last month in office. These were much more satisfactory rules, going much further in the effort to protect people's medical privacy. The Bush administration has kept most of those rules, but in March 2002, it announced that it planned to relax them in some respects, effective in April 2003. In an editorial about the new proposals, former Secretary of Health and Human Services Donna Shalala, who created the Clinton administration rules, thanks the Bush administration for keeping most of them, but she points out the dangers inherent in two of the proposed changes. First, patient consent for routine exchange of information among medical professionals was required under the Clinton rules, but will become optional under the Bush rules. Second,

> In another crucial section of the regulation, I think the Bush administration got it wrong. . . . Any drug company can now pay a pharmacy to mail information about a new drug to its customers, without their knowledge or consent. Even worse, there is no way for the patient to get off the mailing list—ever. Our obscure but important "opt out" provision, under which patients could get off the list has been erased.[98]

In addition, insurers, who fought for the Bush changes, will be able to circumvent paperwork that divulges how information submitted to them will be used and thus avoid dissuading patients from applying for coverage.[99] Thus the passage of the House bill in 1999 and the loosening of protections under the Bush administration together illustrate just how necessary it is to enact laws that will restore confidentiality as a value over the long term, so that it is not subject to the whims of changing administrations. Among other things, the law must forbid the sharing of information about a person by companies without that person's specific permission to do so.[100]

DUTY TO PREVENT TEMPTATION

Jewish law requires that owners of a divided common courtyard erect a wall so that they are not even tempted to invade each other's privacy. Similarly, argued Rabbi Spitz, American law should seek to limit the temptation to take data stored in computers. Some measures that he suggested are laws that permit data to be held no longer than is necessary for the purpose collected, that allow people to examine their personal data files at a nominal fee, that require businesses and government agencies promptly to correct any inaccuracies, that permit anyone to note within the file itself any dispute with information in his or her computer file, and that demand that the data be maintained in a reasonably secure manner to prevent access by any unauthorized person using any device, such as a remote terminal or another computer system.[101]

CONSIDERED RESTRAINT

The preconditions of the Ḥafetz Ḥayyim on revealing confidential information—need, accuracy of the information, proper intent, lack of alternatives, and no unnecessary harm—are, suggested Rabbi Spitz, appropriate measures to be built into civil law. Thus "considered restraint in regard to personal data would allow transfer only if the data subject [that is, the person involved] consented or public need overrode the privacy concern."[102] "Public need" includes not only those occasions when the law compels disclosure but also less legally formal situations. So, for example, disclosure would be permitted when the person had acted adversely to a business interest and it was necessary for the business to protect itself. To give another instance, disclosure would be allowed when it was limited, customary, and usual among businesses; was for the sole purpose of providing business or employment references; and avoided any unnecessary embarrassment of the person involved. Before turning over information about a person to a third party, the business would be required to notify him or her, unless prohibited by law; release only the information legally requested; and, if possible, respond to a subpoena or legal process in a time frame that allows the person on whom the information is being sought to challenge the request in court.

SANCTIONS
Just as Jewish law backed up its demands for preserving confidentiality with threats as severe as social ostracism, so too civil law should provide for fines and/or damages when information is improperly gathered or shared or when businesses refuse to correct information in a timely manner. These remedies should include attorney and court expenses and "restitutionary relief from the violator for the collection of any gain which resulted from the invasion of privacy."[103]

In sum, in place of the piecemeal statutes and the variety of court cases we now have, we need, as Susan Gindin has noted, "a comprehensive federal policy guaranteeing individuals the right to control the collection and distribution of their personal information. Legislation which incorporates the basic tenets of fair information practices is a vital component of this policy."[104]

EDUCATION AND PERSONAL RESPONSIBILITY
To Rabbi Spitz's four suggestions concerning the law and Gindin's call for a comprehensive privacy policy encased in legislation, I would add two comments. First, social practice is not only a matter of law and sanctions, as important as they are, but also a function of what people learn to expect of each other and of themselves, together with the ideals that members of the society share and try to incorporate in their lives. Consequently, educators and religious and political leaders have an important role to play in restoring privacy to contemporary life. This should be done, first, by teaching people to expect and respect reasonable bounds of privacy, not just in the public arena but within their own families as well. The tie between privacy and dignity must be clearly explained so that people understand that this is not just a matter of freedom but also a matter of the quality of life. These lessons must be reiterated in synagogues, churches, mosques, and other religious institutions, where the specific *religious* significance that privacy entails within a given religion's theology should be spelled out, repeated often, and employed in the religious institution's dealings with its members and with others.

Second, American ideology sees privacy as a right, and thus it would permit, but not require, use of encryption software or other electronic tools to protect one's own privacy. Jewish ideology, in contrast, proclaims it a duty to protect our own privacy and that of others. Thus Jewish law applied to modern communications would *require* that we take such measures, at least for information that should not be shared with the public.

Therefore, in addition to working for further legal guarantees of our privacy, we Jews have the responsibility to take whatever steps we personally can to ensure our own privacy and that of others. Concerns for privacy should pervade our own personal use of electronic communications as well as our business interactions, for unless and until state or federal legislation imposes proper safeguards, it will be up to individuals and companies to regulate themselves in this matter.

Thus privacy is a major concern of the Jewish tradition. It is not an absolute right, and I spelled out some of the limits to it in legal, ritual, and professional settings together with the justifications for those limits. Because of the significant importance of protecting privacy for reenforcing both an individual's sense of integrity and the community's sense of respect and morality, however, we as individuals and as a society should take the steps that Rabbi Spitz and I have together suggested to preserve our own privacy and that of others. Through such measures, we can safeguard privacy while still preserving the ability of the community to invade it for specified purposes and while still enjoying the immense gains in communication that modern technology affords us.

CHAPTER THREE

"This Is My Beloved, This Is My Friend": Sex and the Family

S exual issues are certainly one of the prime arenas in life in which we want privacy, and, indeed, sex is a factor that pervades many aspects of our lives. Sex is certainly not the whole of life, but it is an important part of it, and so it should be part of the discussion of the norms by which Jews live.[1]

The Jewish tradition has much to say about human intimacy, and much of what it says is as compelling now as it was to our ancestors. Even within the ranks of those who obey other parts of Jewish law strictly, though, the laws and values of Judaism on matters of sexuality and intimacy are, unfortunately, observed too often in the breach. Those who in other areas are not very religiously committed are not likely to know or follow Jewish norms about sex either.[2] Judaism has a distinctly positive view toward sexuality as the gift of God, and it articulates values and rules that make sex the pleasurable, yet holy, activity it was meant to be. Thus however one understands the authority of the Jewish tradition,[3] its sheer wisdom on this topic recommends that its perspectives and norms be better known and practiced.

This chapter is divided into four major sections. The first presents some of the general values of the Jewish tradition that should

influence all of our relationships, including especially our most intimate ones. This section frames the entire discussion of sex in the
context of our relationships to each other. The next section discusses Jewish norms for marital, heterosexual sex; parenthood, key
problems within families and marriage, divorce, and stepfamilies.
Then I turn to heterosexual sex outside the bonds of marriage, including a note for teenagers. In the last section, I describe the current positions within the Conservative movement on
homosexuality and then I present my own stance on the matter.[4]

SEXUAL RELATIONS: FUNDAMENTAL CONCEPTS
AND VALUES

TWO FUNDAMENTAL CONCEPTS

Two of the fundamental features of the Jewish perspective on
human beings I discussed in Chapter One have direct relevance
to matters of intimacy.

THE HUMAN BEING AS AN INTEGRATED WHOLE CREATED BY
GOD

Many people in our time think of sex as a distinct area of life,
separate from the rest of what we think, feel, and do. Thinking
about sex like that, however, dehumanizes and mechanizes sex:
Sex becomes simply the functioning of a machine with no meaning beyond the immediate pleasures it affords. Judaism very
much prizes the pleasure involved in sexual activity, but that is
not its only meaning.

For the Jewish tradition, God created each one of us *as an integrated whole*, with no part of us capable of living apart from
any other part of us. The body, the mind, the emotions, the will,
and the spirit are all involved, at least to some degree, in everything we do in life, and they affect each other continuously and
pervasively. This integrated view of the human being has an immediate implication for our sexual activities—namely, that on
a level as conscious and deliberate as possible, our sexual acts
ought to reflect our own values as individuals and as Jews.

This means at least four things. First, we should not do what
others are doing, or what they are saying they are doing, just
because that seems to be the socially accepted practice. Our sexual activities should rather flow out of our own values, shaped—

in the case of Jews—by our Jewish heritage and by its aspiration for holiness.

Second, we must recognize that sexual intercourse is not an isolated act with little or no effect on the rest of our lives; it is not the working of a machine that can be turned on or off at will with no consequences for the rest of our lives. Sex should rather be seen in the broader, more accurate way in which Judaism depicts it—as one important part of our human existence tied to all the other parts. Sex, therefore, affects, and is affected by, the totality of our lives.

This means, third, that some of the concepts and norms that guide us as Jews in other parts of our lives are at least as important in our sexual relationships. This should not be surprising. Sex, after all, is one of the ways through which we relate to one another. Emotionally and physically, it is particularly intense, of course, but that only means that the expectations we have for each other in other contexts are all the more important in sex.

Finally, just as each individual is an integrated whole, so too each Jew's identity as a human being critically depends on his or her ties to the community. Indeed, as I described briefly in Chapter One and more extensively elsewhere,[5] Enlightenment ideology depicts communities as voluntary associations, whereas Jewish sources understand each Jew as inextricably connected to the Jewish people.[6] As a result, all of our acts, including our sexual ones, have social consequences. Therefore, while our sexual activities should reflect our own values and not simply peer pressure, when shaping our individual sexual values we must consider the effects of what we do—not only how we affect those with whom we engage in sexual relations but also how we affect the moral character of our people. In this, as in other areas of life, our actions should be a *kiddush hashem* (a sanctification of God's name), by reflecting well on the Jewish tradition, the Jewish people, and the God Jews worship.

THE HUMAN BEING AS CREATED IN THE IMAGE OF GOD

A central concept of Judaism's understanding of ourselves and others is that each of us was created in the image and likeness of God.[7] We are not an accidental happenstance produced by blind forces of nature; we are rather the conscious and purposeful creation of God. Moreover, we share some of God's characteristics. Like God, but, of course, not to the same degree, we are capable of sustained thought, creativity, and awareness of ourselves, our world, and God; the light of God is imminent in our spirit.[8] We share in God's dominion over the earth,[9] and we have the divine attribute of free will,[10] for we can recognize the difference between right and wrong, good and bad. We are privileged to commune with God and, in rabbinic terms, even to be God's partner in ongoing acts of creation.[11]

The various manifestations just delineated of God's image within us give us each divine worth. We have that ultimate source of value regardless of our abilities or disabilities, our wealth or poverty, our personal qualities or defects, or the degree of our usefulness to others. We have divine worth even if we do not think very much of ourselves.

The divine worth granted to each of us is a special blessing; we share in no less than the essence of God. It is also the source of many of our responsibilities to ourselves, to others, to our world, and to God. If we indeed know the difference between right and wrong, we have the responsibility to choose the right. If we are to be God's partners in ongoing acts of creation, we must act accordingly.

This concept has far-reaching implications when applied to the area of intimate relations. The sexual aspects of our being—physical, emotional, intellectual, and spiritual—are not base or obscene; they are part of the entire human being that God termed "very good" after creating us.[12] We must use our sexual faculties, like all other elements of our being, for good purpose, as defined by Jewish law and tradition, to activate their potential for divinity. And we have not only the ability but also the duty to do that. Intimate relations, then, are not seen within Judaism as simply physical release or the product of base, animalistic lust; they are, when carried out in the proper context, no less than an expression of the divine image within us.

SIX FUNDAMENTAL VALUES
MODESTY
The two concepts described above are the basis of some of the values Judaism teaches us. One such value is modesty. Although

Judaism does not construe sexual desires and activity as a corrupting or embarrassing part of our existence, as some other religions and systems of thought do, it does require that we confine sexual activity to private quarters.[13]

I would suggest several reasons for this demand. Keeping sexual activity private distinguishes it from animal sexuality and thereby expresses a respect for the unparalleled, divine image within us. Privacy also imparts a uniqueness and holiness to human sexual acts, for sexual relations then take place with a cognizance of the restrictions that our distinctly human character imposes on us. Moreover, one shares the intimacy of sexual intercourse away from the observation of others so that it can attain an intensity and focus that would otherwise be absent. Privacy thus enables sexual intercourse more effectively to bind the couple together emotionally.

Judaism not only prescribes that sexual activity be confined to private quarters but also demands the converse, that sex should not be flaunted in public. Specifically, the privacy (tzniut, "modesty") that Judaism requires of sex affects our clothing, our speech, and our public activities.

We may dress in accord with the styles of the times, but never should our apparel accentuate the sexually arousing parts of our bodies. Thus sexually suggestive or revealing clothes, including swimwear, for either men or women are not in keeping with Jewish law or sensibilities.

Similarly, our speech patterns should manifest respect for our bodies as creations of God, and this includes the generative parts of our bodies. Crass or violent sexual language bespeaks discomfort with one's own body and disrespect for its divine value. It also cheapens the level of discourse, thereby diminishing the stature of everyone concerned, including especially the speaker. Everyone enjoys a dirty joke from time to time, but that is a far cry from using foul language in every other sentence.

Judaism's expectations of modesty also affect our behavior in public. Sexual activity beyond holding hands, a hug, or a kiss should be reserved for private quarters. This is not to demean sex as something sordid that one must hide; quite the contrary, it is to sanctify it as the intense, intimate, mutual expression of love that it should be. Such love is understood within Jewish sources to be a great good, but a private one.

RESPECT FOR OTHERS

Another implication of being created in the image of God is that we must respect every other human being, regardless of the extent of any given individual's talents, beauty, intelligence, wealth, character traits, or any other factor. The Hebrew term for this value is *"kavod ha-briyyot."*[14] If that is true for everyone else, it certainly should be true for our sexual partners, because sex, after all, is—or should be—an expression of love and intimacy.

Minimally, this requires that sexual relations may not be coercive. While at any given time one partner may want to engage in sexual activities more than the other, and while partners may acquiesce to each other to please one another as part of a long-term relationship, sex should never be a mere usage of the other person for physical release. There is nothing wrong—and, indeed, everything right—with enjoying sex; that sex involves physical pleasure is one of the great gifts that God has given us by creating us as we are. The goal of sexual pleasure, though, may never override mutual respect. Thus neither person may ever make the other the unwilling object of his or her sexual pleasure; even in the context of marriage, that would constitute rape. Moreover, if one member of the couple does not want to engage in sexual activity in a particular way, that wish must be honored.

A more adequate expression of the respect due to each person would restrict sex to those people, and to those times, when both partners honestly feel love for one another. To be respectful of oneself and of others, sexual acts should not be mechanical or casual but should rather express the couple's mutual love.

HONESTY

Judaism demands of us a high standard of honesty, because respect for other human beings entails that we not deceive them. Thus in commerce, advertising must be truthful, scales must be accurate, and descriptions in contracts of products and services must correspond to what the parties really intend. Similarly, in relationships, the talmudic Rabbis require that "one's 'yes' should be yes, and one's 'no' should be no."[15] One must sincerely and honestly communicate what one means at any given time.

There is one exception and one limitation to the tradition's requirement of honesty. When the truth will only hurt someone else, and nobody stands to lose by describing things as nicer than they are, one may choose tact over truth.[16] Moreover, not everything needs to be said or reported. Lying leads to a lack of trust and thus undermines the possibility of long-term relationships. Reporting every feeling or every instance of disagreement at the moment it arises, though, is not the recipe for a healthy relationship either. One must be honest, but not brutally so.

The same norms of honesty apply to sexual activity. People involved in dating should not deceive each other in regard to their intentions. One can and should be tactful, but if one really does not want to continue a relationship, the honest—and, ultimately, the kind—thing to do is to say so. Similarly, people should not pretend to be romantically involved to gain sexual favors. Relationships develop over time, and what begins simply as a friendship may later blossom into romance; but honesty requires that, within the boundaries of tact, people should make their feelings and intentions clear.

This is true within a marital relationship as well. One need not, and indeed should not, say those things that are simply hurtful, even if they are true. Moreover, one is not obliged to correct every mistake one's spouse makes, especially in public. Furthermore, one need not share with one's spouse every fantasy—sexual or otherwise—that one has. At the same time, one must be open and honest about those matters that the spouse has a right to know as part of a trusting relationship, especially matters that affect either or both members of the couple in significant ways and that can be changed to improve the quality of their relationship.

LOVE AND FIDELITY

"You shall love your neighbor as yourself"[17] is, perhaps, the most famous of the Torah's commandments. It is "a great generalization" of all the other commandments in the Torah, according to Rabbi Akiva, all of which, according to Hillel, are but an interpretation and extension of this one.[18] The *siddur*, the traditional

Jewish prayer book, places the blessing of God as One "who blesses His People Israel with love" immediately before the *Shema*, which commands us, in turn, to love God. Human love, then, mirrors the loving relationship between God and the People Israel and, as such, partakes in aspects of divinity.

The Rabbis interpret the command to love our neighbor as ourselves to require us to show concern for our neighbor in concrete ways.[19] We do not have to like everyone, but we do have to extend ourselves in specific ways to aid others. The same is true all the more for those with whom we are romantically involved, for there, presumably, the feelings of attachment are stronger, the interactions more numerous, and the legitimate expectations that each may have of the other are greater. (Responsibilities always increase with increasing depth in a relationship.) Negatively, we may not intentionally offend or annoy that person or take him or her for granted, and we certainly may not harm that person in any way. Positively, love requires that we think of the other's needs and wants in living our own lives and that we make a point of attending to them. We can never, of course, totally escape our egocentricity. Indeed, Jewish law maintains that we must worry about our own health and safety first.[20] We must, however, learn to care for others. As the Jewish theologian Martin Buber said, we are not truly human unless we cultivate I–Thou relationships, wherein we think of others not as a means to our own ends but as ends in themselves.[21]

Part of what it means to love someone is to be faithful to that person. This, in some ways, is a corollary of being honest with each other, but love goes beyond honesty in the extent and depth of its demand for trust. Because of the intensity and intimacy involved, romantic relationships, unlike friendships, involve exclusivity. I am the *only* lover of my spouse and *therefore* am willing to be as open and intimate with her or him as I am. We need that kind of security to expose ourselves to the extent that we do in love relationships. Consequently, fidelity is a critical part of such relationships.

HEALTH AND SAFETY

Contrary to the contemporary notion that my body belongs to me, our tradition teaches that our bodies belong to God. As owner, God can and does demand that we take care of our bodies throughout our lives, very much as the owner of an apartment legitimately requires that those who rent it take reasonable care of it during their occupancy. Jewish law, therefore, prescribes a number of positive obligations that we have to take care of our bodies (proper sleep, exercise, diet, hygiene), and it forbids mutilation of the body, taking undue risks with it, and suicide.[22] As detailed below, these requirements take on added meaning for all those entering sexual relationships in the age of AIDS and other sexually transmitted diseases.

HOLINESS

Judaism demands of us that we live by the highest of moral standards, that we emulate God. The Torah says: "You shall be holy, for I the Lord, your God, am holy."[23] The Hebrew word (*kadosh*) that we translate as "holy" means "special, set apart, unique in character." As Jews, we are to aspire to be God-like, to shape our behavior in ways that sanctify God's Name (*kiddush ha-shem*). Conversely, we must avoid forms of behavior that desecrate God's Name (*hillul ha-shem*). While the tradition is fully aware that no human being can be perfect, that each of us needs the tradition's provisions for making amends, for "returning" (*teshuvah*), we have a mission to strive continually to be exemplary, "a kingdom of priests and a holy nation."[24]

Sex is one important arena where this aspiration must manifest itself. Singling out one person as your marital partner through the Jewish betrothal ceremony is called, in Hebrew, *kiddushin*. The term indicates that each person is now uniquely the marital partner of the other and that their relationship should be one deserving of God's blessing. Sexual acts that violate Judaism's norms can distance a person from God, but sex can also bring people closer to God as they fulfill the divine purposes of companionship and procreation. Indeed, probably the most famous rabbinic letter on sexual morality in the Middle Ages, attributed to Rabbi Moses ben Nahman (Nahmanides), is titled *The Letter of Holiness (Iggeret ha-Kodesh),* and the section of the book on family law by Rabbi Abraham ben David of Posquieres dealing with the moral and theological prisms through which one should approach sexual activity is called

"*Sh'ar ha-Kedushah*" ("The Gate of Holiness").[25] Thus sex, in the Jewish tradition, can be a vehicle not only for pleasure, celebration, and wholeness but also for holiness.

SEX WITHIN MARRIAGE

The Jewish tradition sees two primary purposes for sex within marriage, as evidenced by the two commands in the Torah to engage in sex. One appears in Exodus 21, where the Torah says, at least as the Talmud understood it, that a man taking a woman in marriage must not deprive her of "her food, clothing, or conjugal rights."[26] The other appears in the very first chapter of Genesis, in which God tells the first man and woman to "be fruitful and multiply and fill the earth."[27] Thus companionship and procreation are the two divinely ordained purposes of sex within marriage.

Moreover, these are independent commandments. Thus before, during, and after the years that a couple plans to have children, the duty to have conjugal relations for the sake of companionship continues. God's desire, according to the Torah and the Talmud, is that people should, if at all possible, live in marital partnership, regardless of their ability to procreate.[28]

MARITAL COMPANIONSHIP
THE COMMANDMENT
Adam and Eve, the progenitors of all humanity according to the biblical story, were specifically created for each other, "for it is not good that a person be alone. . . . And therefore a man leaves his father and his mother and clings to his wife so that they become one flesh."[29] The Torah thus recognizes the basic human need for intimate companionship and seeks to satisfy that need through the institution of marriage.

Indeed, Genesis 2 portrays Adam as created by God first as a solitary human person, endowed by himself with all the possibilities of life. Since, according to that story, God eventually created both Adam and Eve, why, we wonder, did God not create them simultaneously? The reason seems to be that God wanted the first person to experience, not just to imagine, what it is like to have every material thing but no person to love. Only after

Adam had experienced the pain of being continually alone would he be ready to appreciate the need for companionship and interdependence as the essential path of personal fulfillment. For him, and for us, his descendants, this is the human norm.[30]

Sex is one of the ways in which the companionship between husband and wife is expressed. In the passage from Exodus 21:10 quoted above, the Torah recognizes the sexual desires of women as well as those of men.[31] While contemporary Westerners might take it for granted that women as well as men have rights to sex within marriage, other societies in the ancient world—and, for that matter, in the medieval and the modern worlds as well—assumed that only men have sexual appetites. Women tolerate the sexual advances of their husbands, in this view, because they want children and economic security. In contrast, the Torah and the Rabbis who later interpret it, in recognition of the couple's mutual desires, structure the laws of marriage so that both spouses have rights to sex with regularity within marriage.[32] Moreover, within the bounds of modesty, Jewish law permits couples to have sex in any way they want.[33] The Torah and the Rabbis thus went quite far to affirm the rights of both members of the couple to the pleasures of each other's sexual company.

On the other hand, when sex becomes a tool for control, a marriage ceases to be the partnership that it is intended to be. Jewish sources specifically proclaim that coercive sex is never allowed, and they disdain either spouse "rebelling" against the other by denying sex. One need not agree to engage in sexual relations each time that one's spouse wants to do so, and a refusal to have conjugal relations must be respected. At the same time, the tradition does not approve denial of each other's sexual rights over a long period of time without due reason, for then the spouse who wants to have sex is being denied the sexual expression of companionship to which each partner is entitled in a marriage.

Marital companionship is, in part, sexual, but it is more than that. In the Jewish marriage ceremony, the only explicit reference to the couple being married describes them as *"re'im ha-ahuvim"* (the loving friends). This description appropriately indicates that the companionship of marriage should extend over a wide scope, such that the husband and wife are not only lovers but also friends. They should take time to enjoy many things together. They should talk with each other about what is going on in their lives and what they are thinking and feeling. They should be, as the marriage ceremony says, loving friends, where the friendship is as strong an element in their relationship as their romantic love.

MUTUALITY IN MARITAL SEX

Sex is a powerful force in our lives. The promise of it, or the denial of it, can be used as potent weapons to get someone to do what you want. In extreme cases, sex can be used for violent ends, as in rape. Clearly, specific prohibitions in Jewish law together with respect for the other as a creature of God, let alone love for the other, would unequivocally rule out such behavior.

Both spouses, however, will not always feel equally motivated to engage in conjugal relations. One partner may acquiesce even when not really in the mood out of love for one's mate and concern to satisfy his or her needs. The Jewish tradition, in fact, instructs men to be sensitive to their wives' intimations of the desire for sex and to satisfy that need whenever possible.[34] Conversely, a woman who is not particularly in the mood for sex may nevertheless consent to have sex with her husband out of love for him; and she should, in any case, be as sensitive to his desires as he should be to hers. If she really does not want to have sexual relations on a given occasion, though, she may refuse, and her husband must honor her wishes.[35] It is hoped that the love the two have for each other will enable them to support each other as much when one of them does not want to engage in conjugal relations as when they both do.

According to Jewish law, sexual intercourse is to take place in private, and it must not subject either spouse to undue medical risk. Furthermore, the Torah has rules that limit conjugal relations to the times when the woman is not having her period.

Within these limits, however, according to the Jewish tradition, couples may engage in sexual relations in whatever way they want. "All forms of intercourse are legitimate," says the Talmud. Later Jewish sources are somewhat embarrassed by this permissiveness, but it remains the law.[36] The Talmud was not prudish; it specifically affirms as one of the legitimate expectations of marriage the right of both spouses to insist on having sex in the nude, with no sheet or other imposition between them ("the Persian custom").[37] On the other hand, if both members of the couple want to have sexual relations in that way or any other—including any sexual position, oral sex, and anal sex—they may do so, as long as it is done in private and with mutual consent.

The Jewish tradition was keenly aware that sexual expression was not confined to intercourse. Beginning with the biblical book Song of Songs, love poetry abounds in the Jewish tradition. It bespeaks the joys of love that can and should be savored in the many ways lovers express their endearment of each other.[38] In our own day, this might include calling one's spouse during the day, acts of love other than intercourse like kissing and hugging, and doing favors for one another. The mutuality of sex, and the strength of marriage, both depend on the couple taking the time to reaffirm their love for each other in all of these ways, and more.

MARITAL PURITY (TOHORAT HA-MISHPAḤAH)

Most Jews do not know much about the rules of marital purity. The Torah includes rules that forbid conjugal relations during a woman's menstrual period.[39] The Torah gives no rationale for these rules apart from saying that they are part of the way in which the people Israel become holy—that is, separated from other peoples and in league with God.[40] While the Torah requires sexual abstinence for seven days, the Rabbis added another five, and so couples who follow these laws do not have conjugal relations for twelve days out of every menstrual month. The woman must immerse herself naked in undrawn waters, which in practice has meant either in a natural body of water or, more commonly, in a mikveh—that is, a pool specially constructed to fulfill the legal requirements.[41]

Throughout much of the twentieth century, it appeared that these laws were slowly passing into disuse, even among otherwise religious Jews. For some, this was a matter of custom; to-horat ha-mishpaḥah simply was not part of the Judaism they were taught or that they, their families, or their friends practiced. For others, it seemed strange to maintain the purity laws in regard to a woman's period when all of us, both men and women, are always in a state of ritual impurity anyway. That is because purification from most forms of impurity requires, according to the Torah, being sprinkled with ashes of a red heifer that had been sacrificed on the Temple altar; but with the destruction of the Temple, that became impossible. Why, then, should we worry about a woman's menstrual impurity when she remains impure on other grounds anyway? Still others objected to these laws on scientific grounds: Isolating a woman during her menstrual period, in this view, expressed an attitude of fear about a perfectly natural and safe process that scientifically oriented people should not perpetuate.

Finally, some have objected to these laws on egalitarian grounds, for there is an inherent inequality in the way in which the Torah and subsequent Jewish law treat the natural emissions of the sexual organs of women and those of men. After a man has a seminal emission, the Torah requires far less of him to regain a state of purity than what it demands of a woman after her menstrual flow: The man need only wash himself (not necessarily in a *mikveh*)[42] and wait until sunset, whereas the woman must wait seven days (twelve according to the Rabbis) and then immerse in a *mikveh* according to specific rules. Indeed, the Talmud says that Ezra instituted a decree that men who emitted semen were required to immerse in a *mikveh* before studying Torah (and, according to some medieval authorities, before praying), but that decree was annulled when it became clear that men were not abiding by it. As a result, the laws governing women's impurity during menstruation continue in force, but not those governing men. These laws, in the eyes of some, therefore degrade women, for they imply that women are periodically sullied by their menstrual functions and thus need monthly cleansing, but men are not subject to such diminishment when they function sexually and do not require such repair.[43]

In recent years, though, some couples have made the laws and practices of *tohorat ha-mishpaḥah* part of their sexual practice, sometimes for the full twelve days followed by immersion in a *mikveh* and sometimes for the more limited, biblical period. In some cases, the reason couples abide by these laws is simply that they are part of Jewish law and should be obeyed as such. Other people are motivated to obey these laws for reasons advanced by some schools of feminist Jewish thought, because some women find this to be one of the distinctly female rituals by which they can affirm their Judaism and reconnect with Jewish women through the ages.

Couples who practice these laws also find other meanings in them. Monthly abstinence forces both members of the couple to appreciate the joys of sex all the more when they resume. Moreover, it reenforces the recognition that neither spouse is just the sex object of the other, for there are times each month when their relationship must be played out on other planes. Sex then becomes one of the arenas in which they relate to each other, but never the only one. Furthermore, following these laws makes the couple particularly anxious to have sex precisely when the woman is most fertile. Consequently, if the couple is not using contraception, the possibility of children, with the ties to past and future generations that children symbolize, is also part of the meaning of these laws. The old and new rationales given for these laws, taken together, have enabled some contemporary couples to see these laws as a way to enhance the sense of ongoing holiness in their marital relationship—just as the Torah declared the purpose of these laws to be.[44]

ADULTERY AND INCEST
The exact opposite of loving, marital companionship is adultery. Adultery is prohibited by the seventh of the Ten Commandments, and adultery and incest are together treated as one of the three prohibitions that, according to the Talmud, a person is not to violate even on pain of losing one's life.[45] Indeed, the Torah prescribes the death penalty for both men and women involved in adultery;[46] and if for some reason that punishment is not carried out, the Talmud maintains that a woman who committed adultery is forbidden to both her husband and her paramour— that is, she may not continue in her marriage and she may not marry her lover.[47] Thus the Jewish tradition clearly forbade adultery in the strictest of terms.

Even though I know of no Conservative or Orthodox rabbinic ruling that has reversed this talmudic stance, in practice rabbis often find ways to maintain that the adultery has not been legally established so that they can pursue efforts to have the couple reconcile, especially if the couple has young children. Sometimes those efforts are successful, and they certainly should be pursued. Divorce, as I discuss below, always brings with it pains of its own for both the couple and for any children involved.

Still, even with the most successful efforts to repair the marriage, adulterous affairs leave indelible scars. Adultery is, after all, a betrayal of the original wedding covenant of holiness (kiddushin), in which both members of the couple promised to engage in sexual relations exclusively with each other. Moreover, adultery constitutes a violation of the trust the couple promised each other in that covenant.[48] As a result, even if the husband and wife manage to reconcile, the extramarital affair becomes part of the couple's story that can never be rewritten for either them or their children. People contemplating adultery should, therefore, seek marital counseling as soon as possible to help them resolve the issues in their marriage that tempt them to have an affair.

Incest is prohibited in very strong and specific language in the Torah and is, along with adultery, one of the three prohibitions that the Rabbis insist one must not violate even at the cost of one's life. The Torah delineates which family relations are forbidden to each other sexually, and the Rabbis added to that list.[49] God prohibits incest, according to the Torah, to distinguish us from the abhorrent sexual practices of the Canaanites, who defiled their land thereby; later Jewish thinkers add other rationales for the prohibition.[50]

The Torah forbids incest both within marriage and outside of it. The particular form of incest that occurs between parents and children, though, is perhaps especially egregious, for it violates what should be the deepest relationship of trust in the human family. As a result, parent–child incest often causes lifelong damage to the children involved, severely impairing their self-esteem and making it impossible for them to form strong, trusting relationships with others. People who are tempted to engage in incestuous relations of any sort *must* get help so that they can avoid inflicting this gross harm on those whom they instead should love and care for.

DIVORCE AND CHILD CUSTODY

When two people stand under the *huppah* (wedding canopy), they intend that their marriage will last for the rest of their lives. The sad reality, though, is that nowadays there is a high rate of divorce.[51]

The Torah provides for divorce,[52] and so from our earliest texts the Jewish tradition has not considered divorce a sin. On the contrary, at times divorce is appropriate and possibly even a Jewish and moral good. That would certainly be true when the marital bond includes abuse or when it causes severe harm to the self-esteem of one or both spouses; but it might even be true when the couple simply cannot get along, despite counseling and other modes of trying to repair their relationship. On the other hand, though, the Talmud teaches that the Temple altar itself sheds tears upon the termination of a marriage,[53] suggesting that divorce is a source of immense sadness to all involved, not only to the couple and the family but even to the community and the world. Divorce is sometimes the right thing to do, sometimes a tragedy, and often both.

The increase in divorce in our day derives from many factors, some cultural, some economic, and some moral. One of those factors is the new economic and emotional equality of women, so that both men and women today are freer than ever before to choose to end their marriage. Another is the unrealistic expectations of constant passionate excitement with which many people enter marriage, largely as a result of the media; marriage may well be romantic and passionate, but people should get married to be companions through life together and to have and raise children, with passion and physical pleasure as accompaniments to those activities rather than the prime motives to get married.[54]

Even when clearly indicated, divorce in most cases is nevertheless a profoundly sad event, shattering the hopes and dreams of both spouses and the sense of continuity in their lives, often destabilizing their self-image and self-confidence, and always requiring a radical change of their lives from within and from without. New living arrangements must be made, and one can no longer depend on the other for emotional support, for sharing, or even for dividing the tasks of life. Married friends of the divorcing couple may no longer remain friends; and, if they do, time spent with them can become awkward.

If the couple has children, divorce has a lifelong impact on the children's sense of self and on how they view relationships. Even the most optimistic of researchers admit that at least 20 percent of children whose parents divorce suffer serious setbacks through the rest of their lives in their ability to relate to others, especially romantically, and so the children's welfare has to be a prime consideration in the decision about whether to divorce in the first place and, if so, in the arrangements to care for the children emotionally as well as physically.[55] Growing up within the context of a fractious marriage also has negative effects on children, though; so if the couple cannot truly reconcile, divorce may be the better option for both themselves and their children.

If a couple with dependent children decides to divorce, it is imperative that they find ways to ensure that their children will suffer as little as possible. The children minimally must not be made to take sides and must not be used as footballs to express the couple's anger with each other. Even when the divorce is not amicable, couples must strive to safeguard the welfare of their children. Often that means resolving to be civil with each other in sharing custody of the children, no matter how much that hurts each member of the couple on the inside. Except in downright abusive situations, children generally do better with continued contact with both parents. Even though this will prevent the couple from having full closure until their children are grown, they should care enough for their children to ensure for them the active love and influence of both their father and their mother.

Because of the negative impact of divorce on both the couple and the children, Judaism clearly stands in opposition to the frivolous or glamorous image of divorce sometimes portrayed in the media. A life partner should never be traded in simply for the sake of "acquiring" a newer model. Such flippancy degrades the full humanity of both spouses and dishonors the sanctity of the marital bond. Furthermore, while contemporary popular books on psychology and some movies teach the value of an individual's personal growth, often in opposition to staying in a marriage,[56] Judaism instead emphasizes the deeply stabilizing, stimulating, and sanctifying effects of marriage, children, and continuity on individuals and on society as a whole. Individuals should certainly seek ways to fulfill their dreams, but that should not come at the cost of marriage and family, which themselves are integral parts of human growth.[57]

Couples who do decide to divorce should obtain a Jewish writ of divorce (a *get*) after fulfilling whatever procedures are demanded by civil law. (In accordance with civil law, rabbis will not process a Jewish writ of divorce until the civil decree has taken effect.) A *get* is required because Jewish law does not recognize the power of any court, American or Jewish, to dissolve a marriage; only the husband can do that by giving his wife a *get*. (The marriage is also dissolved, of course, if the husband dies.) Therefore Conservative and Orthodox rabbis, who are committed to the authority of Jewish law, will not officiate at the marriage of a Jew who has been previously married to another Jew unless the first marriage has been dissolved in Jewish law as well as civil law. Furthermore, if the woman is divorced in civil law but not Jewish law and then remarries in a Reform or a civil ceremony, because she is still officially married in Jewish law to her former husband, her children by her second husband are illegitimate (*mamzerim*), which could cause major problems for them if they later choose to marry in the Orthodox or Conservative communities. American law does not recognize the authority of Jewish law to dissolve a marriage either, and so American Jews who divorce must fulfill the requirements of both legal systems.

For the vast majority of divorcing couples, the procedure of obtaining a *get* happens without any complications. The cost is just a few hundred dollars, which can be reduced if necessary, and the couple does not even have to be in the same room together if they choose to avoid seeing each other or if they are living in different cities.

There is a very small percentage of cases, though, in which the husband either cannot authorize that a *get* be given to his former wife (for example, if he has become insane or is missing in action during a war) or refuses to give his wife a *get*. Either circumstance makes her an *agunah*, a woman chained to her first husband and unable to remarry.

If the man cannot act because he is missing in war, then Jewish courts depend on just one witness (rather than the usual two) to establish that he died. If he cannot act because he is going insane (for example, owing to Alzheimer disease), rabbis will use any moments that he is lucid to gain his authorization to write a *get* for his wife. Ultimately, a decree of one hundred rabbis can free her to remarry.

The more common cases—although not all that common—occur when the husband refuses to give his wife a *get*. Sometimes the husband has good reason to take this stance, for example, to apply pressure to his former wife to abide by the custody arrangements decreed by the civil court. If his motives are less honorable, though, the Conservative movement and some Orthodox rabbis have developed ways that can be used as a last resort to free her from her first marriage so that she can remarry. However, the proper way for a Jewish couple to divorce is through a *get*. Even if former couples feel great anger toward each other, simple fairness as well as Jewish law require that they free each other to get on with their lives through the legal instrument of a *get*.[58]

While custody arrangements for children will nowadays be worked out by the civil courts, Jewish law's perspective on custody may help a couple think through how to approach the matter. The presumption in Jewish law is that children up to the age of six will stay with their mother and that beginning with that age boys will live with their father and girls with their mother.[59] That general pattern of custody arrangements stems from a much more role-differentiated society than we are used to today, in which it was assumed that children of both genders need the mother's special nurturing until age six and that beginning with that age children need to live with the parent who will model what they themselves will become as adults. That, though, is a rebuttable presumption, for ultimately the criterion in Jewish law for custody is the welfare of the child.[60]

We now understand that fathers as well as mothers are important in young children's development and that both parents contribute to all their children's sense of self-identity and self-worth as they grow through latency and adolescence. Thus joint custody arrangements of some sort are probably the best for most children, assuming that the parents can get along well enough to make that work. If that is not possible or, as in the case of an abusive parent, not desirable, some provision for the child to spend time with caring adults of both genders should be sought. Most often that is both parents, but it could also be other members of the family, friends, or a Jewish Big Brother or Big Sister. In any case, the ultimate criterion for child custody in Jewish law as well as in most North American jurisdictions is the welfare of the child.

PREPARATION FOR MARRIAGE
Jews living in an era in which divorce is common must enter into marriage with a higher level of intentionality and care than ever before. The knowledge that one in two marriages ends in divorce should require all couples to be especially mindful of what it takes to make marriage work.

Marriage is the most profound relationship we enter as adults and, therefore, one of our most demanding undertakings. It touches on our deepest human longings for love, trust, and intimacy, and thus it brings out the very best and the very worst of who we are as individuals. Moreover, everyone grows and changes over time, and marital relationships have to adjust to such changes. For these reasons and more, sustaining a successful marriage is indeed hard work, and people contemplating marriage owe it to themselves and to their future spouses and children to prepare for that task. We spend years preparing for our careers, so eight or ten sessions of a marriage preparation course, where available, is a superbly good investment of time. Alternatively, the couple should consider a series of counseling sessions with a rabbi and/or marriage counselor.

The goal of marriage preparation, whether in a course or in premarital counseling, is to encourage the couple to talk to each other about important aspects of their relationship. Adequate preparation might include issues of sexual concern, children, parents, friends, jobs, money, and communal commitments. It might also teach people to learn how to have a quarrel without threatening their marriage; indeed, some couples emerge stronger after they can clear the air in an emotionally expressive, but respectful and positive way. More generally, marriage preparation should help people learn how to communicate with each other. A couple should also discuss how they are going to express their Jewish commitments in their new home and how Judaism can help them with some or all of the issues mentioned above.

Clearly, people cannot reasonably expect to plan their entire lives in the months just before or after their wedding. People appropriately change their minds on some matters as time goes on and circumstances change. But to enter marriage in this era without deeply exploring these areas of concern to all couples is to close one's eyes to reality. Conversely, those who engage in a serious course of preparation for marriage significantly raise the probability that they will stay married; only 8 percent of couples who took the University of Judaism's Preparation for Marriage course during its twenty-five years of existence were ultimately divorced, a far cry from the 50 percent rate for the general population.

Preventive care for marriage does not end with the wedding. On the contrary, successful marriages are unions in which both spouses are mindful on an ongoing basis not only of their own needs but also of the needs of their mate. Spouses must remain cognizant of how important it is to continue to express love and appreciation for the other on a daily basis. This includes freely offering and receiving hugs and compliments; responding generously to each other's requests for help; and refraining from unnecessary criticisms and nasty or sarcastic remarks. In general, the couple must set aside adequate time—amid multiple other demands—to honor and nurture this most important of life's commitments.

When difficulties arise in marriage, couples in our day are well advised to shed any residual sense of embarrassment about seeking help—from friends, family, rabbis, or counselors. This is simply a continuation of the model of preventive care they initiated during the engagement period. Just as one would seek professional care for medical problems, one must do the same to protect the health of a marriage. Couples who do not have specific problems should seriously consider enrolling from time to time in Jewish Marriage Encounter or some such program in which they spend a weekend or more engaged in activities designed to ensure that they are still communicating well.

PARENTHOOD
The Commandment

In addition to the companionship it provides, marriage is also theologically important, as Genesis 1 affirms, for purposes of propagation. The Rabbis later determine that the command to "be fruitful and multiply" is fulfilled when the couple has borne two children, specifically, a boy and a girl.[61] If a couple cannot reproduce, the commandment to procreate no longer applies, for it makes no sense logically or legally to command people to do what they cannot do. Nevertheless, infertile couples should seriously consider adoption, converting the child to Judaism if he or she was not born to a Jewish woman. The Talmud states that adopting and raising children are "as if one has given birth to them" and that adoptive parents "follow the Lord at all times."[62]

Those who can produce or adopt children should see it as a mitzvah of the highest order to have more than the minimal number of two, for nothing less than the future of the Jewish community and of Judaism depends on that. The Jewish community, after all, lost a third of its members in the Holocaust, and, as I describe in some detail in the section on contraception, contemporary Jews are not producing enough children even to maintain their present numbers. Add to these factors the high rate of intermarriage and assimilation among Jews today, and it becomes clear that we Jews are in serious demographic trouble as a people. One needs a Jewish education to become an informed, practicing Jew, of course, but people can be educated only if they exist in the first place. The mitzvah of procreation, like all other commandments, does not apply to those who cannot fulfill it; but for those who can, propagation or adoption is literally a matter of life and death for us not only as individuals and as families but also as a people.

Children, of course, are not only an obligation but also a blessing. Parents inevitably worry about their children, get angry with them on occasion, and suffer with them during their frustrations and missteps, but parents also share in their children's accomplishments and renew their own sense of the joy of life through their offspring.

Moreover, children are our destiny, perhaps our strongest tie to the future. Biblical and rabbinic sources affirm that individuals live on after death in some form[63] and that the influence we have had on others during our lifetime continues after death; but we also, for those sources, live on through our children. We are, after all, linked to the generations, both past and future, and children are one primary form of that bond.

The importance of marriage, within the Jewish tradition, is not only for reasons of propagation and companionship, as important as they are, but also to educate children in the Jewish tradition so it can continue across the generations. Abraham, the Patriarch of the Jewish people, is already charged with teaching his children;[64] and the commandment for each one of us to do likewise, which appears several times in the Torah, is enshrined in the sections chosen for the first two paragraphs of the *Shema*,[65] a prayer that we recite twice daily. Even after schools were established, the primary context for Jewish education remained the home, and to this day parents continue to be responsible for ensuring that their children learn to be educated and practicing Jews. In our own time, we are rediscovering that no schooling, however good, can be adequate; that family education is the key to the continuation of the Jewish heritage; and that parents must continue to educate themselves as they seek to teach their children. This, in fact, is just a subset of the general Jewish duty to study the tradition on a lifelong basis, for Judaism is very much a religion for adults. Parents have the mission to prepare their children for such lifelong learning, whether the parents are married or single, custodial or not; but one of the objectives of marriage within the tradition is to provide the context in which children can best learn how to be Jews.

Teaching our children includes education in sexual behavior. Children learn what it is to be a husband or wife first and foremost from their own parents. Young children begin to understand the special kind of love involved in marriage when they see their parents caring for each other, hugging each other, laughing together, planning things together, sharing the tasks of life, and, yes, even arguing with one another. Older children may learn some of the biological aspects of sex in school, but they need their parents to help them discern the values involved. With the exception of communicating the imperative to protect oneself from AIDS and other sexually transmitted diseases, teachers—especially in public schools—are not authorized to teach what is appropriate in boy–girl relationships and what is not. That is the parents' job, and it is an ongoing one through the child's teenage years. For that matter, even in adulthood children may consult with parents about how to handle specific issues in their romantic relationships.

In these discussions, parents should not feel that their children will ignore them or think them to be outmoded if they advocate precautions or even total abstinence before marriage, especially if they do so calmly and with reason. They certainly should present sex as Judaism does—namely, as one part of our being that is integrated with all other parts of our being, and therefore our sexual behavior should reflect our own values as individuals and as Jews. Peer pressure should not govern the decisions that teenagers or adults make about their sexual activities; decisions about the most personal parts of our lives must come from the depths of who we are individually as people and as Jews, for what we do inevitably reflects on how we see ourselves and how others think of us. Parents should help their children see this linkage between sexual expression and self-image.

While conversations about these matters at all ages should be open and honest, the parents' own example most powerfully educates their children in sexual ethics. Parents, then, should see themselves as Jewish models not only in ritual behaviors but in moral ones too, including the area of sexual morals.[66]

For all of these reasons, then, marriage and children are vital in Jewish thought and practice. Many people, however, do not or cannot get married, and others cannot have children. Unfortunately, the Jewish emphasis on marriage and children all too often amplifies the pain that such people feel. It is thus important in this context to reaffirm the divine significance of everyone's life; we are all created in the image of God, and we all retain divine worth as individuals, whether or not we are married and whether or not we have children.[67]

INFERTILITY
As I indicated earlier, the command to procreate, like all other commands, does not apply to those who cannot fulfill it.

Therefore, the Jewish teachings described above about the importance of having and raising children should not generate guilt or shame in infertile couples. The Jewish tradition should not add to their frustration by holding up an ideal that is impossible for them to fulfill, for Judaism can never be legitimately interpreted to expect the impossible. On the contrary, family, friends, and the Jewish community as a whole should be careful not to add to the burdens of an infertile couple; they should instead help such couples endure the grief, frustration, disappointment, and anger that often accompany infertility.

As I describe in some detail in *Matters of Life and Death*, Jewish law permits infertile couples to avail themselves of the modern medical means to overcome infertility, but it does not require that they do so. Jewish law also endorses adoption as a means of having children, including adoption of children of any age or race. Adopted children who are not known to be Jewish by birth and children born to a non-Jewish surrogate mother must be formally converted to Judaism; but, for a child, that is a simple procedure well worth the joy of having children.[68] There are resources within most Jewish communities, often under the aegis of Jewish Family Service, to help Jewish couples experiencing infertility to explore their options and to provide support and advice. The absence of children, though, does not in the least impugn the divine value of one's individual being or one's marriage.

CONTRACEPTION

Sometimes couples who can procreate choose not to do so, at least for a time. This raises the question of contraception.

Even though the Rabbis of the Mishnah and Talmud knew that both men and women have indispensable roles in procreation and child rearing, they maintain that it is only the man who is legally liable for procreation. The stated reason for that decision is a specific interpretation of a verse in the Torah, but other rationales have been suggested.[69]

This provision of Jewish law has important implications for contraception. Since women are not legally obligated to procreate and men are, contraceptive techniques used by women are more easily permitted than those used by men.

Jewish sources from as early as the second century describe methods of contraception. A rabbinic ruling from that time prescribes the use of birth control devices when pregnancy would endanger either the woman or the infant she is nursing.[70] Subsequent rabbinic opinion splits between those who sanction the use of contraception only when such danger exists and those who mandate it then but allow it also in situations without such risks.

If couples are going to use contraceptives, Jewish law prefers forms that prevent conception in the first place over those that abort an already fertilized egg because, in most cases, Jewish law forbids abortion. For most of gestation, the fetus is considered "like the thigh of its mother," and, because our bodies are God's property, neither men nor women are permitted to amputate their thigh except to preserve their life or health.[71] Jews are often misinformed about this because they have heard, correctly, that Jewish law *requires* abortion when the woman's life or health—physical or mental—is threatened by the pregnancy and that Jewish law *permits* abortion when the risk to the woman's life or health (again, physical or mental) is greater than that of a normal pregnancy but not so great as to constitute a clear and present danger to her.

"Mental health" as a ground for abortion, however, has not been interpreted nearly as broadly in Jewish sources as it has been in American courts; it would not include, for example, the right to abort simply because the woman does not want to have another child, even because of economic pressures. Most rabbis, however, interpret Jewish law to permit an abortion when there is evidence that the child will be severely malformed or afflicted with a lethal genetic disease or when the pregnancy resulted from rape or incest.

Thus from the point of view of Jewish law, the most favored form of contraception is the diaphragm, for it prevents conception and has little, if any, impact on the woman's health. If the contraceptive pill or implant is not contraindicated by the woman's age or body chemistry, those are usually the next most favored forms of contraception. Couples like these forms of birth control because they are easy to use and because they are quite reliable; Jewish authorities recommend them because their success rate minimizes the possibility that the couple will later consider an abortion as a form of retroactive birth control. Contraceptives that retroactively abort an embryo should be used only when pregnancy would threaten the mother's physical or mental health, as defined in the preceding paragraphs.

The only nonpermanent, male form of contraception currently available is the condom. Because Jewish law makes the male legally responsible for propagation, he should refrain from using contraception at least until he has fulfilled that duty.[72] Condoms, moreover, sometimes split or slip off;[73] and even if they remain intact and in place, they do not always work. Nevertheless, condoms must be used if unprotected sexual intercourse poses a medical risk to either spouse, because condoms do offer some measure of protection against the spread of some diseases, and the duty to maintain health and life supersedes the positive duty of the male to propagate. So, for example, if the previous history of either partner suggests the possibility of HIV infection—whether through previous sexual encounters, drug use, or a blood transfusion—the man must use a condom and both partners must take a blood test. If either one tests positive for HIV, the use of condoms is not enough: Abstinence is necessary, for life must take precedence over the joys of sex.[74]

It should be noted, though, that even those medieval rabbis who permit contraception for nontherapeutic reasons never anticipated that Jews would postpone having children for as long as many Jewish couples now do. Even with modern medical advances, the late teens and the twenties are biologically still the best time for the human male and female to conceive and bear children.[75] Couples who wait until their thirties to begin their families will most likely be able to have only one or two children, and all too many couples beyond their twenties find that when they are ready to have children, they cannot. Because Jews attend college and graduate school in percentages far beyond the national norm[76] and, therefore, postpone marriage and attempts to have children until their late twenties, in their thirties or even forties, Jews are more prone to infertility than the general population. This is an excruciating problem for the couples themselves, for with all the techniques to overcome infertility now available, only half of older couples are ultimately able to have a child[77] and then only after enduring substantial marital tension over this issue, which sometimes even leads to divorce.

There are, of course, good reasons why so many Jews wait so long. In addition to long-term schooling, most women in our society find that they must earn money to support themselves and their families, just as their husbands do. Moreover, many people who would love to find a mate and get married in their early twenties may not be so fortunate. This argues for many things, including the following:

- Parents should make sure that their teenagers choose a college attended by many Jews, for social as well as religious and educational reasons.
- College students should understand that the college years are not too early to look for a spouse.
- Young people who find a mate in college should marry in graduate school and begin having their children then, to increase the probability that they will be able to have the children they want and that the Jewish tradition hopes that they will have. Moreover, the pressures of graduate school, however great, are usually no worse than the ones one experiences during the first years in one's profession.
- Members of the Jewish community who are beyond their childbearing years should contribute the funds to make day care and Jewish schooling and camping affordable.
- Even if young couples choose to use contraceptives for a time, they are well advised, both medically and Jewishly, not to wait too long.

Another factor must be mentioned. We Jews numbered approximately 18 million before the Holocaust, and we lost one third of our numbers during those terrible years. Even if we forget about replenishing the numbers we lost, we are currently not even replacing ourselves. To do that, we would need a reproductive rate of 2.3 (that is, statistically 2.3 children for every two adults). The reproductive rate must be more than 2.0 to account for people who never marry, who marry and choose not to have children or cannot have children, who have only one child, and who have two or more children who themselves then do not reproduce. The present overall reproductive rate of Jews in North

America is 1.8, with non-Orthodox Jews averaging 1.6 or 1.7, which means that we are endangering ourselves demographically as a people.[78]

The world's overpopulation problem is real; but Jews, currently at approximately fourteen million of the world's six billion people, are less than 0.25 percent of the world's population.[79] So even if the reproductive rate of Jews increased to the replacement rate, the impact on the world's population problem would be minimal. Indeed, even if, God forbid, the entire Jewish population of the world were wiped off the map tomorrow, the graph mapping the world's population increases would not show more than a temporary, tiny variation. That would still be true even if the Jewish people increased to replenish the six million lost in the Holocaust. Sacrificing the existence of the Jewish people through producing no children at all or only one or two is, therefore, neither an effective solution nor a warranted one to reduce the world's problems of overpopulation and limited resources.

This in no way is intended to diminish the serious problem of overpopulation in the world. Such concerns, however, are better addressed by increasing the availability and usage of contraception worldwide and by fostering the responsible use of resources, because the higher the standard of living, the lower the birth rate. Such measures would simultaneously add immeasurably to the humanity and dignity of the circumstances in which many poor people live.

Thus simply seeking replacement levels for our own Jewish population does not amount to unfair, special pleading; for we are asking the exact same thing of the other nations of the world. The contemporary, demographic problem of the Jewish people, then, must also be a factor that figures into the thinking of Jews using contraception.

The desire for children must also be a factor in communal planning and in extended family finances. If we are serious as a community in our attempt to replenish our numbers, we must develop policies and programs to encourage larger families who are also deeply Jewish. Greater discounts should be given, for example, to each added sibling in Jewish day schools, camps, and youth group programs. Moreover, as Jews, acting out of our own best interests and out of Jewish values, we should support pro-family legislation, such as laws that provide for family leaves for both mothers and fathers and for high-quality, affordable day care. Grandparents should, if they can, pay for their grandchildren's Jewish education, both formal and informal, for two reasons: Practically, they are often able to afford the expense more readily than a young couple can and, religiously, the biblical duty to teach your children diligently, enshrined in the *Shema*, applies, according to the Talmud, to your grandchildren as well.[80] Thus grandparents should be proud and even eager to help to pay for the Jewish education of their grandchildren, knowing that they are fulfilling a mitzvah and aiding their own family at the same time. Both as a community and as families, then, we must put our money where our mouths are.

Jews who use contraception for family planning, then, should give serious thought to having children earlier in their lives than is now common; the pressures of graduate school are not necessarily greater than, and are often less than, those of the first years of one's career. People can always find reasons to postpone childbearing—until we finish our education, or until we have more money, or until we get started in our careers—but by then it is biologically often too late. Indeed, couples should seriously consider having three or four children. Although the obligation in Jewish law to propagate is fulfilled when the man fathers a minimum of two children (specifically, a girl and a boy), he is not supposed to stop there, because Jewish law requires that we have as many children as we can, for, as Maimonides says, "if one adds a soul to the People Israel, it is as if he [or she] has built an entire world."[81] In our current demographic crisis as Jews, this is all the more imperative. Many couples in Conservative Congregation Beth El in Minneapolis, in fact, have what they call their "mitzvah child"—that is, the one extra child they had, in addition to the number they had originally planned on having, to make Jewish physical continuity possible.

Once again, those who cannot have children are exempted from this obligation, but even they should consider adoption. Those who can have children should have three or four. This means using contraceptives for family planning purposes only for a very short time, if at all. In the end, we must all be reminded of the way in which our tradition thinks of children and the way in which many people experience them—that is, as a true blessing from God.

SINGLE PARENTHOOD

Single parents in great numbers are a new phenomenon in Jewish life. In fact, only a small percentage of the Jews of North America live in the previously normative family of mother and father married for the first time sharing a home with two or more children. Instead, many homes with children now consist of blended families, where divorced parents and their new spouses parent children from first and subsequent marriages; I consider Jewish aspects of such families in the next section. Other homes are composed of a single adult parenting one or more children. Some people become single parents through divorce, some through the death of their spouse, some through nonmarital intercourse, some through artificial insemination, and some through adoption. Synagogues, schools, youth groups, and camps are increasingly adjusting to these new realities, but probably much too slowly for the people involved.

While parenting can be enormously fulfilling and rewarding, it is almost always a very hard job, endlessly demanding of the parent's time, energy, patience, and creativity. Single parenting is all the more so. All of us in the Jewish community, therefore, need to make special efforts to help single parents with those responsibilities, pragmatically, psychologically, and financially. This might include ensuring the availability of child care through volunteers, a synagogue program of child care, or financial assistance; creating support groups within the synagogue for single parents; and instituting reduced membership and tuition rates, when needed. It certainly includes recognizing that the family unit of a single parent with his or her children is a family—not an object of pity, but a full-fledged family, albeit one with special needs.

Since single parents often lack extended family members or friends who can help them bear the responsibilities of parenthood, single parents experience distinctive strains on their time, energy, and psyche that inhibit dating and (re)marriage. Thus synagogues particularly need to help single parents who wish to marry to find the time and opportunity to do so. This might include planning social and educational activities where singles in general, and single parents in particular, can meet, and it might also include the provision of child care or baby-sitting services (perhaps as a youth group project) to give single parents time to meet potential mates.

Single people with children have a special responsibility to model for their children sexual behavior that reflects Jewish values. That is understandably harder when one is trying to balance the duties of parenting with carrying on a personal life of one's own, but it is absolutely critical. The biological or adopted children of married parents were not around to witness their parents' dating patterns before marriage, but single parents will find their romantic behavior during dating scrutinized by their children and used as a paradigm for their own. When single parents date, their teenagers, who may also be dating, see them as a directly relevant model. Younger children, when they later become teenagers themselves, will often remember what their parent did when he or she was dating.[82]

Children growing up in single-parent families also undergo special stresses. They often have less of a parent's time, energy, or attention than children growing up in a two-parent home, because a single mom or dad is the sole financial support of the family. Moreover, all children need adult models of both genders to gain a healthy understanding of what it is like to be a man or a woman; single parents by themselves can provide a model of only one gender. For both of these reasons, then, single parents are well advised to find other adults to help with raising their children, either among family or friends or through organizations such as Jewish Big Brothers or Jewish Big Sisters.

Conversely, Jews in our age can no longer assume that their parenting duties have ceased when their children move out of the house; they may well be called on to help with the parenting of nieces, nephews, cousins, or grandchildren. That may upset their dreams and plans for their senior years, but the more conscientiously and enthusiastically they welcome these new tasks, the better it will be for everyone.

Moreover, adult Jews should give serious consideration to volunteering for Jewish Big Brothers or Jewish Big Sisters. In doing so, they not only offer tremendous help to the single parent and to the child but also help the Jewish community as a whole raise well-adjusted children in the new, emotionally and psychologically harder circumstances in which many of them find themselves. The children may not always show appreciation to the extent that one would hope, and they may not seek to keep up the relationship once grown; nevertheless, Jewish Big Brothers and Big Sisters should know that contributing to the emotional and psychological well-being and to the Jewish identity of the next generation of Jews is nothing less than a sacred task.

STEPFAMILIES

In generations past, stepfamilies were most often formed when the mother died in childbirth and the father remarried; nowadays, safe Caesarian sections have meant that few women in North America die in childbirth, but stepfamilies are still formed when one spouse dies and the other remarries. Most stepfamilies, though, are created after either or both partners have gone through a divorce and then married each other.

Stepfamilies offer at least two adults to parent the children, one of each gender, and so stepfamilies often do not face the same lack of time and money and the same lack of adults of both genders for modeling that single-parent families do. On the contrary, in many stepfamilies there are three or more adults competing for the attention and love of the child. The newly married couple has to go through the adjustments that all other couples face, but they often do that in the presence of children and with one or more former spouses in the picture. The complicated family linkages involved inevitably make it harder for the couple to nurture their own marriage. Child custody arrangements have to be managed with former spouses, and so do financial affairs. Holiday times and life-cycle events are often the hardest to negotiate. On an ongoing basis, the children have to adjust to new stepbrothers and stepsisters. The fanciful hope that somehow all of them will love each other immediately and will get along even better than the children of a first marriage do only adds to the frustration and worry for all concerned. As a result, children in blended families often have problems:

> Religion, family finances, diet, discipline—these are all issues that stepfamilies around the country are struggling with every day. And most of them are doing it gracefully. Even so, there is a siz-

able minority of stepfamilies in America that are not doing well at all. A variety of studies have demonstrated that stepkids do more poorly on a variety of measures than do kids who live in traditional, two-parent families—even adjusting for income level. They are more apt to repeat a grade in school, have disciplinary problems, and drop out of school altogether. In fact, these studies collectively indicate that stepchildren do about as well as kids who live with a single parent, which is to say much worse than kids in traditional nuclear families.

And that's not the worst of it. According to extensive research of Martin Daly and Margo Wilson of McMaster University in Ontario, stepchildren are more likely to be abused, both physically and sexually, and even more likely to be killed by a parent—100 times as likely—compared with kids being raised by two biological parents. Another line of research indicates that they are less likely to be provided for. For example, American children living with a stepparent are less likely to go to college and to receive family financial support if they do. New research also shows that biological mothers around the world spend more of family income on food—particularly milk, fruit, and vegetables—and less on tobacco and alcohol, compared with mothers raising nonbiological children. The list goes on.[83]

None of this means, of course, that divorced parents should avoid a second marriage; after all, remarriage fulfills their own needs for sex and companionship, and it provides their children with another caring adult and possibly new stepsiblings and even more financial resources. As a result, most stepfamilies do gracefully overcome the problems involved. The complexities of stepfamilies, however, mean that the adults involved must think carefully about how they will manage their new living arrangements. They need to inculcate in themselves and in their children realistic expectations; most families, for example, spend a lot of time apart, particularly when the children become teenagers, and stepfamilies should be no different. They need to define roles and establish household rules. They need to work out the financial arrangements for their household now and for the children's future education. They need to give the members of the expanded family time to adjust to each other. And the couple needs to cultivate their own relationship, for the family will not last if the parents' relationship does not.

All of this, of course, applies to Jewish families as well as those of other religions. The specifically Jewish aspects of Jewish stepfamilies concern the children's Jewish identity and, with that, their Jewish education, activities, group associations, holiday celebrations, and life-cycle events. If the divorced parents share similar Jewish commitments with each other and with their new spouses, the problems on all fronts are diminished, for they are likely to want the same kind of Jewish upbringing for their children, and they will present the same model of Jewish identity to them. There may still be plenty of other areas to work out, but at least the Jewish aspects of their parenting will coincide.

If one of the spouses is Jewishly committed and the other is not, the child will see different forms and degrees of Jewish identity in each of the parent's homes, and the child will inevitably be faced in later life with picking Mom's way or Dad's way—or of abandoning them both so as not to have to choose between them. To avoid making this a choice between Mom and Dad, the parents should do all that they can during the child's upbringing to show respect for the other parent's way of being Jewish, even while practicing and teaching their own. That will make Judaism a source of positive self-identification and self-worth for the child rather than a spark for further friction and conflict. Parents should also help their teenagers understand that everyone, including those who grow up in homes without divorce, chooses an adult form of Judaism that usually varies somewhat from that of their parents, and so the child need not interpret his or her choices as preferring one parent over the other.

The hardest scenarios occur when one parent is committed to Judaism and the other marries a non-Jew—say, a Christian. Then all of the problems of living a Jewish life and of raising a Jewish child inherent in every mixed marriage affect this one as well, but with the complications of children within the stepfamily being raised in different religions and of the former spouse advocating Jewish identity and, at least to some degree, commitment.

The best strategy, of course, is for both parents to avoid marrying someone of another faith in the first place. Even if one or both marries a non-Jew, the Jewish parents should do their best to provide a serious Jewish education and frequent Jewish experiences for their child within an atmosphere of respect for the differing religion(s) of the new members of the stepfamily. The statistics are not encouraging: The vast majority of children of mixed marriages are not raised as Jews. And that is especially so when other children in the household are Christian.[84] Still, mutual respect can go a long way.

The same watchword affects holiday celebrations and life-cycle events. Even when all the adults involved are Jewish, working out a reasonable arrangement whereby the child alternates holidays with each parent is critical, for holiday times are likely to be remembered by both parents and children as very special occasions. The adults involved also need to work out a mutually agreeable way for them all to participate in the children's bar or bat mitzvah celebrations and, ultimately, their weddings, because those events are even more critical in a person's life and are etched in a person's memory and heart even more deeply. This is easier said than done, of course, for divorced people often rub each other the wrong way, and even those who divorced amicably sometimes move to different cities or marry people who have difficulty accommodating the former spouse and his or her family. Rabbis and others with experience in these matters can often help the couple find ways to plan these events with all of the special parameters of blended families in mind.

In life-cycle celebrations, holidays, and indeed generally, *the adults owe it to their children to focus on their children's welfare.* If the adults manage to keep that goal in mind, they will not only act in the best interests of their children but they will also have a much better chance to find ways of dealing with each other civilly, if not amicably.

BALANCING FAMILY AND WORK

Finally let me address an issue that affects many configurations of families. In contemporary society, marriage and family are often balanced against the values of work. Judaism prizes work: "Six days shall you labor and do all your work" is as much of a commandment as "and the seventh day is a sabbath to the Lord your God [on which] you shall not do any work."[85] Jewish sources make it clear that work is important for the welfare of society as a whole, for its contribution to the psychological health and self-worth of the individual, and for the economic support it affords to oneself and to one's family.[86] For some people, though, the secular work ethic prevalent in contemporary society has made work the sole value, a virtual idol.

Judaism would have us recognize the idolatry inherent in a life devoted exclusively to work and would have us balance our commitments to work with serious time and energy spent on other important values, most especially those of family. Overzealous commitment to work does have a deleterious effect on one's sexual and family relationships,[87] and the Jewish tradition would have us remember that one's family should take precedence over one's job. This is poignantly stated in the Rabbis' comment on Numbers 32:16, where the tribes of Reuben and Gad ask to stay in the lands the Israelites had already conquered on the eastern bank of the Jordan River so that "we might build sheep pens for our flocks and cities for our children." On this the Rabbis comment:

> They were more worried about their possessions than they were about their sons and daughters, for they mentioned their flocks before their children. Moses said to them: "Do not do that; what is primary should be primary and what is secondary, secondary. Build first cities for your children and afterwards pens for your flocks."[88]

As both men and women in our society are increasingly taking on the responsibilities of careers, then, it is important to reaffirm that both men and women have critically important roles to play in providing marital companionship for each other and in raising their children.

Achieving a proper balance of work and family, of course, is not easy. Since most parents in our day do not live with an extended family nearby, the full burden of supporting themselves while simultaneously rearing children falls completely on them. Moreover, especially for men, but increasingly for women as well, American society defines "success" almost totally in terms of climbing the ladder at one's job. Years from now, though, when we look back on our lives, most of us will not feel bad that we did not spend more time working; we will instead regret the time that we did not spend with our spouse and children, particularly when they were young and readily available for interaction.[89] All too often, it is not until children reach their teens or twenties that parents feel secure enough in their jobs to find the time to do things with their children; by that time, however, the children are interested in building their own independent lives and rarely have time or interest in doing things with Mom or Dad. Judaism's long-term vision about what is really important in life, as embedded in the Rabbis' commentary on the requests of the tribes of Reuben and Gad, should help us keep our priorities straight as young adults and as older spouses and parents as well.

NONMARITAL SEX

Judaism posits marriage as the preferred context for sexual intercourse. Many Jews these days, though, are engaging in sexual relations outside the marital bond. They face a number of moral dilemmas in their relationships. How would the Jewish tradition guide them?

First I need to define the group to which this section is addressed. Some nonmarital, sexual acts are adulterous or incestuous; the Jewish tradition resoundingly condemns those forms of sex as a gross violation of Jewish law and of all of the values described at the beginning of this chapter. Casual and promiscuous sexual encounters, while not as egregious as incest and adultery, are also to be avoided, since they involve little or no love or commitment and carry substantial health risks.

The nonmarital relations that this section addresses, then, are not adulterous, incestuous, or promiscuous; they are rather sexual relations between two unmarried adults that take place in the context of an ongoing, loving relationship. People engage in such relations for a number of reasons: Because a suitable mate has not yet been, or may never be, found, often despite painful and heartfelt searching; because for chronological, emotional, educational, economic, or professional reasons, one's life circumstances render marital commitment premature; because experience with divorce or the death of a partner has necessitated a gradual healing process, including experience of several transitional relationships before remarriage; or because, in the case of seniors, Social Security and/or tax regulations make marriage very expensive.

Let me begin with expressions of affection commonly done in public among friends. It is perfectly natural and healthy for unmarried people to hug and kiss each other as signs of friendship

111

and warmth. Thus the Shabbat kiss and embraces meant to convey congratulations, comfort, greeting, or simply camaraderie are perfectly legitimate. Indeed, throughout the Bible not only parents and children but also brothers and sisters, friends and lovers embrace and kiss.[90] Such expressions of human caring give special significance to occasions like Shabbat and life-cycle events, and more generally, they save life from being lonely and isolated and make it instead social, secure, and meaningful. In Martin Buber's words, "All real living is meeting,"[91] and these expressions of fellowship and good wishes help us deepen our relationships with the people who make up our community.

Romantic relationships, from their earliest stages and throughout their unfolding, often use these noncoital forms of affection too. Holding hands, hugging, and kissing are perfectly natural and healthy expressions of both a budding romance and a long-term one. One must take due regard for the sense of modesty and privacy that Judaism would have us preserve in expressing our romantic feelings, and so the more intense forms of these activities should be reserved for private quarters.[92] Within that norm, though, unmarried as well as married people routinely do and should engage in these practices as they build and strengthen the loving relationships that make them distinctly human.

The remainder of this section, then, deals exclusively with the issue of sexual intercourse outside of marriage. Nonmarital sex can provide companionship as well as physical pleasure, which, especially in the context of a long-term relationship, are definite goods. Moreover, sometimes people would like to get married but cannot for any of the reasons mentioned above. While the Jewish tradition very much supports sexual pleasure and companionship as goods, it condemns some settings where those are obtained—namely, adultery and incest—and, on the other end of the spectrum, it sanctifies marriage. Nonmarital, consensual sex falls somewhere in between. It lacks the holiness of marriage, for a wedding signifies that the man and woman intend their relationship to provide not only the pleasure and companionship of sex but also the enduring quality and wide scope of a publicly recognized and sanctified relationship, one intended to be permanent and to include, in the case of young people, the procreation and education of the next generation.

Marriage, of course, does not guarantee that a couple will realize the concepts and values described earlier in this chapter, because life does not come with guarantees. Marriage does provide, though, a structure to help couples actualize them, thus making it all the more probable that Jews will live by Jewish values in even their most intimate interactions. Most human societies have encouraged adults to satisfy their sexual drives in the context of a stable relationship in which they also produce and raise children, for that is in the societies' best interests. After all, marriage contributes to the psychological growth and the responsibility of adults, and it takes much of the burden off of society as a whole to teach children moral behavior and attitudes. In Judaism, these social interests are understood also to be God's will; as the first part of the Jewish marriage ceremony says, God "has forbidden us those who are merely betrothed [and certainly those who lack even that early form of singling out an intended spouse] and permitted us [only] those who are married to us through the wedding canopy and the sacred rites of marriage (*huppah v'kiddushin*)."

Some people, though, either will not or cannot get married, and the physical and psychological pleasures that sex provides lead them to engage in sexual relations with each other. People who engage in such relationships are not fulfilling the Jewish ideal. We often, though, act in less than ideal ways in many areas of our lives—and in the area of sex, as in all others, failing to live up to the ideal does not free people from incorporating as much of the ideal as possible into their lives. That is, Jewish norms in sexual matters, like Jewish norms in other arenas, are not all-or-nothing phenomena. In fact, in the context of nonmarital relationships, some of the concerns described earlier in this chapter take on new significance.

Seeing oneself and one's partner as distinctly human creatures of God created in the divine image. Our bodies are not machines separate and apart from "us"; they are an integral part of who we are. As a result, the ways we gain pleasure from our bodies sexually will inevitably have a significant effect on how we perceive ourselves and how others perceive us. My sexual activity should, therefore, reflect my own value system and the personhood of myself and my sexual partner.

While this recognition is a necessary component in marital sex, it is all the more imperative in nonmarital sex, where the lack of a public, long-term commitment to one another heightens the chances that one or both of the partners will see sex as simply pleasurable release. There is nothing wrong with sexual pleasure per se; indeed, it is one of the great gifts of God. In our sexual activities, though, we need to pay attention to the context and circumstances in which we gain that pleasure to retain our human character—indeed, our divine imprint. The more we value our own divinity and that of our partner, the less like animals we—and our sexual activities—will be.

Modesty. The demand that one be modest in one's sexual activities—as well as in one's speech and dress—is another corollary of seeing oneself in the image of God. For singles, it is especially important to note that modesty requires that one's sexual activities be conducted in private and that they not be discussed with others in ways that compromise the honor, privacy, or integrity of one's partner. Certainly bragging about one's sexual conquests lacks both modesty and decency.

Respect for others. Respect for others means, negatively, that we must avoid coercive sex. We must also avoid deceiving an intended partner to gain sexual satisfaction. For example, saying "I love you" when I do not is a lie that besmirches my own integrity and simultaneously manifests lack of respect for the other person. Positively, respect for others demands that we act in ways that honor the divine image in oneself and in one's partner. Marriage is no guarantee that sexual relations will be respectful and noncoercive. Still, the deep relationship that marriage betokens makes it more probable that the two partners will care for each other in their sexual relations as well as in all of the other arenas of life.

Honesty. Honesty is one corollary of respect for others. Marriage is a public statement of commitment of the partners to each other, and sexual activity is one powerful way in which that commitment is restated and reconfirmed. If one is not married, sex cannot possibly symbolize the same degree of commitment. Unmarried sexual partners must, therefore, openly and honestly confront what their sexual activity means for the length and depth of their relationship.

Fidelity. Fidelity is another corollary of respect for others. Marriage by its very nature demands fidelity. Unmarried relationships, even long-term ones, by their very nature demand a lesser degree of fidelity. The security, intensity, and intimacy that fidelity imparts to a relationship are, therefore, not as accessible in a nonmarital relationship. In the spirit of this value, though, one should avoid short-term sexual encounters and seek, instead, long-term relationships to which one remains faithful for the duration of the relationship. Infidelity breeds pain, distrust, and—in the extreme—inability to form intimate relationships with anyone. The Jewish tradition requires us to respect one another more than that; we minimally must be honest and faithful to our commitments so as to avoid harming one another.

Breaking up a friendship usually produces hurt feelings; where sex has been involved, the potential for anger, self doubt, and feelings of betrayal is all the greater. Therefore, if and when one or both partners decide to end the relationship, that must be done as tactfully and lovingly as possible.

Health and safety. The concern for health and safety within the Jewish tradition is even more critical in nonmarital relationships than it is in married ones, for most sexually transmitted diseases are contracted in sexual liaisons with multiple partners. In our time, this includes not only recurring infections, such as syphilis, but fatal diseases, such as AIDS.

It is, therefore, imperative to recognize that sexual contact with *any* new partner raises the possible risk of contracting sexually transmitted diseases, including lethal ones. Not only is that a pragmatic word to the wise but it comes out of the depths of the Jewish moral and legal tradition, where *pikuah nefesh* (saving a life) is a value of the highest order. Moreover we are commanded by our tradition to take measures to prevent illness in the first place.[93] Fulfilling these commandments in regard to AIDS requires all of the following:

- Full disclosure of each partner's sexual history from 1980 to the present to identify whether a previous partner may have been infected with HIV.

115

- HIV testing for both partners before genital or oral sex is considered, recognizing all the while that a negative test result is valid only after six months have elapsed since the last genital contact.
- Careful and consistent use of condoms and avoidance of oral sex until the risk of infection has been definitively ruled out by either the partner's sexual history or the results of HIV testing.
- Abstinence from coitus and oral sex altogether when there is demonstrated HIV infection in either partner.

One must also recognize that condoms do not prevent the spread of other sexually transmitted diseases and that one can never guarantee safe sex with multiple partners. Still, in response to the Jewish demand that we preserve our health and avoid undue risks, if a person is going to have sex outside of marriage—particularly with multiple partners—then this Jewish imperative requires that one take whatever precautions one can to make one's sexual activity as safe as possible. If any of these requirements in regard to AIDS and other sexually transmitted diseases cannot be met owing to discomfort with open communication, lack of maturity, one partner's reticence to disclose his or her sexual history, or doubts about the trustworthiness of the partner's assurances, then abstinence from sex with this partner is the *only* safe and Jewishly legitimate choice. AIDS, after all, is still lethal; protease inhibitors, while a wonderful new tool in fighting the ravages of the infection, work in only half of AIDS victims, and the drugs are beginning to lose their effectiveness even for those people in whom they have previously worked. Thus protection against AIDS and other sexually transmitted diseases must be part of any sexual decision. We are *always* obligated to take care of our bodies, and that responsibility does not stop at the bedroom door.

The possibility of a child. Unmarried couples should recognize that, even with the use of contraceptives, an unplanned pregnancy is always a possibility. That leaves the possibility of abortion. Jewish law does not classify abortion as murder, as Catholicism does, because Jewish law understands the status of the fetus developmentally: It is "simply water" during the first forty days of gestation, and from then until birth it is "like the thigh of its mother." Legally, then, abortion is normally forbidden not as murder but as self-injury. Even in the first forty days, morally it is to be avoided because the fetus *in utero* is, after all, a potential life. Moreover, even when abortion is justified, women and often their male partners remember abortions with a degree of ambivalence and pain for the rest of their lives. In fact, all of the couple's options—abortion, raising the child, giving the baby up for adoption (the choice that may seem the least onerous)—involve serious psychological consequences for all concerned, and, in the case of abortion, moral and sometimes physical ones as well.[94] Therefore, abortion should not be used flippantly as a retroactive form of birth control, and couples engaged in nonmarital sex must both use contraceptives and must carefully consider the implications of a possible pregnancy if the contraceptives fail.

The Jewish quality of the relationship. Unmarried couples who live together should discuss the Jewish character of their relationship just as much as newlyweds need to do. In addition to all of the theological and moral issues described above, the Jewish character of a long-term, sexual relationship includes the gamut of ritual commandments, such as the dietary laws and Sabbath and festival observance. It also includes considerations of giving any children that came from their union a Jewish education. The couple should create a Jewish home for themselves and their children, including Jewish ritual observances, Jewish books, magazines, and music, and Jewish social and social action activities.

Moreover, Jews should exclusively date other Jews, to ward off the likelihood of intermarriage and the problems it produces for themselves and for the Jewish people as a whole. Intermarriage is a major problem for the contemporary Jewish community, and studies indicate that as many as 82 percent of the children of intermarried couples are not raised as Jews.[95] Furthermore, intermarriage is a problem for the people themselves. Marriage is hard enough as it is, considering the number of compromises that the couple must make; it is even harder if the husband and wife come from different religious backgrounds. It is no wonder, then, that as high as the divorce rate is nowadays

117

among couples of the same religion, it is almost double that among couples consisting of a Jew and a non-Jew.[96] Consequently, single Jews should date only Jews, if they want to enhance their chances of staying together, of ultimately marrying, and of having Jewish children and grandchildren.

To repeat an important point: Jewish norms in regard to sex, like Jewish norms in regard to everything else, are *not* all-or-nothing things. Thus, while marriage is the Jewish ideal, mature singles who engage in sexual activities can and should strive to conduct their sexual lives according to the Jewish ideas and norms described above. Indeed, all Jews should consciously strive to live according to those concepts and values in all of their relationships, including most especially their most intimate ones. Only then can their Jewish identity have some of the meaning it should for the sexual components of their lives.

A SPECIAL NOTE FOR TEENAGERS

If the considerations of nonmarital sex discussed above apply to people in their twenties and beyond, they apply all the more to teenagers, for whom the commitments of marriage and children are simply not possible. This, though, puts teenagers in an especially difficult bind, for their bodies are sexually mature, even though educationally and financially they are not in a position to rear children. Moreover, the level of sexual hormones in males is as high as it will ever get, because hormonal levels in males peak at age eighteen. For females, that occurs between the ages of twenty-six and thirty.

In ages past, people married in their late teens; but young people today go to high school, college, and often graduate school, so marriage is usually not an option as a sexual outlet for them until they reach their mid-twenties. Members of both sexes can usually procreate without difficulty from puberty to age twenty-seven, with somewhat more risk of infertility until age thirty-five, and with considerably more risk of infertility and birth defects after that.

Teenagers throughout history have been driven by their hormones and by their age-appropriate, psychological tasks of differentiating themselves from their parents, of seeking the company of other teenagers, and of exploring their sexuality.

Each of the movements in Judaism has, therefore, aptly created opportunities for Jewish teenagers to meet each other and to learn to feel comfortable in each other's presence. Indeed, given the small numbers of Jewish people in the world, it would be wise for Jewish youth groups to create intergroup activities to maximize the teenagers' sense of belonging to the entirety of the Jewish people (*k'lal yisrael*), to give them expanded opportunities for Jewish friendships, and also, frankly, to increase the pool of Jews among whom the members can find a romantic relationship. As long as such a relationship is voluntary on the part of both partners, and as along as Judaism's norms of modesty and privacy are maintained, holding hands, hugging, and kissing are perfectly legitimate for teenagers as they build romantic relationships.

Even more than single adults, though, teenagers need to refrain from sexual intercourse, for they cannot honestly deal with its implications or results—such as the commitments and responsibilities that sexual relations normally imply for both partners, including, especially, the possibility of children and the risk of AIDS and other sexually transmitted diseases. Abstinence is surely not easy when the physical and social pressures are strong, but it is the only responsible thing to do.[97]

One other matter is that Jewish teenagers should date Jews exclusively. As much as marriage may seem eons away, in modern times dating is the usual way in which young people meet and ultimately marry. Marrying the boy or girl that you first met at school is still a common phenomenon, for such people share experiences from their high school years and perhaps even from early childhood. Thus high school students need to restrict their dates to Jews.

Along the same lines, it is worth repeating that high school juniors and seniors planning for college should be sure to choose a school with a significant number of Jews. That is important for general religious, educational, and social reasons, but the romantic factor is absolutely critical. Although not everyone finds his or her mate in college, a significant number do, and so one important element in a Jew's choice of college should be the availability of other Jews with whom one can form a community and among whom one can date.

MASTURBATION

Especially given the high hormonal levels of teenagers and young adults, refraining from nonmarital sex will almost inevitably mean that they, and, for that matter, older people will masturbate. This is especially true in our own time, when people commonly marry some fifteen years after they become sexually mature. The Mishnah, by contrast, mandates that men marry by the age of eighteen,[98] and the Talmud records how Rabbi Hisda boasted that he was superior to his colleagues because he had married by sixteen, "and had I married at fourteen, I would have said to Satan, 'An arrow in your eye.' "[99] Men in their middle to late teenage years presumably married women who were somewhat younger. Even then, we must presume that nature took its course and that people masturbated at least until marriage.

The Torah is silent about masturbation; the story of Onan[100] that is often cited in this regard is about interrupted coitus, not masturbation. The talmudic Rabbis and the medieval Jewish tradition, however, roundly condemned masturbation, especially by males.[101] Much of that, though, was due to earlier medical beliefs that masturbation would lead to insanity, impotence, loss of hair, and a host of other maladies.[102] We now know that such beliefs are not true. Therefore, even though the tradition was not happy about masturbation, it is preferable that people masturbate than that they engage in nonmarital sex, because masturbation does not involve any of the moral commitments or physical risks of sexual intercourse. Masturbation should be done in private, of course, just as all genital activities should be. In that context, men and women who masturbate rather than engage in nonmarital sex should feel no guilt about it: They are making the morally and Jewishly preferable choice.

HOMOSEXUALITY

Homosexual relationships have become much more public than they ever were in the past, as gays and lesbians in increasing numbers and percentages come out of the closet to declare their sexual orientation. This has prompted intense debate in society generally and in the Jewish community in particular about the status of homosexuals, including such matters as protection from hate crimes and from discrimination in housing and in the workplace as well as affirmative rights of marriage, adoption, health care options, conservatorship, and inheritance.

Since I have written about this matter at some length in *Matters of Life and Death*,[103] I will not repeat that discussion here. Suffice it to say, I believe that homosexuals should be treated in our general and Jewish communities just as heterosexuals are, enjoying the same rights and bearing the same responsibilities. This would mean, among other things, that Jewish gay men and lesbians should endeavor to incorporate the concepts and values discussed in the first section of this chapter in their sexual activities just as Jewish heterosexuals should. Promiscuity should be shunned, careful attention should be paid to ensuring health and safety, and respect for the other must be manifested in the relationship. Ultimately, I believe, society should provide homosexuals the same social support for long-term, monogamous relationships that we afford heterosexuals through the institution of marriage. Interested readers should consult *Matters of Life and Death* for a discussion of the grounds for these positions.

The most liberal Orthodox spokesmen have drawn a distinction between homosexual persons who sin in the same manner as all Jews do and homosexual sexual activities, which are prohibited as an especially egregious sin, an "abomination" in the words of Leviticus.[104] Such rabbis intend this distinction as a way to make room for homosexuals within the Orthodox community—but that welcome comes at the cost of having an integral part of the homosexual's identity and life branded as an abomination. Other Orthodox rabbis are less kind; and, in any case, Orthodox rabbis as a group, with maybe one or two exceptions, condemn homosexual sex.

Conversely, as early as 1973 the Reform movement accepted into its synagogue organization those synagogues with special outreach to gays and lesbians; and in 1990, the Reform rabbinical school, Hebrew Union College, officially adopted a policy opening admission to gays and lesbians on a par with heterosexuals. Thus while individual Reform synagogues or persons may object to gay sex or to gays occupying positions of synagogue leadership, the official policy of the Reform movement does not support either of those stands, maintaining instead that homosexuals should be treated exactly as heterosexuals.

It is thus only in the Conservative movement that heated discussions on this topic continue. While I tend to be somewhere in the middle of the movement in my personal practice and in my stance on all other topics, on this one I am very far on the left end. Nevertheless, it is important to state that in 1990 and 1991, respectively, the Rabbinical Assembly (the organization of Conservative rabbis) and the United Synagogue of Conservative Judaism (the movement's organization of synagogues) passed the following resolution:

GAY AND LESBIAN JEWS

WHEREAS Judaism affirms that the Divine image reflected by every human being must always be cherished and affirmed, and

WHEREAS Jews have always been sensitive to the impact of official and unofficial prejudice and discrimination, wherever directed, and

WHEREAS gay and lesbian Jews have experienced not only the constant threats of physical violence and homophobic rejection, but also the pains of anti-Semitism known to all Jews and, additionally, a sense of painful alienation from our own religious institutions, and

WHEREAS the extended families of gay and lesbian Jews are often members of our congregations who live with concern for the safety, health, and well-being of their children, and

WHEREAS the AIDS crisis has deeply exacerbated the anxiety and suffering of this community of Jews who need in their lives the compassionate concern and support mandated by Jewish tradition,

THEREFORE BE IT RESOLVED that we, The Rabbinical Assembly [or the United Synagogue of Conservative Judaism], while affirming our tradition's prescription for heterosexuality,

1. Support full civil equality for gays and lesbians in our national life, and
2. Deplore the violence against gays and lesbians in our society, and
3. Reiterate that, as are all Jews, gay men and lesbians are welcome as members in our congregations, and
4. Call upon our synagogues and the arms of our movement to increase our awareness, understanding and concern for our fellow Jews who are gay and lesbian.[105]

The Conservative movement, then, as a movement, stands on record for full civil rights for gays and lesbians and for protection from attack and discrimination. It also officially welcomes gays and lesbians, as it welcomes all Jews, to Conservative congregations. Serious disagreement continues within the movement, however, on two issues: admission of gays and lesbians to rabbinical and cantorial schools, and the advisability of creating and using some kind of commitment ceremony for gay or lesbian couples. The very name of such ceremonies is a matter at issue. Options include "commitment ceremony"; *brit re'im* (covenant of friends) or *brit re'im ha-ahuvim* (covenant of loving friends), based on the description of the couple in the seven blessings for a heterosexual marriage; and "marriage" or the Hebrew equivalents, *"kiddushin"* (betrothal) and *"nisu'in"* (marriage). The liturgy for such ceremonies is also at issue, ranging from ceremonies very close to Jewish marriage rites to those very different from them.

While the Conservative movement at this writing officially endorses neither ordination nor commitment ceremonies, some Conservative rabbis on their own authority as rabbis have performed ceremonies joining same-sex couples, and the Conservative movement's Committee on Jewish Law and Standards (CJLS) has been asked to revisit these issues. Moreover, some openly gay and lesbian rabbis serve in a variety of posts within the synagogues and schools of the Conservative movement. Thus the debate goes on.

When the CJLS extensively debated homosexuality in 1991–1992, I suggested that this matter is, at least to some extent, a generational matter. I personally never heard of the word "homosexual," let alone "gay" or "lesbian," when I was growing up in the 1950s. In my freshman year of college (1961) one of the books we read as part of a required great books course was Plato's *Symposium*, in which Socrates lauds homosexual sex between a master and student as an appropriate expression of that relationship. We tittered about that for two days without serious discussion about homosexuality and then moved on to the next book on the syllabus.

It was not until 1973 that I next was confronted with the topic. I was already teaching at the University of Judaism, and an old camp friend who had become a rabbi of a synagogue in Cleveland called. He told me that a fellow who had been a member of his congregation, regional president of United Synagogue Youth, and then a student at the Joint Program between Columbia University and the Jewish Theological Seminary of America had come out as a gay man during the spring of his sophomore year. The man had been shunned by the seminary community at that time and thus had transferred to the University of California at Los Angeles (UCLA). The rabbi asked me to meet with this young man just to reassure him that people in the Jewish community still cared about him. When I did that, I experienced the first and only time that I felt genuinely embarrassed by my tradition. All I knew about Judaism and homosexuality was the verses in Leviticus that condemn gay sex as an abomination.[106] But he, for understandable reasons, had done considerable research on the topic as it had been treated in the later Jewish tradition. He also described to me what it was like being a committed Jew and yet condemned by his own tradition. I do not know what happened to him, and I hope that in the three hours we spent that afternoon I at least conveyed a sense of sympathy and support, but I am afraid that I was dumbfounded by what he told me and did not have much to say to allay his feelings of rejection by his own tradition.

Because I specialize in bioethics, when the AIDS virus was identified in 1981, I found myself on an AIDS task force at UCLA Medical Center. Since the disease as it first manifested itself in North America disproportionally infected gay men, I came to know a number of gays during those years and ultimately served on the board of directors of Nehamah: The Jewish AIDS Project of Los Angeles. It is hard to fear or hate a group of people when you get to know them and discover that, as a group, they are just as intelligent, moral, and Jewishly committed as straight Jews are.

In the meantime, I noticed that my teenage children in the 1980s had a very different experience with this whole topic than the one that I had had. They knew a number of openly gay classmates at school, and it did not seem to phase them. Their attitude was simple: Some people are straight, and some are gay, much the same as the fact that some people have blue eyes and others have brown eyes. They just took it, in other words, as a fact of life.

It was right in the middle of the four meetings of the CJLS, in December 1992, that our daughter told my wife and me that she is a lesbian. As a graduate student in the midst of a doctoral program in psychology, she knew how to present this well—in a calm way, with a description of how she gradually came to know this about herself, lest we think that she was jumping to conclusions; with openness to all of our questions; and with some books for us to read. I was very glad then that I had done some serious thinking about this issue before she told us; I honestly do not know how well I would have reacted without that previous experience and thinking. I am also glad that I had formulated my stance on the matter before she came out to us, so that I could rest assured in my own mind that my stance was not just a case of special pleading. Over the years since then, what I have learned from her and from many other gays and lesbians has only added to the pool of evidence for the liberal stance that I have taken on this issue. Indeed, it is precisely the testimony of gays and lesbians themselves that convinced me in the first place, and now I have my own experience as a parent of a lesbian to add to what I have heard from others.

Even some of my rabbinic colleagues who have taken a more traditional stance on this issue have told me that their own children see the matter very differently. The science on the causes of homosexuality is still soft; the most reliable evidence comes from homosexuals themselves. That evidence is unquestionably reliable because no sane person would intentionally subject himself or herself to the discrimination that contemporary society still heaps on homosexuals. The only evidence that appears to be quite definite, as affirmed now for close to thirty years by the American Psychiatric Association, is that psychiatric interventions to try to change a homosexual's sexual orientation not only do not work but are actually harmful, making the homosexual feel even worse about himself or herself and contributing to the horrendous statistics of suicide among homosexuals.

Aristotle long ago pointed out that it is folly to seek certainty in those areas where certainty cannot reasonably be expected.[107] So as the science develops, perhaps the proper stance at this time is precisely what the Conservative movement has taken— namely, to affirm our commitment to the tradition while at the same time recognizing that as the scientific studies and personal anecdotes increase, we should be continually open to reevaluating the traditional position. In the meantime, the Conservative position is correct in not disallowing either the traditional stance or the liberal one, enabling all of us to continue the discussion with respect as we agree to disagree.

I do hope, though, that we as a movement can soon endorse full acceptance of otherwise qualified gay men and lesbians to our rabbinical schools and of officiating at commitment ceremonies. The current realities of homosexual rabbinical students having to hide in a closet and of rabbis feeling undermined by their movement if they officiate at commitment ceremonies are intolerable.

MAKING SEX MEANINGFUL, JOYFUL, AND HOLY

Sex is one of the gifts God has given us by creating us as we are. Like all of our faculties, we can use it for good or for bad, and Judaism provides us with instruction (Torah) for channeling our sexual energies toward good purpose. Marriage and family are that purpose, for in that context the individual and the community can attain all of the benefits of both. At the same time, in our own day, when we have many people who are single and others who are openly homosexual, we all must remind ourselves that single and homosexual Jews partake of the divine image and the ultimate value it imparts just as much as married heterosexuals do—and so do married people who cannot have children, single-parent families, and blended families. We should all take significant, positive steps to involve people in each of these family configurations in the Jewish community.

Judaism has much to teach all of us about how we should think about sex and how we should behave sexually—whether a person is single or married, heterosexual or homosexual. May each of us enjoy God's gift of our sexuality within the guidelines of Judaism, so that our sexual activities can bring not only pleasure and companionship but also wholeness and holiness; and may each of us be able to say of someone special what the lover says in the Bible, "This is my beloved, this is my friend."[108]

CHAPTER FOUR

Parents and Children

W HILE JUDAISM CONSIDERS PROCREATION TO BE ONE OF THE goals of sex within marriage, it certainly does not leave matters there. It has much to say about the interaction between parents and children. No family will be like any other, of course, and some of what the tradition says about these matters may seem dated to a time when role differentiations were clearer and when economic, educational, and social conditions were considerably different from what they are today. Moreover, even those parts of the traditional materials that we find compelling we may not be able to apply easily and directly to contemporary circumstances. Even so, the Jewish tradition here, as in other areas of personal ethics, has much to suggest to us.

FILIAL DUTIES: THE PERSPECTIVE OF JEWISH CLASSICAL SOURCES

THE TWO BASIC DUTIES: HONOR AND RESPECT

Two of the Torah's commandments frame the relationship of children to their parents: the command to honor one's parents and the command to respect them.[1] While both sound like a demand that children have specific attitudes toward their parents, the Talmud, as is its common practice, translates those attitudes into specific actions.

Jews and others often construe the command to honor parents, the fifth of the Ten Commandments, as chiefly applying to young children and their parents. Although young children should certainly be taught to honor their parents, until children reach the age of bar or bat mitzvah, they cannot be held legally responsible for anything. Thus the Rabbis understood the commandment as primarily governing the interactions of adult children of elderly parents. That makes the commandment even more critical for adults nowadays than it was for our ancestors, for with many people living into their eighties, nineties, and beyond, and with families commonly scattered throughout the country or even the world, adult Jews need clear and wise guidance about what they need to do for their parents and how. This becomes especially urgent for couples who find themselves balancing these duties with obligations to their children and to each other as mates. Many of us today are in that situation, and, frankly, we need all the help we can get.

As the Rabbis understood it, the commandment to honor parents requires that adult children provide food, clothing, and companionship.[2] The Midrash teaches a poignant lesson based on the juxtaposition of this, the fifth of the Ten Commandments, with the prohibition against murder, the sixth:

> "Honor your father and your mother. . . . You shall not murder." Why are these two laws juxtaposed [in Exodus 20:12, 13]? To teach you that if a man has food in his house and does not share it with his father and mother, even when they are young, and most certainly when they are old, then he is considered as if he were a habitual murderer.[3]

Philo, a first-century Jewish thinker, suggested another lesson based on the placement of the fifth commandment within the structure of the ten. The Ten Commandments are commonly divided into two, the first five referring to the relationships between human beings and God, and the second group referring to strictly human relationships. That is because within the first group, the phrase "the Lord your God" is used five times, whereas the second group includes no mention of God. Furthermore, the first group features duties unique to the People Israel, but the second group seems to apply to all people; indeed, the laws of many other peoples of the ancient world specify parallel prohibitions, although it is only in the Torah that they are presented as divine commandments rather than the fruit of human wisdom. Finally, it is striking that the document opens with "the Lord your God" and closes with "your neighbor."[4] This division into two groups of five, then, makes the command to honor parents the last of the commandments governing our relationship with God, just before those relating to the human community exclusively. Noting this, Philo suggested that the command to honor parents is placed in that position so that it acts as a bridge between God and human beings, for it is our parents who teach us both how to behave in human society and how we are to think and act toward God. That is, in the process of growing up, we learn to honor God by first honoring our parents; as we grow older, we continue to experience and honor God each time we do something to honor our parents and behave toward other human beings according to what they first taught us:

> After dealing with the seventh day [the Fourth of the Ten Commandments], God gives the Fifth Commandment on the honor due to parents. This commandment He placed on the borderline between the two sets of five: it is the last of the first set, in which the most sacred injunctions [relating to God] are given, and it adjoins the second set, which contain the duties of human beings to each other. The reason, I think, is this: we see that parents by their nature stand on the borderline between the mortal and the immortal sides of existence—the mortal, because of their kinship with people and other animals through the perishableness of the body; the immortal, because the act of generation assimilates them to God, the progenitor of everything.
>
> Some bolder spirits, glorifying the name of parenthood, say that a father and mother are in fact gods revealed to sight, who copy the Uncreated in His work as the Framer of life. He, they say, is the God or Maker of the world; they [the parents] only of those whom they have begotten. How can reverence be rendered to the invisible God by those who show irreverence to the gods who are near at hand and seen by the eye?[5]

Parents prepare the psyche of the child for the experience of honoring God, and by acting to honor parents, one honors God. Rabbinic literature expresses the same theme:

> Rabbi [Judah the President] says: the honoring of one's father and mother is very dear in the sight of Him by whose word the world came into being, for He declared honoring them to be equal to

honoring Him, revering them to revering Him, and cursing them to cursing Him.[6]

The other commandment in the Torah shaping relationships to parents is this: "You shall each *revere* [respect, fear] his mother and his father and keep my Sabbaths: I the Lord am your God."[7] In analyzing this text, the Rabbis asked two important questions: How is it related to the command to *honor* one's parents, and what are we to learn from its juxtaposition of reverence for parents and keeping the Sabbath? To the first question, they answered this:

> Our Rabbis taught: What is reverence (*mora*) and what is honor (*kavod*)? Reverence means that he [the son] must neither stand in his [the father's] place, nor sit in his place, nor contradict his words, nor tip the scales against him [in an argument with others]. Honor means that he must give him food and drink, clothe and cover him, lead him in and out.[8]

Another rabbinic passage on the same page of Talmud requires that, as an act of reverence, one not address parents by their first names but rather call them, "My father (mother), my teacher." Moreover, the Torah itself says, "He that curses his father or his mother shall surely be put to death,"[9] and "Cursed be he that dishonors his father or his mother."[10] Talmudic and medieval literature maintain that these requirements of honor and respect also apply to one's mother-in-law and father-in-law and to one's grandparents, although to a lesser degree than they apply to one's parents.[11]

In addition to these requirements of respect for parents so that we do not demean them, the Torah forbids harming them outright. Thus the Torah says that "He that strikes his father or his mother shall surely be put to death."[12] (I discuss that extreme of disrespect—striking one's parents—in Chapter Five.)

In these talmudic specifications of the biblical commands, reverence involves *refraining* from certain activities; honor consists in positive obligations to *act*. Both apply throughout one's life. One gets the impression, however, that the duties of reverence primarily fit one's childhood while those of honor apply most often when one is already an adult. Both reverence and honor are, according to the Talmud, demanded of daughters as well as sons and apply to mothers as well as fathers.[13]

Classical Jewish texts understand these commands to teach us not only about proper relationships to parents but also about the nature of, and our relationship to, God. In almost Freudian terms, God serves, in part, as an the extension of our parents. According to the Rabbis, in fact, God is one of our parents:

> There are three partners in the creation of every human being: the Holy One, blessed be He, the father, and the mother. The father provides the white matter [probably because semen is white], from which are formed the bones, sinews, nails, brain, and the white part of the eye. The mother provides the red matter [probably because menstrual blood is red], from which are formed the skin, flesh, hair, and pupil of the eye. The Holy One, blessed be He, infuses into each person breath, soul, features, vision, hearing, speech, power of motion, understanding, and intelligence.[14]

Through showing honor and respect for parents, then, one learns, as Philo noted, how to relate to God. Honor and respect are fitting in each case because both God and parents have a role in bringing us into being, in nurturing us physically and psychologically, and in teaching us how to live. Both also have physical power over us—at least, in the case of parents, in our early years—and both influence us psychologically throughout our lives. We must learn these attitudes and the justifications for them intellectually, incorporating awareness of them into our perspective of ourselves and our relations to others; indeed, a portion of this lesson we must apply even to the inanimate world, recognizing our dependence on it and the aptness of our gratitude for it.

Beyond our intellects, however, this knowledge must penetrate our being, shaping our personalities. Humility, care and concern for others, piety, and gratitude are the virtues one learns from honor and respect for parents.

These lessons are so important that, according to the Rabbis, God puts honor and reverence for parents on a par with the honor and reverence due God; according to one rabbinic text, God makes it even more obligatory:

> Great is the precept to honor parents since the Holy One, blessed be He, attached to it still greater importance than the honoring of Himself. It is written, "Honor your father and mother" (Exodus 20:12), and also "Honor the Lord with your substance" (Proverbs 3:9). With what do you honor God? With that which He has

bestowed upon you, as when you carry out such laws as the forgotten sheaf, the corner of the field, tithes, charity to the poor,
etc. If you possess the means of fulfilling these commandments,
do so; but if you are destitute, you are not under the obligation.
With the honoring of parents, however, no such condition is
made. Whether you have means or not, you must fulfill the commandment, even if you have to go begging from door to door.[15]

There are two exceptions to this ranking of parents above
God. The Torah includes an explicit, positive command to "love
the Lord your God with all your heart, with all your soul, and
with all your might,"[16] a verse that is included in a central
prayer, the *Shema*, recited twice daily. Although one must honor
and revere parents, one important strain in the tradition asserts
that a child is not obligated to love them. Rabbi Shelomo
Yizhaki (Rashi' 1035–1104), the most popular Jewish medieval
commentator on the Bible, and other medieval and modern rabbis claim that children are legally obligated to love their parents,
reasoning that love of parents is included in the command to
honor them or to love one's neighbor as oneself.[17] Maimonides,
however, drew a distinction:

> Know that the Torah has placed us under a heavy obligation in re-
> gard to the proselyte. For we were commanded to honor and re-
> vere our parents, and to obey the prophets. . . . Now it is possible
> for a man to honor and revere and obey those whom he does not
> love. But with the proselyte there is a command to love him with
> a great, heartfelt love . . . much as we are commanded to love God
> Himself.[18]

Clearly, it is best to honor one's parents out of love and to love
them while fulfilling the duties of honoring them, but that is not
always how a child feels. The law demands honor and respect of
parents, but, at least according to Maimonides, it does not demand love of them. It does, however, require not only honor and
reverence for God but also love of God, even when, as in the case
of the biblical Job, one feels anything but love.

There is another way in which honor and respect for God supersedes that for parents, and that is derived from the juxtaposition of the commands to revere one's parents and keep My
Sabbaths in Leviticus 19:3. The Rabbis read the "and" of this
verse such that the second clause is a condition for the first:
"You shall each revere his mother and his father and [that is, *on*

condition that or *as long as*] you keep My Sabbaths." Thus they said:

> Because one might think that one is obliged to obey one's father or mother who desires that one violate a commandment, therefore the Torah says, "and you shall keep My Sabbaths"—[that is,] you are all required to honor Me.
>
> It is possible to think that even if the father ordered his son to defile himself [by going into a cemetery to retrieve the father's possessions if the son has priestly status, i.e., is a *kohen*] or not to return a lost article that he had found, the son is to obey the father. Consequently there is a verse to teach, "You shall each revere his mother and his father, and keep My Sabbaths." All of you are alike bound to honor Me.[19]

Based on this general principle, Rabbi Asher ben Yehiel (the Rosh, d. 1327, Germany and Spain) later ruled that a man should disregard his father's insistence that he not make peace with an enemy, because "The father who commanded his son to hate a man does not have the right to command him to violate the Torah." The Torah commands, after all, "You shall not hate your brother in your heart," and the Rabbis derived from the verse in Psalms "Seek peace and pursue it" that we actively must try to make peace with our enemies.[20] Despite parental objections to a particular school, most scholars permit an adult son to study Torah where he wishes, even though the parents do not object to his studying Torah altogether;[21] and most permit a son or daughter to emigrate to Israel over parental objections so as to fulfill the commandment to live there.[22]

Rabbi Solomon ben Adret (Rashba) used the principle that divine commands supersede parental ones to permit a man to violate his parents' wishes in marrying the woman he loves, even if that means that the son would be precluded from providing the range of services prescribed as part of the honor and respect due to parents. (This does not apply to a marriage that would violate the norms of Jewish law, such as an incestuous marriage or a marriage to a non-Jew; the rabbi is addressing the case in which a Jewish man and woman who are eligible to marry each other want to do so over their parents' objections.) The man has the right to do this, according to Rashba, to fulfill the commandment "Be fruitful and multiply," for which marriage is a legal prerequisite.[23] While some sources disagree,[24] ultimately Rabbi

Moses Isserles, in his authoritative glosses on the important code, the Shulchan Arukh, stated, "If a father opposes the marriage of his son to a woman of his son's desire, the son need not accede to the father."[25] Thus, for all these sources, when there is a conflict, we must choose to honor God rather than our parents.

Obeying God even takes precedence in times when children are confronted by the simultaneous demands of God and parents—although, even then, the law would have the children seek a way to do the parent's command immediately:

> Eleazar bar Matya said: "If one's father says, 'Bring me some water,' while one has a commandment [of God] to perform, one delays the father's honor in order to fulfill the other commandment, for both father and son are subject to the commandments [of God]." Issi ben Judah said: "If it is possible for the other commandment to be done by others, let them do it so the son can engage in the father's honor." Rabbi Matnah said: "The law accords with Issi ben Judah."[26]

Exactly how children are to prioritize other commandments with the ones to honor and respect parents is a matter of some debate elsewhere in talmudic and medieval sources,[27] with every effort to find a way for both to be fulfilled. Throughout this discussion, however, the principle is clear: We *are* children of our human parents, but our divine parentage takes precedence. Even parents are not to be treated as gods; the fitting object for unlimited piety and gratitude is God, on whom one depends for everything during all of one's life.

One other important principle in regard to honor and respect of parents emerges from the sources—namely, that the parents should not make unreasonable demands of their children or punish their children in a way that will lead the child to rebel against them and dishonor them. The Rabbis deduced this from the Torah's command, "Do not put a stumbling block before the blind," which they interpret to include not only the physically blind but also those blinded by their lack of information or by their temptation to do something improper.[28] This is an instance of the latter case, by which unreasonable demands of children or striking an adult child will tempt the child to say or do things that are in violation of the commandments demanding honor and respect for parents. It is a maidservant of Rabbi Judah ha-Nasi, in fact, who saw a man strike his mature son and said, "Let that man be put under a ban of excommunication, for he violates the prohibition, 'Do not put a stumbling block before the blind,' which refers to one who strikes his mature son."[29]

Maimonides codified this as a general principle: "It is forbidden for a man to impose too heavy a yoke upon his children by being overly insistent on his due honor, for he thereby brings them close to sinning. Instead he should forgive and turn aside, for a father may forgo his honor if he wishes."[30] The thirteenth-century anonymous work, *Sefer Hasidim*, takes this principle further by applying it not only to concrete demands but also to emotions: "The father and mother should not so enrage their son [or daughter] that he cannot restrain himself but must rebel against them."[31]

Thus while commandments to honor and respect one's parents make demands of the children, they also require the parents to be reasonable in their expectations. In the end, after all, what Jewish sources really want is loving parent-child relationships in which honor and respect of all parties inheres in the very nature of the relationship. The laws I have been discussing, like law generally, come to define the nature and scope of minimally acceptable behavior when people do not feel loving and generous. Even then, parents must not use these commandments as a weapon against their children or as a tool for self-aggrandizement and power; they should use these norms as guidelines of the acts and attitudes that they should manifest themselves and that they should teach their children.

FULFILLING PARENTS' PHYSICAL NEEDS

In general, food and clothing must be provided according to the parents' needs. To understand the scope of this commandment, it is instructive to compare the duty of a husband to supply food and clothing for his wife with the parallel duty of children to do this for their parents.

Both husbands and children must provide clothing suitable for the season. In both cases, "clothing" is understood broadly to include housing. In the case of the husband, the Mishnah specifies that "housing," in turn, includes house furnishings—a bed, a mattress or mat on which to lie or sit, and utensils for eating and drinking—and Maimonides adds a yard outside for her use and a lavatory.[32]

These, however, are only minimal requirements prescribed in the case of a poor husband; if he is rich, then he must support his wife according to his wealth.[33] This is even more true for a wealthy child of poor parents, for rabbinic sources wax eloquent about how far the commandment of honoring one's parents extends.[34] Similarly, while the law of honoring one's parents may be fulfilled by feeding and clothing them with their own financial resources, it is preferable to use one's own assets, if one can, so as not to vex them.[35]

PERSONAL PRESENCE

"To lead one's parents in and take them out"—part of the definition of honoring parents—denotes a kind of personal service when parents are unable to walk in and out by themselves. Maimonides articulated that tone clearly: "And he [the son] leads [the father] in and out and serves him in the other ways in which we serve a teacher."[36] The medieval moralist Rabbi Israel Alnakawa defined this in terms of adult children and their able parents:

> "Lead them out"—How is this to be done? The son is obliged to accompany his father and mother, and not to turn his back until they are out of sight. "Take them in"—How is this to be done? He is obliged to give them a fitting dwelling, or rent one for them. And when the father or mother enters the son's home, he must rejoice in their coming and receive them happily.[37]

For many of us, though, the implications of this requirement vis-à-vis frail parents are much more extensive, for Jewish law understood honor of parents to include the requirement not to abandon them. The Midrash states this poignantly. At the very beginning of our familiarity with Abraham in the Bible, when he was still called Abram, we read: "The Lord said to Abram, 'Go forth from your native land and from your father's house to the land that I will show you.' "[38] In commenting on this verse, a midrash (a rabbinic interpretation and expansion of a verse) says this:

> Abram was apprehensive, saying, "When I leave, men will profane the name of God because of me, as they will say, 'He left his aged father and went off.' " So God said to Abram, "I release you

from the obligations of honoring your father and your mother, but I will release no other person from this obligation."[39]

The midrash is troubled by the fact that Abram leaves his aged father. What kind of beginning is that for a future patriarch of the Jewish people? And indeed, Abram's own equanimity in the situation is surprising: He is worried only about what others will say, not about the inherent wrongfulness of abandoning his father.

The midrash explains these facts as the result of a specific decree of God so that God could use him as a leader. As Gerald Blidstein points out, "This is typological rather than unique: the young prophet leaves the home of his parents for the company of Elijah, [and] the student of a sage chooses the academy over home and prefers the service of his master to that of his parent."[40] But those are the *exceptions* to the rule: Unless one is engaged directly in God's service as either prophet or rabbinic scholar, one is obligated to accompany one's parents through their old age.

It is important to understand that the duty to be with one's aged parents is not only to be able to take care of their physical needs, a task that presumably could be done by a person hired for the job, but also for the psychological reason that they need company—especially from those who can most directly give them a sense of warmth and continuity. Loneliness is painful for anyone. The presence of friends alleviates that, but nothing can replace seeing members of one's own family. That too is a "need"—or better, an opportunity for honor. Even God, according to the Midrash, exemplifies this value by bidding us to build a sanctuary so that God can dwell among us: "You are my children, and I am your father. . . . It is an honor for children to dwell with their father, and it is an honor for the father to dwell with his children. . . . Make, therefore, a house for the father in which he can dwell with his children."[41] Thus, although the major medieval codes do not directly require that children reside with parents, they undoubtedly assume it.[42]

TWO EXCEPTIONS TO PERSONAL CARE OF PARENTS

There are two exceptions to the rule that we must give personal care to our parents. First, both Maimonides and Joseph Karo permitted a child who cannot bear taking care of a parent who has become mentally disordered to make arrangements for others to provide the requisite care: "If one's father or mother becomes mentally disturbed, he should try to treat them as their mental state demands, until they are pitied by God. But if he finds that he cannot endure the situation because of their extreme madness, he may leave and go away, appointing others to care for them properly."[43] This is not blanket permission to transfer care to others because of the difficulties of old age; it applies only to cases of mental or emotional dysfunction.

Because the Talmud approvingly records two instances in which children took care of their demented parents and one in which a child abandoned such a parent,[44] it is possible that Maimonides meant to permit transferring the care of insane parents to others only when their condition is irreversible, but not otherwise.[45] On the other hand, since Maimonides specifically made the decision depend on whether the child can bear the parent's dementia, perhaps the objective status of the parent's psyche does not matter. One way or the other, Jewish law specifically provides for a transfer of care to others when the child cannot tolerate the parent's mental state.

The first exception thus depends on the parent's mental state and/or the child's reaction to it; the second exception is based instead on the relationship between the parent and child. While parents and children ideally get along well with each other, that is not always the case. As we have seen, Jewish sources specifically demand that a parent not make overly burdensome or provocative demands on a child so that the child is tempted to dishonor or disrespect the parent or perhaps even assault him or her, because in making a demand that evokes that response, the parent would thereby transgress the biblical command of not putting a stumbling block before the blind.[46] Thus if the relationship between the parent and child is not good, Jewish law would find it better for the child to transfer the care of the parent to someone else, as long as the child ensures that the care fulfills the parent's physical and psychological needs at a reasonably good level. Thus, while *Sefer Hasidim* required generally that children live in the vicinity of their parents to minister to their needs, it said this: "It is best that a father and a son separate if they quarrel with each other, for much pain is caused; and I do not mean only the pain of the father or the teacher, but even the pain of the son."[47]

Rabbi Eliezer Pappo, a nineteenth-century moralist, required that both parent and child agree to the separation, but when relations are not good, he encouraged them to do so:

> Inasmuch as the Sages have said that a man should not dwell near his master if he cannot accept his authority, we may infer that if a man cannot honor his parents as they should be honored, then . . . it is best that he no longer share his father's board, provided that his father agrees to this. It is also best that a man—if he can—send his children from his table, lest he be guilty of placing a stumbling block before them . . . and thus there shall be peace in your home.[48]

CARING FOR ELDERLY PARENTS IN TODAY'S WORLD

In modern times, of course, it is often difficult, if not impossible, to live near one's parents. The mobility of contemporary society has meant that children often live and work far away from parents. This may be regrettable, but it is a real phenomenon that traditional sources do not contemplate. Moreover, facilities for caring for the elderly that were not available in the past are increasingly being created today, as the population of the United States, and indeed of the Western world, ages.

Objecting to Maimonides' permission for a child who cannot bear to be with a demented parent to leave his or her care to others, Rabbi Abraham ben David of Posquieres asked: "Whom can he command to take care of him?"[49] That is, who would undertake to perform that which a person's own child refuses to do?

Today we have clear answers to that question in the form of people hired to help in various ways at home or in assisted living facilities or in nursing homes. In part, this is a function of the demise of the extended family, but it is also a result of the large increases in longevity and the numbers of elderly in our society.

The question, then, is whether the use of such facilities constitutes a violation of the traditional demand that care of one's parents must be personal. It seems to me that it depends largely on the intent of all concerned. In one of the most sensitive comments that the Talmud makes about the commandment to honor parents, the Rabbis point out that even the demands for physical care must be carried out with a proper attitude:

> A man may feed his father on fattened chickens and inherit Hell [as his reward], and another may put his father to work in a mill and inherit Paradise.
>
> How is it possible that a man might feed his father fattened chickens and inherit Hell? It once happened that a man used to feed his father fattened chickens. Once his father said to him: "My son, where did you get these?" He answered: "Old man, old man, eat and be silent, just as dogs eat and are silent." In such an instance, he feeds his father fattened chickens, but he inherits Hell.
>
> How is it possible that a man might put his father to work in a mill and inherit Paradise? It once happened that a man was working in a mill. The king decreed that his aged father should be brought to work for him. The son said to his father: "Father, go and work in the mill in place of me [and I will go to work for the king]. For it may be [that the workers for the king will be] ill-treated, in which case let me be ill-treated instead of you. And it may be [that the workers for the king will be] beaten, in which case let me be beaten instead of you." In such an instance, he puts his father to work in a mill, but he inherits Paradise.[50]

If attitudinal factors are crucial in regard to physical care, how much more are they relevant to fulfilling the tradition's demands that one satisfy one's parents' psychological needs for proximity and interaction. Thus if children cannot realistically care for their parents themselves, or if the parents would be better off and happier living in their own home or in a facility for the elderly, then placing them in such a facility is not only permissible but possibly the most desirable option, *provided* that the tone with which this arrangement is made and carried out is one of honor, respect, and ideally even love. Such an attitude must be expressed in concrete actions by making sure that the living arrangements for one's parents meet their physical and psychological needs as much as possible and, most especially, by visiting and/or calling them reasonably frequently.

Increasing numbers of Jews, however, are finding that as their parents become unable to care for themselves, the best option is to house them at one of their children's homes. This is especially so when the parents are mentally fine but suffer from some physical disabilities that make it hard or even impossible for them to live on their own. Under such circumstances, housing elderly parents at one of the children's homes provides an opportunity for the grandchildren to have continuing interaction with them and possibly to help in their care. This graphically models what the Jewish norms of honor and respect are all about, an important lesson for the grandchildren to learn for the future care of the adult children.

Even as the parents' physical condition worsens, adult children may care for them at home in a form of care called "hospice." When people suffer from chronic diseases like cancer, they often come to a stage when the attending physicians judge the disease to be incurable. At that point, patients have two choices. They can try "heroic" measures, such as experimental surgeries or drugs, or they can acquiesce to their impending death and seek only palliative care.

Jewish law permits *both* options. If someone wants to pull out all the stops, as it were, he or she may do so, even if the medications or procedures to be tried have a high risk of involving complications that may, in fact, hasten the onset of death. As long as the intention is not suicide but cure, subjecting oneself to the high risks of experimental therapies is permissible.

On the other hand, one may also decide not to engage in that mode of treatment, but simply receive medications to alleviate pain. One is still seeking medical aid, as Jewish law requires every sick Jew to do, but the intent and form of that aid is different. *When one has a terminal, incurable disease,* palliative care is appropriate and sufficient to satisfy the dictates of Jewish law; for while Jewish law requires sick Jews to avail themselves of medical care, it does not require that they have unrealistic hopes for cure or engage in therapies unlikely to bring cure. Similarly, we are not expected to be omniscient, knowing what cures will be developed tomorrow. When the attending physician(s) judge the illness to be incurable, medical treatment exclusively to alleviate pain is both moral and legal for observant Jews to employ.

Such care can usually be done on an outpatient basis, with the patient living at home. This enables families to spend the last time they have together in familiar and comfortable environs. This is often much less expensive financially, but that is not the primary reason that families choose hospice care. It is rather because of its comfort, dignity, and humanity. In hospice care, people live as long as possible among those whom they know and love. They do not spend a large portion of their last months and weeks in hospitals, but rather devote their time to whatever interests them for as long as they are able. Dying of a chronic illness is never pleasant, but hospice care makes it as humane as possible.

Hospice care at home, though, is not right for everyone. Some will choose to fight the noble battle against a disease diagnosed as incurable, and they have that right. Others will prefer to live in assisted living facilities or nursing homes, or their children's jobs or location may require that. But Jewish parents and their adult children should know that hospice care at home falls within the rules of Jewish medical ethics, and it has the added advantage of enabling children not to delegate their parent's care to others but rather to do it directly and personally as an act of honor and love.[51]

In sum, the Jewish tradition has developed a number of specific rules to give content to the feelings of honor and respect that we are to have for our parents. Housing elderly parents who cannot care for themselves at one's own home may no longer be possible, necessary, or desirable. That may be because both the adult and his or her spouse may work outside the home during the day and cannot afford to arrange for private care for the parent all day long. Moreover, because of the increasing number of elderly people in contemporary society, long-term-care facilities have become available, and often elderly parents would prefer the company of their peers to living with people much their junior, even if they happen to be members of their own family. Furthermore, people with professional medical and social work skills staff such facilities and provide activities suited to the interests of elderly people, all of which are not available at the adult child's home. Finally, some parents and children do not get along very well.

On the other hand, some families may find that many of the traditional measures of personal care have a refreshingly modern ring to them, articulating modes of behavior that moderns would do well to follow. That is especially true when parents and children get along well and when grandchildren can benefit from the experience of close ties with their grandparents and of aiding in their care. Whatever the decision on the particular arrangement that a family uses to care for their elderly parents, the crucial element is one of tone, for, as we have seen, even supplying one's parents with a basic need like food is only an act of honor if it is done in that spirit.

PARENTAL DUTIES: APPLYING JEWISH CLASSICAL SOURCES TO CONTEMPORARY CIRCUMSTANCES

Just as children have duties toward their parents, so too do parents have obligations toward their children. The classic talmudic text delineating those duties is this:

> Our Rabbis taught: A man is responsible to circumcise his son, to redeem him [from Temple service if he is the first born, "*pidyon ha-ben*"], to teach him Torah, to marry him off to a woman, and to teach him a trade, and there are those who say that he must also teach him to swim. Rabbi Judah says: Anyone who fails to teach his son a trade teaches him to steal.[52]

The Talmud then proceeds to specify the details about each of these parental obligations. So, for example, it says that if the father fails to have his son circumcised, then the communal court has the duty to ensure that it is done, and if the court fails in that task, then ultimately it is the boy himself who, upon reaching adulthood, must arrange to have himself circumcised. In what follows, though, I would like to focus on several parental duties in this list that pose problems for contemporary parents and their children—namely, teaching Torah, teaching a trade, and marrying the children off.

TEACHING TORAH AND TEACHING A TRADE

As one might expect, in the eyes of the Rabbis teaching Torah is a cardinal duty of parents. It is embedded in two of the Torah's paragraphs that the Rabbis chose for the *Shema*, recited twice daily,[53] and so this was clearly a duty that the Rabbis wanted to impress on parents. It was not only that God's command obligated parents to do this but also, as the Rabbis recognized, because the Jewish tradition requires considerable knowledge to practice it well, and hence "He who denies a child religious knowledge robs him of his heritage."[54] Indeed, God gave the Torah to Israel only because He was convinced that children would learn it:

> Rabbi Meir said: When the Israelites came to receive the Torah, God said to them: "Bring to Me good sureties that you will observe it." They answered: "Our ancestors will be our sureties." God answered: "Your sureties need sureties themselves, for I have found fault with them." They answered: "Our Prophets will be our sureties." God replied: "I have found fault with them also." Then the Israelites said: "Our children will be our sureties." They proved acceptable, and God gave the Torah to Israel.[55]

The Rabbis went still further: They believed that the creation and continued existence of the whole world depends on children learning the Torah: "The world itself rests upon the breath of the children in the schoolhouse."[56] In a manner typical of them, the Rabbis then sought to define the scope of this obligation:

> To what extent is a man obliged to teach his son Torah? Rav Judah said in Samuel's name: For example, Zevulun, the son of Dan, whom his grandfather taught Scripture, Mishnah, Talmud, laws and legends.—An objection was raised: [We have a tradition that] If he [his father] taught him Scripture, he need not teach him Mishnah . . .—[The law, then, is] like Zevulun, son of Dan, yet not altogether so. . . . [F]or whereas there [he was taught] Scripture, Mishnah, Talmud, laws, and legends, here [i.e., as a general rule] Scripture alone [suffices].[57]

That is, the father must teach his son minimally Scripture, but ideally he should teach him all the things that Zevulun, son of Dan, learned. The Mishnah, in its description of a person's overall development, spells out the ages at which it is appropriate to begin study of various parts of the ideal curriculum:

> He [Yehudah ben Tema] used to say: At five years of age—the study of Bible; at ten—the study of Mishnah; at thirteen—responsibility for the commandments; at fifteen—the study of Talmud; at eighteen—marriage; at twenty—pursuit of a livelihood; at thirty—the peak of one's powers; at forty—the age of understanding; at fifty—the age of giving counsel; at sixty—old age; at seventy—the hoary head [or, white old age]; at eighty—the age of strength [or, rare old age]; at ninety—the bent back; at one hundred—as one dead and out of this world.[58]

Parents, though, were not generally schooled themselves, and some children did not have parents altogether. Consequently, toward the end of the first century C.E. Jews had already established schools that parents could use as their agent in fulfilling this obligation:

> Rabbi Judah said in the name of Rav: Rabbi Joshua ben Gamla should be remembered for good, for had it not been for him the Torah would have been forgotten in Israel. For at first, the boy who had a father was taught Torah by him, while the boy who had no father did not learn. Later, they appointed teachers of boys in Jerusalem, and the boys who had fathers were brought by them [to the teachers] and were taught; those who had no fathers were still not brought. So then they ordered that teachers should be appointed in every district, and they brought to them lads of the age of sixteen or seventeen. And when the teacher was cross with any of the lads, the lad would kick at him and run away. So then Rabbi Joshua ben Gamla ordered that teachers should be appointed in every district and in every city and that the boys should be sent to them at the age of six or seven years.[39]

In past generations, Jews were much too poor to provide much formal education for their children. Girls generally got little, if any, formal education. Boys were not treated much better, for by age ten or so they had to help the family earn a living. Except in the very specific times and places in which Jews were tolerated and allowed to become members of general society, Jews of the Middle Ages and the early modern period who did manage to study beyond the age of ten usually focused on Jewish texts alone. There were, of course, exceptions, especially in regard to medicine: Jews (including many rabbis) were often at the forefront of both clinical medicine and medical research.[60] Even those who became doctors, though, had considerably less to learn than contemporary doctors do; Thomas Jefferson's Medical School at the University of Virginia trained doctors in one year!

Much has changed in the last century. In the United States, in 1910, only 13 percent of the population graduated from high school and only 3 percent from college; in 1999, 83 percent of Americans had graduated from high school and 25 percent from college. In 1910, 24 percent of the population had less than five years of schooling; in 1998 only 2 percent of Americans had had less than five years of schooling.[61] The United States could afford to have its children engaged in extended years of schooling only because of a marked improvement in its economic conditions, for even if education ultimately improves productivity, during students' years of schooling they are economically unproductive.

Because the world's largest Jewish community after World War II was in the United States, the extent and content of Jews' formal education changed alongside that of other Americans. In fact, because Jews and Judaism treasure education so deeply, and because Jews in the early and middle of the twentieth century found education to be their path into America's middle and upper classes, Jews tended to be ahead of the curve. For that matter, to this day much higher percentages of Jews complete college and professional schools than is true of the general American population.[62]

Contrary to times past, Jews now fully expect their children to learn general subjects as least as well as Jewish materials. Some might see that as a mark of the increasing secularization of the Jewish community; but it can be justified in very Jewish terms as an expression of the parents' duty to teach the child a trade. In our own time, that increasingly means providing a college and even a professional education, for more and more jobs depend on extensive education. Thus it is not somehow anti-Jewish for parents who send their children to Jewish day schools to insist on a top-notch general education as well as intensive Jewish education; it is just that the Jewish tradition demands at least as much that parents teach their children Torah, and so the curriculum of their children's education should devote considerable time and resources to that task.

But many Jewish children and teenagers receive no Jewish education at all, and very few outside the Orthodox world spend as much time in Jewish studies as in general studies. A national study conducted by Jack Wertheimer in 1999 claims that there are approximately 180,000 Jews under eighteen years of age in the United States enrolled in Jewish day schools and 260,000 in supplementary schools.[63] There are, however, between 1.0 and 1.2 million Jews of that age in the United States, and so somewhere between 37 and 44 percent of young Jews are currently getting some kind of Jewish education. An extensive study of Los Angeles Jewry in 1997 found that 51 percent of Jews between five and seventeen years old were receiving some sort of Jewish education, with 21 percent of those in day schools (or about 11 percent of the total number of Jewish youth).[64] Of the total group, another 24 percent received some Jewish education in the past, and 25 percent received or are receiving no Jewish education at all.

While the parents' Jewish commitments are a significant factor in how much Jewish education their children receive, another big factor is money. Providing extensive education in both general and Jewish studies is very expensive. The most Jewishly committed parents are faced not only with Jewish day school tuition but also the costs of Jewish summer camping and eventually Jewish youth groups. Current day school tuition for the elementary grades is typically $10,000 to $11,000 a year and as much as $18,000 or even $20,000 a year for the high school grades. Gerald Bubis, founder and former director of the Irwin Daniels School of Jewish Communal Service at Hebrew Union College in Los Angeles, estimated that the total annual Jewish costs for such families with just two children would be between $25,000 and $35,000;[65] a typical budget is as follows:

Synagogue dues and assessments	$ 1,100
Tuition for two children in day school	22,000
Average day camp fees (two weeks, two children)	1,200
Average resident camp (one month, two children)	5,000
Jewish Community Center dues	500
Minimal Federation gift	200
Total	$30,000

The median household income among Jews in Los Angeles, though, is $50,000; only about 22 percent of households report over $100,000 in annual income, and many of those consist of older adults whose children have finished their schooling. Even for young couples with that much money, however, it is not easy to cope with these costs; as Bubis said, "it is unlikely that households whose gross incomes are under $125,000 could manage to spend 25 percent to 30 percent of their gross income on Jewish services. After all, most families pay a mortgage, save for college, drive cars, give to other charities, and even choose to go to concerts, take vacations, subscribe to magazines, and the like."[66]

The high cost of day school tuition is not because the schools are profligate or inefficient or that teachers and administrators are too highly paid. Quite the contrary, there is a severe shortage of teachers of Jewish subjects, and those who enter the profession do so only because they have tremendous dedication and commitment to the Jewish tradition and community. The teacher shortage will not disappear until schools pay high enough salaries to induce Jewish parents to encourage their own children to become Jewish educators. In any case, Jewish day schools are all nonprofit institutions; in fact, tuition even at those high rates does not usually cover the costs involved, and day schools must supplement their tuition income with fundraising of various sorts to make ends meet.

Even though tuition rates do not accurately reflect costs, many parents cannot afford that much, and so they have to make choices about how they are going to teach Judaism to their children. That demands that parents set their goals clearly. If, as Bubis wrote, the ultimate objective is not so much that their children know a great deal about the Jewish tradition but rather that they identify as Jews strongly enough to motivate them to seek Jews to marry, then recent research suggests that parents spend their limited dollars on getting their children involved in Jewish camping and youth groups and use the synagogue's supplementary school (that is, supplementary to public school education) rather than the local day school.[67] Bruce Phillips, professor of Jewish Communal Service at Hebrew Union College in Los Angeles, who has worked on a recent research project on this issue, put it this way:

> Our study has shown that the third and fourth generation Jews most likely to marry other Jews are those who, as teenagers, *planned* to marry Jews; and that specific Jewish experiences during their teen years help create Jewish teen peer groups that encourage this motivation toward endogamy.[68]

Even then, as Bubis noted, "those who choose to send their children to supplementary religious schools instead of day schools have a dramatically lower cost, but still could spend $5-$8,000 on synagogue, camping fees, JCC dues, and a Federation gift."[69]

Choosing between intensive Jewish education and merely Jewish identity is not a happy choice for many parents; after all, the day schools do a much better job at providing the knowledge and skills of Jewish living than the afternoon schools do, if only because they can and do devote more time to Jewish studies at more productive times of the day. That might argue for parents caught in this situation to get more actively involved in their children's Jewish education themselves, studying with them for some time on the weekends, for example. This would resurrect the Torah's Jewish model of parents teaching their children themselves, at least for part of the child's Jewish education, and that, in turn, would stimulate the parents to study themselves. Studying together with their children would, in fact, be a good idea for parents of day school students too. But if families cannot afford day school tuition, even with financial aid from the school or other sources, they should not give up on their children's education; they should rather choose the less expensive option of Jewish supplementary schools and combine that with Jewish camping and youth groups.

One other important lesson of the Jewish tradition should inform the practices of at least some Jewish families. Usually, the young adults who are having children are at the early stages of their earning capacities and, therefore, are unable to afford the high costs of day school tuition, Jewish camps, and youth groups on top of paying synagogue dues, let alone the other costs of life. The children's grandparents, though, are often at the height of their earning capacity, and sometimes that means that they could afford to contribute substantially to their grandchildren's Jewish formal and informal education, perhaps even paying the entire bill. Jewish law sees this not only as a nice and generous thing to do; it actually obligates grandparents to assume these costs if they are at all able to do so. The Rabbis based this duty of grandparents on Deuteronomy 4:9: "Take utmost care and watch yourselves scrupulously, so that you do not forget the things that you saw with your own eyes and so that they do not fade from your mind as long as you live. And make them known to your children and to your children's children." On that verse the Rabbis said:

> Are grandparents responsible for teaching their grandchildren? . . .
> "And you shall teach your children" (Deuteronomy 11:19), from

> that I only know that I must teach my children; how do I know
> that I must also teach my grandchildren? Because the Torah says,
> "and make them known to your children and to your children's
> children" (Deuteronomy 4:9).[70]

Thus grandparents who have the economic means to contribute to the Jewish education of their grandchildren should see it as their duty to do so. They should also see it, of course, as their distinct privilege, for they are thereby making concrete contributions to the ongoing chain of the Jewish tradition in the most personal way possible, through their own posterity.

"MARRYING HIM OFF TO A WIFE"

The Talmud clearly assumes that marriages are arranged by parents of both the bride and the groom, and hence it announces the parental duty of finding a mate for their children. While that system lasted a very long time (my own grandparents had an arranged marriage), it no longer is the way young Jews find their spouses. Current dating patterns have the immense benefit of leaving it to the people themselves to decide, thus maximizing individual autonomy; but the old way guaranteed a marriage for virtually everyone when they were in their late teens or early twenties. That took away much of the pressure and uncertainty that today's high school and college students have. It also ensured marriage at the time when both the men and the women were biologically at the most fertile stages of their lives, thus avoiding some of the infertility problems that current couples face when they get married in their late twenties and do not even begin to try to have children until their thirties.

For better or worse, though, the old way is not coming back. That leaves current adult children and their parents with a real problem. High school and college provide a natural environment in which people can meet each other, and for some, graduate school lengthens yet further the time in which school can be the venue for meeting one's mate. Once schooling is over, though, there is no good place for people to meet each other.

People in their early and middle twenties—the first generation to pass through adolescence in a world with E-mail—are using the Internet for this purpose to an extent that older generations find intimidating. These young adults "have few of the scruples older

Americans have about putting their photographs and personal descriptions on the Web"; and so, for them, using on-line personals is "not a somber, mildly terrifying business of pairing off before you die," says Rufus Griscom, the founder of Nerve.com. "It's entertainment."[71] Although personal ads in newspapers and magazines were formerly seen as last-ditch attempts by the desperate, Americans younger than thirty are using on-line services earlier in their dating careers and more casually—simply to make friends or to date outside their established circles. Thus, while 1.6 million people had posted personal ads as of April 2001, a year later that figure had nearly doubled, with fully half of the new users under the age of thirty. This has changed the assumptions of getting to know a potential spouse. Dating once implied "a very long process where you disclose things over time," said Robert Rosenwein, a professor of social psychology at Lehigh University. "The Internet speeds that up considerably. There's a renegotiation of the concept of intimacy." Moreover, even with pictures, which young people usually demand before they will respond to an ad, there is always the problem of leaving out pertinent information, for the ads often represent "the author's aspirations, more than the reality."

Although the Internet can surely help people meet each other, especially those who no longer have school as a venue to make connections, it is not a panacea. Some people will not find a suitable spouse in the traditional places (work, the synagogue, or parties of mutual friends) or on the new place (the Net). Parents must not hesitate, then, to help their children find someone, even if the children first object to any parental interventions. Parents can suggest, for example, that their children attend services or some other activities at the synagogue for the specific motive of trying to meet someone; after all, the synagogue is not only a *Bet Tefillah* (house of prayer) and *Bet Midrash* (house of study) but is most commonly called a *Bet Knesset* (house of meeting, although not usually intended in quite this way!). They can also suggest that their children get involved as volunteers in various Jewish communal activities through the Federation or other groups that have young adult divisions. I know of two families—the Salters and the Wagners—who formed the S&W Good Company when their children were reaching their mid-twenties with no marital prospects on the horizon. The parents simply had their children invite all of their friends and friends' friends to their homes once a month for some kind of program—social, social action, intellectual, or religious (like a holiday celebration)—and lo and behold, all of them found their spouses that way. The method particular parents will use may be different, but the message is the same: You need not stand idly by if your children are having trouble meeting potential spouses.

The problem in fulfilling this talmudic duty for parents in our own day, though, goes beyond *finding* someone for their children to marry; it also involves nuturing their children's *intention* to marry at a young enough age to have a reasonable chance of having children themselves without difficulty. Because of young Jews' extensive educational programs, which are expressions of their commitment to the value of education as well as professional achievement, they rarely plan to marry before their late twenties. Because of the modern techniques that have been developed to overcome infertility, young adult Jews often simply assume that they can have children into their forties, and so there is no rush to get married and procreate.

That is a false assumption, however, for biologically the optimal age for both men and women to procreate is still age twenty-two; infertility problems increase somewhat by age twenty-seven; significantly between ages thirty and thirty-five; and geometrically after that, when birth defects and developmental problems (such as Down's syndrome) become more prevalent. Moreover, only about half of the couples who suffer from infertility can ultimately bring home a baby with the assisted reproductive techniques currently available, and some 85 percent of those have a child through the least technologically sophisticated of the methods used—namely, artificial insemination with either the husband's or a donor's sperm. Moreover, the younger the couple is, the greater the chances that those assisted reproductive techniques will be effective.

The misconceptions about the power of modern medicine to overcome infertility are so great that in April 2002, *Time* magazine ran a cover story on the pitfalls of waiting too long to reproduce.[72] It unfortunately did not document the problems for men as well as women. It should have done so, for the problem is just as prevalent in men as they age as it is in women: 40 percent of infertile couples cannot have children because of a problem in the man, 40 percent because of a problem in the woman, 10 percent due to a problem in both, and for 10 percent the doctors cannot diagnose the problem that is preventing the couple from procreating. In men, sperm counts and sperm motility go down with age, sperm becomes misshapen, and impotence begins; in women, eggs become less viable, blockages develop in the fallopian tubes, implantation becomes more iffy, and miscarriages increase. These problems impose immense strains on the marriage, for each month the couple faces a final examination, as it were, and if they are infertile they are likely to fail most of those final exams. This causes the couple to wonder about some deeply personal things: Who am I as a man? Who am I as a woman? Who are we as a couple? Do we have a future together without the children we dreamed of having? If so, what is our future together supposed to be like? All too many marriages break up over these issues.[73]

Marrying and beginning the process of procreation earlier does not guarantee freedom from reproductive problems, but it certainly increases the likelihood of reproductive success. This, then, suggests several approaches for parents in a kind of modern interpolation of their talmudic duty to marry off their children. I discussed these directions for parents in Chapter Three, but they bear repeating, because of their deep, personal significance for couples, for their parents, and for the Jewish people as a whole.

- Make sure that your teenage children actively participate in a Jewish youth group and date only Jews. Intermarriage always starts with a date, and the intention to seek someone Jewish to marry gets formed primarily during one's teenage years.
- Make sure that your children apply to, and ultimately go to, a college with a large number of other Jews.
- Communicate to your children that it is not too early to look for a mate while in college and to get married and begin to have children while in graduate school.
- Then we older Jews must put our money where our mouths are by ensuring that Jewish venues are available and affordable for day care for young children and that formal and

informal Jewish schooling is affordable as well. Since charity begins at home, grandparents have a special role in contributing to their grandchildren's care and Jewish education.

Thus even though parents no longer "marry off" their children by choosing a mate for them, parents still have a major role to play in carrying out this talmudic duty. For everyone's sake, may they succeed!

CHAPTER FIVE

Family Violence

S EX AND FAMILY LIFE DO NOT ALWAYS CORRESPOND TO THE IDEALS
described in the last two chapters.[1] Human beings, after all,
are fallible, and so their lives do not fully mirror moral and
Jewish ideals. And sometimes people's behavior not only fails to
achieve the ideal but even goes to the extreme opposite end of
the spectrum, where meanness, cruelty, and inhumanity reign.
It is to that sort of behavior that I turn now to explore Jewish
sources and values in response to physical, sexual, and verbal
abuse of others.

TYPES OF ABUSE AND THEIR JEWISH LEGAL STATUS

THE IMPORTANCE OF THE CONSERVATIVE LEGAL METHOD TO ABUSE ISSUES

In some ways, it would seem absolutely obvious that Judaism
would not allow an individual to beat another, especially a family member. After all, in its opening chapters, the Torah tells us
that we are all created in the image of God.[2] That fundamental
tenet would seem to require that, at a very minimum, we do not
physically abuse others. The classical Rabbis of the Jewish tradition certainly understood that to be the case, for in the Mishnah and Talmud they specify five sorts of compensation for
personal injuries. Specifically, assailants must pay their victims

for their lost capital value, their time missed from work, their pain and suffering, their medical expenses, and the embarrassment they suffered.[3] Courts may impose lashes for trespasses of the law, but in doing so, even they had to take due care to preserve the dignity of God and of the culprit, who is, still, God's human creature.[4]

Nowadays, when Jews live under the jurisdiction of national legal systems that treat Jews as equal citizens and do not carve out separate civil and criminal authority for Jewish courts over Jews, even Jewish courts no longer have the authority to beat others; individuals have even less authorization to do so. Indeed, the Rabbis took the notion of the integrity of the individual so far as to say that those who slander others (and certainly those who cause them physical injury) are as though they had denied the existence of God.[5] Conversely, Rabbi Eliezer said, "Let your fellow's honor be as dear to you as your own."[6]

Given these underlying principles, one would expect that any family violence that occurred within the Jewish community would be based on misinformation about the Jewish tradition, neglect of it, or simply the foibles of individuals. Surprisingly and unfortunately, when we probe the sources, we find that some rabbis permitted forms of family violence, and others actually encouraged it. Consequently, before I address this subject directly, it is critical to remind readers of a core methodological conviction of Conservative Judaism and, indeed, also of this book: *We must understand sources within their historical context and make judgments about when and how to use them that are appropriate to our own time and to our moral and theological convictions.*

The Jewish tradition, after all, has spanned many centuries. During that time, it has not remained the same. Sometimes its development has been an internal unfolding of its inherent commitments in thought and in practice, and sometimes the example of other peoples among whom Jews lived produced changes within Judaism. Moreover, not all of the tradition is of an everlasting and compelling quality, and so generations of Jews have reinterpreted some parts of the tradition, all but ignored some, added other elements, and even taken steps to make some portions of the tradition effectively inoperative. These changes sometimes occurred through conscious, judicial decisions and sometimes through the changing customs and ideas of the people Israel in many times and climes.

Such a historical understanding of Judaism is critical for identifying its contemporary message on any subject, and the topic of family violence is no exception. Contemporary Jews look to the tradition for enlightenment and guidance, and we often find it in a simple, straightforward manner. Moreover, if our own stance is to have any reasonable claim to Jewish authenticity, the Jewish tradition as it has come down to us must exert a primary claim on our allegiance as our People's understanding of what God wants of us, with the burden of proof resting squarely on the shoulders of those who would change it.

Sometimes, however, traditional sources say things that we find obsolete or even offensive. When that occurs, we have not only the right but also the duty to exercise judgment. We must determine whether such a mode of thinking or acting recorded in the tradition is a historical remnant that must be altered because contemporary circumstances or moral sensitivities have changed or whether the tradition as it stands is instead an indictment of our own way of doing things and a challenge for us to change. If we are to be taught by the tradition and to be responsible exemplars of it, we must be aware of the twin duties we have as its heirs: We must learn it and preserve it, and, at the same time, we must evaluate it and reinterpret it when necessary. Only then can Judaism continue to speak to us with wisdom and power.

This chapter is written in answer to Jews asking about the status of family violence in Jewish law. Jews expect their tradition to give them guidance beyond the demands of civil law, for we aspire to holiness. We certainly cannot interpret Jewish law to allow us to be less moral than what civil law requires.[7] Since civil law in most areas of the Western world now prohibits most forms of family violence, Jews must eschew it for that reason—in addition to the grounds afforded by the Jewish tradition.

ACKNOWLEDGING FAMILY VIOLENCE WITHIN OUR COMMUNITY

Not only is family violence an unpleasant memory from sources of the past but it afflicts contemporary Jewish families as well.

That has not been part of the Jewish community's self-image; it is only in recent years, in fact, that Jewish communal institutions and individual Jews are openly admitting that family violence occurs within our midst. Somehow Jews were supposed to be immune from such behavior; that was, our sources assure us, what non-Jews do, not how Jews behave.

Family violence is indeed rampant in society. According to a report covering twenty countries and two thousand domestic violence studies, one out of every three women worldwide has been beaten, raped, or physically mistreated in some other way. Beyond the women's immediate physical injuries, abuse has been linked to problem pregnancies (including miscarriages, premature labor, and fetal distress), substance abuse, gastrointestinal disorders, and chronic pain syndromes.[8] Violence also affects children. In each of the past several years in the United States more than four hundred thousand reports of verifiable sexual assaults against children have been filed with authorities by teachers and doctors who deal with battered and traumatized youngsters, and studies indicate that at least one out of every three girls and one out of every five boys is sexually abused before age eighteen.[9] Moreover, the number of cases of battered children reported to state agencies per year grew from roughly two million in 1986 to three million in 1994, with continuing increases thereafter.[10] Furthermore, some two thousand children, most of them under age four, die each year at the hands of parents or caretakers.[11]

We have no good statistics to know whether Jews engage in these and other forms of family violence to the same degree as do other groups within the general population, but the disturbingly frequent cases of family violence brought to Jewish Family Service agencies across North America and to similar institutions in Israel afford good evidence that Jews suffer from all modes of this malady and that the problem is not confined to isolated cases. Moreover, family violence occurs among the Orthodox at least as much as it does among Conservative, Reconstructionist, and Reform Jews. Devotion to tradition has not, unfortunately, prevented violent behavior within the family.

I have been a member of the board of directors of the Jewish Family Service of Los Angeles since 1985, with special interest in its Family Violence Project. Similar projects are now in place or in the planning stages in New York, Chicago, and other cities as Jewish communities throughout North America, Israel, and indeed the world finally acknowledge the problem and begin to take steps to deal with it.[12]

BEATING WIVES OR HUSBANDS

In the area of spousal violence, as in all the areas I discuss in this chapter, we must be careful to distinguish acceptable forms of physical contact from abuse. Affectionate or supportive forms of touching between spouses are certainly not included in the category of abuse; they are easily differentiated from objectionable behavior by their motive, the willingness and the eagerness of the partner to be touched in that way, and the lack of physical and emotional wounds that normally result from violent behavior. Even a one-time slap in anger, while not pleasant or ideal, does not constitute abuse. When I speak in this section of beating a spouse, then, I am referring to repetitive blows, delivered out of anger, a desire to control, or some other motive inimical to the welfare of the victim that often inflict bleeding or bruising.

Naomi Graetz wrote a book on rabbinic rulings about wife beating through the ages.[13] She divided the rulings into five categories, discussed below.

Acceptance

Some rabbis accept that some Jewish husbands beat their wives, and they permit it. They justify such blows either as a means for the husband to educate his wife in proper behavior or as a way to obtain domestic harmony (*shelom bayit*). The rabbis who permitted husbands to beat their wives when the women failed to perform the duties required of them by Jewish law or when they violated prohibitions in the law include Rabbi Yehudai Gaon (eighth century, Babylonia), Rabbi Shmuel Hanagid (936–1056, Spain), "the Gaon" reported by Rabbenu Nissim, and Maimonides, who wrote: "A wife who refuses to perform any kind of work that she is obligated to do may be compelled to perform it, even by scourging her with a rod."[14] Later, Rabbi Israel Isserlein (1390–1460, Germany/Austria) permitted a husband to beat his wife if she cursed her own parents, "in order to keep her away from [violating] this strict prohibition."[15]

A variation on this approach permitted a husband to beat his wife if she had hurt him, presumably so that after he vented his anger in this way, domestic harmony would return. That is how Rabbi Shelomo ben Adret (Rashba, c. 1235–c. 1310, Spain) ruled,[16] as did Rabbi Moses Isserles (Rema, c. 1525–1572, Poland), who condoned wife beating as a response to taunting or degradation. Thus, on the one hand, Rabbi Isserles maintained that when the beating is rooted in the husband's aggression, it is not acceptable and the court should compel him either to desist or to divorce his wife:

> A man who strikes his wife commits a sin, just as if he were to strike anyone else. If he does this often, the court may punish him, excommunicate him, and flog him using every manner of punishment and force. The court may also make him swear that he will no longer do it. If he does not obey the court's decree, there are some authorities who say that we force him to divorce her, if he has been warned once or twice, because it is not the way of Jews to strike their wives; that is a Gentile form of behavior.[17]

On the other hand, when the beating is caused by the wife's antagonistic behavior, then the husband is subjected to no such penalties:

> But if she is the cause of it—for example, if she curses him or denigrates his father and mother—and he scolds her calmly at first but it does not help, then it is obvious that he is permitted to beat her and castigate her. And if it is not known who is the cause, the husband is not considered a reliable source when he says that she is the cause and portrays her as a harlot, for all women are presumed to be law-abiding [kesherot].[18]

DENIAL

Some rabbis deny altogether that Jewish husbands beat their wives. We saw that in Rabbi Isserles's comment that wife beating "is a Gentile form of behavior"—even though he then condoned it for Jews under specific circumstances.[19] Rabbi Abraham ben David of Posquieres (Rabad, c. 1125–1198, France) was more consistent. In commenting on the passage in which Maimonides permitted a husband to beat his wife if she refused to do the housework required of her by law,[20] he expressed great surprise and said, "I have never heard of women being scourged with a rod."

APOLOGETICS
Another group of rabbis seek to defend the honor of the Jewish community by whitewashing the facts. This usually involves a heavy dose of denial. When the facts cannot be ignored, though, apologists seek to marginalize the phenomenon, stating that Jews who engage in wife beating do so less frequently and less violently than non-Jews do. Alternatively, this group of rabbis seeks to justify such behavior, maintaining that Jews who actually engage in such behavior do not really hurt their wives or do so for a good reason. Yet another approach that falls within this rubric comes from those rabbis who displace the blame by shifting it to the surrounding culture. Often, even while acknowledging some of the evidence of wife beating, apologists ignore other pieces of it that do not fit their thesis. Graetz noted Rabbi Joseph Hertz as an example of such an apologist.[21]

REJECTION
Some rabbis declare that wife beating is unconditionally unacceptable. This is the strain of rabbinic rulings most in keeping with our own modern point of view. The three medieval rabbis who were most articulate in taking this stance were Rabbi Simha ben Samuel of Speyer (late twelfth to early thirteenth century, Germany), Rabbi Meir ben Barukh of Rothenburg (Maharam, c. 1215–1293, Germany), and Rabbi Perez ben Elijah of Corbeil (d. c. 1295, France). Rabbi Simhah condemned wife beating in the strongest of terms. He saw wife beating as more serious an offense than assaulting any other person, because in the marriage contract (ketubbah) a husband takes on a specific obligation to honor his wife beyond the normal obligations we all have to respect the integrity of other creatures of God. Consequently, Rabbi Simhah decreed penalties for wife beating that are considerably more severe than the five remedies for general assault. He said: "Therefore penalize him severely, whether physically or financially, for what has happened. Great repentance is necessary, and deal severely with him in the future as you see fit."[22]

Rabbi Joseph Karo recorded Rabbi Simhah's opinion more fully:

> I found in a responsum of Rabbenu Simhah that "it is an accepted view that we have to treat a man who beats his wife more severely than we treat a man who beats another man, for he is not obligated to honor the other man but is obligated to honor his wife—more, in fact, than himself. And a man who beats his wife should be put under a ban and excommunicated and flogged and punished with various forms of torment; one should even cut off his hand if he is accustomed to it [wife beating]. And if he wants to divorce her, let him divorce her and give her the *ketubbah* payment."

Further on Rabbi Karo wrote: "You should impose peace between them, and if the husband does not fulfill his part in maintaining the peace but rather continues to beat her and denigrate her, let him be excommunicated, and let him be forced by gentile [authorities] to give her a writ of divorce."[23]

Rabbi Meir of Rothenburg follows Rabbi Simhah's lead. He, too, ruled that "a man who beats his wife . . . is compelled [by the court] to give her a divorce."[24] Moreover, he said that "The batterer must be boycotted and excommunicated, beaten and punished will all sorts of beatings, and his hand should be cut off if he used it to beat her."[25]

Finally, in proposed legislation (*takkanah*), Rabbi Perez ben Elijah of Corbeil, noted that "The cry of the daughters of our people has been heard concerning the sons of Israel who raise their hands to strike their wives. Is it not rather forbidden to strike any person in Israel?" Citing the authority of the Tosafists, Rabbi Samuel, Rabbi Jacob Tam, and Rabbi Isaac, Rabbi Perez then decreed that one who beats his wife must, on complaint of his wife or one of her relatives, "undertake on pain of excommunication not to beat his wife in anger or cruelty or so as to disgrace her, for that is against Jewish practice." Furthermore, if the husband disobeys, the court will assign the wife alimony as if the husband were away on a journey.[26]

EVASIVENESS

The final group of rabbis evades responsibility for the phenomenon of domestic abuse within their communities or display what Graetz called "the wringing hands syndrome." They recognize that wife beating is wrong, but they maintain that they are pow-erless to do anything about it. So, for example, Rabbi Solomon ben Abraham Adret (Rashba, 1235–1310, Spain) said:

> A question was asked of him: What is the ruling for a husband who regularly beats his wife, so that she has to leave his home and return to her father's home?
>
> The answer is: The husband should not beat his wife. She was given to him for life, not for sorrow. He should honor her more than his own body. The court investigates to determine who is re-sponsible. If he beats her, she is allowed to run away, for a person does not have to live with a snake. But if she curses him for no reason, the law is with him, for the woman who curses her hus-band leaves without collecting the money promised in her mar-riage contract (*ketubbah*). At any rate, I do not see that the court can do more than tell him in strong language not to beat her and warn him that if he beats her not according to law, he will have to divorce her and give her the money of her marriage contract.[27]

Similarly, Rabbi David ben Solomon ibn Avi Zimra (Radbaz, 1479–1573, Spain/Egypt), affirmed the right of a husband to beat his wife "if she behaves improperly, according to our Torah, in order to bring her back to the right path, for she is under his ju-risdiction." He added the condition, though, that there must be witnesses to the wife's violation of the law, and he asserted that "he is not allowed to beat her for matters that pertain to him personally, for she is not his servant." Moreover, "if he habitu-ally beats her, he should be punished." In a clear reference to Rabbi Simhah, however, he noted, "There is one who exagger-ated in his teaching and said that we can force him to divorce her, even by use of non-Jewish courts." In another ruling, Radbaz went so far as to say that if the court does force the husband to divorce his wife on this ground, her children by a second mar-riage would be illegitimate (*mamzerim*).[28] In other words, the husband's actions may be wrong, and the court may even punish him for that, but it cannot free the woman to marry someone else on that ground. This Graetz rightly classifies as evasion of responsibility on the part of the court.

In sum, then, the sources are not as unified in their stance against wife beating as we probably would have expected and certainly would have hoped. In general, rabbis living in Muslim countries were the most permissive of wife beating, those in France less so, and those in Germany not at all. According to contemporary historian Avraham Grossman, wife beating among Jews in Muslim countries was frequent, especially among the lower social strata and particularly when economic times were hard. Moreover, the phenomenon of early marriage for girls contributed to this, for the older men who were their husbands may have assumed that they were not only partners, but also substitute parents for their wives. Undoubtedly, rabbis in Muslim countries were also influenced by Muslim practices, for the Koran calls on the husband to beat his wife if he suspects that she is behaving immodestly or disobeying him.[29] Even so, Grossman asserted, "the situation of Jewish women in Muslim countries was better than that of the Muslim women."[30]

Conversely, in Germany in the eleventh to thirteenth centuries, women enjoyed high social status. That was reflected in the Jewish community in the legislation of Rabbenu Gershon prohibiting polygamy; restricting divorce against the will of the woman; and providing a fixed, high sum in the woman's marriage contract. Moreover, Jewish women in medieval Germany played a significant role in supporting the family. In addition, the Ashkenazic Hasidim made any insult or shame caused to a person, including wife beating, not only a crime but a sin, where repentance was inflicted measure for measure. This attitude clearly influenced those outside the community of Hasidim as well.[31]

In addition to these historical factors, there is an important legal institution underlying whatever permission exists in some sources for a husband to beat his wife, namely, that Jewish law assumes that the husband owns his wife. The Mishnah and Talmud went very far to protect the rights of the woman; but, after all is said and done, the very language for betrothal in classical Jewish law is that a man "acquires" (koneh) his wife.[32] It is precisely this aspect of Jewish marriage law that Graetz, Hauptman, and others suggest that we change to uproot the underlying legal context that sets the stage for the permission of wife beating.

Even the Conservative Jews who do not want to go that far in altering institutions from the past no longer think of marriage as the husband's acquisition of the wife, despite the fact that that terminology (*kinyan*) is still used in our marriage rituals. Husbands in our day have no more right to discipline their wives than wives have to discipline their husbands. In our times, then, the opinions of Maimonides and Isserles on this issue, among others, must be set aside as no longer applicable. Instead, relying on opinions like those of Rabbis Simhah, Meir of Rothenburg, and Perez ben Elijah of Corbeil, as well as our own judgment, the Conservative movement's Committee on Jewish Law and Standards (CJLS) *has unanimously declared that wife beating is prohibited by Jewish law.* Indeed, in traditional Jewish marital law, when a husband "acquires" his wife, he thereby takes on a number of binding legal and moral obligations to her, and, as the Conservative movement interprets them, wife beating is not only inconsistent with but also contrary to those duties.

Moreover, in cases in which wife beating occurs and cannot be corrected through therapy for the husband, the Conservative rabbinate has devised ways, consistent with traditional Jewish law, to help the woman free herself from the marriage. That includes counseling to help her make the decision to extricate herself from the abusive situation, referrals to Jewish Family Service or other such agencies that can facilitate that process and show her how to protect herself (and her children) from further harassment, guidance (if necessary) in obtaining legal help to dissolve the marriage in civil law, and then appropriate actions within Jewish law to dissolve the marriage by a formal Jewish writ of divorce (*get*), if possible, or by an annulment (*hafka'at kiddushin*), if necessary. A commitment to the life and health of the woman demands no less.

The same is true in the opposite direction. While there is not, to my knowledge, any source within our tradition that ever allowed the wife to beat her husband, it does occur. Indeed, if women are reluctant to report instances of being beaten because of worries of shame, slander, and economic support, men are even more reticent to report being beaten by their wives, because they are too embarrassed to admit that they have been battered by a woman. Since childhood, after all, boys are taught that they are supposed to be the physically stronger gender.[33]

165

Sometimes even professional athletes are assaulted and in-jured by their wives. One such case involved Tawny Kitaen, a forty-year-old movie star, who was arrested

> on misdemeanor charges of battery and abusing her husband, Cleveland Indians pitcher Chuck Finley, 39. The Orange County [California] district attorney's office says a high-heeled Kitaen re-peatedly kicked Finley and brutally scratched his face and arms. She was released from jail April 3 and faces up to a year in jail if convicted.[34]

Although spousal abuse is much more often perpetrated by men than by women, this case is not an isolated incident. In 1996, the *Los Angeles Times* reported that arrests in Los Angeles County of women who beat their husbands had risen sharply be-tween 1987 and 1995.[35]

Thus it is worthwhile to mention here that *husband beating is also prohibited by Jewish law*[36] *and is equally as reprehensible as wife beating.* Rabbis and lay Jews must do all in their power to help the battered man free himself from the abusive situation in ways similar to those delineated above for a wife suffering abuse.

BEATING CHILDREN

If a man's wife was construed as his possession in the past, all the more were his children. While this may seem unreasonable and even archaic to many people nowadays, American law shares that view, first challenged in the early 1990s in the court case of *Gre-gory K.* As a *Newsweek* article put it," 'Portable property' was Emerson's term for children, and most people believe kids do be-long to their parents, body and soul. As a practical matter, the courts have tended to uphold that view."[37] That presumption un-derlies the approach of many of the classical Jewish sources on children. If, according to Maimonides, discipline was the major justification for beating a wife, that rationale applies all the more for children—at least in some Jewish sources. "Spare the rod and spoil the child" has firm roots in the Book of Proverbs:

> *Do not withhold discipline from a child;*
> *If you beat him with a rod, he will not die.*
> *Beat him with a rod,*
> *And you will save him from the grave.*[38]

This applied to mothers as well as fathers:

Rod and reproof produce wisdom,
But a lad out of control is a disgrace to his mother.[39]

Along these lines, the Rabbis specifically exempt parents and teachers from the monetary damages usually imposed on those who commit assault on the theory that beating a child is sometimes necessary to carry out the parental duty of teaching the child Torah in its widest sense, including the difference between right and wrong.[40] (The teacher is, in the Rabbis' view, simply an agent to enable the parents to fulfill this responsibility of theirs.) Deuteronomy, the fifth book of the Torah, goes even further: It states that parents may bring a "wayward and defiant son, who does not heed his father and mother and does not obey them even after they discipline him" to the town elders to be stoned.[41] In this case, of course, the physical damage to the child is to be inflicted not by the parents but by public authorities, and that is clearly a significant difference. The parents, though, are still the instigators of this procedure.

One must immediately distinguish, though, between discipline of a child and child abuse. It is arguable whether striking a child is ever a good way to discipline a child. I am among those who think that it is not, for it teaches the child that might makes right. I recognize, though, that Jewish law and, indeed, the law of many societies throughout history have accepted hitting a child as an appropriate method of discipline. Striking a child for that purpose constitutes one end of a spectrum. Presumably, parents would hit the child only when the child's behavior was so unusually vile or the child was so out of control that, in the estimation of the parents, milder forms of reprimand would not work.

At the other end of the spectrum is child abuse, wherein the parent's striking of the child is frequent, uncontrollable, unprovoked, and excessively severe. Hitting the child is not responsive to the child's behavior or needs, but rather acting out the parent's frustration. This occurs especially when the parent either does not understand the needs of the developing child or has expectations of behavior that do not match the child's capabilities. Parents also abuse children when they do not know effective methods of discipline. Striking the child, then, is the parent's misdirected attempt to calm his or her own inner anxiety and is either not responsive at all, or is not properly responsive, to the child's behavior in his or her social and developmental context.

In between those extremes are cases in which the line between legitimate discipline and child abuse is harder to discern. Even granted such ambiguities in the middle of the spectrum, though, we surely have a problem in our society when 10 to 20 percent of university students retrospectively report that as they were growing up both they and other family members were beaten to the point of producing, at a minimum, bruises or bleeding.[42]

At most, then, verses like the ones from Proverbs cited above legitimate striking a child only for reasons of discipline, and then only when no milder form has been effective in correcting the child's behavior. Included within acceptable (even if not ideal) discipline are a light smack on the buttocks (a "potch") or even striking the child elsewhere on the body with an open hand (but not punching or pommeling with a fist), and even then only those types of contact that do not produce bleeding or a bruise. In contrast to the verses cited from Proverbs and to the practice permitted in times past, however, the Conservative rabbinate has declared that, in its interpretation and application of Jewish law to our times, striking a child with a rod, belt, or instrument of any kind is forbidden. Moreover, Jewish law, in its Conservative interpretation, clearly and emphatically prohibits a parent's use of corporal punishment to the point of abuse—that is, when the child is seriously harmed or when the punishment is clearly excessive as a response to the child's misdeed.[43]

After all is said and done, though, the use of corporal punishment, even within permissible parameters, is questionable. The same Book of Proverbs that advocates the use of physical force in raising children also says, "Educate a child according to his own way."[44] The Talmud understands this to mean that parents should make age-appropriate demands so as not to put their children into a situation in which corporal punishment would be called for. In other words, parents have a duty to set reasonable standards for their children so they avoid even being tempted to use physical forms of discipline. As the Talmud says, parents must not make it difficult for their children to fulfill the commandment of honoring them.[45]

Even in the worst of cases—the kind described by Deuteronomy—the Talmud could not accept anything like the death penalty. The Rabbis therefore legislated evidentiary procedures that made it impossible ever to attain a capital conviction in such a case. Once having created these barriers, they themselves said, "A wayward and defiant son [subject to execution according to Deuteronomy 21:18–21] never was and never will be."[46] If the Rabbis insisted that even courts not go to the limit available to them under biblical law in physically punishing children, parents should certainly limit the physical punishment they inflict—or, even better, refrain from it altogether. After all, if the parents' duty is to teach the child proper behavior, they should not, in the process of doing so, do to the child exactly what they do not want the child to do to others. Educationally and pragmatically, then, as well as Jewishly, the best policy is not to use physical punishment at all.

One especially troubling aspect of this picture occurs in instances in which parents beat developmentally disabled children. While there is at most minimal justification for beating a normally intelligent child for purposes of discipline, children with less-than-normal intelligence or with other developmental disabilities often cannot even understand why they are being subjected to blows, and so the abuse loses much of its justificatory cover. One can understand the extra measure of frustration that parents might feel in raising such a child, and one can certainly appreciate the additional demands that rearing him or her entails over raising a child of normal intelligence; but parents of special-needs children need to get help so that they can parent these children in appropriate, nonviolent ways.[47]

The same rules that apply to the discipline of children—but with even less endorsement for striking the child—apply to family-like situations outside the family where adults are in charge of children. Thus teachers, youth group leaders, coaches, camp counselors, and the like may, at the very most, give a light slap on the buttocks to children to get them going to the next activity. They may not strike the child in any form of corporal punishment.

According to a recent study,[48] parents should think twice and three times before spanking their children. After analyzing six decades of expert research on corporal punishment, including eighty-eight studies of corporal punishment conducted since 1938, psychologist Elizabeth Gershoff of Columbia University's National Center for Children in Poverty found links between spanking and ten negative behaviors or experiences, including aggression, antisocial behavior, and mental health problems. The one positive result of spanking that she identified was quick compliance with parental demands. As Gershoff noted, "Americans need to re-evaluate why we believe it is reasonable to hit young, vulnerable children, when it is against the law to hit other adults, prisoners, and even animals."[49] When parents are in a situation in which they are considering spanking, they should "think of something else to do—leave the room, count to 10 and come back again. The risk is just too great."[50] Even other psychologists who critiqued Gershoff's study defended only mild to moderate spanking as a disciplinary option for children aged two to six, but they advise parents with abusive tendencies to avoid spanking altogether.[51]

This certainly does not support the 61 percent of parents of children under the age of seven who, according to a survey of three thousand adults, believe spanking is an appropriate "regular form of discipline."[52] Moreover, the survey revealed that parents often spank their children because they have completely unrealistic expectations: More than 25 percent think that a three-year-old child should be able to sit quietly for an hour; 51 percent expect a fifteen-month-old to share her toys with other children. The burden of the Jewish tradition and of the best psychological evidence available would instead admonish parents to find other more effective and less risky forms of discipline.

None of the above, of course, is intended to prohibit parents or even other adults in charge of children from hugging them or putting an arm around children's shoulders to comfort them or to express congratulations in, for example, a ball game. On the contrary, we all need such support from those who care for us and mentor us. Parents, in particular, should be sure to hug their children and kiss them; for children who grow up without such expressions of love, especially in the first years of life, are at risk for developing affective disorders that prevent them from relating to other people with any degree of attachment or love.

A small percentage of people in authority abuse children, and those children and their parents rightly then sue not only the people involved but also the institutions that were negligent in preventing the abuse. That unfortunately makes all teachers, counselors, and clergy reticent to give children reassurance, congratulations, and, frankly, love through any form of touching them. Contemporary societies and legal systems need to find a way to prevent abuse while not also making appropriate and desirable touching impossible. Even parents, of course, may not abuse their children, but they must appropriately express their affection not only with words but also with touch.

All of the above strictures, then, are with reference to acts of violence against the child, differentiated from acts of love or friendship by both the intention and context of the parties and the form and energy of the physical contact.[53] Those criteria should help us craft reasonably clear behavioral lines between appropriate and inappropriate touch, especially for authority figures outside the family, so that this important social bonding mechanism does not get lost in our efforts to prevent abuse.

BEATING PARENTS

Abuse of elderly or infirm parents is, unfortunately, a growing phenomenon in our society, especially as people live longer and suffer from the mental and physical disabilities of old age. The Jewish tradition has no room for maltreatment of parents. Parents, of course, are human beings and are, therefore, protected under the provisions of Jewish law prohibiting assault and demanding monetary remedies for it. The Torah, though, makes parents special. It specifically prohibits striking one's father or mother, and it prescribes the death penalty for one who does so.[54] That leaves little room for doubt about the Torah's view of striking parents.

If any more grounding is sought for prohibiting parental abuse, it would come from the Torah's positive commandments to honor and respect one's parents. As discussed at some length in Chapter Four, the Torah specifically mentions that mothers as well as fathers are to be revered and honored, and the Rabbis construed these commands to be demanded of daughters as well as sons.[55] The Rabbis understood "respect" to require that children not harm parents and "honor" to insist that they actively provide for them.[56] So, for example, if the child has food and the parent does not, the law permits forcing the child to provide food for the parent.

The Talmud, as we have seen, sets limits to these obligations, so that, for example, one may provide for one's parents out of their assets rather than from one's own.[58] On the other hand, stories in the Talmud recount instances in which specific people went to extraordinary lengths to honor and respect their parents, and these are taken as models for us all.[59] With this as a background, one can understand that the tradition, which prized honor and respect of parents so much, would in no way countenance parental abuse.

These laws stand on their own, independent of any assessment of the quality of the parenting provided. There are at least two rationales in Jewish sources to justify a duty to honor even bad parents. One is that the parents, along with God, are the three partners in the creation of their children; thus the Talmud noted: "If people honor their father and mother, God says, 'I reckon it to them as if I dwelled among them and as if they honored Me.' "[60]

Second, parents are commanded to teach their children how to behave according to the dictates of the Torah. Some parents fail miserably in this task; nevertheless, to the extent that they carry out this obligation, they fulfill a God-like role and are to be respected as such. As discussed in Chapter Four (see page 128), Philo made this point well.[61]

Thus abuse of parents is even more specifically and severely denounced in the Jewish tradition than abuse of other people or even other family members.[62] The positive obligations to honor and respect one's parents add yet more strength to the general obligation to respect the divine element in each one of us. Since respect of a person would certainly preclude abuse, we are doubly warned in the case of parents against beating them.

Not all parents, of course, are model human beings or paradigm parents; some are nasty or even abusive. When parents have abused their children or violated the law, a number of Ashkenazic sources (Rashi, Tosafot, Rabbenu Tam, Rabbi Moses Isserles) assert that the Torah's commands to honor and respect them no longer apply. Sephardic sources, however, generally assert that the commands to honor and respect parents continue even in the face of abuse or other illegality. This is true for Rabbi Alfas, Maimonides, and Rabbi Karo.[63]

Thus, although one may, according to some authorities, fail to honor or respect one's parents when they have been absent or abusive, beating them is another matter. The former is failing to do one's normal duty; the latter is violating an explicit interdiction—actually, a host of them. The specific prohibitions of the Torah against parental abuse and the concepts and laws of reverence and honor for parents add to the general laws punishing assault in Judaism's unequivocal condemnation of parental abuse.

In sum, then, within the dictates of Jewish law Jews may withhold love from their parents, either for cause or just as a function of the personalities involved, and if the cause is severe enough, they may even be released from the commands to honor and respect them. Jews may also arrange for the care of their parents at the hands of others, assuming that personal caring is either physically or emotionally impossible; if the nature of their relationship permits it, children should visit their parents and call them often. At no time, though, do children have the right to assault their parents.

SEXUAL ABUSE

Sexual abuse, as applied to children, is defined in psychological literature as "sexual contact, ranging from fondling to intercourse, between a child in mid-adolescence or younger and a person at least five years older." When defined that way, "at least 20% of American women and 5% to 10% of American men experienced some form of sexual abuse as children."[64] Among adults, sexual abuse is usually understood to be any nonconsensual sexual act or behavior. This definition assumes that we fully acknowledge the well-known ambiguities of some expressions of agreement or refusal, but it asserts that such ambiguity does not affect all or even most expressions of one's desires. For either age group, sexual abuse demeans and humiliates, making one feel shameful and exposed, particularly in regard to one's sexuality.

Some forms of sexual molestation leave physical wounds, including permanent ones that preclude the victim's future ability to procreate. Even those attacks that do not leave such wounds fall under the category of physical abuse, for they represent unwanted and often violent invasions of one's body. Consequently, all of the objections described above to beating a family member would also apply to sexual assault.

Sexual violation, however, is objectionable on other grounds as well. First, it represents the exact opposite of the holiness that we are to aspire to achieve. Thus, in regard to sexual abuse of family members, the Torah states unequivocally, "None of you shall come near anyone of his own flesh to uncover nakedness: I am the Lord."[65] After a long list of such forbidden relationships, it then states that such were the abhorrent practices of the nations that occupied the Promised Land before the Israelites. The land thus became defiled and is now spewing them out—almost as if the land had an allergic reaction to toxic food. The Israelites themselves may remain in the Holy Land only if they eschew such practices and act as a holy people. Furthermore, "All who do any of those abhorrent things shall be cut off from their people. You shall keep My charge not to engage in any of the abhorrent practices that were carried on before you, and you shall not defile yourselves through them: I the Lord am your God."[66] Part of what it means to be a People chosen by God as a model for others, then, is that Jews must not engage in incest or sexual abuse. To do so violates the standards by which a holy people covenanted to God should live and warrants excommunication from the People Israel. Jews are expected to behave better than that.

Why does the Torah speak of incest and sexual abuse as "defilement" and "abomination" in addition to its usual language of transgression? In part, it is because the Promised Land was itself seen as alive and violated by such conduct, but surely the words refer to the human beings involved too. One's bodily integrity is compromised when one is sexually abused. Sexual abuse is experienced not only as an assault on one's body but also—and usually more devastatingly—as an onslaught on one's person. One has lost one's integrity—not only in body but in soul. One no longer feels safe in the world; at any moment, one can be invaded in the most intimate of ways. The abuse is thus indeed a defilement: What was sacred and whole before is now desecrated and broken.[67]

Sexual abuse is also the source of much embarrassment. The Torah makes this exceedingly clear: "If two men get into a fight with each other, and the wife of one comes up to save her husband from his antagonist and puts out her hand and seizes him by his genitals, you shall cut off her hand; show no pity."[68] Despite the special justification the woman had for shaming her husband's assailant, the Torah demands drastic steps in retribution for the degradation she caused—although the Rabbis transformed this to a monetary payment that she had to pay.[69] (Incidentally, note that, as the Torah recognized, feelings of shame and embarrassment are experienced by men who are sexually abused just as much as they are by women.) The Talmud, when determining the payment to be exacted for the shame involved whenever one person assaults another, uses this case as the paradigm for what embarrassment means. We are humiliated when we are sexually abused—even just touched in our private parts against our will—for we feel that our sense of self has been invaded, that our honor has been compromised in the most fundamental way possible.

When children are sexually abused, the damage is even worse. Children depend on the adults in their lives—parents, other family members and friends, teachers, clergy, camp counselors, coaches—to help them master the skills of living. Their psychological well-being depends on their ability to trust such people to act for their welfare, for that is the only way that children can learn to trust themselves and others. Thus, when an adult sexually abuses a child, the child may not at first experience it as an assault; for young children, it may even seem like an interesting, pleasurable game. Whether immediately or gradually, however, children come to recognize sexual activity with adults as an abuse of their bodies and their wills, and they feel

175

not only violated but *betrayed*. This often leads to difficulty later on in forming relationships with others, especially sexual ones; and, in some cases, it even undermines the person's ability to trust the world enough to go out into it for any productive activity.

This kind of frontal assault on not only the body but also the psyche of the child is clearly prohibited by all the Jewish laws discussed earlier prohibiting assault, sexual contact with one's family members, sexual contact outside marriage, and embarrassment of others. The Jewish tradition understands the Torah to ban not only sexual penetration but also any form of illicit fondling or inappropriate behavior for the purpose of gratifying sexual desire.[70] Indeed, in light of the extensive damage it causes to the future ability of the child to cope with life, without too much exaggeration I would say that, in the case of children, sexual abuse is akin to murder.[71]

VERBAL ABUSE

Verbal abuse of either one's spouse or one's children is not treated as an offense special and apart from the offense of verbally abusing any other person, but it certainly is included within the latter, more general prohibition. By "verbal abuse" we commonly mean comments that degrade a person, especially if they are said constantly. "You never get it right," "You are simply stupid," and "How could anyone like you?" are examples of such abuse. Overly harsh criticism, name calling, and intimidating speech are also included in the category of verbal abuse. (Sexual harassment may include elements of verbal abuse and, in some cases, job discrimination as well.)

Some call this "emotional abuse" or "psychological abuse," and psychological literature includes definitions that point to a number of identifying dysfunctions.[72] While I have no doubt that such abuse happens and that this phenomenon needs further study and refining, both as to identification and cure, I hesitate to use either of those terms now for fear that some will understand them to include any instance in which someone makes someone else feel bad. Doing that as part of justified and constructive criticism may actually be a good thing for everyone concerned—although even then tact should be used. Consequently, to make the offense as clearly identifiable as possible, I retain the phrase "verbal abuse," insisting that there be objectively recognizable behavior that makes the culprit guilty of an offense.

One must first distinguish justifiable rebuke for errors from verbal abuse. That distinction follows more or less along the same lines as the one between reasonable discipline and physical abuse. Specifically, verbal abuse is constant, uncontrolled, and unprovoked, while a warranted reprimand occurs only when an error is made and when the reproach is proportionate to the error. At their best, negative evaluations are also constructive, with suggestions for change, a factor that is always absent in cases of verbal abuse. While verbal abuse is often perpetrated by one who has power over the other, it can occur among equals as well, as, for instance, when "friends" insult each other, not in jest or good humor but in an effort to embarrass, humiliate, or harm the other in some way, perhaps as part of making oneself feel superior.

Verbal abuse of anyone is forbidden by the Jewish tradition under the biblical command, "and you shall not wrong one another."[73] This prohibition precludes verbal abuse of minors as well as adults,[74] an important point to note especially by teachers and parents.

In addition to these general interdictions of verbal abuse, Jewish sources tell a man to be especially careful not to abuse his wife verbally, "for since she cries easily, it is all too easy to oppress her."[75] Similarly, the Talmud says that a man's wife is given to him so that he might realize life's plan together with her; he certainly does not have the right to vex or grieve her continually and without cause. "Vex her not, for God notes her tears."[76] These commands are derived, in part, from the promise that the man is required to make in the wedding contract to honor his wife. Indeed, "He who loves his wife as himself and honors her more than himself is granted the Scriptural promise, 'You shall know that your tent is in peace.' "[77] Contemporary readers may be justifiably offended by the sexism of some of these remarks, but that modern sensitivity should lead us to argue that wives as well as husbands are duty bound to avoid verbally abusing their spouses, for husbands, too, can and do feel hurt by such shaming.[78]

Moreover, the sexism in some of these rabbinic comments should not blind us to the power they gain from the theological basis they explicitly invoke: Verbal abuse violates not only the relationship among the human beings involved but also that between the individual and God, for God commands us not to oppress others. One honors God and the Jewish people (*kiddush ha-shem*) when one honors others; conversely, one dishonors God and desecrates God's people (*hillul ha-shem*) when one verbally abuses a human being created in the divine image.

There is a related, more general category, though, that is framed in a combination of legal and theological terms. That category is *ona'at devarim*, oppression by means of words. The Torah includes two verses prohibiting oppression of our neighbor.[79] Since the talmudic Rabbis presumed that no biblical verse was superfluous, they understood the first verse to prohibit financial oppression and the second verse to ban verbal abuse. As illustrations of the latter, they say that one may not remind repentant sinners of their past sins or converts of their previous non-Jewish lives. Similarly, one may not call people by an opprobrious nickname, even if the people so named say they do not mind, and one may not taunt people about their illnesses or the loss of their children.

In that same section, the Talmud points out that verbal abuse is a more serious offense than is financial deception, for the latter affects what one owns while the former affects one's very being. Moreover, misappropriated money or property can often be returned, while defamatory words can never be fully retrieved or recompensed. That is because one never knows how many people have heard or have later been told of the negative remarks, and thus even a repentant speaker can never correct the negative impression in the minds of all who heard the original remarks or a report of them. The Torah itself reflects this increased severity of verbal abuse over monetary crimes, for it specifically warns us to fear God when denouncing verbal oppression but does not include that admonition when forbidding financial deception. None of this, of course, justifies monetary cheating in any way, but it does underscore how much the Rabbis wanted us to avoid verbal abuse.

As violations of a negative biblical command, acts of verbal abuse would make a person subject to lashes inflicted by the court in addition to the opprobrium of the community and of God. It would not justify victims striking back with physical blows or with verbal abuse of one's own—although, as I discuss at greater length later, one may and should defend oneself from such abuse by either telling the abuser off or by removing oneself, if possible, from the context of the abuse.

To my knowledge, verbal abuse of one's spouse and children is never developed as an independent violation of Jewish law. It is certainly included, though, in the more general prohibition proscribing verbal oppression of any member of the community. Logic, in fact, dictates that if we are prohibited from verbally abusing anyone, we are even more duty bound to avoid abusing family members, to whom we have increased levels of responsibility.

Parents, again, occupy a special place in these matters. In Chapter Four, I quoted the full text of the remarkable story the Talmud tells to illustrate verbal abuse against parents: "A man may feed his father on fattened chickens and inherit Hell [as his reward], and another may put his father to work in a mill and inherit Paradise."[80] The Rabbis thus vividly described the attitudes that the biblical duty to respect our parents entails. The story is also a rabbinic extension of one of the Torah's prohibitions—namely, that if one actually curses one's parents, the Torah decrees nothing less than the death penalty.[81] Even if one did not go quite that far, the story is saying, it is wrong to insult one's parents. Thus verbal abuse of parents, aside from sharing in the more general prohibition of oppressive speech (ona'at devarim), involves the added violations of the positive commandment to respect our parents and the prohibition of cursing them.

WITNESSES TO THE ACT OR RESULTS OF ABUSE

As I mentioned earlier, the Talmud interprets the Torah's command not to stand idly by the blood of our neighbor[82] to mean that we must take positive steps to save people's lives. Furthermore, the Torah's command to come forward with testimony[83] would make it seem obvious that Jews who witness abuse or its results must testify to it and help people extricate themselves from it. The following four commands within Judaism, though, are sometimes misinterpreted to prevent witnesses to abuse from testifying to government officials or to others in authority about an abusive situation:

- The prohibition against defaming another human being (*lashon ha-ra*).
- The prohibition against shaming someone else (*boshet*).
- The prohibition against handing a Jew over to non-Jewish authorities (*mesirah*).
- The prohibition against desecrating God (*hillul ha-Shem*).

In addition, in the specific case of child abuse, some Jews worry that informing the authorities will violate the prerogatives of parents and make it impossible for them to carry out their biblical duties to educate their children. I shall examine each of these concerns in turn.

DEFAMING ANOTHER HUMAN BEING
The Jewish tradition forbids several kinds of speech: lies (*sheker*); truths that it is nobody's business to know (*rekhilut*, or gossip); and truths that, for all their truth, are defamatory (*lashon ha-ra*). It is this last prohibition that some people invoke to claim that Judaism prohibits witnesses to abuse from informing authorities. Since complaints about the abuse, the argument goes, will inevitably defame the abuser, witnesses may not describe to others what is going on.

Defamatory speech is an important thing to avoid as much as possible, but there are some very clear exceptions to the prohibition. One exception occurs when failure to defame the person will result in harm to someone else. If someone routinely defrauds customers, for example, you are duty bound to warn potential victims and to inform the authorities, however negative your report may be. In fact, as a general rule, when failure to disclose a financial or physical abuse to the proper authorities will result in continued illegal activities, the victim and anyone who notices the wrongdoing are obliged to report such activities. Even though that will inevitably defame the abuser, such action is not only permissible but mandatory when it is done in an effort to prevent harm to oneself or someone else.[84] As Maimonides wrote:

> Anyone who can save [someone's life] and does not do so transgresses "You shall not stand idly by the blood of your neighbor" (Leviticus 19:16). Similarly, if one sees his brother drowning in the sea, accosted by robbers, or attacked by wild animals and can save him personally or can hire others to save him, and does not save him, or he heard non-Jews or informers plotting evil or attempting to entrap another and he does not inform him . . . transgresses "You shall not stand idly by the blood of your neighbor."[85]

Indeed, the Talmud says that if one person (A) is attacking another (B), any third party (C) has not only the right but also the obligation to stop A—even at the cost of A's life, if that is necessary. This is the law of the pursuer (rodef).[86] Unlike the law in many American states, Jewish law would thus justify C in even killing an abusive spouse or parent if that were the sole way to stop constant assaults on B, but only when there is imminent danger of the death, rape, or serious injury of B. In other words, Jewish law allows a third party (C) to do what B himself or herself could legally do according to both American and Jewish law as an act of self-defense.[87]

The law of the pursuer is based on a broader principle in Jewish law, that of pikkuah nefesh (saving a life). Specifically, the Torah proclaims the command to follow God's commands and to live by them.[88] The Rabbis interpreted this to mean that we must live by them and not die by them. Toward that end, the Rabbis determined that we not only may but must violate all but three of the commandments if that is necessary to save a life. As I have noted, the three prohibitions that we may not violate even to save a life are murder, incest/adultery, and idolatry. The first of the exceptions, however, applies only when we would be murdering an innocent person to save our own or someone else's life. If, instead, the person in question is threatening us, we both may and must seek to kill him or her first, and if the person in question is pursuing another, we must intervene, even to the point of killing the pursuer, as the law of rodef demands.[89]

Now, these, of course, are extreme cases. The law of the pursuer demonstrates, however, exactly how far Jewish law was willing to go to stop attacks. And if it justifies even homicide to prevent an assault, it certainly expects third parties to intervene in less violent ways to protect victims from further abuse.

That includes reporting cases of abuse to legal authorities. This is not only required as a part of the effort to save lives but is also specifically demanded in the Torah according to the Talmud's interpretation of the Torah's verses cited at the beginning of this section. "One may not stand idly by the blood of one's neighbor" demands coming forward to help someone who is being attacked.[90] One who has information to report and fails to do so also violates Leviticus 5:1: "If he does not come forth with his information, then he shall be subject to punishment."[91] While in monetary affairs, the witness may wait until summoned, in other matters, such as abuse, the witness must come forward voluntarily to "destroy the evil from your midst."[92] For that matter, even *suspicions* of abuse must be reported to the authorities, for Jewish law maintains that Jewish law, including the law against defamation, must be violated even when the threat to someone's life is not certain (*safek nefashot*).[93]

The positive duty to inform authorities applies to witnesses of abuse by a spouse, a parent, a teacher, or anyone else. Witnesses to spousal abuse or to its results may understandably feel reticent to intervene in what might be construed as the couple's private affairs, especially since raising the issue may cause one to lose a friend, particularly if the abused party refuses to acknowledge the abuse and becomes defensive. Even if the abused spouse admits the abuse to a friend, neither the abused party nor the witness may want to expose the family to the humiliation involved in making the abuse public, preferring instead to deal with it within the family. That, however, almost never works; if there is any chance that the marriage can and should be saved, it will have to be with outside, professional help.

More often the abused party needs help in extricating herself (usually) from the marriage altogether. Thus for all their understandable hesitation, witnesses to spousal abuse *must* inform the authorities, for failing to do that exposes the abused party to the risk of further maiming and even death. Defamation of the abuser will probably occur, but that concern is definitely superseded in Jewish law by the need to save the physical integrity and the very life of the victim.

The same is true for child abuse. People who observe child abuse by parents or its physical manifestations must set aside concerns for the privacy of the family and its possible defamation to save the child from further battery or even death. Similarly, witnesses to child abuse perpetrated by teachers, counselors, or youth group leaders must report even suspicions of such abuse to the authorities.

This raises one complication in cases of child abuse. Typically, the teacher or friend who reports the abuse is doing so on the testimony of the child together with supportive evidence in the form of bruises on the child's body. Rabbi Israel Meir Ha-Kohen (the Ḥafetz Ḥayyim, 1838–1933, Poland), who specialized in the laws of defamation, ruled that any information that would cause harm to the accused must be revealed only if it could be legitimately introduced into a Jewish court of law,[94] Since the testimony of minors is usually inadmissible,[95] this would preclude many interventions to redeem a child from an abusive situation.

Some Jewish authorities, however, accept the testimony of minors if supported by other evidence,[96] and that is the way the CJLS has ruled. Children, after all, are not to be presumed untruthful, especially in matters as painful and personal as this, and corroborating external evidence can alleviate any doubt we might otherwise have. In any case, the report that must be given to civil authorities generally remains confidential and goes only to the governmental agencies responsible for child welfare, who must investigate further. Consequently, even if one takes the ruling of the Ḥafetz Ḥayyim as being authoritative, this should not prevent adults who listen to abused children tell their story or who see evidence of abuse from taking steps to have such complaints examined and, if proven accurate, acted on.

SHAMING ANOTHER
Similar remarks apply to the issue of shame. Judaism certainly prohibits embarrassing someone else publicly. Indeed, rabbinic statements compare public shaming of a person to killing him

or her, for one Hebrew way of saying "shaming another" is *malbin p'nai havero b'rabbim*—literally, "making his friend's face white in public," just as it becomes white in death.[97] Moreover, as mentioned earlier, an assailant must pay for the embarrassment caused to the victim and his or her family as part of the remedies for causing a personal injury. The Talmud, in fact, engages in a sophisticated discussion of the nature of shame, asking whether the heart of it is the victim's degradation in the public's esteem, in the victim's own sense of self-worth, or in the victim's family's embarrassment. These sources within the tradition that proscribe shaming others are all corollaries to the underlying theological principle of Judaism that human beings are worthy of respect as creatures of God created in the Divine image.[98]

Some things, though, take priority over this prohibition. Specifically, as in the case of defamatory speech, when shaming another is not done out of meanness or indifference but is rather an outgrowth of a practical or moral necessity, it is justified, permitted, and, in some cases, required. For example, if someone is committing fraud, a person who discovers this is not only allowed but also duty bound to expose the fraud. Even though that will inevitably embarrass the perpetrator, the overriding needs are to protect any future victims and to enable those who have already been defrauded to recover what they can.

If such monetary protections supersede the concern of shaming another, preventing bodily injury or even death does so all the more. As in the case of defamatory speech, we may not stand idly by but must rather expose the abuser so as to stop the abuse and get help for his or her victims. This is demanded, as explained above, both under the laws of *rodef* (the pursuer) and also under its legal root, the requirement to violate all but three of the commandments of the Torah in order to save the life of another (*pikkuah nefesh*). Identifying an abuser will inevitably cause him or her shame, and we should not do that any more than necessary. The Torah, after all, demands that we respect even the executed body of a murderer by not letting it remain unburied overnight.[99] But we are not only permitted but also required to override our concern for embarrassing the perpetrator to stop the abuse and to get help for the victims.

INFORMING CIVIL AUTHORITIES: THE ISSUE OF
MESIRAH

Traditional Jewish law forbids *mesirah*, turning Jews over to non-Jewish courts for judgment.[100] This prohibition undoubtedly arose out of two concerns. First, rampant discrimination against Jews in society generally made it unlikely that Jewish litigants would get a fair hearing. On the contrary, a dispute among Jews aired in a gentile court might provide the excuse for punishing both Jewish litigants and perhaps the entire Jewish community. Better that we Jews not call attention to ourselves altogether.

Moreover, rabbis over the generations wanted to make sure that Jewish law remained authoritative. In some times and places and for some purposes, Jews were forced to use non-Jewish law and courts. Specifically, if Jews were to engage in business with non-Jews, they had to use non-Jewish law, and it then became too cumbersome and too confusing to switch to Jewish law for their inter-Jewish trade. Moreover, doing so might well be unfair if all other business was regularly conducted according to the norms of another legal system, leading Jews to assume that the same rules applied to their trade with other Jews.

For these political and moral reasons, Samuel, a rabbi of the early third century, announced the principle of *dina de'-malkhuta dina*, "the law of the land is the law." That was restricted, though, to civil matters; and until the Enlightenment, Jews did, in fact, use Jewish courts to adjudicate even their own civil disputes, although often by the generally accepted, non-Jewish laws of commerce in force at the time. Since the permission to use non-Jewish courts embedded in the principle of *dina d'-malkhuta dina* applies only to commercial affairs, how then can a Jew in good conscience inform civil authorities about another Jew who is apparently abusing his or her family member, a child, or someone else?

Since the advent of the Enlightenment, a number of rabbis have ruled that the laws of *mesirah* no longer apply. Some, like the Shulchan Arukh, have maintained that using non-Jewish courts was prohibited only when they were unfair to Jews (and perhaps to others as well), and when the prosecution of a Jew in a non-Jewish court would be the occasion for persecution of the entire Jewish community. Since neither of these factors characterizes courts in modern Western democracies, Jews may use non-Jewish courts.[101]

Even if one maintains that the prohibition of using non-Jewish courts still holds, it would not apply to criminal matters, over which Jewish courts have no jurisdiction or power to punish. Thus Rabbi Moses Isserles, who lived in a pre-Enlightenment society (sixteenth-century Poland), cites others who lived even earlier who held that "if a person is struck by another, he may go to complain before the non-Jewish court even though he will thereby cause great harm to the assailant."[102] Since Jewish courts in our day have even less power and authority to handle such matters than they did in pre-Enlightenment times, Ashkenazic Jews, those whose ancestors came from central and eastern Europe, can rely on that ruling.

Sephardic Jews generally follow Rabbi Joseph Karo, author of the Shulchan Arukh on which Rabbi Isserles commented. Rabbi Karo asserted that the prohibition of *mesirah* continues to his day, making it illegal for a Jew who is being harassed to report that to the civil authorities. Even Karo, though, maintained that when there is a *meitzar ha-tzibbur*, a menace to the community as a whole, *mesirah* is permissible.[103] He was probably talking about non-Jews attacking the Jewish community as a whole for the reprehensible action of one of its members. Legal authorities in Western democracies in our day are unlikely to inflict penalties on the Jewish community as a group on the excuse that there are some Jews who are batterers; governments in the Americas, Europe, and other places are much more likely to prosecute such people as individuals, just as they would any other citizen who violated the law.

In our time, though, abuse of spouses, elderly parents, and especially, children has unfortunately reached the extent of a *meitzar ha-tzibbur* in three other senses. First, those who abuse others constitute a physical threat not just to the ones they have already abused but to all potential, future victims as well—and therefore to the entire community. Second, abusers pose a threat to the sense of well-being of the community as a whole by making it an unsafe place to live. Third, abusers within our community defame us as a community and the God whom we worship, and the desecration of the Divine Name (*hillul ha-Shem*) involved is also a source of pain and suffering for the community as a whole.

Consequently, it is certainly within the spirit of these precedents, if not their letter, to assert that for both Sephardic as well as Ashkenazic Jews, witnesses to abuse may, and indeed should, enlist the help of governmental agencies to stop the abuse. The Conservative movement's CJLS has accordingly ruled that witnesses to abuse should inform the police so that victims can avail themselves of the remedies and protections that civil law affords.[104]

Rabbis who are witness to abuse present a special case, for American law recognizes a clergy–client (usually called priest–penitent) privilege. Thus if a Jew in the course of counseling with his or her rabbi disclosed that he or she had engaged in spousal or child abuse, American law would protect the confidentiality of that disclosure unless the counselee waived that right or indicated his or her intention to engage in future abuse of the same kind. Absent either of those conditions, the rabbi might be successfully sued for breaching the counselee's privacy by reporting the past abuse to civil authorities, although some states interpret the immunity of clergy to the child abuse reporting laws very narrowly.[105] Suffice it to say, then, that the provisions in Jewish law demanding that we save life and limb would require those who know about an abusive situation to report it to the civil authorities so that it might end and, from the perspective of Jewish law, that would apply to rabbis no less than to any other Jew. Rabbis who become aware of an abusive situation in a counseling setting, however, should consult with an attorney to determine whether civil law in their jurisdiction grants them the right to report the matter in the specific case before them; if not, they should seek to end the abusive situation in some other way.[106]

DEFAMING GOD

Sometimes Jews' objections to reporting abuse to the civil authorities are not based on the specific law prohibiting handing Jews over to the non-Jewish courts (*mesirah*) but rather on one of the concerns that led to that law, specifically, *hillul ha-shem*, the prohibition of defaming the reputation of God and, by extension, of God's chosen people. Even if fair treatment can be ensured in the courts of modern Western democracies, the argument goes, reporting to governmental authorities that some Jews abuse their family members and thus making that fact public reflects poorly on the entire Jewish community and may even become the excuse for acts of anti-Semitism.

Hillul ha-Shem, though, cuts both ways. The Mishnah already cautions us that attempting to sequester a *hillul ha-Shem* will always be unsuccessful: "Whoever desecrates the name of Heaven in private will ultimately be punished in public; whether the desecration was committed unintentionally or intentionally, it is all the same when God's name is profaned."[107] That is especially so when civil law requires reporting abuse, for then Jews trying to hide the abuse will be correctly perceived as engaged in illegal, cover-up activities as well as unwise and uncaring conduct. This would be an even greater defamation of God's reputation (*hillul ha-Shem*) and, in addition, a threat to the welfare of the community (*meitzar ha-tzibbur*).

The Jewish community, like all other human communities, is not perfect. Jews cannot reasonably expect perfection of themselves, and non-Jews must likewise not expect that of Jews any more than they do of themselves. Jews and others should certainly strive to be God-like, but ultimately no human being is God. Therefore, we ultimately do more for our own reputation as a community and for the Name of God, our covenanted partner, if we own up to the problems in our community and try to deal with them honestly. *Hillul ha-Shem*, then, far from prompting us to try to hide the abuse that is going on among us, should instead motivate us to confront it and to root it out. Everyone worldwide knows that people sometimes do bad things and that some people do worse things than others; what gains respect is the honesty, sensitivity, and energy that a community shows in facing that problem squarely by making sure that justice is done and that safety is ensured within a context of human healing and repair for all concerned.

THE SCOPE OF PARENTAL PREROGATIVES

"And you shall teach your children diligently,"[108] a part of the first paragraph of the *Shema*, is an obligation that Jews know well. To fulfill that duty, parents may enlist the aid of teachers, but ultimately the responsibility rests with the parents. Consequently, Jewish law assumes that children would ordinarily reside with their parents so that they could fulfill this duty—in addition, of course, to providing the emotional bonding that is so vital to the well-being of the child.

Custody of children, however, is not automatically a parental right in Jewish law. It depends on the welfare of the child. Thus in divorce proceedings, for example, there is a *presumption* in the law that children beyond their sixth birthday are served best when they are living with the parent of the same gender.[109] The social situation in modern times has changed considerably, and that in itself may call this presumption into question in regard to contemporary custody decisions. The important thing for our purposes here, though, is that even in traditional Jewish law the presumption is rebuttable.[110] In particular, the welfare of the child and, as a corollary, the need to maintain close ties among all of the children can and often do override these gender-based assumptions.[111] A parent's right to have custody of his or her children, then, applies only when the welfare of the child is served by that arrangement.

In our case, if the child is in any danger of physical or sexual abuse, the welfare of the child would certainly supersede any parental claim to custody. Even if removal from the parental home would lead to the child's placement in a foster home or a non-Jewish institution, that must be done to save the life of the child. *Pikkuah nefesh* takes precedence over the positive obligation to teach one's children Torah and the negative command prohibiting the placing of a stumbling block before the blind, which, as I have discussed, was interpreted to include the educationally and morally blind.[112] Moreover, the one who reports the apparent abuse does not know that the child will be raised by non-Jews: The court may determine that abuse did not, in fact, take place, or, if it did, the court may (and probably will) place the child with other family members or other Jews, if possible. The Jewish community should certainly see it as an obligation to offer such Jewish facilities for children and adults who need them, as Jewish Family Service of Los Angeles, for example, does through Vista Del Mar (for children) and Grammercy Place and

Hope Cottage (for abused wives and their children). Even in the extreme case, however, when the child is ultimately taken from his or her parents and raised by non-Jews, one who reports such abuse to the authorities is correctly preferring the saving of the child's life over the other commandments mentioned above.

Thus the upshot of this section is that Jews must report both their own abuse and that of others to the civil authorities. None of the concerns usually proffered for failing to do that stands up under legal examination, for the prohibitions against defaming or shaming another person, handing over a Jew to non-Jewish authorities, and desecrating God's Name are all either set aside or more effectively fulfilled by ensuring that abused people get help. Similarly, saving the physical integrity and life of a child overrides the prerogatives of parents to retain custody. Ultimately, saving one's own life and safety and those of others supersedes all of these concerns and makes it imperative that we report the abuse of ourselves or others so as to extricate victims from life-threatening situations.

THE ABUSED PARTY: MAKING ONE'S WAY OUT OF AN ABUSIVE SITUATION

Victims of abuse in large percentages keep the abuse to themselves. Thus in the twenty countries studied in the report cited earlier, between 22 and 70 percent of women, depending on the country, never told anyone about the abuse.[113] Children are even more reticent to come forward with accusations of abuse.

With both women and children, several factors make this happen. Often they depend economically on their abusers and therefore worry that they will not be able to sustain themselves if they take steps to leave the abusive situation. Many times they feel attached to the abuser and thus hope that their lives together can continue but without the abuse. In such cases, they certainly do not want to embarrass or otherwise harm the abuser. Sometimes they feel at least partly to blame for the abuse themselves, however unwarranted that feeling may be. Ironically, the very laws mandating doctors, clergy, and psychological professionals to report suspected abuse may be stopping victims from getting help, because they fear that once the case becomes public in that way, their abuser will wreak revenge on them.[114] And children, in particular, need to mature considerably before they can recognize abuse for what it is and gain the strength and the information to seek ways to stop it.

Men who suffer abuse by their wives may be reticent to attest to the abuse and to get help in redressing it for all the reasons that apply to women, but for men there is an additional factor. Because men are acculturated to think that they are supposed to be the stronger sex, the shame involved for a man in admitting that he could not defend himself against a woman acts as a powerful deterrent to making the abuse public.

Although all these reasons for remaining in an abusive situation are understandable, the abused party has an even stronger duty in Jewish law to disclose the abuse than other people do. "Avoiding danger is a stronger obligation than any prohibition," the Talmud says.[115] As I have noted, saving a life supersedes all but three commandments and saving your own life is even more compulsory—if you can save only your own life or that of someone else, the Talmud rules that "your life takes precedence."[116] This imperative to extricate oneself from abuse applies even to cases in which the issue is not physical or sexual harm, but the victim is constantly subjected to verbal abuse. Thus if a parent becomes insane and continuously hurls insults at adult children, the Talmud and codes even permit the children to distance themselves from the verbally abusive parent as long as the children fulfill the command to honor their parents by providing for the parent's care at the hands of another.[117] Contemporary circumstances involving demented patients come immediately to mind, for this precedent makes it clear that one may, and probably should, place a parent in the advanced stages of dementia in a facility designed for that purpose so that the parent can be continuously protected against harming herself or himself and, when applicable, so that the children need not suffer the parent's verbal abuse.

These Jewish legal principles together mean that abused adults have a positive obligation to ignore all the issues discussed in the previous section—the prohibitions of defaming or shaming another, of handing someone over to governmental authorities, and of desecrating God—to save their own lives. Indeed, their duty to report an abuser to save their own lives is even greater than their responsibility to help others suffering abuse.

Minor children cannot be made legally responsible for extricating themselves from an abusive situation any more than they can be made responsible for any other command, but they certainly have the sanction of the tradition to reveal parental abuse to those who can help them, despite the defamation and shame involved and the undermining of parental prerogatives. The Talmud tells a story in which an elderly woman publicly shames her adult son and yet the son continues to honor her. In approving the son's actions, the Talmud was not sanctioning public degradation of children; quite the contrary, the story can make its point only if the reader assumes that normally parents should not publicly humiliate their children.[118] The concern for honor of parents, then, may not get in the way of preserving life and health, least of all one's own.

Consequently, abused adults must muster the courage to disclose the abuse to those who can help them out of the abusive circumstances in which they live, however much shame they initially feel in doing so. Abused, minor children, while not legally liable in Jewish law for doing this, are encouraged to do so. Both children and adults caught in this painful situation can take heart in the fact that ultimately such bravery not only may restore whatever dignity they lost in the process but also may actually increase their self-respect and honor as they escape the cycle of abuse and mistaken self-blame in which so many are unfortunately enmeshed.

THE ABUSER

INVESTIGATING AN ALLEGATION OF ABUSE

Until now, I have assumed that it is clear that a given person has abused another. While physical evidence and/or admission by the culprit make that so in many cases, the claim is not always undisputed. After all, multiple bruises attest to abuse, but they do not identify who inflicted it, and the accused may deny that he or she caused the harm. In some cases of alleged physical or sexual abuse, there may be no physical evidence at all. In recent, highly publicized cases before the American courts, the incidents happened years, if not decades, ago. What steps, then, must we take to confirm the abuse and the identity of the abuser?

In Jewish law, even more than in American law, a person is innocent until proven guilty. Thus, while American law accepts confession as proof in all matters, in Jewish law self-incrimination is "like a hundred witnesses" in civil matters,[119] but in criminal matters it is not accepted as a ground for court action.[120] Indeed, long before we get to the standards of evidence required in Jewish legal actions, we have the overarching principle that we may not slander people (*motzi shem ra*), let alone deprive them of their jobs or their freedom on the basis of such slander. While the Torah explicitly prohibits talebearing,[121] the Talmud hesitates to impose legal remedies for slander, owing to its general principle that legal redress can be exacted only if damage is done to another directly.[122] Nevertheless, later courts decreed severe legal remedies for slander, basing themselves on the Talmud's granting of power to inflict sanctions beyond the letter of the law if it is for the benefit of society.[123] Thus Rabbi Asher ben Jehiel (d. 1327, Germany/Spain) stated that in his time it was the custom of the courts everywhere to impose fines on "those who put others to shame with their words" and to assess the damages according to the social status of the offender and the victim.[124] Rabbis Karo and Isserles in the sixteenth century went further yet:

> If a man spits on his neighbor, he is liable to pay damages, but he should not pay if he only spits on his neighbor's garments or if he shames him verbally. But the courts everywhere and at all times should introduce legislation for this matter as they see fit. Some say that he is to be placed under a ban of excommunication until he pacifies the victim of his insult. [Gloss] And some say that he is to be flogged.[125]

Legal procedures exist, of course, to identify and punish those who commit wrongs. Mere suspicion of wrongdoing, however, does not constitute guilt, and slandering a person to make others incorrectly think that he or she committed an offense—or that it is confirmed that she or he did when that has not yet been determined—is thus itself a punishable crime.

Nowadays, rabbis outside the State of Israel do not have the authority to impose fines or lashes, but appropriate sanctions should be imposed on people who knowingly allege false charges to harm the accused or gain sympathy for themselves. So, for example, falsely accused people should avail themselves of any and all remedies prescribed in civil law. In addition, though, they have a right to expect the Jewish community to demonstrate its disgust at such behavior and its unwillingness to tolerate it. Depending on the situation, that might include dismissal from a job in the Jewish community (on grounds of moral turpitude); expulsion from the camp, school, or synagogue in which the incident took place; and, minimally, a demand for a public apology. In the process of dealing with such an instance within a community, the relevant laws prohibiting defamation (*motzi shem ra*), lying (*sheker*), and even the related law about plotting witnesses (*edim zomemim*)[126] should be taught, along with their rabbinic developments, so that this instance may become the occasion to teach people the kinds of speech the Jewish tradition expects Jews to avoid.

All sanctions imposed on the accuser, of course, apply only to cases where no abuse had occurred and the accuser knew that; they would not be appropriate in cases where there is reasonable question as to whether the defendant's actions constitute abuse or not. In such cases, the accuser, in lodging the complaint, acted out of an honest, even if mistaken, understanding of the situation and is blameless for doing so. The defendant can then dispute that understanding in a judicial tribunal if she or he thinks that the accuser misconstrued the situation, and the judges can decide.

I know of a case in which a youngster at a Jewish camp accused his teacher of hitting him. There were no witnesses, there was no bruise, and the teacher denied it altogether. Even though the camper had been in trouble with other staff members on other occasions, and even though the teacher had had an unblemished record in these matters, the camp authorities chose to remove the teacher from his position for fear of a lawsuit by the youngster's parents. I certainly understand that fear, especially given today's litigious society, but Jewish law would not countenance that action. In our zeal to protect our students and families from abuse, we must not ride roughshod over the reputations, the livelihoods, and the very lives of the accused simply because they are accused.

However, other elements of Jewish law create a real tension surrounding these concerns. While the law rightly puts the burden of proof on an accuser, in cases of family violence we must recognize that it takes an immense amount of courage just to assert the abuse publicly, let alone to find ways to stop it. We might, therefore, have good reason to trust the innocence and trustworthiness of those who accuse others of abuse more than we normally trust accusers. Moreover, as much as we are commanded by our tradition to assume the innocence of the accused, we are also commanded not to stand idly by while the life or safety of others is threatened and, indeed, to take steps to save them. Child and spousal abuse, after all, are real. Nobody is disputing that. Indeed, family violence of all types is an enormous problem in contemporary society, and it clearly must stop. In the process of rooting it out, however, we must be diligent in preserving the presumption of innocence firmly embedded in the Jewish and American traditions while we also take steps to protect those who may have been harmed and may be hurt again.

In all of these matters, it would be well for us to remember *both* sides of Sir Mathew Hale's famous eighteenth-century dictum to a jury: Rape "is an accusation easily to be made and once made, hard to be proved, and harder to be defended by the party accused, tho [sic] never so innocent."[127] We must, on the one hand, not dismiss out of hand the accusations of children and adults of physical, sexual, or verbal abuse. Indeed, given the courage required to come forward, we must afford them our credence and trust. On the other hand, though, we must remember that, in the many cases in which there are no witnesses or physical evidence, the credibility of such accusations must be weighed against a strong presumption of the innocence of the accused until and unless a finding of guilt is reached by an appropriate tribunal.

Although attaining such a balance of duties can be very hard when the matter is approached legally, most often legal guilt or innocence is not the issue facing the rabbi, educator, or lay leader of the Jewish community. Instead, someone comes forward and asserts abuse at the hands of another person, perhaps a family member. Rabbis, teachers, and other Jews must not simply send the person home with the instructions to do what he or she can to restore peace in the home; that only reinforces the sense that the Jewish community does not want to acknowledge family violence within its ranks and will not protect its victims. Worse, it also tells victims that they are to blame for the abuse, which, if it is true abuse, is never the case.

Without prejudging the accuracy of the person's claims, the rabbi, family member, teacher, counselor, or friend is better advised to accept the accusation at face value, leaving it to the legal authorities to determine its truth later, and immediately help the person extricate herself or himself from the abuse. In the case of children, many states require reporting the suspicion of abuse to the civil authorities. With both children and adults, it will mean attentively listening to victims, expressing trust in them and support for them, and finding ways for them to extricate themselves from the abusive situation. If the abuse occurred years ago, it will require finding an effective response to the wounds that it caused, whether through legal action, personal or family counseling, the abuser's active steps to make amends, or some combination of these and other measures. In diagnosing abuse and in discerning an appropriate response, Jewish Family Service and other such agencies with expertise in these matters can be of immense help.

When people come forward with claims of abuse, probably the key things for rabbis and other Jewish professionals to understand is that they should *not* immediately assume a legal posture and endeavor to determine whether the claim is true or not, and they definitely should *not* deny the claim outright or become defensive. We do, indeed, need to ascertain the guilt or innocence of the accused carefully and fairly, but the immediate task at hand in most cases is to help people extricate themselves from what they at least perceive to be situations of abuse. The difficulty of coming forward and the intense demand that the Jewish tradition puts on us of saving people from danger must be paramount in our minds and in our actions.

MAKING AMENDS
When a fair hearing determines that there is sufficient evidence that a given person has abused another, in addition to whatever civil or criminal penalties apply, Jewish families and communi-

ties need to take steps to ensure that the offender cannot continue the abuse. This may mean, for a family, moving out of the quarters occupied by the abuser or forcing him or her to move out of theirs, and it may mean, for a Jewish school, youth group, or camp, relieving the person of her or his job and perhaps even ostracizing the abuser from the community.

At the same time, the Jewish tradition puts great faith in the ability of those who do wrong to make amends and correct their behavior. It never expects us to be perfect: Jewish liturgy, after all, has us say three times each day, "Forgive us, our Father, for we have sinned," and every Yom Kippur evening we know full well that next year we will be back trying to cleanse our souls once again. The date is already scheduled! That does not mean, however, that efforts to improve oneself are fruitless and that we, therefore, have no duty to try. Quite the contrary, Judaism imposes a positive obligation on us to do *teshuvah*, to take steps to return to the proper path, and it assumes that we can do it if we really try.

What are those steps? Although I describe them in some detail in the next chapter, suffice it to say here that the process includes the following:

1. Acknowledgment of the wrong.
2. Remorse.
3. Public confession.
4. Asking for forgiveness from the aggrieved party.
5. Restitution to the extent that that is possible.
6. Refraining from committing the wrongful act the next time the opportunity arises.[128]

The famous twelve-step programs used to help people with addictions of various sorts have strong echoes with these traditional steps in Judaism; that is why Jewish forms of those programs have quite naturally emerged.[129] They offer one form of changing abusive behavior. In addition, Parents Anonymous for those who physically abuse their children and Parents United for those who sexually abuse their children are also built on some of the same wisdom embodied in the Jewish process of *teshuvah*. Going through such a program, of course, is anything but easy, for it seeks to change long-standing behavior.

Indeed, unless successful therapy has intervened through programs such as these, people who were themselves abused as children are more likely than the general population to abuse their own children. At the same time, most people who have been abused do not abuse others, usually because they have found a caring community who confirm their own self-worth despite the degradation they suffered from the abuse. That fact makes it all the more imperative for synagogues to extricate victims from the contexts in which they suffer abuse and to find them supportive environments so that they can begin to rebuild their self-esteem. It also argues for synagogues to sponsor groups such as Parents Anonymous and Parents United—or at least to refer those of their members who abuse family members to such groups.

In regard to the abuser, it is critical for synagogues to accept the steps of *teshuvah* as making the person worthy of reinstatement into the community as a whole. *Teshuvah*, after all, is difficult, especially when it involves deeply rooted behavior patterns such as the ones we are discussing. No wonder, then, that the Talmud says that fully righteous people (*zaddikim*) cannot stand in the same place as those who have repented, for the strength needed to repent is much greater than the strength needed to be good in the first place.[130]

If one succeeds in reversing a history of abuse, one attains the status of a person who has returned (*ba'al teshuvah*). American law makes convicts who have served their sentence indicate their criminal past on all sorts of documents, and such people often continue to be denied voting privileges, the right to apply for a government job, etc. Jewish law requires us to trust the process of return (*teshuvah*) much more strongly. It mandates that Jews not even mention the person's past violations, let alone bar him or her from full participation in society. Such recounting of the person's wrongful deeds is categorized as verbal abuse (*ona'at devarim*) itself. Moreover, it puts obstacles in the way of those who try to do better, a violation of the biblical command, "Before a blind person you may not put an obstacle."[131] Thus the Jewish tradition strongly encourages abusers to seek help to control their abusive drives, promising full restitution in legal, social, and theological status if they succeed.

The abuser, however, must go through all these steps to be accorded the renewed status of good standing within the community. Punishment by the civil authorities is not sufficient. For example, I was consulted in a case in which a man who for years was head of his synagogue's Cub Scout troop was later accused by a number of his former charges of sexual abuse. On the strength of the testimony of these teenagers, he was sent to prison. When he was released, he wanted to join the synagogue once again. He refused, however, to acknowledge that he had ever done anything wrong. That does not constitute *teshuvah*, despite the time he had spent in prison, and so the congregation was right in refusing to readmit him to membership.

If the man in this example had instead fulfilled the requirements of *teshuvah*, the congregation would be duty bound to readmit him to membership but would not be obliged to reinstate him as its Cub Scout leader. Although one may not routinely remind the offender or anyone else of his or her past offense, one both may and should invoke that information in making decisions about the ways in which that person is permitted to interact with others. People may fully meet the requirements of *teshuvah* and yet continue to be sorely tempted to repeat their offense if the opportunity arises. For such people, it is a favor neither to the offender nor to the people he or she may harm to put the culprit in a situation in which such temptation exists; that would be "putting an obstacle before the blind." The past offense is enough of a ground to suspect that the offender may remain weak willed in this area and likely to harm others once again. This is especially true for child abusers, whose behavior is so deeply rooted in their psyche that it is often impossible to undo.

Therefore, even though we may not gratuitously mention an offense or bar the person from activities irrelevant to the offense, we both may and should use that knowledge to help the offender avoid tempting situations and to protect others at the same time.[132] We need to support people in their efforts to return to proper behavior, but we are not obligated to give such people opportunities to test their new resolve, especially when the welfare of others is at stake.

As a result, it may well be that, for some abusers, full *teshuvah* may not be possible. For its own protection and for the sake of the abuser too, the community may not afford the abuser the opportunity to complete the last stage of *teshuvah*, where the sinner confronts the same situation in which he or she previously sinned and acts differently. In such cases, the community, recognizing that that is the case not because of a failure in the abuser's resolve to do *teshuvah* but rather because of its own decision, may reinstate the abuser into the community, despite his or her failure to complete the process of *teshuvah*, for all purposes except for functioning in situations in which he or she was previously abusive. The process of *teshuvah*, as described in the sources, may not be possible or appropriate for all cases, and the community's norms must respond accordingly.[133]

THE ROLE OF RABBIS, EDUCATORS, AND LAY LEADERS

What can rabbis and Jewish educators do to prevent abuse or at least alleviate its consequences? The Clergy Advisory Board of the California Department of Social Services produced a short pamphlet that was distributed to clergy of all religions throughout the state.[134] It focuses on child abuse, but its recommendations can easily be adapted to spousal or parental abuse as well. In this section, I paraphrase and embellish on the pamphlet's instructions, generalizing them to apply to spousal abuse as well as child abuse, to jurisdictions outside California, to educators and lay leaders as well as rabbis, and to specifically Jewish concerns and contexts.

Learn to recognize abuse. If you fail to recognize the signs of abuse in your congregation, school, camp, or youth group, the abuse will undoubtedly continue. The opportunity to protect people from future abuse is often lost because of ignorance, denial, or fear of interference. Professional schools should mandate training for their students, and professional organizations should provide continuing education for their members, regarding how to discern potentially abusive situations, how to take family histories that include instances of abuse, how to provide religious counseling for abusers and their victims, and how to know which other professionals within the community should be called on to help in both preventive and curative actions.

Do not assume that you can handle the situation alone. While clergy can be critical in helping victims and perpetrators of abuse, they should not try to do this alone. If abuse is going to be stopped and its effects ameliorated, professionals of various sorts must be called on. One clergy member is quoted in the pamphlet as saying, "A father divulged to me that he was molesting his daughter. He was repentant. I prayed with him, but did not seek further help to protect the victim. She later made a serious attempt on her life because, even after repentance and prayer, the father had continued to molest. It shook me."

Know and obey your government's requirements to report abuse to legal authorities. Many states, provinces, and cities have enacted laws that require clergy and teachers, as well as physicians, to report abuse to legal authorities. Exactly what must be reported, and to whom, varies. California law, for instance, wants rabbis and teachers to err on the side of caution in that it specifies that educational and religious professionals must report even *suspicions* of abuse and leave it to legal authorities to determine whether those suspicions are well founded. The laws in other places may be different, going further in the direction of protecting the accused. In cases of spousal abuse, reports are generally made to the police, and in some locations that is true for child abuse as well; in other places, instances of child abuse are to be reported to the Office of Children's Protective Services (or the equivalent agency of state or local government).

Sometimes clergy or teachers become aware of abuse through the confession of a congregant in a private counseling setting, and that raises questions of confidentiality. As I discussed in Chapter Two, though, the law of most jurisdictions follows the California *Tarasoff* case in specifically requiring professionals to break professional–client confidentiality when the client (congregant) plans to threaten the safety or physical welfare of anyone in the future, and the law protects professionals from lawsuits complaining of such a breach of confidentiality.

In any case, rabbis and teachers everywhere have a legal responsibility to be on the alert for instances of family violence and to report such cases to legal authorities when civil law requires it. Failure to do so may subject rabbis or teachers personally, as well as the religious or educational institution for which they work, to both civil and criminal prosecution. Insurance companies are increasingly restricting their coverage so that they can avoid liability for such suits, thus making the institutions and their personnel all the more legally exposed.

Protect your congregation or school from potential abusers. People who prey on children often seek positions that will give them access to, and authority over, children. Potential molesters cannot, of course, be identified by appearance alone. Synagogues, schools, youth groups, and camps, though, should, as part of their hiring policies and procedures, take measures to screen out those likely to molest the children under their care. This is important not only for the institutions and their charges but also for the molester as a function of the ban on putting a stumbling block before the blind—in this case, the morally blind who might be tempted to use their position of authority to abuse those in their care.

This, of course, is easier said than done, for as much as institutions must prevent molesters from being part of their staff, they also must avoid making unfair and unwarranted judgments of applicants. They certainly must not base their decisions on prejudices—say, against males or against homosexuals (the overwhelming majority of convicted child molesters are heterosexual). At the same time, though, background checks should include attention to this aspect of a person's history.

The abuser may be a colleague. Rabbis, cantors, and Jewish educators as well as clergy of other faiths have unfortunately been involved in some highly publicized cases of abuse of various sorts. Due process, of course, must be applied in any investigation of such allegations, and the presumption of innocence must be preserved. If child, spousal, or other abuse by a rabbi, cantor, or educator is confirmed, however, other Jewish professionals on the staff and in the vicinity must be prepared to respond to the scandal and the public outrage. As the California pamphlet puts it, "While the needs of the victim are primary, compassion needs to be extended to the injured religious community and the perpetrator as well." In addition, steps must be taken to heal the community, help it avoid such incidents in the future, and bring the perpetrator both to justice and to the process of *teshuvah.*

Clergy and educators can take specific steps to prevent and alleviate this problem. In addition to the steps described above, the California pamphlet mentions several others. First, provide child and spousal abuse services, and support other communal efforts to do the same:

> Anything that your community of faith does to strengthen families is child [and spousal] abuse prevention. For some at-risk families, participation in religious services is their only real support system. You can reach out to families in isolation and turmoil by addressing parenting [and spousal] issues through sermons, study groups, or by sponsoring public forums.[135]

Such discussions may well center on some of the topics I covered in Chapter Three, because that material provides a safe forum for opening people up to talking about all issues of human intimacy, including these troubling ones, and it does so in the context of Jewish conceptions, laws, and values. In addition, Mother's Day or Father's Day or the story of the binding of Isaac read on Rosh Hashanah or during the year may be used as an occasion for a worship service, forum, sermon, or readings on these subjects.

In addition, synagogues and Jewish federations should support efforts, typically by Jewish Family Service agencies, to establish safe houses with kosher facilities for victims of abuse. As a joint effort of synagogues and Jewish Family Service, synagogue services should be made available to residents in such facilities, and experts in this area from Jewish Family Service should be called on for preventive and educational programs within our synagogues and educational institutions.

Second, use the power of the religion and the community to deter abuse. Rabbi Simhah spoke of excommunicating a wife beater from the congregation, exactly what the synagogue did in the case of the child abuser who was imprisoned and later wanted to rejoin the synagogue without doing full *teshuvah*. Others might argue that there is a better chance that continued membership within the community will more likely bring a change in behavior; if a synagogue follows that course, it can and should still express its disgust for abuse by, for example, refusing to give honors or positions of leadership to those known to be physically or verbally abusive to others. Rabbis should not hesitate to use theological language in explaining to abusers that such behavior is not only a violation of a Jewish communal norm but also a transgression of God's will as embedded in Jewish law and values.

Third, counsel adult survivors of abuse. Adults who abuse others were often abused themselves as children. If they are going to be able to break the cycle of abuse, they will need considerable counseling, instruction in good patterns of family interactions (since, by hypothesis, while growing up they never saw firsthand how families can handle their tensions in a healthy way), and positive reinforcement for dealing with problems in nonabusive ways. Synagogues can, for example, form support groups for adult children of abuse, with opportunities to express their rage and to learn how to create a healthy family life; Jewish Family Service may be of aid in establishing and staffing such groups.

Fourth, address the spiritual aspect of healing. Rabbis and other Jews all too often underestimate the role of religious conviction in aiding the healing process. Virtually all of the twelve-step programs place heavy reliance on faith in God, not only because historically such programs emerged from Christian faith communities but also because healing is assisted greatly when a person feels aided not only by other people who have the same problem but also by God. We Jews need to cease to be embarrassed by such religious language. We should unself-consciously invoke the religious tenets of our tradition to help people who have been abused to heal the wounds of the past and to reconstruct and redirect their lives.[136]

RECONNECTING WITH GOD'S IMAGE WITHIN US

The Jewish responses to family violence that I explored in this chapter are all deeply rooted in Jewish views of God and humanity. In secular systems of thought, abuse is problematic because it violates the Golden Rule and more generous, humanitarian concerns. When the topic is abuse within the family, further matters arise, including the resultant inability of the family to provide the safety, warmth, and education on which society depends and the inherent violation of the sanctity of the family. Judaism shares all of these concerns, but it also believes that abuse of another represents a denial of God's image in every human being.

In conceiving of the situation in that way, Judaism also can provide a real source of strength for abused people struggling to escape from their situation and to rebuild their lives. No matter how much someone else has diminished your self-image, Judaism is telling you that you were created in the image of God. Among other things, that means that, like God, you have inherent worth, regardless of what anyone else says or does. That Divine value represents a challenge, for we must all strive throughout our lives to realize the Divine within us. It is a challenge, though, that gives life meaning and hope.

The following "High Holy Day Message" from the Jewish Theological Seminary of America—published in *Newsweek*, *The New York Times*, and *The Wall Street Journal*—summarizes these themes nicely:

> "Know whom you put to shame, for in the likeness of God is (s)he made." (*Genesis Rabbah* 24:8)
>
> Some people who are reading this were beaten yesterday, or terrorized, or kept in isolation.
>
> Some who tormented them are reading this now.
>
> And they are not strangers to each other; they are family.
>
> Intimates. People like us. Us.
>
> Home should be a haven, the place where you can count on being valued and protected.
>
> If instead it is a place where the people closest to you beat you up, or keep you on edge with threats, or isolate and demean you— then what is safe?
>
> Violence in the family is not love; it is not discipline; it is not deserved. It is an abuse of power, and it is wrong—because decent people don't behave that way; because it is against the law, and for one more reason: we are all made in the image of God.
>
> To lash out in violence—especially against someone whose life is linked with yours—is to violate a likeness of God, and to degrade that likeness in yourself.
>
> **Are you being hurt or humiliated by the person you are closest to?**
>
> **Believe that you do not deserve the abuse.**

No one has the right to tell you that you are worthless: your worth comes from God.

Have you been taking out your anger and frustration against the people who depend on you?

Know that you are better than that; you are made in the image of God. You have the power to stop hurting and belittling them. God gives it to you.

To all who read this, we ask:

- Look at yourself, at your partner, at your elderly parents, at your children, as images of God. Treat each of them with the respect which that demands.

- Make your home a haven. Instead of raising your hand or your voice, raise your own dignity and the self-esteem of the people who turn to you for love. You may not be able to perfect the world, but this much you can do.

- Help your religious community to face the fact of domestic violence and to offer active support to those who have been enduring abuse, threats, and humiliation. A house of God should be a place for teaching restraint, decency, and reverence; make yours that place.

- *Behave as though God made you worthy; it is true. Behave as though the world depends on your humanity and decency. It does.*

". . . for the sin which we have committed before Thee, openly and in secret . . ."

High Holy Day Liturgy[137]

CHAPTER SIX

The Elements of Forgiveness

OR SIXTEEN YEARS, I SPENT PART OF MY SUMMERS AS THE RABBI in residence at Camp Ramah in California, a camp affiliated with the Conservative movement in Judaism. In addition to teaching staff classes, I made it a point to get involved in as many camp activities as I could.

One summer, there was an immense feud between two bunks of twelve-year-old boys. The counselors, the division head, and even the camp psychologist had tried to bring some peace, but to no avail. As a last resort, they asked me to do what I could.

GOD'S ROLE IN FORGIVENESS: THE GUIDANCE OF THE PRAYER BOOK

When I met with both groups of boys together, I handed out prayer books. I could see the boys' eyes roll and their eyebrows lift: Here was the rabbi doing his thing again!

I had them look at a section of the weekday *Amidah*, which, together with the *Shema* and its attached blessings, constitutes the core of the morning service. The *Amidah* is built on nineteen blessings of God together with accompanying paragraphs that expand on the themes of those blessings. In the first three paragraphs, the parties to the prayers that follow are identified together with their primary relationships: the people praying are the descendants of Abraham, for whom God was a shield; God is the source of power, even to the point of resurrecting the dead in the future; and just as God was manifest in the past and will be in the future, so too we now experience God as holy—that is, as wholly Other.

Immediately after identifying the parties to Jewish prayer in that way, the *Amidah* turns to these three blessings, the fourth, fifth and sixth of the *Amidah*:

4. You graciously give human beings knowledge and teach people understanding. Graciously grant us of Your knowledge, discernment, and wisdom. Blessed are You, Lord, who graciously grants knowledge.

5. Return us, our Father, to Your Torah, and bring us close, Our Sovereign, to Your worship. And bring us back in complete return (*teshuvah*) to You. Blessed are You, Lord, who wants return.

6. Forgive us, our Father, for we have missed the mark; have compassion on us, Our Sovereign, for we have transgressed, for You show compassion and forgive. Blessed are You, Lord, compassionate One who forgives often.

The fourth blessing articulates our gratitude for what we are first aware of after identifying who we are and who God is—namely, that we know things. Specifically, we have, as the prayer says, *de'ah* (information), *binah* (the ability to distinguish the difference between things, or analytical knowledge), and *haskel* (the wisdom gained from experience). We thank God immediately for such forms of knowledge because, in the mode of Descartes, our consciousness of knowing things is one of the first and most fundamental things we recognize about ourselves and, probably, also because our knowledge distinguishes us from the other animals and is a prerequisite for our free will.

The very next blessing, though, has us asking God to help us return to Him. That is, as soon as we think about what we know about ourselves, we recognize that we make mistakes and even deliberately sin. The blessing, then, asks God to help us return to Him. We have hope that God will indeed aid us in this task because we know God to be, as the prayer says, One who desires human return.[1]

Finally, in the sixth blessing, having invoked God's aid in helping us return to Him, we ask God for forgiveness. We can do that because God is not only One who wants our return, but also One who is known to be compassionate and forgiving when we take steps to return.

OBSTACLES TO ASKING FOR FORGIVENESS

After studying these paragraphs with the boys from camp (twenty-four of them altogether), I asked them why they thought that the prayer book asks God to help us return to Him. I suggested that instead of thinking about offending God, which may be difficult to fathom, they should think about parallel situations in human relationships. When the question was posed that way, the boys were amazingly forthcoming and astute in identifying the factors that make asking for forgiveness hard. I rephrase, summarize, and add to that discussion here, but I continue to be impressed by how much of this list the boys themselves articulated. Specifically, then, to ask for forgiveness is hard because you must do the following:

- Give up your self-image of being morally innocent, together with any defenses that you may have established to reinforce that self-image. This is very hard on the ego.
- Give up any moral claims to the effect that you were in the right after all. This requires you to relinquish your superior moral position in the argument, thus dramatically diminishing your status and power in the relationship with the person you have wronged.
- Acknowledge that you have done wrong—that is, asking for forgiveness requires that you not only abandon the general, positive view that you have of yourself but accept a negative evaluation of what you did. None of us likes to admit that.
- Articulate that admission to the wronged party. It is not enough to realize in your own mind that you have done something wrong to another; you must admit that fact openly to the wronged party. This is humiliating.
- Trust the other person to be both willing and able to overcome the many impediments to forgiveness (delineated below) so that the other person can and will extend himself or herself in response to your request for forgiveness. If the wronged party refuses to forgive you, that only compounds the

humiliation you feel. In fact, if that happens, you wonder whether you should have admitted the wrong in the first place, for now you have lost your edge in the argument. You inevitably also feel angry that your willingness to humble yourself to seek forgiveness was not met by a reciprocal willingness on the part of the wronged party to take steps to repair the relationship. Indeed, you may feel that now you are the wronged party.

These factors in human interactions, I pointed out to the two groups of boys, amply explain why the prayer book begins with asking God to be willing to forgive. Only if God—and, by extension, people—are open to the possibility of forgiveness can it ever happen. Given the numerous and difficult obstacles to such openness, one can understand why the prayer book first has us ask God to be open to our return. Otherwise, no request for forgiveness can even be heard, let alone granted. And if it is hard to ask forgiveness from God, who, after all, is known to desire our return, it is all the more difficult to ask forgiveness from human beings we have wronged; in that context, no such openness is ensured and, on the contrary, the offender has every reason to fear that the victim will shun him or her.

OBSTACLES TO FORGIVING

Turning then to the sixth blessing, I asked the boys to tell me why the other side of the coin is hard, too. Once again, I rephrase and add to the answers they gave me, but the boys were amazingly astute in identifying the factors that make forgiving someone hard.

You, as the victim, have to give up your claims to justice, that you have been wronged and that the offender owes you something. Some of the reticence to do this stems from the human penchant to want to get even and to carry a grudge—characteristics that the Torah specifically requires us to suppress in commanding us "Do not take vengeance or carry a grudge, but rather love your neighbor as yourself; I am the Lord."[2] Even if you can overcome your desire to get back at the offender in the mode of "an eye for an eye," you still may feel reluctant to forgive because you rightfully feel that he or she owes you something.

That is, even if retribution may not be in order, compensation may be—and, indeed, the Rabbis of the Mishnah and Talmud specifically interpret "an eye for an eye" to mean *not* that the victim should exact retribution on the offender but rather that the offender must compensate the victim monetarily.[3] For these legitimate expressions of the demand for justice to be fulfilled, then, the victim may justifiably require the offender to pay for monetary damages and perhaps also a fine (what we would call today punitive damages). Even with such compensation, though, it is often hard to overcome the sense that no compensation can adequately make up for your loss—either because that actually is the case, as, for example, when something has been damaged that had emotional attachments for you, or simply because you like the old and familiar thing rather than the new replacement.

You, the victim, have to overcome your feelings of vulnerability. After all, the offender has invaded your space, as it were, and has harmed you in a way that you were not able to prevent. That inevitably compromises your own feelings of safety and integrity.

You have to trust that the offender will not harm you (or anyone else) again. Given the inherent fallibility and selfishness of people, nobody and nothing can provide an ironclad guarantee that people will not harm others, but since you were just recently injured by this particular person, it is especially difficult to muster such trust in regard to him or her. Toward that end, you might require that, to the extent that it is possible, the person take concrete steps to lessen the chances that the behavior will be repeated.

FACTORS PROMOTING FORGIVENESS

With all three of these factors mitigating against forgiveness, why would anyone forgive anyone else? Here, too, my twelve-year-olds had a keen sense of the matter, although I expand on their comments somewhat. You forgive someone else because of the following reasons.

You yourself do bad things and want to be forgiven when that happens. This was by far the most prevalent rationale for

211

forgiving others offered by the boys, stemming out of a painful but conscious recognition on their part that each of us is just as fallible as the next person.

You want to restore your relationship with the offender, albeit on a different footing. After all, if you never forgive someone who wrongs you, you will never have any friends.

You need to get past this incident to get on with your life. You, therefore, forgive the other person even if you would really prefer that the offender never darken your doorstep again. This is admittedly a selfish rationale for forgiveness, and it does not bode well for the future of your relationship with the offender, but sometimes you decide that it does not matter, especially when you were not that close to the person in the first place.

You want to do the right thing. Even if you still feel vulnerable and lack trust in the ability or even the intention of the offender to act differently in the future, you might forgive the person as an act of moral principle or, as I suggested to the boys, as a way of imitating God.

PARDON, FORGIVE, AND RECONCILE

One other issue emerged from our discussion that day. The very words we were using needed to be more carefully defined so that we were sure we understood what we were thinking and saying.

The words "pardon" and "excuse" are often used interchangeably, as, for example, when you brush up against someone accidentally and say either "Pardon me" or "Excuse me." In legal contexts the two terms are used in different settings but nevertheless denote a similar phenomenon. Specifically, I might have violated the law but will not be punished because I had a valid excuse—for example, if I drove through many stop lights to get my wife to the hospital in time to deliver our baby or if I killed someone in self-defense. The violation still stands, but no punishment is warranted. Similarly, when a governor pardons a prisoner, the record will still show that the prisoner violated the law; that does not go away. Only the punishment is curtailed.

Forgiveness involves one step more: The original violation is itself removed and thus certainly any punishment that might have resulted from that violation. The injured parties might still remember the transgression and even take some precautions to make sure that they will not suffer that way again; but if they forgive the perpetrator, they accept him or her into their good graces once again and treat that person as they did before the violation—with, of course, the possible exception of taking precautions against being violated that way again. Thus forgiveness prepares the parties for resuming their relationship as fully as they can.

Finally, in reconciliation the transgressor becomes part of the friendship, family, or community again, despite the bad feelings that have been generated by what he or she did. Neither pardon nor forgiveness alone produces reconciliation; they only help the parties set aside the bad feelings that have soured their relationship. Pardon or forgiveness, in other words, brings the parties back to neutral ground. Once that is done, both parties must take positive steps to rebuild the relationship and restore genuinely good feelings. Note also that while forgiveness is totally within the power of the victim, reconciliation can happen only if both parties agree to resume their relationship.

Reconciliation can take place whether or not the sin remains—that is, whether the reconciliation has been preceded by pardon or forgiveness. The terms of the reconciliation, though, will usually be more generous and open-handed if the sin is wiped away—that is, if forgiveness, and not just pardon, has occurred.

If the sin remains and only pardon has been achieved, the conditions under which the transgressor may function in the relationship are often restricted. This, in effect, is what the United States does with felons who have served their time: They are returned to the community, but they may not become police officers or vote, and they must report their crime each time they apply for employment. In contrast to this, Jewish law requires that once a transgressor has endured what the court decrees his or her punishment to be, members of the community may not even mention the crime, unless such discussion is geared to the practical purpose of safeguarding the community from future violation. Speaking about the person's former crime to anyone for any other reason is, from the point of Jewish law, itself a violation of the commandment prohibiting us from oppressing our neighbors—this being a form of verbal oppression.[4] In other words, Jewish law requires that transgressors be forgiven and not just pardoned.

This distinction between reconciliation based on pardon or grounded in forgiveness is exactly parallel to how the sin offering worked in the sacrificial cult in the ancient Temple. As Professor Jacob Milgrom pointed out, the offerings that Leviticus 4 demands of the community, the chieftain, and the commoner to induce God's forgiveness for an unintentional sin do not really bring forgiveness—that is, the wiping away of sin—but rather reconciliation based on pardon:

> The rendering "forgive" for *salah* is, in reality, not accurate. When God grants *salah* to Moses' request for it (Numbers 14:19–20), it cannot connote forgiveness, considering that God qualifies it by declaring that all of adult Israel, with the exception of Caleb, will perish in the wilderness (vv. 21–24). Furthermore, in the entire Bible only God dispenses *salah*, never humans. Thus, we confront a concept that must be set apart from anthropopathic notions: it does not convey the pardon or forgiveness that humans are capable of extending. Finally, because Moses invokes God's dreaded attribute of vertical retribution (v. 18; cf. Exod. 34:7), he clearly does not have forgiveness in mind. All he asks is that God be reconciled with his people; punish Israel, yes, but do not abandon it. Indeed, in the episode of the golden calf, God answers Moses' request for *salah* by renewing the covenant (Exod. 34:9–10). . . .
>
> By the same token, the offender who brings the *hatta't* [sin offering] does so because he knows that his wrong, though committed inadvertently, has polluted the altar and hence, has alienated him from God. By his sacrifice he hopes to repair the broken relationship. He therefore seeks more than forgiveness. If God will accept his sacrifice, he will be once again restored to grace, at one with his deity.[5]

In his penultimate sentence here, Milgrom calls "forgiveness" what I have called "pardon." Indeed, the sinner wants exactly what forgiveness entails—namely, restoring the relationship to as much of its former strength as possible.

In any case, I did not go over this biblical material with the boys, but we did distinguish these various forms of rapprochement. At the end of this discussion, I scheduled another session with them and asked them to think, in the meantime, of the concrete things the two groups might do to overcome the obstacles to forgiveness—that is, those things that would open them up to forgiving others and those things that would prompt them to ask for forgiveness themselves.

In that session, after hearing and discussing their suggestions, I explained that Judaism does not assume that we are perfect. On the other hand, it does not proclaim that we are innately sinful either, very much contrary to the Christian doctrine of Original Sin. Instead, the Rabbis assert that we each have two inclinations, one to do good and one to do bad,[6] and God gives us instruction in the Torah (the literal meaning of the word "Torah" is precisely "instruction") to help us control our penchant to harm others and to foster our desire to do good. That is, we cannot expect ourselves or others to be perfect; indeed, we ask God for forgiveness not only on the High Holy Days, when we concentrate on that part of our religious lives, but three times each day when we recite the three paragraphs of the *Amidah* that we had studied. We must, then, not be overly hard on ourselves or others. At the same time, we must demand of ourselves and others that we all do what we can to avoid or at least repair any wrong or bad act that we have done, and we must actively seek to do right and good things.[7] As Rabbi Tarfon said, in one of my favorite rabbinic sayings, "Yours is not to finish the task, but neither are you free to desist from it."[8]

THE PROCESS OF RETURN (*TESHUVAH*): BECOMING WORTHY OF FORGIVENESS

How does one make amends? This is well described in the Jewish concept of *teshuvah* (return). This is not just repentance, from the Latin root meaning "to pay back." It is a full-blown return to the right path and to good standing with the community and, indeed, with God. Hence the prayer that we had studied blesses God for accepting us back in His good graces when we endure a punishment, and it says that God "desires return"— that is, a return to the relationship we had with God before sinning. Jewish sources then prescribe that the same process for returning to God be used when we need to repair our relationship with another human being.

To explain that concept to the boys from camp, I handed out paragraphs from Maimonides' famous formulation of it.

Maimonides (1140–1204), the great rabbi, physician, and philosopher, wrote a code of Jewish law, the *Mishneh Torah,* in which he organized and summarized the Jewish legal tradition to his time, combining elements from the Bible, Mishnah, Talmud, responsa (rabbinic rulings in specific cases), customs, and the ongoing tradition. In the section on the process of return, his philosophical as well as his legal skills are in evidence, because he defined the elements of return as clearly and carefully as possible. Maimonides did not, however, provide a simple list of the elements of return, as one might expect from a systematizer like him, undoubtedly because the appropriate process of return depends, in part, on the specific nature of the transgression. I nevertheless asked the boys to identify the elements of the process of return as they appear in these paragraphs and then put them in the order that they would most likely occur.

Below is an English translation of the paragraphs I distributed to the boys. The extract is from the section of Maimonides' code titled "Laws of Return." I retained the masculine language to be true to the original, even though, as the first biblical passage Maimonides quoted makes clear, women are subject to the same laws in Judaism, whether as perpetrators or as victims.

Chapter One

1. [For] all of the commandments of the Torah, whether positive [that is, commanding someone to do something] or negative [commanding someone not to do something], if a person transgressed one of them, whether intentionally or unknowingly, when he goes through the process of return and returns from his transgression, he must confess before God, blessed be He, for the Torah says, "When a man or a woman commits any wrong toward a fellow person . . . he must confess the wrong that he has done" (Numbers 5:6-7). This is a confession expressed in words [and not just thought]. Such a confession is a positive commandment. . . . And similarly anyone who injures his fellow or damages his property—even though he paid him what he owes him—does not atone until he confesses and returns [refrains] from ever doing anything similar again, for the Torah says, "*any* wrong [literally, "from *all* the wrongs of a person" or "from *all* the wrongs toward a fellow person"—and not just those against God]. . . .

3. In our time, when the Temple does not exist and we do not have its altar of atonement [through animal sacrifices], we have no alternative but the process of return. The process of return

atones for all transgressions. Even if a person was wicked all his days and engaged in the process of return only in the end, we do not mention anything about his wickedness, as the Bible says, "the wickedness of the wicked shall not cause him to stumble when he turns back from his wickedness" (Ezekiel 33:12). The essence of the Day of Atonement also atones for those who engage in the process of return, as the Torah says, "For on this day He will wipe your slate clean" (Leviticus 16:30). . . .

Chapter Two

1. What is complete return? [It occurs when] a person encounters something in which he transgressed [previously] and it is possible for him to do it [again] but he separates himself from it and does not do it, not because of fear and not because of failure of strength, but rather because he has undergone the process of return. For example, if a man had forbidden sexual relations with a woman, and after some time he was alone with her and still loved her and still had strength of body and was [even] in the same locale where he had transgressed previously with her, but he separated himself [from her] and did not transgress, that is a person who has effected complete return. . . . And if he did not engage in the process of return until his old age, when it was impossible for him to do what he used to do, even though that is not the best kind of return, nevertheless it is effective for him and he attains the status of one who has returned. Even if he transgressed all his days and engaged in the process of return on the day of his death and then died in a state of return, all his sins are forgiven, as the Bible says, "Before the sun and light and moon and stars grow dark, and the clouds come back again after the rain" (Ecclesiastes 12:2)—that is, the day of death. From this we learn that if he remembered his Creator and engaged in the process of return before he died, he is forgiven.

2. And what is return? It is that the sinner abandon his sin, remove it from his thoughts, and resolve in his heart that he will not do it any more, as the Bible says, "Let the wicked give up his ways . . ." (Isaiah 55:7). Moreover, he will have remorse over the fact that he transgressed, as the Bible says, "Now that I have turned back, I am filled with remorse" (Jeremiah 31:18 [31:19 in some English translations]). And the One who knows all secrets must testify that he will not return to this sin ever, as the Bible says, ["Return, O Israel, to the Lord your God, for you have fallen because of your sin. Take words with you and return to the Lord. Say to Him, 'Forgive all guilt and accept what is good; instead of bulls we will pay the offering of our lips. Assyria will not save us . . .] nor ever again will we call our handiwork our god [since in You alone orphans find pity]" (Hosea 4:2-4). And he must make oral confession, articulating the resolutions that he made in his heart.

3. Anyone who confessed with words but did not resolve in his heart to forsake [his former ways] is like one who immerses himself [in a ritual pool of water to regain a state of ritual purity] but has a reptile in his hands [which makes him impure again immediately], for the immersion will not benefit him until he throws away the reptile. And so the Bible says: "[He who conceals his transgressions will not succeed, but] He who confesses and gives them up will find mercy" (Proverbs 28:13). And he must spell out the sin in detail, as the Bible says, "Alas, this people is guilty of a great sin in making for themselves a god of gold" (Exodus 32:31) [thus specifying "the great sin"].

4. Some of the modes of manifesting repentance are: (a) the penitent cries continuously before God in tears and supplications; (b) performs acts of charity as much as he can; (c) distances himself greatly from the matter in which he sinned; (d) changes his name, as if to say: "I am a different person, not the same person who committed those deeds;" (e) changes all of his actions for the good and for the right path; and (f) exiles himself from his place [of residence], for exile wipes away sin, for it causes one to be submissive and to be humble and meek in spirit.[9]

5. It is highly praiseworthy in a penitent to make public confession, proclaiming his sins to them [the community], revealing his transgressions against other people [Rashi on B. *Yoma* 86b: so that they will intercede with the victim to ask him to forgive the perpetrator]. He [the one engaged in the process of return] says to them: "Truly, I have sinned against so-and-so, and did this and that to him, but today I repent [return] and feel remorse." He, however, who is proud and does not publish his trespasses but conceals them, has not achieved complete return, as the Bible says, "He who conceals his transgressions will not succeed" (Proverbs 28:13). This only applies to transgressions of one person against another, but with regard to sins committed against God, the person need not publish them [to the community]. Indeed, it is a mark of effrontery on his part if he publicizes them [Rashi on B. *Yoma* 86b: for he diminishes the Name, or reputation, of God through his public proclamation of his willful transgression of God's commands. Moreover, as B. *Berakhot* 34b maintains, publicly proclaiming sins against God makes it seem as if he is not embarrassed by them]. He should rather repent of them before the Almighty, blessed be He, declaring in detail his sins before Him, and make public confession in general terms; and it is well for him that his iniquity has not become known, as it is said, "Happy is he whose transgression is forgiven, whose sin is covered over" (Psalms 32:1).[10]

6. Even though return and supplication are always good, they are particularly so and are immediately accepted during the ten days

between Rosh Hashanah (New Year) and Yom Kippur (the Day of Atonement), as the Bible says, "Seek the Lord when He may be found" (Isaiah 55:6). This only applies, however, to an individual. But as for a community, whenever its members return and offer supplications with sincere hearts, they are answered, as the Torah says, "For what great nation is there that has a god so close at hand as is the Lord our God whenever we call upon Him?" (Deuteronomy 4:7). . . .

9. The process of return and the Day of Atonement only atone for transgressions against God, as, for example, when one has eaten a forbidden food or indulged in illicit sexual relations. But transgressions against another person—as, for example, if one wounds, curses, or robs someone are never forgiven until the injured party has received the [monetary] compensation due him and has been appeased. Even if the perpetrator has compensated the victim, the wrongdoer must also appease the one he has injured and ask his forgiveness. Even if a person only annoyed another in words, he has to pacify the latter and entreat him until he has obtained his forgiveness. If, however, the injured party is unwilling to forgive, he [the perpetrator] should bring three of his [the victim's] friends at one time, and they should entreat the person offended and solicit his pardon. If they fail, he [the offender] should take with him a second and even a third group. If the offended person continues obdurate, the wrongdoer leaves him alone and goes away; the one who refused to forgive is now the sinner. But if the victim was the offender's teacher, the pupil has to go to him again and again, even a thousand times, until pardon has been granted.

10. It is forbidden to be obdurate and not allow oneself to be appeased. On the contrary, one should be easily pacified and difficult to anger. Moreover, when asked by an offender for forgiveness, one should forgive with a sincere mind and a willing spirit. Even if one had been much vexed and grievously wronged, he is not to avenge nor bear a grudge (Leviticus 19:18). . . .

11. If a person sinned against another and the latter died before pardon was sought, the offender should bring ten men, station them at the grave of the deceased, and, in their presence, declare: "I sinned against the Lord, God of Israel, and against this individual, having committed such-and-such a wrong against him." If he owed the deceased money, he should pay it to the heirs. If he did not know any of the heirs, he should deposit the amount in court and confess.

What, then, are the elements of the process of forgiveness as described by Maimonides? While the order and even the elements on the list may differ according to the specific offense and the particular way in which one interprets Maimonides, one possible interpretation is the following:

1. Acknowledgment that one has done something wrong.
2. Public confession of one's wrongdoing to both God and the community.
3. Public expression of remorse.
4. Resolve by the offender not to sin in this way again (perhaps announced publicly).
5. Compensation of the victim for the injury inflicted accompanied by acts of charity to others.
6. Sincere request of forgiveness by the victim—with the help of the victim's friends and up to three times, if necessary (and even more if the victim is one's teacher).
7. Avoidance of the conditions that caused the offense, perhaps even to the point of moving to a new locale.
8. Acting differently when confronted with the same situation in which the offender sinned the first time.

The first four steps may possibly take place amid crying and entreaties for forgiveness and, in the most serious of cases, may even include changing one's name.

RETURN: ITS PROBLEMS AND PROMISE
Avoidance Versus Confrontation of Temptation

Of the elements of forgiveness just delineated, steps seven and eight are mutually contradictory, for offenders cannot possibly act differently in the same situation if they have intentionally removed themselves from tempting contexts. My own reading of this makes the proper course depend on the circumstances. It is undoubtedly right and proper, for example, for pedophiles to remove themselves from children as much as possible. That will mean that they will never be able to effect full return, but they can surely accomplish a great measure of return, and it is more important to protect innocent children from abuse than to enable pedophiles to achieve full return. One would certainly not want to entrust such a person with a position of responsibility for children, such as a teacher, coach, youth group leader, or camp counselor.[11] Thus the return of which Jewish sources speak is *not* necessarily to the same position that the person occupied before committing the offense; it is rather to good standing with God and within the community—albeit a standing that the community can and should limit for its own protection.

This strategy of avoidance is also commonly invoked in twelve-step programs for those addicted to alcohol, drugs, gambling, overeating, and the like. Similarly, placing convicted gang members in a new city after they are released from prison may remove the possibility of full return, in that we will never know whether these people are now strong enough to resist all of the lures of their old neighborhood. However, this may be completely acceptable if it also gives them a stronger chance to begin a new life free from gang activities. On the other hand, when the risk cannot be avoided without curtailing human interaction altogether—for example, when the offense is gossip or petty theft or illicit sexual intercourse—then avoiding the risks of recurring sin is impossible (the bad news) but full return becomes possible (the good news).

THE DUTY VERSUS THE GRACE TO FORGIVE

Note too that forgiveness becomes the *duty* of the victim after the offender has done his or her best to make amends and to act differently in the future and has asked for forgiveness at most three times. In many cases, the victim may hesitate to forgive for all the reasons that I enumerated earlier, but when the offender has undergone the entire process of return, forgiveness is required, even when the wrong can never be fully righted.

It certainly makes sense that God should impose a duty on us to forgive each other. We thereby become closer replicas of Him, and we also overcome our alienation from each other. A good God would presumably want such things.

Forgiving, though, requires one to overcome feelings of hostility and revenge. Experientially, then, forgiveness seems more like an act that goes beyond moral duty, a supererogatory act rooted not in our sense of duty but in our capability for charity and benevolence. How can these feelings be reconciled with Judaism's insistence that forgiveness is a moral duty?

The answer lies in the Jewish approach to moral education. Optimally, of course, you should do the right thing for the right reason. When that is not possible, though, should you wait to act until you acquire the right motivation, or should you do the right act now even though it is for the wrong rationale? Immanuel Kant, who emphasized intention as the key element in determining the moral character of an act, would say the former: Wait to act until you can do so out of a sense of moral principle. Judaism, though, stands at the opposite end of that spectrum: "A person should always do the right thing even for the wrong reason," the Rabbis said, "for in doing the right thing for an ulterior motive one will come to do it for the right motive."[12] Thus even though one feels like anything but forgiving someone, once the transgressor has gone through the process of return, the victim must do all in his or her power to forgive the person. In such cases, it is duty that is at work rather than charity; at some point, we hope, the victim will be able to forgive out of a sense of charity too.[13]

This means, of course, that for Judaism forgiveness is not exclusively, or even primarily, an internal, psychological process. Typical of Judaism's emphasis on action, the concept of forgiveness that emerges out of the Jewish tradition stresses the actions that the perpetrator must take to return to God and the community and, in turn, the actions that the community must take in welcoming him or her back. It is, in other words, an *interpersonal* process, not an internal, psychological one. Judaism certainly harbors the hope that the feelings of the perpetrator, the victim, and the community will ultimately follow along, thereby creating the foundation for reconciliation and even renewed friendship; but the essence of forgiveness, for the Jewish tradition, is not acquiring a new feeling about each other, but rather acting on the demands that the duty of forgiveness imposes on us so that we can live together as a community worthy of God's presence.

THE SCOPE OF THE DUTY TO FORGIVE

The Jewish tradition's description of the process of return also helps us define those cases in which forgiveness should not be granted. So, for example, if the offender never admits wrongdoing, then even if he or she has served a prison term, the very first step in return has not been achieved and no forgiveness can legitimately be demanded of the victims. I described just such a case in Chapter Five, in which a synagogue's Cub Scout leader was convicted of sexually abusing the boys in his den. Because he never admitted that he had done anything wrong, the community was under no obligation to forgive him or to restore his membership to the synagogue.

JUSTICE AND MERCY

Even in cases in which the person does not complete the process of *teshuvah*, though, it is not always easy to identify a proper response to the perpetrator, for just as Judaism values justice, so too it values compassion and mercy. This flies in the face of many Christian stereotypes of Judaism, which see Judaism as a religion of law and Christianity as a religion of love. Neither is exclusively true. Christianity speaks much of God's love, but it also values justice. Conversely, Judaism places great emphasis on justice and law, but only because it understands love to be most effectively expressed in families and societies where there are good laws.

Even so, sometimes the requirements of law must be set aside in an act of mercy. Thus on the Day of Atonement we Jews ask God Himself to move from his seat of justice to his seat of mercy in judging us, and since God is our paradigm, we too must manifest such compassion. The Rabbis said this explicitly:

> "To walk in all His ways" (Deuteronomy 11:22). These are the ways of the Holy One: "gracious and compassionate, patient, abounding in kindness and faithfulness, assuring love for a thousand generations, forgiving iniquity, transgression, and sin, and granting pardon . . ." (Exodus 34:6). This means that just as God is gracious and compassionate, you too must be gracious and compassionate. "The Lord is righteous in all His ways and loving in all His deeds" (Psalms 145:17). As the Holy One is righteous, you too must be righteous. As the Holy One is loving, you too must be loving.[14]

Note that the Rabbis, in this famous homily, cut off the biblical passage in the middle. According to the Bible, God is "gracious and compassionate . . . forgiving iniquity, transgression, and sin; yet He does *not* remit all punishment, but visits the iniquity of fathers upon children and children's children, upon the third and fourth generations." The Rabbis, in one of their most audacious moments, stop the sentence in the middle and thereby change the biblical view of God into a much more forgiving, rabbinic view—and it is this rabbinic editing of the biblical verse that is repeated many times in the High Holy Day liturgy. Even for the Rabbis, though, God is *both* righteous and compassionate, and His love is a product of His ability to balance both.

Similarly, although gross offenses should probably not be forgiven without sincere attempts to engage in the process of return, one might be prone to forgive more minor offenses without such a process, both as a pragmatic way of getting on with one's life and possibly of restoring a friendship and also as an expression of the religious demand that we imitate God. Such free forgiveness, though, becomes harder to justify as the offense grows larger, especially if it affects not only one's property but also one's person and especially if its nasty effects persist. Then God's righteousness seems to be the divine attribute that we should emulate. Knowing just how to strike the requisite balance between justice and mercy when deciding when and whom to forgive, though, is often easier said than done—and is itself an expression of the godly in us.

LIMITS TO FORGIVENESS
Are there sins for which no forgiveness is justified even after going through the process of return?

Communities
In defining who may, and who may not, join the Israelite community, the Torah itself forbids forgiveness to three specific communities and insists that Israelites actively seek to destroy one of them:

> No Ammonite or Moabite shall be admitted into the congregation of the Lord; none of their descendants, even in the tenth generation, shall ever be admitted into the congregation of the Lord, because they did not meet you with food and water on your journey after you left Egypt, and because they hired Balaam, son of Beor, from Pethor of Aram-naharaim to curse you. . . . You shall never concern yourself with their welfare or benefit as long as you live. . . .
>
> Remember what Amalek did to you on your journey, after you left Egypt—how, undeterred by fear of God, he surprised you on the march, when you were famished and weary, and cut down all the stragglers in your rear. Therefore, when the Lord your God

grants you safety from all your enemies around you in the land that the Lord your God is giving you as a hereditary portion, you shall blot out the memory of Amalek from under heaven. Do not forget![15]

On the other hand, that same passage in Deuteronomy prescribes that the Edomites be forgiven for not allowing the Israelites to pass through their territory on their trek from Egypt, "for he is your kinsman." Presumably kinsmen are owed a greater measure of forgiveness than other people deserve. Deuteronomy even insists that the Israelites forgive the Egyptians—despite the fact that they enslaved the Israelites for hundreds of years—"for you were a stranger in his land." Thus the fact that the Egyptians provided a place to live, albeit under terrible conditions, also requires the Israelites ultimately to forgive them. In both these cases, though, three generations must elapse before they can be fully admitted to the Israelite community, for by then the community that committed the trespasses and the community of Israelites that suffered them will have passed out of existence: "You shall not abhor an Edomite, for he is your kinsman. You shall not abhor an Egyptian, for you were a stranger in his land. Children born to them may be admitted into the congregation of the Lord in the third generation."[16]

Thus there are apparently some communities that do such egregious acts that they may never be forgiven, but other nations can and should be forgiven, at least after the passage of some time. The Torah does not describe in any more detail the criteria by which to judge which communities of the future are to be forgiven their trespasses against the People Israel and which not. This, of course, raises major issues in our own time, when Jews need to decide how they are going to reconcile with present-day Germans, Poles, Austrians, and others. Many of the problems concern moral standing: The people asking for forgiveness—or at least for reconciliation—were, for the most part, not even born during the atrocities of the Holocaust, let alone responsible for them; and, conversely, the people being asked for forgiveness were likewise, for the most part, not even born during the Holocaust and therefore did not suffer directly from it—although members of their immediate or extended families may well have done so. Do we inherit our ancestors' guilt and thus their ability to ask for forgiveness? Do we inherit our ancestors' pain and injury and thus their standing to forgive? If not, is forgiveness possible a generation or two later? Even if forgiveness is impossible, is reconciliation attainable then? I dealt with these issues elsewhere,[17] but suffice it to say here that the Torah clearly draws distinctions between communities that can and should be forgiven and those that cannot and should not be, and the latter group constitutes a limit to the scope of forgiveness.

Individuals

Since forgiveness is completely within the power of victims, they *can* forgive any offender, whether or not he or she deserves it—assuming, of course, that the victim survived the offense.[18] Are there any individuals, though, who *should not* be forgiven even if they go through the process of return? That is, are there any offenses that are so egregious that the process of return is not powerful enough to cleanse the offender and make him or her worthy of restoration to the community? Are there any offenses that even God does not and should not forgive?

Maimonides reflected the ambivalence of the tradition on this issue. On the one hand, relying on a number of talmudic passages, he compiled a list of offenses that are so heinous that even God does not forgive their perpetrators, and he stated this in very strong language:

> The following have no portion in the world to come, but are cut off and perish, and for their great wickedness and sinfulness are condemned for ever and ever: heretics and scoffing skeptics; those who deny the [authority of the] Torah, the resurrection of the dead, or the coming of the Redeemer; apostates; those who cause a multitude to sin; those who secede from the ways of the community; anyone who commits transgressions like [King] Jehoiakim, in high-handed fashion and openly; informers [against the Jewish community to the government]; those who terrorize a community for other than religious purposes; murderers and slanderers; and those who pull down their foreskin [to obliterate the circumcision, the physical mark of Israel's Covenant with God].[19]

In the following paragraphs of his code, Maimonides defines each of these categories, specifying what each category means and the various classes of people who fall under each one, for a total of twenty-four groups. At the end, though, he said this:

> When it is said that one who commits any of these sins has no portion in the world to come, that statement is to be understood as applying only to the sinner who dies without going through the process of return. If he returned from his wickedness and died while in the process of return, though, he is of those who will have a portion in the world to come; for there is nothing that stands in the way of return.[20]

When one thinks of contemporary history, Hitler and Stalin come to mind as people to whom forgiveness should be permanently denied. Similarly, those who have committed genocide in Cambodia, Bosnia, and Rwanda fall under this category. Their actions were depraved, repeated, and with malice aforethought, and we have no evidence of any remorse, let alone the other steps of return.

How far, though, does this stretch? Would it be improper ever to forgive, for example, fathers who sexually abuse their daughters or mothers who abandon their newborn infants in garbage dumps? What about mass murderers? More generally, is the number of people affected a factor? The seriousness of the offense? The lack of mitigating circumstances? The lack of remorse or any attempts at return? On the other hand, should there *ever* be those to whom we deny return altogether? Would that be in keeping with modeling ourselves after a just, but compassionate, God? Jewish sources do not resolve these issues. What emerges is a strong belief that people can change for the better and that they must be given the opportunity to do so. This is grounded in Judaism's strong assertion of human free will. Maimonides, in fact, maintained that it is only "stupid gentiles and mentally incompetent Israelites" who deny that people have the ability to choose good or evil, for if that were not the case, he pointed out,

> how could the Almighty have charged us, through the Prophets, "Do this and do not do that, improve your ways, do not follow your wicked impulses," when, from the beginning of his existence, his destiny had already been decreed, or his innate constitution irresistibly drew him to that from which he could not set himself free? What room would there be for the whole of the Torah? By what right or justice could God punish the wicked or reward the righteous?[21]

Along with free will, though, comes responsibility, and so forgiveness is deserved only by those who accept responsibility for their wrongful actions, show remorse for them, and seek to make amends through the process of return described above. Even then, according to some sources, certain offenses cannot be atoned for; people who commit them can never repair the wrong that they have done and warrant restoration to friendship and good standing in the community. These sources suggest that even God does not forgive such offenses. According to other Jewish sources, though, the possibility of return exists even for those who have committed the most egregious sins.

That tension in the sources, is, in my view, right on target, for in truth we do not know in such cases whether forgiveness is possible or warranted. Probably the most eloquent expression of that dilemma is Simon Wiesenthal's story "The Sunflower." In it, a Nazi who was a member of the SS and admitted to having killed Jews is on his deathbed. He asks Wiesenthal to be his confessor and grant him forgiveness. The story is followed by a symposium of thirty-two people, including such important religious thinkers as Edward Flannery, Abraham Heschel, Primo Levi, Martin Marty, John Oesterreicher, and Cynthia Ozick.[22]

Although some of the respondents were sure that Wiesenthal had the right to forgive but then took differing stances as to whether he should have, others were not sure that he even had that standing in the first place. What emerges from the symposium is thus not clear guidance at all, but rather deep ambivalence—an ambivalence that is, in my judgment, exactly appropriate. Sometimes we simply do not know who, if anyone, has the authority to forgive; at other times, we know who can forgive but do not know whether forgiveness is warranted.

THE PROMISE OF FORGIVENESS

Fortunately, though, in most of our lives, the instances when we are called on to ask for forgiveness or to forgive others are not nearly as serious as the mass murders committed by the ex-Nazi asking for forgiveness on his deathbed. Moreover, usually it is the victim who is asked, not a surrogate, and that removes the hard issue of whether anyone can forgive an offense against someone else, even a relative. Forgiveness is often hard, and asking for forgiveness is also hard, but fortunately in most of our lives the degree of difficulty does not approach that in Wiesenthal's story. For that alone we should be thankful.

To return to the camp boys whose conflict started this chapter, I surely cannot report utopian results. After our sessions, though, they did find ways to become civil to each other and even to do some things together with a sense of cooperation, respect, and, yes, by the end of the summer, even friendship. Through it all, it was truly amazing for me to see how the liturgy and the recipe for return in classical Jewish sources could take on deep emotional, intellectual, and practical meanings in the lives of modern-day people.

CHAPTER SEVEN

Hope and Destiny

ASIDE FROM THE FORGIVENESS AND RECONCILIATION THAT WE strive to achieve in our interpersonal relations, what should we hope for? How should we imagine our ultimate destiny?

These questions may sound very remote and even metaphysical, and in certain respects they are. They have, though, an important effect on how we live our lives, just as goals always have on our efforts to achieve them. To make this concrete, I focus on how these matters affect the way in which Jewish tradition would have Jews think about and approach the end of life. In doing so, I do not repeat the specifically medical matters that I discussed at some length in *Matters of Life and Death*, except to the extent that that is necessary to explain issues of hope and destiny. I instead am interested in the end of life as one clear example of how Jewish views of hope and destiny frame all moral and personal decisions in life. To make the point even stronger, I intersperse some other examples as well. In this way I demonstrate in this last chapter of the book that its topic, hope and destiny, frames the whole of life and affects all of our concrete decisions; we need only look beyond the immediate concern and think, as Judaism would have us do, from the perspective of Judaism's ultimate goals and ends.

Hope is a central Jewish concept. The anthem of the modern State of Israel, in fact, is titled *Ha-Tikvah*, "The Hope." Traditional Jewish expressions of hope apply to what can be attained in this life, in a Messianic future, and in life after death. Such hopes, according to the Jewish tradition, are not unrealistic or Pollyannish: They are grounded in reality as Judaism perceives it—its understanding of God, of individuals and communities, and of human destiny. These convictions also define the *limits* of legitimate hope as they shape Jewish moral directives for life in general and for medical decisions in particular. I thus describe each of those perceptions in turn, indicating how each affects what Judaism would have us do and feel in difficult moral situations.

GOD

While God in the Jewish tradition is transcendent and awesome, the dominant emphases in Jewish theology are on God's immanence and beneficence. God is portrayed in the Bible as morally good, and God describes Himself as "a God compassionate and gracious, slow to anger, abounding in kindness and faithfulness, extending kindness to the thousandth generation, forgiving iniquity, transgression, and sin."[1] Moreover, God is described many times in the Bible as our Healer,[2] and the Torah promises that if we obey God's commandments, God will prevent illness in the first place.[3] Indeed, in thinking about the relationship between God and illness, we must remember that most of us for most of our lives are healthy. We dare not take that for granted. It is a strong piece of evidence for a benevolent and compassionate God. These aspects of God can and should buoy up a sick person's hope.

The biblical God, however, also enforces moral norms, and illness is listed as one of the punishments God inflicts for sin.[4] This aspect of Jewish theology can actually undermine the hope of the ill. If someone has indeed sinned—and who of us has not?—this doctrine can dampen hope for recovery and any effort to achieve it, prompting instead resignation to the just punishment of God.

Worse, the apparently innocent get sick, sometimes seriously so. Then, too, some of us are born with disabilities, including painful ones. When such things happen, the traditional tie between illness and sin causes perplexity and anger. Moreover, the ill and disabled and their relatives and friends conclude from such occurrences that nothing makes moral sense in the world, that God is capricious and that, therefore, no matter how innocent a disabled infant is, and no matter how good a person has been, God cannot be trusted to help people to overcome disabilities or illness.

These reactions are particularly evident in the biblical Book of Job, where Job's wife, responding to the multiple calamities that had befallen her husband, advises him to blaspheme God and die rather than endure further pain and suffering.[5] Job reproaches her for expecting only good from God, and he says "Naked came I out of my mother's womb, and naked shall I return there; the Lord has given, and the Lord has taken away; blessed be the name of the Lord."[6] Nevertheless, he cursed the day of his birth,[7] for he could find no meaning in his suffering and no explanation to exonerate God. The theological doctrine of the linkage of illness with sin, then, coupled with the manifest evidence of innocent people suffering, makes God arbitrary and immoral at worst and inscrutable at best, and neither of those results supports the plausibility of hope by the disabled or ill or by those who care for them.

Balancing these perspectives between God as the compassionate Healer and God as the stern and sometimes enigmatic enforcer of moral norms is the ongoing task not only of Jewish theologians but also of rabbis and other Jews as they minister to the disabled and the sick. We often are not able to explain God's role in the cause of disability and illness. That has led some Jewish theologians to revise their concept of God, so that God is either not personal at all and, therefore, cannot be expected to apply or even know of morality or that God, while personal and moral, is limited in power and, therefore, disability and illness occur despite God's will that they should not. Hope, then, to the extent that it is available, springs from human bonding in facing the disability or illness and, depending on the theology, possibly from God's ability (even if limited) to achieve some good results.[8]

However, most contemporary Jewish theologians, even in the face of the Holocaust, have reaffirmed the traditional concept of a personal God who is inherently moral and demands morality of us. To reconcile that belief with the phenomenon of innocent people suffering, such theologians either invoke the world to come as the place where our moral accounts will be rectified and the unjustifiably disabled or sick will reap their due reward, or they maintain that we simply do not know why God inflicts unjustified pain or at least permits the innocent to suffer. In maintaining either or both of these tenets, they are reiterating classical rabbinic theology found in the Talmud and Midrash, although often with new twists. In any case, according to these theologians, we, like Job, must continue to have faith in God for other compelling reasons, including especially the many good things that most of us enjoy in much of our life, with health and love as prime examples.[9]

INDIVIDUALS AND COMMUNITY

PROVIDING PHYSICAL SUPPORT

According to the Jewish tradition, God created and owns everything in the universe.[10] This includes our bodies throughout our lives and even in death. God has granted us the normal use of our bodies during our lifetimes, and that inevitably involves some dangers and risks; but God, as owner, imposes specific requirements and prohibitions intended to preserve our life and health as much as possible. That requires, negatively, that we do not abuse our bodies[11] and, positively, that we take steps to prevent illness through proper diet, exercise, sleep, and hygiene.[12]

God's ownership of our bodies is also behind every Jew's obligation to help other people escape sickness, injury, and death.[13] This duty does not rest on some general (and vague) humanitarian reason or on anticipated reciprocity; it rather grows out of our role in helping God preserve what is His. Specialized training makes physicians especially able and, therefore, especially obligated to aid people in overcoming illness,[14] but we all share in that duty. On the basis of Leviticus 19:16 ("Nor shall you stand idly by the blood of your fellow"), the Talmud proclaims that obligation to provide medical aid encompasses expenditure of the community's financial resources for this purpose. And Nahmanides understood the community's obligation to provide medical care as one of many applications of the Torah's principle "And you shall love your neighbor as yourself."[15]

Conversely, the individual Jew, when ill, has the reciprocal obligation to seek medical care. Thus Jews may not live in a community without a physician,[16] for to live outside easy reach of a physician would be to endanger our bodies unduly and thus to renege on our duty to preserve God's property.

We should certainly pray for God's help in bringing healing, for God is the ultimate Healer, but we may not merely depend on God: We must also take steps to prevent illness in ourselves and in the public at large, and we must consult physicians and follow their advice to restore health when we fall ill. God's partnership with each of us, and with health care workers in particular, in preserving and restoring health provides theological grounding for our hope for a healthy life, for recovery from illness when it occurs, and for the strength to cope with disabilities. In addition to these divine characteristics that should buttress hope, the duty of the community to care for each other should provide the physical support disabled and sick people need, thus buoying their hope for recovery or at least amelioration of their disability or disease.

PROVIDING EMOTIONAL AND SOCIAL SUPPORT

The Jewish tradition has always asserted an intimate interaction among all human faculties—body, mind, emotions, will. Instead of dividing body from soul, the Bible differentiates one's *shem* (usually translated as "one's name," but meaning one's identity to the outside world) from one's *nefesh* (usually translated "soul" but meaning one's inner being, one's own understanding of oneself). We do differ in our own eyes and thoughts from the picture that others have of us. The Rabbis, who knew Greek thought, used the language of body and soul, but in a number of rabbinic sources they strongly affirmed the intertwining of our faculties, either explicitly or implicitly. So, for example, according to one popular rabbinic story, God does not judge the body and soul of a person separately but rather as one, united whole;[17] and the rabbinic recipe for life is to combine study with a worldly occupation: "An excellent thing is the study of Torah combined with some worldly occupation, for the labor demanded by both of them causes sinful inclinations to be forgotten. All study of Torah without work must, in the end, be futile and become the cause of sin."[18]

Given the strong emphasis on the integration of body and soul, it is not surprising that in Jewish law the community's obligations to support healing include not only medical ministrations but psychological and social support as well. The major advances in contemporary medicine, and the American culture of seeking technological solutions for every problem, have accustomed us to focus exclusively on the physical aspects of healing. Long before medicine could do very much to conquer illness, though, the Rabbis realized that social support could make a big difference in the struggle to regain health. They thus decreed the obligation of visiting the sick (biqqur holim), claiming that in visiting the sick we imitate God:

> "Follow the Lord your God" (Deuteronomy 13:5). What does this mean? Is it possible for a mortal to follow God's Presence? The verse means to teach us that we should follow the attributes of the Holy One, praised be He. As He clothed the naked, for it is written, "And the Lord God made for Adam and for his wife coats of skin and clothed them" (Genesis 3:21), so you should clothe the naked. The Holy One, blessed be He, visited the sick, for it is written [after the description of Abraham's circumcision], "And the Lord appeared to him near the oaks of Mamre" (Genesis 18:1), so you should visit the sick. The Holy One, blessed be He, comforted those who mourned . . . and so should you comfort mourners. The Holy One, blessed be He, buried the dead . . . and so should you bury the dead.[19]

Moreover, visiting the sick, as an act of both loyalty and kindness (hesed), is one of a small list of commandments for which there is no limit and that "yield immediate fruit and continue to yield fruit in time to come" (or "in the world to come").[20]

What, though, does one do when visiting the sick? Both patients and visitors quickly tire of talking about the weather and the food served. The visitors already feel uncomfortable being around someone who reminds them of their own vulnerability; the need to find a topic of conversation other than what may be a grim prognosis makes matters even worse—and deters many from coming for a visit in the first place.

The Rabbis recognized this in their directions for such visits. First, visitors should not stand over the patient. That body language says that the visitor is powerful and the patient is weak. The patient already feels incapacitated and diminished in stature, and continually having to look up at those who enter the room only reinforces such feelings. Visitors and health care personnel (including, or perhaps especially, doctors) instead should sit down at the bedside so that their heads are on a more or less equal plane with the patient's.[21]

Family and friends should concentrate on what can make the remainder of the patient's life meaningful. Some topics that should be raised are practical in nature, such as the way they want their property distributed and their preferred course of medical treatment.

Visitors should also give permission to the patient to talk about his or her illness. This is in many ways parallel to what visitors should do in a house of mourning during the seven-day mourning period (shivah). As a child, I was taught that you should discuss anything but the deceased to get the mourners' minds off the death in the family that they just suffered. That is exactly wrong. Mourners are reticent to burden their visitors with their sad feelings and their memories of the deceased, and so if visitors do not raise that topic, mourners will presume that visitors do not want to hear about it. Many times I have visited houses of mourning on the third or fourth day of shivah and sim ply asked a mourner a question. For example, if the deceased was the mourner's parent, I might ask, "What is the earliest mem ory you have of him (or her)?" If the deceased was a spouse, I might ask, "When did you meet?" Usually it is forty-five min utes before I have to ask another question, for my first question indicated that I was indeed willing to be a listening ear.

The same is true for a sick person: He or she will presume that visitors do not want to hear about the illness unless they specif- ically ask about it. The way to do that is not to say, "How are you?"—because the answer to that question is either fine or lousy, both of which are conversation stoppers. Ask instead, "What did the doctor say?" If the prognosis is good, then you can rejoice with the patient and talk about his or her return home and to the normal activities of life. If the prognosis is bad, even terrible, then the visitor can ask what he or she can do to help the patient see that there are still things to reasonably hope for.

237

As Rabbi Maurice Lamm so eloquently articulated, when medically there is nothing to hope for, hope should be directed to these seven goals:

- Hope that you will be able to cope with suffering.
- Hope that something good will come from it.
- Hope for remission—if not a cure.
- Hope for an extension of time.
- Hope for the future welfare of your family.
- Hope to keep your dignity.
- Hope for life after life.[22]

To these I would add several things. First, one may also hope and even pray for death to come soon. Although Jewish law forbids committing or assisting a sucide, it does permit asking God to put an end to the pain and suffering of the last stages of life.[23]

In the meantime, though, once patients have had the opportunity to discuss the implications of their disease frankly so that they can deal with their fears and gain help identifying and achieving their hopes, visitors can buoy patients' spirits by treating them as adults, respecting them enough to engage in conversation about the same adult topics that previously interested them—and even some that they had not previously explored. One of the most enlightening experiences of my early rabbinic career was teaching a series of classes on Jewish theology to residents of a Jewish nursing home. The group consisted completely of college graduates. Even though none of them had ever studied Jewish theology before, they had specifically asked for these classes because, as the social workers who had arranged these lectures told me, the residents were sick of playing Bingo! They had been intellectually active at earlier stages of their lives, and their physical illnesses now did not significantly change their intellectual interests or even their mental capacity—except that I had to speak just a little more slowly than I usually do. The students even read assignments in preparation for the class from specially prepared sheets with enlarged print. I wish my younger students were always as well prepared!

Visitors do not normally discuss Jewish theology, of course, but this example indicates just how seriously I mean to make the point that conversations with patients should be challenging and should cover a wide variety of topics. The very normalcy of such discussions communicates that the illness has not diminished the visitor's respect for the patient's intelligence and humanity, and that the remainder of one's life can still be filled with meaningful conversation.

The Jewish tradition has also provided another mechanism for making the lives of terminal patients meaningful. That is the ethical will. In times past, ethical wills were written, but now they can be taped or even videotaped. Patients who know that they have a task to accomplish in leaving their children and (especially) their grandchildren a record of their family history and their own experiences, values, thoughts, dreams, and hopes will redouble their efforts to live as long as they can so that they can complete this important project.[21]

Moreover, if the patient suffers from a serious illness, especially one that will most likely take his or her life, some families can heal troubling relationships under those circumstances that they were not able to resolve earlier in their lives. The limited term of life remaining for the patient becomes patently clear in such a setting, and that often motivates all concerned to be more forthcoming in their relationships with family and friends than they were previously. It may be sad that family members and friends could not repair their relationships earlier, but the last stage of life, even if physically painful, may be emotionally among the most significant days the person has lived.

In an age when Americans live largely as individuals or in nuclear families, far away from extended family and even many friends, this duty of visiting the sick becomes all the more imperative. Requests for assisted suicide are prompted in part by the sheer loneliness and the sense of abandonment patients feel in living with a long-term illness: "If nobody cares if I live or die," the patient all too often thinks, "then why should I bother to go on living in this diminished state?" Sufficient pain medication must also, of course, be supplied to ameliorate the patient's physical condition, but social support is key to the patient's will to continue living. Although that is dramatically true for patients suffering from chronic, long-term illnesses, it is no less true for those afflicted with other forms of illness, even those from which most people readily recover. After it is all said and done, we need each other's presence and company to support our will to live.

The Jewish tradition, then, conceives of health care as a communal effort. The community must provide the funds for medical care as well as the human support and warmth needed by the sick through fulfilling the commandment to visit them (*biqqur holim*). Both the physical and emotional ministrations of the community are rich sources of healing and hope.

INDIVIDUAL DESTINY

THE JOURNEY TO DEATH AND THE HEREAFTER

Just as a religion's stance on the morality of birth control, abortion, and the various techniques of overcoming infertility depends critically on its perception of the gestational process and the role of sex in life generally and in producing children in particular, so too medical decisions that affect the end of life grow out of a tradition's perception of how we die and what happens thereafter. Similarly, the reservoirs of hope that can be tapped in a religious tradition depend, in part, on how the tradition perceives the nature of life, death, and their sequel.

In Chapter Three, I noted that classical Jewish sources speak of several stages through which we come into life, including the first forty days of gestation, the forty-first day until birth, and then the first thirty days after birth. As the embryo became the fetus and then ultimately the child, different rules applied as to whether its life could legitimately be prevented through contraceptives or terminated. In the same way, Jewish sources portray several stages in the dying process, with legal and theological consequences attached to each one.

Specifically, when first diagnosed with an irreversible, terminal disease, the person is a *terefah;* there is a deficiency in the person's organs that will eventually bring death. In the very last moments of life, when one's life is like "a flickering candle," one is a *goses.* Death follows, defined traditionally as the cessation of breath and heartbeat, but more recently as the absence of all brain wave activity, including the brainstem. The soul does not abandon the body, however, until three days after death. Jews have had a variety of beliefs as to what happens to the person after that.

Let us now examine each of these stages in turn to identify both the medical treatment and appropriate goals of hope at each stage. When a person is diagnosed with a life-threatening disease but one for which there is some hope for recovery, the Jewish tradition encourages every effort to gain healing. Rooted in reliance on God as our Healer together with confidence in God's human agents, this stance of Jewish faith requires not only whatever medical treatment offers a chance of recovery but also the full social and psychological support of family and friends. Moreover, the patient himself or herself should hope and trust that recovery will come. Reading Psalms or other spiritually fortifying Jewish or general texts can help with this, and so can prayer. Such an attitude is important not only religiously as a statement of faith but also medically as a method of regaining health, for some studies have indicated that people in the same physical condition have a greater chance to recuperate if they themselves and those around them believe that it will happen. It is, as it were, a self-fulfilling prophecy. Some diseases, of course, cannot be overcome; we are all, in the end, mortal. But when a cure is medically possible, faith in recovery is itself an important element in the prognosis for cure.[25]

When a person's disease is diagnosed by several doctors as incurable, the person in the first phase of demise is called a *terefah*. When applied to animals other than human beings, that term refers to an animal suffering from a fatal organic defect, such as a pierced windpipe or gullet.[26] It is presumed that a *terefah* animal will die within twelve months.[27]

A human *terefah* is also defined on the basis of medical evidence—specifically, as Maimonides said, "it is known for certain that he had a fatal organic disease and physicians say that his disease is incurable by human agency and that he would have died of it even if he had not been killed in another way."[28] While most authorities classify a person as a *terefah* when death is expected within twelve months, analogous to the presumption regarding an animal,[29] others argue that fundamental physiological differences between humans and other animals (and, I would add, the expenditure of considerably more human energy and resources in caring for sick humans) often enable people who have an incurable illness to survive for a longer period.[30]

241

The twelve-month period in regard to humans is thus only an estimate, and the crucial factor in the definition of *terefah* is the medical diagnosis of incurability.

Of course, one might say that since we are all mortal, life itself is a terminal illness! That would put us all in the category of *terefah*. Expanding the category of illness and therefore of *terefah* that broadly, however, does not help us portray what happens in human life, for then we cannot distinguish healthy people from sick people. Indeed, the whole point in inventing the words "ill" and "sick" in the first place was to enable us to describe people at different stages of health so that we could then know how to respond to them. Sick people require our medical ministrations and exemptions from the duties of day-to-day life; healthy people do not require special medical attention and can be expected to fulfill their responsibilities in life. Thus the lexicographical choice that we have made in all languages I know is to distinguish between illness and health. As a result, even though life itself is terminal, the category of *terefah* refers only to those whose illness has made their demise expected in the near future.

This category is important legally in Jewish law, because while killing an incurably ill person is not permitted, one who does so cannot be convicted of murder, for it is presumed that the victim's illness was part of the cause of his or her death. Instead, according to Maimonides, one is subject to divine sanction and to extralegal sanctions imposed by the court or king.[31]

Put another way, the Talmud establishes the general principle of the sanctity of each and every human life by posing the rhetorical question, "How do you know that your blood is redder? Perhaps the blood of the other person is redder!"[32] As Rabbi Joseph Babad said, the provision in Jewish law exempting the killer of a *terefah* from the death penalty effectively makes the *terefah* an exception to this tenet of the equality of all human lives. That is, while a *terefah* is definitely *not* considered a dead person, his or her blood *is* considered "less red" than that of a viable human being.[33]

This led to a specific ruling during the Holocaust. In those excruciating times, rabbis permitted Jews to acquiesce to Nazi commands to throw victims of the gas chambers into crematoria rather than be shot themselves, despite the fact that the gassed people still exhibited some signs of life. As people with terminal illnesses, the lives of the gassed could be sacrificed for others who were still fully alive.[34]

In all but extreme triage situations such as that, though, the incurably ill person has a call on our medical care. After all, Jewish sources make him or her *analogous* to a dead person, *not equated* to one.[35] In light of the impossibility of cure, though, the aim of our medical ministrations at that time will be to provide comfort, including the nonmedical support of family and friends. Hope in that setting, should not be directed to cure, for by hypothesis in these cases there is good medical evidence that that is impossible, and Jewish law forbids us to pray for God to reverse that which cannot be changed.[36] Instead, we should direct our hopes to things that are still possible for the *terefah* to do, things like the ones listed earlier.

In the early stages of being a *terefah*, though, one may be able to do quite a bit. I was once asked by a congregational rabbi in the Los Angeles area to meet with him and a congregant of his. The congregant, a man in his late fifties, had been diagnosed with an inoperable, malignant brain tumor. As soon as the diagnosis was confirmed, he quit his job as an engineer with a major aeronautical firm, and he and his wife went on the trip abroad that they had dreamed of but never taken. Now, after the trip, he was asking his rabbi and me to lead him to Jewish sources describing the dying process—not death and mourning, but how Judaism would have us think, feel, and act while we are still alive and conscious but terminally ill. He wanted to be guided by that material in his own life and to include it in a memoir he was writing for his family. It was that man who prompted me to write this chapter: Not only did he ask a question that I had not thought of before but he demonstrated just how much one can do while being a *terefah*.

The same nonmedical responses apply to the next stage in the dying process, but the medical treatment may change. When one is about to die, one is a *goses*. A *goses* "brings up a secretion in his throat on account of the narrowing of his chest."[37] Rabbinic sources describe the life of a *goses* like that of a flickering candle, such that even moving the person to prevent bed sores is prohibited lest the motion bring on death. Even then, the patient is to be treated as a living person in most respects.[38]

Since Jewish law permits medical inaction (passive euthanasia) such as withholding or withdrawing medications and machines once a person becomes a *goses*, however, there has been intense interest in defining the moment of the onset of that category. The most stringent contemporary rabbis, the ones who permit medical inaction least often, are those who define it as the stage within three days of death.[39] More liberal rabbis, who want to extend our ability to withhold or withdraw medical interventions and let nature take its course, have expanded it to as much as a year. Some have instead argued that the relevant issue in defining *goses* should not be the time the person is expected to live, but the incurability of the disease.[40] I have argued elsewhere, though, that the sources' analogy to a flickering candle, such that even moving the patient becomes life-threatening, suggests that a *goses* is literally in the last hours of life and that rabbis like me who would like to rule liberally in medical matters at the end of life must instead use the category of *terefah*.[41]

However one defines *goses*, the moment of death comes next. As noted above, death is traditionally defined as the cessation of breath and heartbeat; according to many modern authorities, the cessation of all brain function, including the brainstem, suffices to determine death.[42] Even then, though, the story is not over. Early rabbinic sources speak of death as "the going out of the soul," but rabbinic lore maintains that the association between body and soul is not altogether severed until three days after death. During that time, according to the classical Rabbis, the soul hovers over the grave, hoping to be restored to the body. It departs only when the body begins to decompose and the face changes in character. This, it was believed, was why mourners' grief often reaches its emotional climax on the third day after a loved one's death.[43] This belief, though, did not diminish Jewish law's insistence on burying the body as soon after death as possible in a closed casket as the proper way to honor the dead.

LIFE AFTER DEATH

Until the Book of Daniel, written about 165 B.C.E. and thus chronologically the last book of the Hebrew Bible, Jews believed that those who died did not survive their death. The dead descended to a murky place called Sheol, a term often left untranslated or rendered as "the grave" with no specification of what the dead experience there.[44] From there, though, they might be recalled by the living in a vision, as the deceased Samuel speaks to Saul with the help of the witch of En-dor.[45] The dead reside there to eternity, though, never to return to life as we know it again. The dead cannot even praise God, let alone hope for anything for themselves.[46] Late biblical books like Job (c. 400 B.C.E.) and Ecclesiastes (Kohelet, c. 250 B.C.E.), in fact, know of the doctrine of a resurrection of the dead, but they explicitly deny it.[47]

Thus, except for the Book of Daniel, biblical theology confines the individual's eternity to manifestations in life as human beings know it. Specifically, according to the theology of all biblical books except for Daniel, you live on after death in just two ways: through the memory people have of you and your deeds and through your children. Thus God's blessings of the Patriarchs explicitly includes both of these factors: "Abraham is to become a great and populous nation, and all the nations of the earth are to bless themselves by him." The levirate marriage, whereby the brother of a man who died childless marries his widow, is specifically designed to perpetuate the name of the deceased because the law specifies that the children of the widow and the brother will bear the name of the deceased man as their father. Indeed, childlessness is a source of tremendous frustration and despair in the biblical stories in part because it prevents a claim on eternity through one's progeny. Along these lines, the Rabbis, who believed in life after death, nevertheless thought of a childless man as if he were dead, and they interpreted the biblical punishment of *karet* (being cut off) to mean that the sinner's children would die in his lifetime, leaving him without endurance after death.[48]

Later Jewish tradition continues to put great emphasis on the importance of children as a mode of our personal and communal continuity. That is, rabbinic doctrines affirming that each person has a life after death added to, but did not replace, the biblical sense that our continuity as a religion and a people depends on procreation and education in this life. This has been stressed even more in our own times, when, as I discussed in Chapter Three, Jews face a major demographic crisis as a people and all too many of our young couples suffer the personal heartache of infertility. Children, whether acquired through normal sexual intercourse, infertility treatments, or adoption, are thus still a crucial element in the continuity of individuals and the Jewish people as a whole, just as they were in biblical times.

The biblical denial of life after death changes with the Book of Daniel, several books of the Apocrypha written shortly thereafter, and ultimately with rabbinic (Pharisaic) Judaism, for it is in the last two centuries B.C.E. and the first two centuries C.E. that the doctrine of a life after death becomes embedded in Judaism. Thus Daniel declared: "Many of those that sleep in the dust of the earth will awake, some to eternal life, others to reproaches, to everlasting abhorrence. And the knowledgeable will be radiant like the bright expanse of sky, and those who lead the many to righteousness will be like the stars forever and ever."[49]

In the Apocrypha, the idea of heavenly immortality, either awarded to all Israel or to the righteous alone, vies with the resurrection of the dead. Thus 4 Maccabees promises everlasting life with God to those Jewish martyrs who preferred death to the violation of the Torah and does not mention resurrection. In contrast, 2 Maccabees proclaims resurrection.[50] Either way, though, the person was to live on after death.

The Pharisees, the rabbis who shaped the Jewish tradition, troubled by the fact that the righteous suffer and the evil prosper (tzadik ve'ra lo, rasha ve'tov lo),[51] believed in an ultimate squaring of the accounts, as it were, in a life after death. This doctrine preserved God's justice and reassured people of the ongoing significance of their lives, even after death.[52]

Since there was no biblical or empirical evidence about what a life after death might be like, no prophet, even Moses, could know what would take place there.[53] That, of course, did not stop people from speculating about this, and Maimonides, an important twelfth-century rabbi and philosopher, parodied such speculations:

> Concerning this strange world to come, you will rarely find anyone to whom it occurs to think about it seriously or to adopt it as a fundamental doctrine of our faith, or to inquire what it really

means, whether the world to come is the ultimate good or whether some other possibility. Nor does one often find persons who distinguish between the ultimate good itself and the means that lead to the ultimate good. What everybody always wants to know, both the masses and the learned, is how the dead will arise. They want to know whether they will be naked or clothed, whether they will rise in the same shrouds in which they were buried, with the same embroidery, style, and beauty of sewing, or in a plain garment that just covers their bodies. Or they ask whether, when the Messiah comes, there will still be rich and poor people, weak and strong people, and other similar questions.[54]

While the Rabbis never tried to reconcile all of their various pictures into one systematic whole, in all their comments they wrote their own values large. This is perhaps most evident when they proclaim that in the world to come, we will all study Torah, but, unlike the current world in which even the best of human teachers have faults, in the world to come God will be our teacher. Those who could not study much during their lives because they had to earn a living but nevertheless learned as much as they could will be privileged to study with God, and scholars in this world will have the ultimate joy of God resolving all of their unsolved intellectual puzzles![55] In sum, "In the World to Come, there is neither eating nor drinking, nor procreation of children nor business transactions, nor envy or hatred or rivalry; but the righteous sit enthroned, their crowns on their heads, and enjoy the luster of the Divine Presence."[56]

In times of severe illness, Jews often explore these Jewish beliefs about the end of life and the possibility of existence thereafter. This can provide sick people and their caregivers with yet another reservoir of hope: "Even if I do not survive this illness, life will go on in another form, and so I should not become too despondent now."[57]

As the quotation from Maimonides indicates, though, these doctrines of life after death never became the central focus of Judaism, as they did in Christianity. Both Judaism and Christianity believe in living a good life now and in the promise of a future life after death, but the emphasis in the two traditions is significantly different. To be a Christian, by definition, one must in some sense believe in Jesus as the Christ (Messiah), and that immediately focuses one's attention on concepts of the Messiah and the afterlife. The central story of Judaism, in contrast, is the Exodus and Sinai, beckoning us to trust that God will redeem us and teach us *in this life*.[58] Thus Jews generally think of Torah, God's commandments, the People Israel, and God's mission for us to improve the world as the center of their faith, with ideas of the Messiah and the afterlife, if mentioned at all, much farther down the list and much fainter in their consciousness.[59] Some modern Jews, in fact, like to ignore Judaism's beliefs in a life after death altogether, as if they did not exist. That, of course, is simply incorrect.[60] Nevertheless, Judaism's hope for a future Messianic end time in human history devoid of illness as well as other human failings and frustrations, together with its roots in the social activism of Exodus and Sinai, make Judaism's emphasis—contrary to that of Christianity—the duty to improve this life.

One manifestation of this is that Jewish belief in a life after death has not diminished Jews' fight to remain alive. I once asked a friend of mine who is an oncologist whether there is any difference between his Jewish and his Christian patients. Without hesitating a moment, he said, "Sure. When I tell Christians that they have an inoperable tumor, they are not happy, but they resign themselves to that because they are going to meet Jesus. When I tell Jews that, though, they ask for a second opinion, a third opinion . . . !"

Jews do tend to be aggressive in medical care, often to a fault. Hospice care, in fact, is a relatively new phenomenon among Jews, with some Orthodox rabbis still doubting that it is permissible, because it presumes that there is no hope for recovery.[61] Undoubtedly, the Jewish emphasis on this life undergirds such attitudes.

Clearly, some balance must be restored. After all is said and done, we are mortal. Adam and Eve ate of the Tree of Knowledge of Good and Evil, but they were prevented from eating of the Tree of Life. That means that in medical decisions we should have reasonable but not unrealistic hope. We should clearly try to cure people when we can; and, in any case, we must strive to alleviate their pain and suffering through medication and personal contact. We need not, however, exercise every possible option to keep a person's body functioning. On the contrary, to do that would be to challenge the mortality God embedded in our creation. At some point, we pass from being God's partner in healing to building a medical Tower of Babel. A proper theological perspective should warn us against playing God in that way.

COMMUNAL DESTINY

The biblical Book of Ecclesiastes espouses a circular view of history. For Ecclesiastes, there is nothing new under the sun, everything that exists now already was, and everything that will be in the future already exists. That leads him to the conclusion that all is vanity, that there is nothing to strive or hope for.

All of the rest of the books of the Hebrew Bible, though, embrace a linear view of history, in which the world moves from creation through the period of revelation to the promise of redemption. The Prophets hold out the hope for a future time when there will be no war among human beings or even between humans and the animals now hostile to them. Instead, all humans will learn Torah from Zion and will behave accordingly.[62] Indeed, the Torah itself promises that if we abide by God's commandments, God will bless us with peace, prosperity, and the assurance that "The Lord will ward off from you all sickness; He will not bring upon you any of the dreadful diseases of Egypt."[63]

This splendid Messianic age can occur, though, only if the impediments to its realization are first removed. Thus many biblical and rabbinic visions of the end time include a war against the forces of evil.[64] Similarly, significant strides in improving the communal level of health can happen only if sources of pollution are removed or at least ameliorated and if common social practices like smoking and driving while drunk are curtailed. Eliminating obstacles to health must accompany the positive steps we take to ensure it.

Jewish Messianic expectations must be differentiated from Jewish beliefs about life after death. The latter concept, described briefly above, applies primarily to individuals after their physical death. Jewish Messianic beliefs, in contrast, apply to men and women—like human beings now—living in a future, idyllic time. Visions of that future time within Jewish sources range

from minimalist versions, where the only thing that differentiates that time from today is Jewish political autonomy, to max-
imalist descriptions, by which there is universal peace and
prosperity—when even the wolf lies down with the lamb, when
all Jews will be reunited in Israel, and when all peoples learn
Torah from Jerusalem. This latter account of the hoped-for end
time in human history can, according to some, be initiated only
by God, whereas others, including the progenitors of modern
Zionism, maintain that human beings can and should help God
make that day happen.

In any case, the prospect and promise of a Messianic time undergirds the Jewish hope that ultimately we may merit a world
devoid of sickness altogether. Whether Jews are aware of it or
not, the biblical motifs of Exodus and Sinai and of the Messianic
hope for the future are the ideological underpinnings for much of
what Jews actually do in their lives. These beliefs explain and
justify the serious involvement of Jews in *tiqqun olam*, "fixing
the world," understood in our own time as social action, including the widespread and serious involvement of Jews in medical
research. They also provide the ideological framework for Jews of
all stripes of religious belief and practice to support medical research financially and to use medicine aggressively in their own
lives and in those of family and friends. God permits us and even
requires us to engage in medical care, holding out the hope of a
time in the future when no illness will occur.

Similarly, our aspiration for creating a Messianic world must
include efforts to overcome poverty and ignorance of all kinds.[65]
A peaceful world can happen only if everyone has sufficient food,
water, clothing, and shelter; a means of gainful employment
(and, one hopes, a meaningful one at that); the intellectual background necessary to obtain such a job; the liberal arts education
and social experience necessary to understand and appreciate
people of different backgrounds; and the moral character and
commitment to care for others. The vision of Jewish classical
sources of a world of peace, prosperity, and knowledge of God's
ways embraces all these factors. Even if we cannot attain all
these aims, the sources provide us with a goal toward which we
must strive, a challenge to us to make this world as much like
this Messianic ideal as we can.

250

As most Jews understand the Jewish belief in a future Messianic time, it is our job now to help God make that day happen. Our trust in God as our partner in creating such a day does not eliminate or even diminish our duty to be active partners in that effort. On the contrary, through the commandments God calls on us to create such an ideal world. Ultimately, then, it is the fact that God created us with the ability to envision an ideal world and with the free will and faculties to make it happen that forms the basis for Jewish social activism and the Jewish hope for the future.

Notes

KEY TO NOTES

The following abbreviations are used in the notes to the text:

B. = Babylonian Talmud (edited by Ravina and Rav Ashi, c. 500 C.E.)

J. = Jerusalem (Palestinian) Talmud (editor unknown, c. 400 C.E.)

M. = Mishnah (edited by Rabbi Judah ha Nasi [Judah the Prince], president of the Sanhedrin in c. 200 C.E.)

M.T. = Maimonides' *Mishneh Torah* (completed 1177)

S.A. = Shulchan Arukh (completed in 1565 by Yosef Karo, a Spanish [Sephardic] Jew, with glosses by Moses Isserles, a Polish Jew from Cracow, indicating where German and eastern European [Ashkenazic] Jewish practice differed)

T. = Tosefta (edited by Rabbi Hiyya and Rabbi Oshaiya in c. 200 C.E.)

Modern works are referred to by author (or editor) and publication date. Full bibliographical information can be found in the Bibliography.

NOTES TO CHAPTER ONE

1. The story is cited in MacIntyre (1967), 2:463.
2. Mill (1863), 298–300.
3. Kant (1994), 279.
4. Ibid., 281.
5. Ibid., 282.
6. Ross (1930), 41.
7. Heschel (1982), 9.
8. Psalms 1:1.
9. Psalms 34:13–15. The word translated "integrity" here is *shalom,* usually understood as meaning "peace," which it may mean here as well.

10. Ecclesiastes 5:17, 7:16–18, 9:7–10.

11. Nietzsche (1885), 334.

12. Ibid., 333.

13. Gilligan (1982), Held (2002), and Noddings (1984).

14. For a more detailed analysis of the biblical and rabbinic rationales for abiding by Jewish moral norms, see Dorff (1989).

15. Rosenzweig (1955).

16. For example, B. *Bava Metz'ia* 30b. To explore the relationship between Jewish law and morality further, see Dorff (1998), 395–417. For other Conservative views, see Gordis (1990), 50–68, and Greenberg (1977), 157–218. For unusual, but thoughtful, left-wing Orthodox approaches to this issue, see Hartman (1997), 89–108, and Spero (1983), 166–200.

Since, for Reform Judaism, Jewish law is, according to Freehof (1960), 22, "not directive, but advisory" and involves "our guidance, but not our governance," moral norms, however they are construed, always take precedence over Jewish law, because moral norms are binding but Jewish law is not. A more recent Reform platform, *A Centenary Perspective*, issued in 1976, says, "Our founders stressed that the Jewish ethical responsibilities, personal and social, are enjoined by God. The past century has taught us that the claims made upon us may begin with our ethical obligations, but they extend to many other aspects of Jewish living." Reform Jews are, therefore, "to confront the claims of Jewish tradition, however differently perceived, and to exercise their individual autonomy, choosing and creating on the basis of commitment and knowledge." This represents a wider commitment to Jewish practice but not a conviction that Jewish law per se is binding, and so the relationship between Jewish law and morality does not bother Reform thinkers nearly as much as it does those in the Conservative and Orthodox movements, who hold that Jewish law is binding. See Borowitz (1983), xxii–xxiii.

17. Genesis 18:25.

18. Borowitz (1991), 284–299. See also the exchange between Rabbi Borowitz and me on the extent to which his theory is indeed Reform, beginning with my review of his book in Dorff (1996a) and our exchange of letters in Borowitz (1997) and Dorff (1997).

19. See note 16.

20. See Dorff (1998), 7–13, 395–423; and Mackler (1995).

21. See Buber (1970). *Ethics and Infinity* (1985) is one good source among Levinas's many works for his ethical views. A good analysis and application of his views in feminist terms is Zoloth-Dorfman (1995).

22. See, for example, Exodus 19:5; Deuteronomy 10:14; and Psalms 24:1. See also Genesis 14:19,22, where the Hebrew word for "creator" (*koneh*) also means "possessor," and where "heaven and earth" is a merism for those and everything in between, and Psalms 104:24, where the same word is used with the same meaning. The following verses have the same theme, although not quite as explicitly or as expansively: Exodus 20:11; Leviticus 25:23,42,55; and Deuteronomy 4:35,39, 32:6.

23. Bathing, for example, is a commandment according to Hillel (*Leviticus Rabbah* 34:3). Maimonides summarized and codified the rules requiring proper care of the body in M.T. *Laws of Ethics* (*De'ot*), chaps. 3–5. He spells out there in remarkable clarity that the purpose of these positive duties to maintain health is not to feel good and live a long life but rather to have a healthy body so that one can then serve God.

24. B. *Shabbat* 32a; B. *Bava Kamma* 15b, 80a, 91b; M.T. *Laws of Murder* 11:4–5; S.A. *Yoreh De'ah* 116:5 gloss.; S.A. *Hoshen Mishpat* 427:8–10.

25. B. *Hullin* 10a; S.A. *Orah Hayyim* 173:2; S.A. *Yoreh De'ah* 116:5 gloss.

26. Bleich (1977a); Freehof (1977), chap. 11; and Rabbinical Assembly (1983), 182.

27. Genesis 9:5; M. *Semahot* 2:2; B. *Bava Kamma* 91b; *Genesis Rabbah* 34:19 (states that the ban against suicide includes not only cases where blood was shed but also self-inflicted death through strangulation and the like); M.T. *Laws of Murder* 2:3; M.T. *Laws of Injury and Damage* 5:1; S.A. *Yoreh De'ah* 345:1–3. Compare Bleich (1981), chap. 26.

28. Specifically, forty-four states currently have laws that make aiding a person to commit suicide a felony; see Savage (1996).

29. Genesis 1:27; see also Genesis 5:1.

30. See Genesis 1:26–27; 3:1–7,22–24.

31. See Genesis 2:18–24; Numbers 12:1–16; and Deuteronomy 22:13–19. Note also that "*ha-middaber*" (the speaker) is a synonym for the human being (in contrast to animals) in medieval Jewish philosophy.

32. Maimonides, *Guide of the Perplexed*, part 1, chap. 1.

33. See Deuteronomy 6:5 and Leviticus 19:18,33–34, and note that the traditional prayer book juxtaposes the paragraph just before the *Shema*, which speaks of God's love for us, with the first paragraph of the *Shema*, which commands us to love God.

34. Consider the prayer in the traditional early-morning weekday service: "*Elohai neshamah she-natata bi,*" "My God, the soul [or life breath] which you have imparted to me is pure. You created it, You formed it, You breathed it into me; You guard it within me" (Harlow, 1985, 8–11). Similarly, the Rabbis describe the human being as part divine and part animal, the latter consisting of the material aspects of the human being and the former consisting of that which we share with God; see *Sifrei Deuteronomy*, par. 306; 132a. Or consider this rabbinic statement in *Genesis Rabbah* 8:11: "In four respects man resembles the creatures above, and in four respects the creatures below. Like the animals he eats and drinks, propagates his species, relieves himself, and dies. Like the ministering angels he stands erect, speaks, possesses intellect, and sees [in front of him and not on the side like an animal]."

35. *Genesis Rabbah* 24:7.

36. M. *Sanhedrin* 4:5. Some manuscripts are less universalistic; they read: "Anyone who destroys one *Israelite* soul is described in Scripture as if he destroyed an entire world, and anyone who sustains one *Israelite* soul is described in Scripture as if he sustained an entire world." A Hasidic *bon mot* (from Buber,

1961, 2:249–250) reminds us that we must balance this recognition of our divine worth with a proper dose of humility:

> Rabbi Bunam said: A person should always have two pieces of paper, one in each pocket. On one should be written, "For me the world was created." On the other should be written, "I am but dust and ashes" (Genesis 18:27).

37. For a thorough discussion of this blessing and concept in the Jewish tradition, see Astor (1985).

38. Deuteronomy 21:22–23. For Rabbinic comments on the value of respect inherent in this law and further legal applications of it, see, for example, B. *Mo'ed Katan* 16a; J. *Kiddushin* 4:1; and J. *Nazir* 7:5

39. *Genesis Rabbah* 24:7. Consider also: "Great is human dignity, for it overrides a negative prohibition of the Torah" (B. *Berakhot* 19b, for example). "The Holy One, blessed be He, has concern for the honor of all His creatures, including non-Jews and even wicked people like Balaam" (*Numbers Rabbah* 20:14). "All the Holy One, blessed be He, created, He created for His own honor" (B. *Yoma* 38a, based on Isaiah 43:7).

40. Romans 6–8, esp. 6:12; 7:14–24, 8:3,10,12–13; and Galatians 5:16–24; see also 1 Corinthians 7:2,9,36–38.

41. 1 Corinthians 6:19.

42. Romans 7:23.

43. The Greek side of Maimonides is most in evidence in his *Guide of the Perplexed*, where he states this flatly (part 3, chap. 33):

> It is also the object of the perfect Law to make man reject, despise, and reduce his desires as much as is in his power. He should only give way to them when absolutely necessary. It is well known that it is intemperance in eating, drinking, and sexual intercourse that people mostly rave and indulge in; and these very things counteract the ulterior perfection of man, impede at the same time the development of his first perfection [i.e., bodily health], and generally disturb the social order of the country and the economy of the family. For by following entirely the guidance of lust, in the manner of fools, man loses his intellectual energy, injures his body, and perishes before his natural time; sighs and cares multiply; and there is an increase of envy, hatred, and warfare for the purpose of taking what another possesses. The cause of all this is the circumstance that the ignorant considers physical enjoyment as an object to be sought for its own sake. God in His wisdom has therefore given us such commandments as would counteract that object, and prevent us altogether from directing our attention to it. . . . For the chief object of the Law is to [teach man to] diminish his desires.

Philo's views can be found, in part, in the selections from his writings reprinted in Lewy et al. (1960), part 1, esp. 42–51, 54–55, 71–75. He calls the body a "prison house" (72).

44. Genesis 2:7; B. *Ta'anit* 22b; and *Genesis Rabbah* 14:9. On the different parts that the mother, father, and God contribute to the newborn, see B. *Niddah* 31a. See also B. *Sanhedrin* 90b–91a. The departure of the soul and its return on waking is articulated in the first words that a person is supposed to say upon regaining consciousness after sleep: "I am grateful to You, living, enduring Sovereign, for restoring my soul (life-breath, *nishmati*) to me in compassion. You are faithful (trustworthy) beyond measure" (Harlow, 1985, 2–3). It is also articulated in another early prayer in the daily morning liturgy, *"Elohai neshamah she-natata bi"* (Harlow, 1985, 8–11), with roots in *Leviticus Rabbah* 18:1 (toward the end) and Midrash *Shahar Tov*, chap. 25. The blessing at its conclusion most probably refers not to resurrection after death but to the return of consciousness after sleep, as in the prayer cited above, which also speaks of God restoring the soul to the body at that time.

45. The predominant view seems to be that it can (compare B. *Berakhot* 18b–19a; *Hagigah* 12b; *Ketubbot* 77b), but even such sources depict the soul in terms of physical imagery, thereby enabling it to perform many of the functions of the body. Some sources, in the meantime, assert that the soul cannot exist without the body, or the body without the soul (for example, *Tanhuma* Va-yikra' 11).

46. *Leviticus Rabbah* 34:3.

47. B. *Sanhedrin* 91a–91b. See also *Mekhilta* Be-shallah, Shirah, chap. 2 (ed. Horowitz-Rabin, 1960); *Leviticus Rabbah* 4:5; *Yalkut Shimoni* on Leviticus 4:2 (#464); *Tanhuma* Va-yikra' 6. The very development of the term *"neshamah"* from meaning "physical breath" to "one's inner being" bespeaks Judaism's view that the physical and the spiritual are integrated.

48. M. *Pe·ah* 1:1 and B. *Kiddushin* 40b.

49. M. *Avot* 2:1. See B. *Berakhot* 35b, esp. the comment of Abayae there in responding to the earlier theories of Rabbi Ishmael and Rabbi Shimon bar Yohai.

50. B. *Berakhot* 17a; the earlier rabbinic teaching cited at the end of this source as what we have previously learned appears in B. *Menahot* 110a. While a few of the classical Rabbis belonged to wealthy families, most were menial laborers and studied when they could. Hillel, for example, was so poor that he became the symbol of the poor man who nevertheless found the time and money to study Torah (B. *Yoma* 35b). Akiva had been a shepherd before he devoted himself to study at age forty, subsisting on the price he received for the bundle of wood he collected each day (*Avot de-Rabbi Natan*, chap. 6); Joshua was a charcoal burner (B. *Berakhot* 28a); Yose bar Halafta worked in leather (B. *Shabbat* 49b); Yohanan was a sandal maker (M. *Avot* 4:14); Judah was a baker (J. *Hagigah* 77b); and Abba Saul kneaded dough (B. *Pesahim* 34a) and had been a grave digger (B. *Niddah* 24b).

51. See Leviticus 23:32; M. *Yoma*, chap. 8; and later rabbinic commentaries and codes based on that. Similarly, although there is a rabbinic doctrine of *yissurim shel ahavah*, "pain of love" (*Genesis Rabbah* 92:1), it is always used to explain, post facto, why the good suffer. It is *not* a directive to experience pain. Thus Rabbi Hiyya bar Abba, Rabbi Yohanan, and Rabbi Eliezer all say that neither their sufferings nor the reward promised in the world to come for enduring

them are welcome—that is, they would rather live without both the suffering and the anticipated reward; see B. *Berakhot* 5b. See also Jakobovits (1975), chap. 8.

52. See M.T. *Laws of the Sabbath,* chap. 30.

53. The law of the Nazirite appears in Numbers 6:11. The rabbinic derivation from that law that abstinence is prohibited appears first in B. *Ta'anit* 11a. See also M.T. *Laws of Ethics (De'ot)* 3:1.

54. M.T. *Laws of Ethics (De'ot)* 3:3.

55. Genesis 2:24.

56. M. *Ketubbot* 5:6–7.

57. Genesis 2:18 and B. *Yevamot* 61b.

58. *Genesis Rabbah* 17:2; B. *Yevamot* 62b–63a; and *Midrash Psalms* on Psalms 59:2.

59. B. *Kiddushin* 29b–30a.

60. Genesis 1:28.

61. On the minimum of two, see M. *Yevamot* 6:6 (61b); M.T. *Laws of Marriage* 15:4; and S.A. *Even Ha'ezer* 1:5. On the ideal of having more, see B. *Yevamot* 62b (based on Isaiah 45:18 and Ecclesiastes 11:6) and M.T. *Laws of Marriage* 15:16.

62. Deuteronomy 6:7,20–25, 11:19. This was already one of Abraham's duties (Genesis 18:19).

63. Deuteronomy 5:1.

64. Deuteronomy 31:10–13.

65. On Moses as a prophet, see Deuteronomy 34:10. According to my own computer search, the phrase "Moses, our teacher" appears fifty-six times in the Babylonian Talmud! For example, B. *Berakhot* 3b, 12b, 33b, 55a, 55b; and B. *Shabbat* 30a, 92a.

66. M. *Avot* 5:24.

67. Hirsch (1956), 2:245–250.

68. For more on this, see Dorff (1987), esp. 12–19; Konvitz (1978), chap. 5; and Dorff (2002), chap. 1.

69. B. *Sanhedrin* 17b.

70. B. *Bava Batra* 89a; M.T. *Laws of Theft* 8:20; and S.A. *Hoshen Mishpat* 231:2.

71. This prayer is found in the prayer books of all Jewish denominations, but see, for example, Harlow (1985), 162 f.

72. Half of American Jews from across the nation polled by the *Los Angeles Times* listed a commitment to social equality as the factor most important to their sense of Jewish identity, whereas only 17 percent cited religious observance and another 17 percent cited support for Israel; see Scheer (1988).

73. Deuteronomy 30:11–14.

NOTES TO CHAPTER TWO

1. Gindin (1997), 1173, and generally for this and many of the other legal aspects of privacy, especially regarding access to personal information. I would like

to thank Tracee Rosen, a former rabbinical student at the University of Judaism and now a rabbi, for alerting me to this article. For an extensive bibliography that includes sections on personal privacy and the information age; privacy legislation and data regulation; databank accuracy and access and the sale of personal information; and record matching, surveillance, encryption, and social control, see Tavani (1996).

2. M. *Sanhedrin* 4:5.

3. Fried (1968).

4. Gavison (1980), 447.

5. Shils (1956), 22–24; Bulmer (1979); and Westin and Allan (1967). Spitz (1986), 1, lists these sources and those cited in notes 3 and 4. Much of the material included in my exposition of the Jewish sources was collected by Rabbi Spitz in that article, and I am indebted to him for his thorough and insightful work. I cite some of his conclusions based on this material later in this chapter.

6. *Mekhilta* Yitro on Exodus 20:23 (ed. Horovitz-Rabin, 1960, 245); *Sifra* Kedoshim on Leviticus 19:18 (also in J. *Nedarim* 9:4 and *Genesis Rabbah* 24:7); and *Deuteronomy Rabbah* 4:4.

7. Exodus 19:6.

8. Deuteronomy 24:10–13 and Leviticus 19:16.

9. Leviticus 19:2 and Deuteronomy 11:22, 13:5.

10. *Sifrei Deuteronomy* 'Ekev; see also *Mekhilta* Be-shallaḥ 3; B. *Shabbat* 133b; and B. *Sotah* 14a.

11. Exodus 3:6, 33:20–23. See also Deuteronomy 29:28, according to which "secret matters belong to the Lord our God, while revealed matters are for us and for our children forever to carry out the words of this Torah." Similarly, in the visions of the Heavenly Chariot in Isaiah 6 and Ezekiel 1, both prophets can see only God's attendants and not God Himself.

12. M. *Hagigah* 2:1 and J. *Hagigah* 2:1 (8b).

13. Lamm (1967), esp. 302–303, makes this point.

14. *Roe v. Wade*, 410 U.S. 113 (1973). In 1976, the U.S. Supreme Court, in *Paul v. Davis*, 424 U.S. 693, 713 (1976), identified the personal decisions protected by the constitutional guarantee of privacy as those concerning "matters relating to marriage, procreation, contraception, family relationships, and child rearing and education." In subsequent rulings, the court extended the liberty right of the Fourteenth Amendment to include the right to refuse medical treatment (*Cruzan v. Director, Missouri Department of Health* 497 U.S. 261 [1990]) but not to demand the right to assistance in committing suicide (*Washington v. Glucksberg* 521 U.S. 702 [1997]; 117 S.Ct. 2258 [1997]) and not even to guarantee the right to homosexual sex within one's own home (*Bowers v. Hardwick*, 478 U.S. 186 [1986]—although in Georgia, from which the latter case came, the state supreme court more recently ruled that such private sexual activity was guaranteed under the state constitution (*Powell v. State*, 1998 WL 878550 [Ga.], decided November 23, 1998). Other states have followed suit, including Kentucky, Michigan, Tennessee, and Louisiana.

In Kentucky: *Commonwealth v. Wasson*, Supreme Court of Kentucky, 842 S.W.2d 487 (1992). In Michigan: *Michigan Organization for Human Rights v. Kelly*, No. 88-815820, Wayne County Circuit Ct., July 9, 1990, in which a decision by a state trial judge was not appealed by the state. The court based its ruling on the state constitution; because the attorney general did not appeal this ruling, it remains binding on all Michigan prosecutors until and unless there is further litigation or the legislature changes the constitution. In Tennessee: *Campbell v. McWherter*, No. 93C-1547 (Davidson Cty., Tenn.), 1994, in which a trial judge ruled that the sodomy law violated the state constitution's right to privacy—a ruling that was affirmed by the Court of Appeals of Tennessee in *Campbell v. Sundquist*, 926 S.W.2d 250 (Tenn. App. 1996), and permission to appeal to the Tennessee Supreme Court was denied. In Louisiana: see "Court Throws Out State's Sodomy Law" (1999), according to which a New Orleans appeals court threw out "a 194-year-old Louisiana law against sodomy, saying that consensual oral and anal sex is protected by the right to privacy in the state constitution." See Rubenstein (1997), 256 ff., esp. 263, n. 1.

15. For more on the Jewish approach to abortion, see Dorff (1998), 128–133. See also Feldman (1973), esp. chaps. 14–15.

16. *Bowers v. Hardwick*, 478 U.S. 186 (1986). See note 14.

17. Other grounds to change Jewish law on these matters have been suggested. I myself have made such an argument in regard to homosexuality in *Matters of Life and Death*, 139–151, but with full understanding that the burden of proof rests on me, since I am arguing against explicit prohibitions in the Torah and rabbinic literature. Although I have not seen a convincing argument justifying nonmarital sex, the fact of the matter is that the vast majority of Jews in our time actually live together for months or even years before they marry. In that light, I have tried to introduce a measure of morality and Jewish sensitivity into such relationships through the rabbinic letter I wrote on human intimacy together with the Rabbinical Assembly's Commission on Human Sexuality (Dorff, 1996b). See also Chapter Three herein. Adultery, although permitted in most American states, cannot find even that measure of Jewish approval.

18. *Olmstead v. United States* 277 U.S. 438 (1928); 466 (Brandeis, J., dissenting).

19. Deuteronomy 24:10–11.

20. That Jews may not charge interest on loans to fellow Jews, see Exodus 22:24; Leviticus 25:35–38; Deuteronomy 23:20–21; and M. *Bava Metz'ia* chap. 5. The concern to keep loans available appears, for example, in the leniencies instituted by the Rabbis in the laws of testimony governing the determination that A loaned an object or money to B (B. *Sanhedrin* 2b–3a). That a debtor's home could be invaded when the creditor suspected that collectable items were being hidden there, see Tur, *Hoshen Mishpat* 97:15. See also B. *Bava Metz'ia* 115a, where the right against intrusion is held to apply only to debts arising from loans, not to debts stemming from contracts or other obligations. According to M.T. *Laws of the Creditor and Debtor* 3:7, only the home of the debtor was protected, not that of his surety.

21. He is, however, liable for any injuries he causes, "for he has the right to eject him, but not the right to injure him" (M.T. *Laws of the One Who Injures or Damages [Hovel u'Mazik]* 1:15). If the landlord did not intentionally injure the trespasser, however, he is not held liable (B. *Bava Kamma* 48b; S.A. *Hoshen Mishpat* 421:7), even though a person is generally responsible for unintentional wrongs (M. *Bava Kamma* 2:6; M.T. *Laws of the One Who Injures or Damages [Hovel u'Mazik]* 1:11).

22. B. *Pesaḥim* 112a and B. *Niddah* 16b. The rationale of not surprising and embarrassing someone inside is articulated by Rashi, commenting on both of those passages. See also *Avot de-Rabbi Natan* 7:3.

23. *Derekh Eretz Rabbah* 5:2.

24. Numbers 24:5; M. *Bava Batra* 3:7; and B. *Bava Batra* 60a, 2b, 3a; see also M.T. *Laws of Neighbors* 2:14, 5:6; and S.A. *Hoshen Mishpat* 154:3. The legal requirements mentioned were enforced through monetary fines and, if necessary, excommunication; see Rakover (n.d.), 7, 8. See also *Encyclopedia Talmudit* 8:559–602 at *Hezek Re'iya* (Hebrew) and Lamm (1971), 294–295.

25. B. *Bava Batra* 59b–60a and Tur, *Hoshen Mishpat* 154:16. Nahmanides and Alfasi, commenting on the latter passage, make the point that it is not just the individual's interest but the public interest that is at stake.

26. Leviticus 19:16.

27. Finkelstein (1924), 31, 171 ff., 178, 189. *Encyclopedia Talmudit* 7:153, nn. 877–904 at *Herem d'Rabbenu Gershom* (Hebrew), cites Ashkenazic and Sephardic codes and responsa that adopted and extended Rabbenu Gershom's mail decree.

Jewish communities also sought to ensure confidentiality in the collection of taxes. Some demanded that the collectors be sequestered while working. The Frankfurt Jewish tax collectors refused to reveal entries in their books even to their superiors, the city treasurers, and the Hamburg community imposed severe fines for breaches of confidence; see Baron (1942), 2:281.

28. Lamm (1971), 295. The comment of Rabbi Menahem Meiri is in his *Bet Ha-behirah* to *Bava Batra* (ed. Sofer), 6.

29. *Olmstead v. United States,* 277 U.S. 438, 466 (1928) (Brandeis, J., dissenting) and *Katz v. United States,* 389 U.S. 347 (1967). Brandeis had already voiced this opinion in an article he wrote with Samuel D. Warren (1890), in which they advocated a common law right to privacy and warned that technological innovations would decrease the personal dignity of the individual if such privacy protections were not provided.

30. Sturman (1992) wrote a humorous spoof of these invasions of privacy mandated by Jewish practice. There are, of course, many truths revealed in humor.

31. Sturman (1992) points out another common Jewish practice that is, frankly, harder to justify. When a woman goes to the *mikveh* (ritual pool) to become ritually cleansed after her menstrual flow so that she and her husband can resume conjugal relations, she is often witnessed by other such women and greeted with good wishes of fertility. In regard to a wedding, though, the Rabbis specifically point out that everyone knows that the bride and groom are getting married, at least in part, in order to be allowed to engage in sexual relations, but

the wedding guests are forbidden to mention that out of respect for the couple's privacy and dignity; see B. *Shabbat* 33a.

32. See "E-Mail Snooping" (1996), for the figure of 36 percent, and Piller (1993), for the claim that two-thirds of employers monitor their employees' E-mail.

33. On this and a number of the other legal aspects of privacy, see Gindin (1997):. "E-mail messages can usually be retrieved from a variety of locations, including the network, local hard drives, and backup tapes, even if they have been deleted. E-mail sent or received on an employer's computer system is also discoverable and is subject to review by law enforcement officials in criminal investigations" (1166–1167).

34. Gindin (1997), 1210–1213. For the Supreme Court test of "reasonable expectation of privacy," see *Katz v. United States*, 389 U.S. 347 (1967).

35. Helm (1999), A13. The study was conducted by Media Metrix, a company that monitors Internet usage.

36. That effort included an interview on NBC's *Today* show (February 3, 1999), in which the entire cast repeatedly expressed its disgust at the very thought of being invaded in that way.

37. B. *Yoma* 85a–b (with Rashi there); B. *Sanhedrin* 74a–b; and *Mekhilta* on Exodus 31:13. For a general discussion of the topic, see Jakobovits (1975), 45–98. As for murder, incest/adultery, and idolatry, one must give up one's life rather than commit those offenses. That no civil or theological culpability attaches to violating other Jewish laws in the effort to save a life, see S.A. *Hoshen Mishpat* 359:4, 380:3; and compare Jakobovits (1972), 95–96.

38. M.T. *Laws of Idolatry* 5:3. The provisions that are waived include the requirement to warn the culprit before he commits the act, the prohibition of entrapment, and the plea for clemency. Cohen (1984), 231, makes this analogy.

39. Aftergood (1999), M2.

40. Ibid.

41. See Crossette (1999), A15, A17.

42. Ibid., A17.

43. Ibid.

44. M. *Sanhedrin* 3:7 and B. *Sanhedrin* 31a.

45. Exodus 23:7 includes the prohibition against lying, and Leviticus 19:16 has the ban against gossip. See M.T. *Laws of Ethics (De'ot)* 7:2 for Maimonides' definition of the ban against gossip.

46. B. *Yoma* 4b. According to Magen Avraham (S.A. *Orah Hayyim* 156:2), even if the party revealed the matter publicly, the listener is still bound by an implied confidence until expressly released. See also *Hafetz Hayyim* 10:6.

47. Thus some say that a widow or widower who remarries should not continue to observe the anniversary of death (the yahrzeit) of his or her first spouse. The second spouse clearly knows of the previous marriage, but graphic reminders of it may undermine the second marriage; see *Kol Bo al Avelut*, 2:4, par. 34, and Rabbi Eliezer Waldenberg, *Tzitz Eliezer* 405:34. I, though, disagree with these opinions. While constant reminders of the first marriage are clearly detrimental

to the health of the second marriage, yearly memorials are not only acceptable but also appropriate.

The general rule that tact trumps truth when there is no practical necessity to tell the truth is established in the debate between the Schools of Shammai and Hillel as to what one tells the bride about how she looks on her wedding day. The School of Shammai demands the truth, whether that hurts the bride's feelings or not; but the School of Hillel maintains that, no matter how she looks, people should tell the bride that she looks beautiful. The law follows the ruling of the School of Hillel (B. *Ketubbot* 16b–17a). That would apply even to private conversations, but when the remark is made in public, the more general prohibition of shaming someone in public is also involved. According to the Talmud, one who shames someone else in public is akin to a murderer, for he or she kills the person spoken about in the estimation of the speaker, the hearers, and the person himself or herself; see B. *Bava Metz'ia* 58b and the extended discussion there of this topic through 59b, and see B. *Sanhedrin* 11a.

48. See the commentary of *Metzudat David* on Micah 7:5; B. *Ta'anit* 11b; and B. *Ḥagigah* 16b. Here, and in much of this section, I am indebted to Cohen (1984).

49. *Whalen v. Roe*, 429 U.S. 589 (1977), at 605; compare. also 598–600 and nn. 22–26 (noting that the courts have recognized a privacy interest in avoiding disclosure of personal matters).

50. Gindin (1997) provides a detailed record and analysis of the various federal acts dealing with these subjects (1196–1209) and suggests this use of that provision (1187–1188).

51. The states are Alaska, Arizona, California, Florida, Hawaii, Illinois, Louisiana, Montana, South Carolina, and Washington; ibid., 1188, nn. 179–180.

52. Restatement (Second) of Torts 652A-652I (1977), at 652B, 652D, 652E, and 652C, respectively. These common law torts were first described by Prosser (1960), 389. See Gindin (1997), 1188–1196, for further discussion of these torts and for other common law bases for protecting privacy, including breach of contract; negligence; breach of confidentiality; intentional or reckless disregard of safety; fraud; infliction of emotional distress; right of publicity; trade secret misappropriation; and trespass to chattels, conversion, and unjust enrichment.

53. Leviticus 5:1. See also B. *Bava Kamma* 56a; Tucker (1984), 105; and Cohen (1949), 307. This may be parallel to the U.S. Supreme Court's concept, quoted earlier, of rights having effect only within a context of "ordered liberty."

54. Leviticus 19:16. The Rabbis' interpretation (in the *Sifra* on that verse and in *Targum Pseudo-Jonathan* there) was, "Do not stand idly by when your neighbor's blood is shed. If you see someone in danger of drowning or being attacked by robbers or by a wild beast, you are obligated to rescue that person." See also B. *Sanhedrin* 73a.

55. Note that the Talmud specifically applies the Torah's demand that we not stand idly by our neighbor's blood to assert not only that we must help someone drowning but also that we must help someone beset by bandits (B. *Sanhedrin* 73a). Thus we have a positive duty to protect not only other people's lives but also their property.

56. B. *Arakhin* 15a–16a and M.T. *Laws of Ethics* (*De'ot*) 7:2-4. According to Maimonides there, if one utters negative things about a person occasionally, each time it is the sin of *lashon ha-ra*; if one besmirches a particular person continually, however, it is the graver sin of *motzi shem ra*.

57. For "reprove your kinsman," see Leviticus 19:17. For exposing the sins of leaders, see B. *Berakhot* 63–63b; Rashi to B. *Yoma* 87b; Rabbenu Yonah, *Sha'are Teshuvah* (*Gates of Repentance*), par. 218; and Hafetz Hayyim, *Shmirat Ha-Lashon*, "The Laws of the Prohibitions of Evil Speech," 4:6, 6:4.

58. B. *Bava Batra* 89b.

59. Ibid., 39b.

60. Leviticus 19:17; *Sifra*, Kedoshim 4:8; and B. *Arakhin* 16b.

61. Rosh on B. *Niddah* 61a. This is based on the story of Gedaliah, governor of Judah after the destruction of the First Temple, who ignored rumors of assassins and was subsequently murdered.

62. Thus, according to the Talmud (B. *Sanhedrin* 11a), God refused to tell Joshua who had stolen booty, telling him rather to cast lots to find out for himself.

63. Hafetz Hayyim, *Hilkhot Shmirat Ha-Lashon* 4:1, cited by Pliskin (1975), 164. On this last condition, see Chapter Six herein.

64. Cohen (1984).

65. I discuss this concern in regard to sperm and egg donors in Dorff (1998), 81–90, 103–107.

66. One article that describes just such a situation is Cloud (1999).

67. In the case of children born through donor insemination and egg donation, sharing this information is also required to avoid unintentional incest in the next generation; see Dorff (1998), 69–72.

68. The rabbinic interpretation of the biblical commandments to honor and respect parents (found in Exodus 20:12 and Leviticus 19:3), appears in B. *Kiddushin* 31b; see generally 30b–32a. For a more extended discussion of Jewish filial duties, see *Encylcopedia Judaica* 13:95–100 at *Parent and Child*, Schereschewsky (1972), and Blidstein (1975). See also Chapter Four herein.

69. B. *Ketubbot* 103a and S.A. *Yoreh De'ah* 240:21 ff.

70. For Rashi, see B. *Sanhedrin* 47a, s.v. *'al*, and B. *Berakhot* 10b, s.v. *girer*. For Rabbenu Tam, see *Tosafot* to B. *Yevamot* 22b, s.v. *ke-she-'asah*, and *Mordecai* to B. *Yevamot*, sec. 13. For Rabbi Alfas, see B. *Yevamot* 22b. For Maimonides, see M.T. *Laws of Rebels* (*Mamrim*) 5:12; see also 6:11. For Karo and Isserles, see S.A. *Yoreh De'ah* 240:18 (with gloss). Generally, see Blidstein (1975), 130–136 and Lappe (1993).

71. Allen (1999), S4.

72. Courts have generally held that a physician–patient privilege does not exist at common law, and so it rests on the statutes of those jurisdictions that grant it, either explicitly or implicitly through the public policies announced in various statutes. Zelin (1986) lists the following as examples of such court actions:

Alabama: *Horne v. Patton* (1973) 291 Ala 701, 287 So 2d 82.

Arizona: *Valencia v. Duval Corp.* (1982 App) 132 Ariz 348, 645 P2d 1262.

Colorado: *Anderson v. Glismann* (1984, DC Colo) 577 F Supp 1506 (applying Colorado law).

District of Columbia: *Logan v. District of Columbia* (1978, DC Dist Col) 477 F Supp 1328, 3 Media L R 2094 (applying District of Columbia law); *Vassiliades v. Garfinckel's, Brooks Bros.* (1985, Dist Col App) 492 A2d 580.

Illinois: *Bond v. Pecaut* (1983, ND Ill) 561 F Supp 1037, affirmed without opposition (CA7 Ill) 734 F2d 18 (applying Illinois law).

Louisiana: *Pennison v. Provident Life and Accident Insurance Company* (1963, La App 4th Cir) 154 So 2d 617, cert den 244 La 1019, 156 So 2d 226; *Acosta v. Cary* (1978, La App 4th Cir) 365 So 2d 4; *Leger v. Spurlock* (1991, La App 1st Cir) 589 So 2d 40.

Massachusetts: *Bratt v. International Business Machines Corp.* (1984) 392 Mass 508, 467 NE2d 126.

Missouri: *Mikel v. Abrams* (1982, WD Mo) 541 F Supp 591, affirmed without opposition (CA 8 Mo) 716 F2d 907 (applying Missouri law).

New York: *Feeney v. Young* (1920) 191 App Div 501, 181 NYS 481; *Doe v. Roe* (1977) 93 Misc 2d 201, 400 NYS2d 668; *Anker v. Brodnitz* (1979) 98 Misc 2d 148, 413 NYS2d, 582, affirmed (2d Dept) 73 App Div 2d 589, 422 NYS2d 887, appeal dismissed 51 NY2d 743, 432 NYS2d 743; 432 NYS2d 364, 411 NE2d 783 (recognizing rule); *Griffin v. Medical Society of State* (1939, Sup) 11 NYS2d 109.

Ohio: *Hammonds v. Aetna Casualty and Surety Company* (1965, ND Ohio) 237 F Supp 96, 3 Ohio Misc 83, 31 Ohio Ops 2d 174 (applying Ohio law); *Prince v. St. Francis—St. George Hospital, Inc.* (1985, Hamilton Co) 20 Ohio App 3d 4, 20 Ohio BR 4, 484 NE2d 265.

Oregon: *Humphers v. First Interstate Bank* (1985) 298 Or 706, 696 P2d 527, 48 ALR4th, 651.

Pennsylvania: *Clayman v. Bernstein* (1940) 38 Pa D&C 543.

I would like to thank Rabbi Mark Ankcorn, a lawyer and a 2002 graduate of the Ziegler School of Rabbinic Studies at the University of Judaism, for finding the Zelin article for me.

In California, which has a patchwork of protections principally governing patients with mental illness, substance abuse, HIV and AIDS, seventeen bills on medical confidentiality were introduced in the state legislature between 1996 and 1999. Statutes have already been legislated that establish a physician–patient privilege (Evidence Code sec. 994), a psychotherapist–patient privilege (Evidence Code sec. 1014), and a sexual assault victim–counselor privilege (Evidence Code sec. 1035.8), and this privilege applies to anyone authorized to function in those roles or reasonably believed by the patient to be authorized to function in those roles (Evidence Code, sec. 990 [for physicians], sec. 1010 [for psychotherapists], and sec. 1035.2 [for counselors for sexual assault victims]. Some people are mounting efforts to pass federal legislation to protect patients' medical records, but others are worried that federal law will establish a "ceiling" of privacy, making it impossible for states to legislate stronger guarantees. See Allen (1999), S4.

73. *Tarasoff v. Board of Regents of the University of California* 529 P. 2d 553 (Cal. 1974); modified 551 P. 2d 334 (Cal. 1976), 131 California Reporter 14 (July 1, 1976). That case also affirmed the general privilege itself. The California Evidence Code, art. 8, sec. 1033, now states: "Subject to Section 912, a penitent, whether or not a party [that is, litigant in the case before the court], has a privilege to refuse to disclose, and to prevent another from disclosing, a penitential communication if he claims the privilege"; and sec. 1034 states: "Subject to Section 912, a clergyman, whether or not a party, has a privilege to refuse to disclose a penitential communication if he claims the privilege."

The parallel Arkansas statute reads: "No minister of the gospel or priest of any denomination shall be compelled to testify in relation to any confession made to him in his professional character, in the course of discipline by the rule of practice of such denomination." New York and Michigan, like California, substitute "allowed" for "compelled," thus giving the penitent the right to prevent the clergy from revealing confessions made to them in their capacity as members of the clergy.

This "seal of the confessional" has been generally recognized by the civil courts even in those states that do not have such a privilege written into their evidence codes, even though by common law confessions were not considered privileged. New York is possibly the first of all English-speaking states from the time of the Reformation to grant this protection, for De Witt Clinton affirmed such a privilege in a decision he made in June 1813; see Louisell et al. (1976), 666–667. I would like to thank Rabbi Ben Zion Bergman for these references.

74. For a discussion of the *Tarasoff* case, see Wasserstrum (1985), 243–262. The resulting rule of that case was later legislated in California as Welfare and Institutions Code sec. 8105(c), with a specific provision that "a serious threat of physical violence against a reasonably identifiable victim or victims" that is revealed in counseling must be communicated by the therapist to local law enforcement officials, and that "the duty to warn of the threat takes precedence over the confidentiality of medical record provisions and the psychotherapist-patient privilege. A 'licensed psychotherapist' for purposes of this requirement includes psychiatrists, psychologists, LCSWs, MFCCs, and other persons specified in Evidence Code section 1010."

75. California Health and Safety Code sections 1795.10(c), 1795.14(a). On confidentiality for minors generally, see Weinstein et al. (1996) and Katner (1996). I would like to thank Rabbi Eric Rosin, a lawyer and a 2002 graduate of the Ziegler School of Rabbinic Studies at the University of Judaism, for making these materials available for me.

76. Health and Safety Code sec. 1795.14(a).

77. Title 42, Code of Federal Regulations, sec. 2.14(b).

78. For drugs and alcohol, see Family Code sec. 6929(4)(b). For HIV, see ibid., sec. 6926.

79. Ibid., sec. 6950(g), a 1996 amendment to the California law, however, states:

> Notwithstanding any other provision of law, in cases where a parent or legal guardian has sought the medical care and counseling for a drug- or alcohol-related problem of a minor child, the physician shall disclose medical information concerning such care to the minor's parents or legal guardian upon their request, even if the minor child does not consent to disclosure, without liability for such disclosure.

I am not sure how this squares with the federal regulations discussed in the text.

80. Health and Safety Code sec. 199.27(a)(1).

81. Family Code sec. 6929(4)(c).

82. Ibid., sec. 6929(e) and 6950(e). For the requirement that minors seeking abortion must first inform their parents, see Healy (1999), A13, which notes that a 1987 law in California "established a parental consent requirement, but the state Supreme Court struck it down 10 years later, saying it violated privacy rights."

83. Title 42, Code of Federal Regulations, sec. 2.14(c)(1).

84. Ibid., sec. 2.14(c)(2).

85. Ibid. sec. 2.14(d).

86. Pear (1999).

87. S.A. *Yoreh De'ah* 251:7-8; 252:1.

88. J. *Terumot* 7:20 (47a) and *Genesis Rabbah* 94:9. See Dorff (1998), 291–299, for an extended discussion of how this precedent fits into a contemporary Jewish approach to the distribution of medical care.

89. B. *Sanhedrin* 2b. For the ban on collecting interest from fellow Jews, see Exodus 22:24; Leviticus 25:36–37; Deuteronomy 23:20–21; and M. *Bava Metz'ia*, chap. 5. The command nevertheless to lend to fellow Jews in need is based, in rabbinic literature, on Exodus 22:24, where the "if" clause in that verse is understood as a commandment rather than an option on the basis of the command to lend to the poor in Deuteronomy 15:8; see *Mekhilta* Mishpatim, par. 19; M.T. *Laws of the Lender and Borrower* 1:1; and S.A. *Hoshen Mishpat* 93:1. See also Dorff (2002), chap. 6.

90. Many of them are listed in M. *Gittin*, chaps. 4–5, and the talmudic discussion of those chapters; but see also B. *Sanhedrin* 81b.

91. Cohen (1984), 224–227, takes this position, and I agree with it.

92. Numbers 27:3.

93. B. *Shabbat* 96b. The Talmud (at the top of the next page) goes on to tell a parallel story about Rabbi Akiva's view that Aaron turned leprous just as Miriam did (Numbers 12:10), for which Rabbi Judah ben Betaira again castigates Rabbi Akiva for maligning someone.

94. Gindin (1997), 1180, n. 139.

95. Clausing (1999), C10.

96. Miller (1999), A-8.

97. Williams (1999), A5. See also Gindin (1997), 1182–1183. The European law is Directive 95/46, 1995 O.J. (L281) 31.

98. Shalala (2002), A1.

99. "What It Means" (2002).

100. Rubin (1999). According to an editorial in *USA Today* (1999), 25A, "Early indications suggest it [the Department of Health and Human Services] would produce weaker privacy rules than those in the leading Senate bill. For instance, medical records could be used for many purposes without a patient's consent." The editorial continues:

> The fix isn't complicated. A law stipulating that patients must be asked before a health plan releases private medical data—and that the police force face some hurdles before obtaining records—would go a long way toward protecting patients' health histories without harming medical research or health care. Congress already guarantees the privacy of far less sensitive information, including data on consumers' cable-viewing habits, which can only be released with a subscriber's OK.

101. Spitz (1986), p. 12.
102. Ibid., 12–13.
103. Ibid., 13.
104. Gindin (1997), 1222.

NOTES TO CHAPTER THREE

1. I wrote the original version of this chapter with the Rabbinical Assembly's Commission on Human Sexuality. It was published by the Rabbinical Assembly in 1996 (see Dorff, 1996b). Although I have revised the language and some of the content of that rabbinic letter in creating this chapter, I would like to thank the Rabbinical Assembly for permission to reprint much of that letter here, and I would like to thank the members of the commission for their significant and sensitive input in revising the various drafts of this document. I was privileged to serve as a member of that commission; the other members of the commission, which did its work from 1992 to 1994, were Rabbi Arnold Goodman, chair; Rabbi Michael Gold, co-chair; and Rabbis Morris J. Allen, Stephanie Dickstein, Amy Eilberg, Alan B. Lettofsky, Mark G. Loeb, Noam E. Marans, Arnold E. Resnicoff, Barry Dov Schwartz, and Jeffrey Wohlberg. I would especially like to thank Rabbi Joel Meyers, executive vice president of the Rabbinical Assembly, for his indispensable help in creating the commission and in making its work bear fruit, and Rabbi Gerald Zelizer, who was president of the Rabbinical Assembly during the years of the work of the commission and who handled the many difficult political issues in establishing it and in gaining approval for its products with aplomb. Finally, I would like to thank the members of the Conservative Movement's Committee on Jewish Law and Standards (CJLS) and, indeed, of the Rabbinical Assembly as a whole, because the revisions in the last two drafts of this rabbinic letter were almost entirely suggested by them. I would especially like to thank those who wrote detailed and extensive comments to the sixth and seventh drafts of the letter, namely, Dr. Anne Lerner and Rabbis Arthur Green, David Lieber, Lionel Moses, Avram Reisner, Benjamin Segal, Matthew Simon, and Robert Slosberg.

2. Orthodox rabbis are increasingly getting questions from unmarried couples who are living together about the necessity of *mikveh* (ritual bath) and the like, and it is no longer a secret that family violence is at least as common among the Orthodox as it is among the other streams of Judaism. The Jewish Family Service of Los Angeles, for example, has a special program to combat family violence within the Orthodox community. The latest and, from all accounts, the most scientific study of American sexual behavior indicates that Jews have more sexual partners between the ages of eighteen and forty-four than any other American religious group, including even the unchurched; see Michael et al. (1994), 103. This may well be because Jews tend to go to college and even graduate school and, therefore, marry later. But, even so, this finding and the phenomena mentioned above clearly indicate that, for both the observant and not, the current situation among Jews in regard to sexuality and family relations is considerably different from the norms of Jewish law and well worth a fresh look as to how Judaism can inform our behavior, thought, and feelings in this arena in our own times.

3. In an earlier work, I discussed nine different biblical rationales for the authority of Jewish law together with some additional ones that the Rabbis suggested; see Dorff (1989).

4. The Commission on Human Sexuality specifically did not intend to break new ground in Jewish law on these issues; as per its mandate, it referred matters that, in its judgment, needed more discussion to the CJLS for its research and ruling. Those topics included, for example, whether we should alter the tradition's stance opposing masturbation and whether, in the case of extramarital affairs, we should, contrary to traditional Jewish law, encourage the couple to seek reconciliation, especially when young children were involved. The letter was rather intended to present the gist of the Jewish tradition on sexuality and intimacy in the areas where Conservative rabbis are more or less unified in their interpretation and application of Judaism, as indicated by previous rulings of the CJLS and/or by long-standing practice.

5. Dorff (2002), chap. 1, and Dorff (1987). See also Konvitz (1978), esp. chap. 5.

6. *Genesis Rabbah* 43:7 (43:8 in some editions) and see B. *Shabbat* 10a.

7. Genesis 1:27, 5:1.

8. Proverbs 20:27.

9. Genesis 1:26,28.

10. Genesis 3:5 and Deuteronomy 30:19.

11. B. *Shabbat* 10a, 119b. In the first of those passages, it is the judge who judges justly who is called God's partner; in the second, it is anyone who recites Genesis 2:1–3 (about God resting on the seventh day) on Friday night who thereby participates in God's ongoing act of creation. The Talmud (B. *Sanhedrin* 38a) specifically wanted the Sadducees *not* to be able to say that angels or any being other than humans participated with God in creation.

12. Genesis 1:31.

13. Jewish sources require that even within the privacy of one's home, a couple should engage in sex only if nobody else is awake and there is at least a par-

tition between the couple and other members of the household; see S.A. *Oraḥ Ḥayyim* 240:6, 11 (and see the commentary of Rabbi Moses Isserles and of Magen Avraham there); *Kitzur* Shulchan Arukh 150:3, 4; and B. *Niddah* 17a. Thus the modesty appropriate to sexual activities applies even to one's home and, all the more so, to the public sphere.

14. So, for example, "Great is human dignity, for it overrides a negative prohibition in the Torah" (B. *Berakhot* 19b; compare B. *Shabbat* 81b and B. *Menahot* 37b); "Love your fellow-creatures and honor them" (*Derekh Eretz Zuta* 1:9); and the Holy One, blessed be He, has concern for the honor of all His creatures, including non-Jews and even wicked people like Balaam (*Numbers Rabbah* 20:14; compare *Sifre*, Shofetim, #192). See also B. *Bava Kamma* 79b; *Genesis Rabbah* 48:9; and *Leviticus Rabbah* 17:5. The underlying theological basis for the honor due to all other human beings is, as the Rabbis say, "All that the Holy One, Blessed be He, created, He created for His own honor" (B. *Yoma* 38a, based on Isaiah 43:7).

15. B. *Bava Metz'ia* 49a. For a summary of Jewish laws of commerce, see Solomon Ganzfried, *Kitzur* Shulchan Arukh chap. 62 (trans. Goldin, 1961, 2:36–39).

16. B. *Ketubbot* 17a.

17. Leviticus 19:18.

18. For Rabbi Akiva, see *Sifra* Kedoshim 4:12 on Leviticus 19:18; J. *Nedarim* 9:4; and *Genesis Rabbah* 24:7. For Hillel, see B. *Shabbat* 31a. Hillel answered the heathen who wanted to be taught the whole Torah while the rabbi stood on one foot with the negative version of this commandment: "What is hateful to you, do not do to your neighbor. That is the whole Torah; all the rest is commentary. Go and learn."

19. So, for example, in the spirit of this law—and according to some authorities, on the basis of it—we are required to visit the sick, comfort mourners, assist in making funeral arrangements, help the bride and groom rejoice and contribute to their wedding arrangements, and extend hospitality to guests; see M.T. *Laws of Mourning* 14:1; *Laws of Gifts to the Poor* 8:10; and *Sefer ha-Ḥinnukh*, Commandment #243. In general, see *Encyclopedia Talmudit* 1:211-215 at *Ahavat Yisrael* (Hebrew). Conversely, this law is the foundation for a number of rabbinic prohibitions, forbidding harm to our neighbor's person or property and requiring positive steps to preserve both; see M.T. *Laws of Ethics (De'ot)* 6:3; Maimonides, *Sefer Hamitzvot (The Book of the Commandments)*, Positive Commandment #206; and *Sefer ha-Ḥinnukh*, Commandment #206.

20. B. *Bava Metz'ia* 62a.

21. Buber (1970), esp. 62 ("All actual life is encounter."), 85 ("And in all the seriousness of truth, listen: without It a human being cannot live. But whoever lives only with that is not human."), 111–115 ("How much of a person a man is depends on how strong the I of the basic word I-You is in the human duality of his I"), and 123–124. Buber takes pains to point out that the I–Thou relationship is to be distinguished not only from the I–It relationship but also from a mystical I–I relationship, for genuine encounter requires two separate beings; see 56, 119–120, 126–127, 131, 134–137 ("In lived actuality there is no unity of being.

Actuality is to be found only in effective activity; strength and depth of the former only in that of the latter. 'Inner' actuality, too, is only where there is reciprocal activity."), and 148 ("But in the perfect relationship my You embraces my self without being it; my limited recognition is merged into a boundless being-recognized"). See also Fromm (1956) for a more extended analysis of love along the lines of Buber's thought.

22. For God owns our bodies, see Genesis 14:19,22; Exodus 19:5, 20:11; and Deuteronomy 10:14. The duty to take care of our bodies is summarized best in M.T. *Laws of Ethics (Hilkhot De'ot)*, chaps. 3–5. The Rabbis derive that from Deuteronomy 4:9 and 4:15. For the commandment not to harm yourself, see M. *Bava Kamma* 8:6 and B. *Hullin* 10a. For the prohibition of committing suicide, see *Semahot* (Evel Rabbati) 2:1–5; M.T. *Laws of Murder* 2:3; *Laws of Courts (Sanhedrin)* 18:6; *Laws of Mourning* 1:11; S.A. *Yoreh De'ah* 345:1-3; and *Encyclopedia Judaica* 15:489–491 at *Suicide*. On these topics generally, see Dorff (1998), chap. 2.

23. Leviticus 19:2.

24. Exodus 19:6.

25. In times past, great rabbinic authorities wrote letters to the Jews of their generation to convey Judaism's message concerning human sexuality and intimate relations. Probably the most famous is *Iggeret ha-Kodesh*, attributed to Nahmanides (1194–1270), but we also have manuals on these matters written by, or attributed to, Rabbi Moses ben Maimon (Maimonides, 1135–1204), Rabbi Abraham ben David of Posquieres (1125–1198), and others. They used the format of a letter (*iggeret*) or a manual rather than a rabbinic legal ruling (responsum, *teshuvah*) because in these essays they were not asked to rule on a specific question in Jewish law but rather to educate their readers about the accepted rules of Jewish law and the concepts and values that underlie them. Their audience, then, was not primarily other rabbis, but the general Jewish community. Moreover, these rabbis used the form of a letter because they wanted to be personal in tone as well as in content regarding this most personal of areas.

26. Exodus 21:10.

27. Genesis 1:28.

28. B. *Yevamot* 61b, where Rabbi Nahman, quoting Genesis 2:18, asserts that "although a man may have many children, he must not remain without a wife, for the Torah says, 'It is not good that a man should be alone.' " Later Jewish law codes take this as authoritative law; see M.T. *Laws of Marriage* 15:16; *Laws of Forbidden Intercourse* 21:26; and S.A. *Even Ha'ezer* 1:8.

29. Genesis 2:18,24.

30. I want to thank Rabbi Mark Loeb for suggesting this interpretation.

31. The Septuagint, Peshitta, and Targums all understood the last of the words in this biblical phrase, "*onah*," to refer to conjugal rights, and so did the rabbinic tradition. Rashbam (Rabbi Samuel ben Meir, c. 1080–1174, northern France) and Bekhor Shor (Joseph ben Isaac, twelfth century, France) understand it to mean "dwelling" or "shelter," based on the Hebrew noun "*ma'on*." Paul (1969) of Hebrew University argued persuasively that this phrase in the Torah originally meant "and her ointments," parallel to Hosea 2:7, Ecclesiastes 9:7–9, and many ancient Near Eastern texts—including the Egyptian wisdom text known as "The

Instruction of the Vizier Ptah-hotep," which advises "a man of standing" to fill his wife's belly, clothe her back, and provide ointment for her body. In any case, the rabbis of the Mishnah, the Talmud, and the later Jewish tradition all understood it as meaning conjugal rights, and, as I describe shortly, they determined Jewish law on that basis.

32. For the wife's rights to sex, see M. *Ketubbot* 5:6; M.T. *Laws of Marriage* 14:4–7, 15; S.A. *Yoreh De'ah* 235:1, and *Even Ha-ezer* 76, 77:1. For the husband's rights to sex, see M. *Ketubbot* 5:7; M.T. *Laws of Marriage* 14:8–14; and S.A. *Even Ha'ezer* 77:2–3.

33. That the man may not force himself upon his wife, see M.T. *Laws of Marriage* 14:15. That the couple may have conjugal relations any way they want, see S.A. *Even Ha'ezer* 25:2, gloss, where Isserles says that "he may do what he wants with his wife," but this is a comment on the same paragraph of the Shulchan Arukh that asserts, "he may not have intercourse with her except with her consent (literally, 'desire')." So the upshot is that both members of the couple must agree to the way they are having sex, presumably for the mutual satisfaction of both.

34. B. *Eruvin* 100b; B. *Yevamot* 62b; S.A. *Orah Hayyim* 240:1; and S.A. *Yoreh De'ah* 184:10.

35. B. *Eruvin* 100b; *Leviticus Rabbah* 9:6; *Numbers Rabbah* 13:2; *Pesikta de Rav Kahana*, "And When Moses Finished" (on Hanukkah), Piska (ed. Mandelbaum), 1.1; M.T. *Laws of Ethics* (*De'ot*) 5:4; M.T. *Laws of Forbidden Intercourse* 21:11; S.A. *Orah Hayyim* 240:10; and S.A. *Even Ha'ezer* 25:2.

36. B. *Nedarim* 20b and B. *Sanhedrin* 58b. See Feldman (1973), 155 ff., for the history of the "yes–but" stance that medieval Jewish writers took to this talmudic permissiveness.

37. B. *Ketubbot* 48a.

38. See, for example, Scheindlin (1986).

39. Leviticus 15:19–24, 18:19, 20:18.

40. If one looks at these practices from an anthropological perspective, they probably arise out of ancient fears of emissions from the body, even natural ones, lest the life force of the individual ebb with the emission. The placement of these laws in Leviticus 15, immediately after laws governing emissions due to disease, supports this interpretation.

41. Leviticus 11:36 indicates that a special pool must be constructed. The specific rules for that pool were later spelled out by the Rabbis; for a summary, see S.A. *Yoreh De'ah* 201. See also Klein (1979), 518–522.

42. B. *Berakhot* 22a, according to which nine *kabs* of water, rather than the usual forty of the *mikveh*, is sufficient for the man to use to remove his status of impurity. Furthermore, the Mishnah (M. *Mikvaot* 8:1) asserts that even a pool of water that was filled with a hose and thus definitely unkosher as a *mikveh* is, for those living outside the land of Israel, kosher for the purification of a man who has had a seminal emission. Moreover, the decree of Ezra, requiring such men to immerse themselves specifically in a *mikveh* before reading the Torah (and, perhaps, before reciting the *Shema* or the *Amidah*) was annulled precisely because Jewish men who otherwise abided by Jewish law were simply not fulfilling this decree. See also note 43.

43. See note 39 for the biblical rules for both men and women. Leviticus 22:4 and Deuteronomy 23:11–12 pertain to seminal emissions.

The Mishnah prohibits a man who has had a seminal emission from reciting the *Shema* or the *Amidah* (M. *Berakhot* 3:4-5). According to the Talmud (for example, B. *Bava Kamma* 82a and J. *Yoma* 1:1), it was Ezra who instituted the decree that men who have had a seminal emission immerse themselves in a *mikveh* before reading the Torah. For some interpreters, this meant studying any classical Jewish text (see B. *Berakhot* 22a), and according to some Rishonim (rabbis of the eleventh through sixteenth centuries), a later court also required such men to immerse in a *mikveh* before they prayed; see M.T. *Laws of Prayer* 4:4 (but see the comment of the *Kesef Mishneh* there); Meiri on *Berakhot* 20a; and Rosh on *Bava Kamma*, chap. 7, #19. This is not required by the Torah, for people in a state of impurity of any sort are permitted by the Torah, as the Rabbis understand it, to engage in study and prayer; see Rif, *Berakhot*, chap. 3; M.T. *Laws of Reading the Shema* 4:8; and M.T. *Laws of Prayer* 4:5. Indeed, the purpose of this decree was not, according to these interpreters, motivated by concerns of purity at all but rather to ensure that rabbinic scholars would not have conjugal relations with their wives as often as roosters do with chickens or, alternatively, to make Torah study like the Revelation at Sinai, where men were not to have relations with their wives in preparation for the event (Exodus 19:15) and in honor of the Torah that they were to receive and learn.

Ezra's decree was annulled; see B. *Berakhot* 22a; Bertinoro on M. *Berakhot* 3:4; M.T. *Laws of Reading the Shema* 4:8; M.T. *Laws of Prayer* 4:4-6; S.A. *Orah Hayyim* 88:1; and the commentaries on M.T. and S.A. there. As the *Kesef Mishneh* to M.T. *Laws of Reading the Shema* 4:8, asserts and demonstrates, the annulment occurred not because the rabbis voted to do so, for no later court had the authority to overturn a decree of Ezra's court, but rather, "because there was not enough strength in the majority of the community to uphold it, the Sages did not force the men to immerse, and it was annulled by itself." Maimonides, however, records the laws concerning a man's impurity through seminal emission fully; see M.T. *Laws of the Other Forms of Impurity*, chap. 5, based primarily on M. *Mikvaot* 8:1–4. To my knowledge, those laws have never been formally abrogated but simply have fallen into disuse. On this entire subject, see *Encyclopedia Talmudit* 4:130–148 at *Ba'al Keri* (Hebrew).

The inequality imposed by these laws is most apparent in a comment by Rabbi Moses Isserles (S.A. *Orah Hayyim* 88:1, gloss), according to which even though men who had had a seminal emission could read the Torah and recite the *Shema* and *Amidah* because Ezra's decree had been annulled, the custom in Ashkenazic communities was that women who were in their menstrual flow could not do any of those things (even though Ezra's decree never applied to them!). Moreover, except for the High Holy Days and similar events, when everyone else was attending services and when remaining at home would thus cause great pain, women were even asked to stay away from synagogue services altogether during their menstrual period. This presents quite a gap between what women and men were allowed to do after emissions from their sexual organs.

44. Even if the general custom among the observant Conservative community may be to ignore these laws, rabbinic couples may continue to uphold them, if only because they remain the law on the books. In this, there is a nice parallel in the comment of the *Kesef Mishneh* to M.T. *Laws of Reading the Shema* 4:8, according to which even after the men of the Jewish community had effectively abrogated Ezra's decree through their failure to observe it, the Rabbis continued to observe it, for no court had officially abrogated it. The laws of menstrual purity, of course, have their root in the Torah, whereas Ezra's decree was only rabbinic in origin and authority; but the parallel discrepancy between rabbinic practice, in deference to the standing law, and the custom of the community is both interesting and instructive for matters of ritual purity and, more generally, for the ways in which law and custom intersect.

45. Exodus 20:13 and Deuteronomy 5:17. Compare Leviticus 18:20, 20:10, the latter of which prescribes the death penalty for both parties to the adultery. For the three prohibitions (murder, idolatry, and adultery/incest), see B. *Sanhedrin* 74a.

Until approximately the year 1000, Jewish law allowed men to take more than one wife, and so a married man who had intercourse with an unmarried woman would not, strictly speaking, be committing adultery. He would either be engaging in prostitution or he would be taking another wife through his intercourse with her. A woman, on the other hand, could have only one husband, and so a married woman who had intercourse with any other man, married or not, would be committing adultery. Since the amendment (*takkanah*) of Rabbenu Gershom in 968, however, both men (at least in the Ashkenazic communities) and women are prohibited from having more than one marital partner at any time, and so it should now be seen as equally wrong for a married man or woman to have sexual relations with someone other than his or her spouse. (The State of Israel prohibits polygamy, but it allowed Sephardic men who had emigrated to Israel from Arab countries that permitted the practice to keep their wives.)

46. See Leviticus 20:10 and Deuteronomy 22:22. Compare Exodus 20:13; Deuteronomy 5:17; and Leviticus 18:20 for the prohibition of adultery without specification of the penalty. Because a man could have more than one wife, however, a married man would be classified as an adulterer only if he had sexual intercourse with a woman married to another man, not if he had sex with a single woman, until the decree of Rabbenu Gershom; see note 45.

47. S.A. *Even Ha'ezer* 11:1.

48. Wasserstrum (1985) noted that adultery represents a violation of a couple's promise and trust only if they make promises of exclusive fidelity to each other at the time of the marriage; an "open marriage," in which the couple at the outset mutually agrees on rules whereby either member may have a sexual affair with someone else, would not be subject to such a critique. Wasserstrum is logically correct, of course, but marriage as understood in Judaism entails just such promises, especially after Rabbenu Gershom prohibited polygyny; and so Judaism is logically correct in treating adultery as it does—namely, as a breach of both a mutual promise and mutual trust. Even Wasserstrum, toward the end of his article, argues for monogamy, and in the years since he wrote

his article, couples' experiences with open marriages have not generally been positive.

49. Leviticus 18; 20. A good summary of the rabbinic expansion of the rules of incest can be found in M.T. *Laws of Marriage* 1:6.

50. See, for example, Gaon (1960), part 2, 102, who says that it is to prevent sexual license (in light of the intimacy of family life) and "to prevent men from being attracted only by those women who are of beautiful appearance and rejecting those who are not, when they see that their own relatives do not desire them [!]." Maimonides, in *Guide of the Perplexed*, part 3, to take another example, repeats Saadia's first reason (chap. 49) but adds two more: "The purpose of this is to bring about a decrease of sexual intercourse and to diminish the desire for mating as far as possible, so that it should not be taken as an end, as is done by the ignorant" (chap. 35) and "to respect the sentiment of shame. For it would be a most shameless thing if this act would take place between the root and the branch, I refer to sexual intercourse with the mother or the daughter. . . . Being brother and sister is like being root and branch . . . or even are considered to be one and the same individual" (chap. 49).

51. I would especially like to thank Rabbi Amy Eilberg for her help with this and the next sections.

52. Deuteronomy 24:1–4.

53. B. *Gittin* 90b. The Talmud there actually speaks of a first marriage, but the sentiment undoubtedly applies to subsequent marriages as well.

54. Compare, for illustration, the assumptions about marriage embedded in two Broadway musical numbers: "Some Enchanted Evening" in *South Pacific* and "Do You Love Me?" in *Fiddler on the Roof*. Newly married couples who expect an uninterrupted series of enchanted evenings are bound to be disappointed when they find out that in the best of marriages there are indeed some enchanted evenings, but most are emotionally neutral, and some are downright unenchanting! If people begin, on the other hand, with the expectation of living life with all its tasks together and in a generally loving and supportive environment but with the full spectrum of emotions accompanying their lives as a couple, as the song in *Fiddler* depicts, then they are far less likely to think that their marriage has not met the standards they set for it at the outset.

55. Judith Wallerstein has been the primary voice asserting the harms of divorce, based on her study of 131 children of divorced parents whom she followed from 1970 on while at the School of Social Welfare at the University of California at Berkeley; see Wallerstein et al. (2000a). Others, like University of Pennsylvania professor Frank Furstenburg Jr., claim that "The overall effect of divorce is modest to moderate" (cited in Gleick, 1995, 53). And a lengthy University of Virginia study found that children of divorce were better off than those of highly dysfunctional mariages (Gleick, 1995).

56. Perhaps the most famous effort on this subject, one that depicted the real costs in pursuing one's own personal career at the expense of the family but also the real need for some people to do so, was the film *Kramer v. Kramer*.

57. In recognition of that fact, the Rabbis rule that a man who does not have children of his own may not serve as a judge in a capital case, for his lack of ex-

perience in having and raising children makes him insufficiently appreciative of human life generally; see T. *Sanhedrin* 7:3; B. *Sanhedrin* 36b; and M.T. *Laws of Courts (Sanhedrin)* 2:3.

58. For a more thorough discussion of the details of divorce as understood and practiced by all the modern movements, see Dorff and Rosett (1988), 515–545. In recent years, some Orthodox rabbis have adopted two of the methods that the Conservative movement has used for decades—namely, a prenuptial agreement (*t'ani b'kiddushin*), in which the husband either agrees that the marriage will automatically be dissolved six months after a divorce decree in the civil courts if he has not given his wife a *get* by that time or agrees to pay her a substantial sum of money for her maintenance for each day that he fails to give her a *get*. If no such prenuptial agreement has been signed, Rabbi Emanuel Rackman, former president of Bar Ilan University, has convened a court to annul such marriages as a last resort, just as the Conservative movement's Bet Din (court) has done, basing their authority for doing so on the talmudic principle that every marriage is valid only as long as the rabbis say it is (*kol d'mikadesh, a'da'ta d'rabbanan mikaddesh*); see B. *Ketubbot* 50a; and B. *Gittin* 33a, 73a.

59. B. *Eruvin* 82a and B. *Ketubbot* 65b, 122b–123a. For these and other relevant sources as well as a discussion about them, see Herring (1989), 177 ff.

60. See Schochetman (1992) and Broyde (1994).

61. M. *Yevamot* 6:6 (61b). In that mishnah, the School of Shammai says that one has to have two boys and the School of Hillel says that one must have a boy and a girl. The Talmud understands the School of Shammai's position to be based on the fact that Moses had two sons, Gershom and Eliezer (1 Chronicles 23:15), and the mishnah itself states that the School of Hillel's ruling is based on Genesis 1:27, according to which God created the human being, "male and female God created them." A Tosefta (T. *Yevamot* 8:3) included in the Talmud (B. *Yevamot* 62a) asserts that the School of Shammai actually requires two males and two females, whereas the School of Hillel requires only one male and one female. Yet another talmudic tradition (B. *Yevamot* 62a), in the name of Rabbi Nathan, states that the School of Shammai requires a male and a female, while the School of Hillel requires either a male or a female. The Jerusalem Talmud (J. *Yevamot* 6:6 [7c]) records the position of Rabbi Bun (Abun), which takes note of the context of the School of Hillel's ruling right after that of the School of Shammai's ruling requiring two boys. Rabbi Bun, therefore, read the School of Hillel as agreeing that two boys would suffice to fulfill the obligation, but "*even a boy and a girl*" would; thus the School of Hillel is offering a leniency over the School of Shammai's requirement of two boys, in line with the School of Hillel's general reputation. Rabbi Bun also noted that if that were not the case, so that the School of Hillel were saying that *only* both a boy and a girl would fulfill the obligation, then this ruling should appear in the various lists of the stringencies of the School of Hillel in chapters 4 and 5 of M. *Eduyot*, but it does not. Despite Rabbi Bun's arguments, the codes rule that the obligation is fulfilled only when a man has fathered both a boy and a girl; see M.T. *Laws of Marriage* 15:4 and S.A. *Even Ha'ezer* 1:5.

Ironically, in our own day, when modern technology has suddenly provided us with some control over the gender of our children but when the Jewish community simultaneously suffers from a major population deficit, the Conservative rabbinate, though approving the letter on which this chapter is based and my earlier responsum on artificial insemination, egg donation, and adoption (Dorff, 1996c), has affirmed that technologically assisted gender selection should *not* take place (except, perhaps, when a couple has already had several children of one gender and wants a child of the other gender), that we should welcome children into our midst regardless of their gender, that we see any two children as fulfillment of the commandment to procreate, but that we encourage Jewish couples who can have more than two children to do so.

62. B. *Megillah* 13a and B. *Ketubbot* 50a. See also *Exodus Rabbah,* chap. 4; S.A. *Orah Hayyim* 139:3; Abraham Gumbiner, *Magen Avraham,* on S.A. *Orah Hayyim* 156; and Moshe Feinstein, *Igrot Moshe* on *Yoreh De'ah* 161. Compare B. *Sanhedrin* 19b, where the adopted parent is described as "a person who raises *another's* child." Thus, although highly praised, adoption does not change the legal status of the child's parentage (see also B. *Sotah* 43b), despite several instances in the Bible in which adopted parents are called actual parents (B. *Sanhedrin* 9b, referring to 1 Chronicles 4:18; Ruth 4:17; Psalms 77:16; and 2 Samuel 21:8). Instead, the adopted parents are seen as the agents of the natural parents for most purposes. See Broyde (1993). Even so, CJLS in 1988 approved a responsum by Reisner (2001), esp. 168–169 and 174, according to which an adopted child may use the patronymic and matronymic of his or her adopted parents. On adoption in Jewish law generally, see Dorff (1998), 107–111, which was originally part of my responsum on infertility, approved without a dissenting vote by the CJLS in March 1994; see also Dorff (1996c).

63. See *Encyclopedia Judaica* 2:336–339 at *Afterlife* and 14:97–98 at *Resurrection—In the Bible.* While early biblical sources affirm the existence of Sheol, a murky place to which people's spirits descend after death, resurrection of the body after death is first affirmed by what is chronologically the last book of the Bible (circa 165 B.C.E.), the Book of Daniel (12:1–3). Isaiah 26:19, which also affirms it, is understood by almost all commentators to be a much later addition (*Encyclopedia Judaica* at *Resurrection—In the Bible*). Job (for example, 7:7–10, 9:20–22, and 14:7–22), written in about 400 B.C.E., and Ecclesiastes (9:4–5; compare 3:19–21), written about 250 B.C.E., explicitly deny resurrection and perhaps even any form of life after death. It thus appears that bodily resurrection made its first appearance in Judaism in the second century B.C.E. The Rabbis (Pharisees), though, made it a cardinal doctrine, even asserting that biblical sources—which are, at best, ambiguous about this—clearly and definitively affirm it; see M. *Sanhedrin* 10:1 and B. *Sanhedrin* 90a ff.

64. Genesis 18:19.

65. Deuteronomy 6:4-9, 11:13–21.

66. I especially recommend Ruffman (2001).

67. Another rabbinic text that argues for respecting those who cannot have children but who contribute to the Jewish education of other people's children is this passage from B. *Sanhedrin* 19b:

Rabbi Samuel bar Nahmani said in the name of Rabbi Jonathan: Scripture ascribes merit to anyone who teaches the child of his friend Torah as if he gave birth to him, for it says: "These are the generations of Aaron and Moses," (Numbers 3:1) and it is written, "These are the names of the children of Aaron," (Numbers 3:3) [without mentioning Moses because the text there lists Aaron's children and not the two sons of Moses] to tell you that Aaron gave birth [begat] while Moses taught [a play on the Hebrew, *lamad* and *lemed*]; therefore they [Aaron's children] are called by his [Moses'] name [as well as Aaron's in verse 1 even though Moses was not their biological father].

68. Dorff (1998), chaps. 3–4; based on Dorff (1996c). See also Gold (1988).

69. Both the Mishnah and the Talmud have difficulty finding a biblical verse to support the ruling. See M. *Yevamot* 6:6 (61b), where the ruling is recorded as the majority opinion (that is, without ascription) but without textual support and where Rabbi Yohanon ben Beroka immediately objects: "With regard to both of them [i.e., the male and female God first created] the Torah says, 'And God blessed them and said to them . . . Be fruitful and multiply' (Genesis 1:28)." The Talmud (B. *Yevamot* 65b–66a) brings conflicting evidence as to whether or not a woman is legally responsible for procreation and ultimately does not decide the matter. That is left for the later codes; see M.T. *Laws of Marriage* 15:2 and S.A. *Even Ha'ezer* 1:1, 13, which rule that the duty falls only on the man, but the woman must enable the man to fulfill it.

The Talmud there also brings conflicting exegetical grounds for the Mishnah's ruling, basing it alternatively on "Replenish the earth and subdue it" (Genesis 1:28) or on "I am God Almighty, be fruitful and multiply" (Genesis 35:11). There are problems in using both texts, however. The traditional pronunciation of the first is in the plural, making propagation a commandment for both the man and the woman; it is only the written form of the text that is in the masculine singular (and even that can apply, according to the rules of Hebrew grammar, to either men alone or to both men and women). The second text is indeed in the masculine singular, but that may be only because God is there talking to Jacob; the fact that Jacob is subject to the commandment proves nothing in regard to whether his wives were. These problems prove that the real reason for limiting the commandment of procreation to men is not exegetical at all, and we have to look elsewhere for what motivated the Rabbis to limit it in that way.

The real reason may have been economic: Since a man was legally responsible to support his children, it was against his financial interests to have them in the first place, and so the law had to command him to do so. Alternatively, since biologically the man has to offer to have conjugal relations with his wife for procreation to take place, it may be that anatomical factor that prompted the Rabbis to impose the commandment on men. Conversely, some argue that the Rabbis would not have imposed the commandment on a woman because they would not have legally obligated her to undertake the risks of pregnancy and childbirth, risks that were considerably greater in times past than they are now. Whatever the reason, Jewish law ultimately places legal responsibility for procreation on the man.

70. T. *Niddah* 2; B. *Yevamot* 12b, 100b; B. *Ketubbot* 39a; B. *Niddah* 45a; and B. *Nedarim* 35b. On this entire topic, see Feldman (1973), chaps. 9–13. On the question of assessing the dangers posed to the woman or child by sexual intercourse such that contraception is, according to that Baraita, permitted or required, see ibid.,185–187.

71. B. *Hullin* 58a and elsewhere. According to B. *Yevamot* 69b, during the first forty days of gestation, the zygote is "simply water," but even then the Rabbis required justification for an abortion based on the mother's life or health. On this topic generally, see Feldman (1973), chaps. 14–15.

72. The language of the Mishnah (M. *Yevamot* 6:6) suggests that the man may use contraceptives after fulfilling the commandment with two children. It reads: "A man may not cease from being fruitful and multiplying *unless* he has children. The School of Shammai says: two males; the School of Hillel says: a male and a female." That, however, was not the position of later Jewish law (B. *Yevamot* 62b), which encouraged as many children as possible on the basis of Isaiah 45:18 ("Not for void did He create the world, but for habitation [*lashevet*] did He form it") and Ecclesiastes 11:6 ("In the morning, sow your seed, and in the evening [*la'erev*] do not withhold your hand"). Subsequently these precepts were codified by Maimonides, M.T. *Laws of Marriage* (*Ishut*) 15:16 ("Although a man has fulfilled the commandment of being fruitful and multiplying, he is commanded by the Rabbis not to desist from procreation while he yet has strength, for whoever adds even one Jewish soul is considered as having created an entire world."). See note 81.

73. British researchers, citing World Health Organization statistics and their own study of three hundred men at a south London clinic, suggested that the failure of condoms may largely be due to the use of the same size for all men, a size too small for one third of the men of the world. See "One Size of Condom" (1994), 27.

74. For more on the Jewish imperative of safe sex, see Gold (1992), 112 ff.

75. The optimal age is twenty-two (Weinhouse, 1994). Weinhouse presents a helpful description of the physical factors in pregnancy through a woman's twenties, thirties, and forties. Infertility rate increases with the woman's age: 13.9 percent of couples are infertile when the wife is between thirty and thirty-four; 24.6 percent, when the wife is between thirty-five and thirty-nine; and 27.2 percent, when the wife is between forty and forty-four; see U.S. Congress (1988), 1–6. Recent evidence suggests that a woman's fertility begins to decrease as early as age twenty-seven; see Gibbs (2002).

76. According to Kosmin et al. (1991), 10–11, 34.9 percent of born-Jewish males between twenty-five and forty-four years of age had completed college as their highest degree, and an additional 38.7 percent of that age group had completed postgraduate education; in other words, 73.6 percent had at least completed college. In comparison, only 13.2 percent of the general U.S. white male population aged twenty-five and above had completed college as their highest degree, and only an additional 11.3 percent had received postgraduate education, for a total of 24.5 percent with college degrees—roughly a third of the Jewish percentage. For born-Jewish women, 29.6 percent between the ages of twenty-

five and forty-four had completed a bachelor's degree as their highest level of education, and an additional 37.3 percent had attended postgraduate school, for a total of 66.9 percent with at least a college degree; of the general U.S. white female population, only 10.8 percent had a bachelor's degree as their highest level of education, and an additional 6.3 percent had received postgraduate education, for a total of 17.1 percent with at least a bachelor's degree—roughly a quarter of the Jewish percentage.

77. Yovich and Grudzinskas (1990), 1–2.

78. United Jewish Communities (2002), 3.

79. The best estimate of the current number of Jews in the world is 13,254,100; see Singer and Grossman (2001), 101:540.

80. B. *Kiddushin* 30a.

81. M.T. *Laws of Marriage* 15:16. The Talmud (B. *Yevamot* 62b) bases the requirement to continue having children beyond the minimum of two on Ecclesiastes 11:6; see note 72. Maimonides' theme of a whole world being created with the birth of a child is echoed in M. *Sanhedrin* 4:5, "If anyone sustains a soul within the People Israel, it is as if he has sustained an entire world," and the converse appears in B. *Yevamot* 63b: "If someone refrains from propagation, it is as if he commits murder (literally, 'spills blood') and diminishes the image of God."

82. Sauerwein (1994), E4. Schulman and Mekler (1985) pointed out that as early as age four children scrutinize the person their parent is dating and the interactions between them, including the most mundane verbal or body communications. These authors noted how important it is for parents to remember that they are indeed parents and that they should act as such when dating, because children do not have respect for parents who act like teenagers. Sauerwein (1994, E4) also cites an Iowa State University study, released in summer 1994, that "found that a single mother's dating behavior can sway teen sons into early sexual experimentation and relax teen daughters' attitudes about promiscuity." Furthermore, "a 1987 study found that recently divorced mothers, adjusting from married to single life, are at their peak in promiscuity; consequently, so are their teen daughters. Experts speculated that this would also be true for fathers and sons" (ibid.). Nevertheless, it is "crucial" for single parents to date, according to Les B. Whitbeck, co-researcher for the study, "because half of the country's marriages end in divorce and almost three-quarters of teenagers have sex." Therefore children "need to see a single parent model caring and responsible relationships" (cited by Sauerwein, 1994, E4).

83. Herbert (1999), 61–62. See also Kirn (2000) and Wallerstein et al. (2000b).

84. Kosmin et al. (1991), 16, reported that 28 percent of children of interfaith couples were raised Jewish, and the remaining 72 percent were raised with the other faith or with no faith. A later study reported this: 18 percent were raised Jewish exclusively, 25 percent were raised Jewish and Christian, 33 percent were raised Christian exclusively, and 24 percent were raised with no religion; see Phillips (1997), 49.

85. Exodus 20:9–10.

86. See, for example, M. *Ketubbot* 5:5; *Avot (Ethics of the Fathers)* 2:2; *Avot de-Rabbi Natan* 11; B. *Nedarim* 49b; and *Tanhuma Vayetze*, sec. 13.

87. Classical Jewish law recognized this in demanding that a man who wanted to change to a job that would require him to be home less often could do so only with his wife's permission, even if the new job meant he would earn more money. His wife's permission was also necessary if he wanted to ply his trade in a faraway place rather than a near one. See B. *Ketubbot* 61b, 62b; M.T. *Laws of Marriage* 14:2; and S.A. *Even Ha'ezer* 76:5. Although this is phrased in terms of only the companionship and sex that the man is obligated to provide for his wife, in our society, where women are members of the work force as well, the same would clearly apply to women. People of both genders must consider the needs of their spouse and children when making career choices.

88. *Tanhuma*, Mattot, 1:7, and see Rashi on this verse and *Numbers Rabbah* 22:9. The comment is based on the fact that when Moses responds to Reuben and Gad in Numbers 32:24, he puts building cities for their children before erecting pens for their flocks. The Hebrew words *"ikkar"* and *"tafel,"* which I have here translated "primary" and "secondary," in other contexts mean "essential" and "trivial," respectively; but in light of the Rabbis' esteem for work, the words are clearly being used here comparatively, and hence "primary" and "secondary."

89. Aries (1962) documents the fact that our notion of childhood as a specific set of stages in life is radically different from that of the past, when children were seen as miniature adults. It is, therefore, not clear that the Rabbis of the Talmud or the Middle Ages would have valued time spent with children. They did, however, mandate that parents teach their children. Furthermore, except for sailors and men in the import–export trade, who were often away from home for long stretches of time, the lack of distractions at night virtually guaranteed that parents spent much more time with their young children than we do now. I want to thank Dr. Anne Lerner for calling my attention to this.

90. For example, Genesis 27:26–7, 29:11,13, 31:28,55, 33:4, 45:14–5, 48:10; Exodus 4:27, 18:7; 1 Samuel 20:41; 2 Samuel 14:33, 15:5, 19:40; Ruth 1:9,14; and many, many times, of course, in the love poetry of Song of Songs (for example, 1:2, 2:6, 8:3).

91. Buber (1970), 11–12.

92. Note that even in the Bible's book of love poetry, The Song of Songs, the lover (at 8:1) *wishes* that her lover were her brother so that she could kiss him in public without reproach, but the fact that he is not prevents her from doing so:

> *If only it could be as with a brother,*
> *As if you had nursed at my mother's breast:*
> *Then I could kiss you*
> *When I met you in the street,*
> *And no one would despise me.*

At Ecclesiastes 3:5 we read: "There is a time for embracing and a time for shunning embraces."

93. To save a life, we must, if necessary, violate all but three commandments (murder, adultery/incest, and idolatry); see B. *Sanhedrin* 74a. Furthermore, the Talmud demands that we avoid danger and injury (see also B. *Shabbat* 32a; B.

Bava Kamma 15b, 80a, 91b; M.T. *Laws of Murder* 11:4–5; and S.A. *Hoshen Mishpat* 427:8–10), proclaiming that "endangering oneself is more stringently [prohibited] than the [explicit] prohibitions [of the law]" (*hamira sakkanta meisurah*) (B. *Hullin* 10a). The Talmud also includes many injunctions that apply these preventive principles in practice, as, for example, the command not to go out alone at night (B. *Pesahim* 112b). Conversely, we are commanded to take care of ourselves in the first place so as to prevent illness, based on the Rabbis' understanding of Deuteronomy 4:9,15; see, for example, M.T. *Laws of Ethics* (*De'ot*), chaps. 3–5.

94. See Junod (1994) for a powerful account of the feelings of a woman who gave up her first child for adoption because it was conceived in a nonmarital relation and she could not raise it. Years later, she still feels that people who adopt are like those who take someone else's eyes in order to see, and if her teenage daughter became pregnant, she would advise her to keep the baby, abort, or commit suicide (in that order) before giving up the baby for adoption. This woman, Carole Anderson, founded Concerned United Birthparents in an attempt to convince parents to keep their babies, even when born out of wedlock. I am citing this here neither to dissuade people from trying to adopt children if they cannot have them on their own nor even to dissuade people from giving up children they cannot raise for adoption, Anderson notwithstanding; rather I am citing it to indicate that serious consequences result more often than we might like to assume when unmarried couples have to face these choices. For a more wideranging critique of premarital sex, see Whitman (1997).

95. See note 84.

96. Phillips (1998), 64–65.

97. Teenagers—and, for that matter, adults—might consult Novick (1980), the United Synagogue Youth's source book on this subject.

98. M. *Avot* 5:21; see also note 93.

99. B. *Kiddushin* 29b–30a. In other words, if he had married at an even younger age, his sexual needs would never have led him to do anything wrong.

100. Genesis 38.

101. See Feldman (1973), 109–131, and Dorff (1998), 116–120.

102. See, for example, M.T. *Laws of Ethics* (*De'ot*) 4:19.

103. Dorff (1998), 139–151.

104. At 18:22 and 20:13.

105. The discussion began in the mid-1980s, and it evolved into the resolution of the Rabbinical Assembly quoted here, agreed on in May 1990. A similar, subsequent resolution was adopted in November 1991, by the United Synagogue of Conservative Judaism, the Conservative movement's synagogue arm. The United Synagogue resolution uses the same language as the Rabbinical Assembly resolution that preceded it, but it leaves out the fifth "Whereas" clause and the fourth resolution of the Rabbinical Assembly version. Still, the substance and actual wording of the bulk of the United Synagogue resolution is the same as the fuller version reprinted here from Rabbinical Assembly (1990), 275.

106. See note 104.

107. Aristotle, *Nicomachean Ethics*, book 1, chap. 3, 1094b12–28:

Our discussion will be adequate if it has as much clearness as the subject-matter admits of, for precision is not to be sought for alike in all discussions, any more than in all the products of the crafts. Now fine and just actions, which political science investigates, admit of much variety and fluctuation of opinion, so that they may be thought to exist only by convention, and not by nature. And goods also give rise to a similar fluctuation because they bring harm to many people; for before now men have been undone by reason of their wealth, and others by reason of their courage. We must be content, then, in speaking of such subjects and with such premises to indicate the truth roughly and in outline, and in speaking about things which are only for the most part true and with premises of the same kind to reach conclusions that are not better. In the same spirit, therefore, should each type of statement be *received*; for it is the mark of an educated man to look for precision in each class of things just so far as the nature of the subject admits; it is evidently equally foolish to accept probable reasoning from a mathematician and to demand from a rhetorician scientific proofs.

108. Song of Songs 5:16.

NOTES TO CHAPTER FOUR

1. For the command to honor parents, see Exodus 20:12 and Deuteronomy 5:16. For the command to respect parents, see Leviticus 19:3.

2. B. *Kiddushin* 31b. Compare M.T. *Laws of Rebels (Mamrim)* 6:3 and S.A. *Yoreh De'ah* 240:2,4, 228:11. The text of this talmudic passage is quoted later in this chapter, at note 8.

3. *Tanna d'bei Eliyahu* 26. Compare M.T. *Laws of Rebels (Mamrim)* 6:3 and S.A. *Yoreh De'ah* 240:5 for the law forcing the child to provide food.

4. The Decalogue was, according to the Torah, recorded on two tablets; see Exodus 24:12, 31:18, 32:15, 34:1,4 and Deuteronomy 4:13, 9:10,11,15, 10:1–5; compare Exodus 32:19, 34:28; 1 Kings 8:9; and 2 Chronicles 5:10. For the common view that five of the commandments were recorded on each tablet, see *Mekhilta de-Rabbi Yishmael* Yitro, section 8 (immediately after comment on Exodus 20:13) (ed. Horovitz-Rabin, 233–234); J. *Shekalim* 6:1 (49d); and *Exodus Rabbah* 47:6. This tradition has been reflected in Jewish art since the thirteenth-century Spanish illuminated Bible manuscripts, and a representation of the two tablets in that configuration commonly appears on or above the ark in contemporary synagogues. Such an arrangement, however, would have been hard to engrave, for the first tablet would have had 146 Hebrew words and the second only 26.

The Jerusalem Talmud has a different tradition, preserved as the majority view, that each tablet contained the entire Decalogue; see J. *Shekalim* 6:1 (49d) and J. *Sotah* 8:3 (22d). Saadia maintained that one of the two tablets had the version of the Decalogue found in Exodus 20 and the other had the variant version found in Deuteronomy 5. This note is based on Sarna (1991), 108 and nn.

5. Philo, *Treatise on the Decalogue* (ed. and trans. Colson; Loeb Classical Library, 1929), 7:61, 67, 69.

6. *Mekhilta* Yitro, section 8 on Exodus 20:12. This is followed by biblical proof texts to demonstrate exactly how one can learn that God has equated these. Compare B. *Kiddushin* 30b, where this is in the name of the Rabbis generally.

7. Leviticus 19:3.

8. B. *Kiddushin* 31b. Compare M.T. *Laws of Rebels* 6:3 and S.A. *Yoreh De'ah* 240:2,4, 228:11.

9. Exodus 21:17.

10. Deuteronomy 27:16.

11. S.A. *Yoreh De'ah* 240:24 (with gloss), 374:6. Honor is also due to one's older brothers; see M.T. *Laws of Rebels* (*Mamrim*) 6:15 and S.A. *Yoreh De'ah* 240:22,23.

12. Exodus 21:15.

13. Both the mother and children, though, are supposed to honor the man of the house; see M. *Kiddushin* 1:7; B. *Kiddushin* 29a, 30b, 31a; M.T. *Laws of Rebels* (*Mamrim*) 6:6, 14; and S.A. *Yoreh De'ah* 240:14,17.

14. B. *Niddah* 31a.

15. J. *Pe'ah* 15d. Honor of God and parents are put on a par in B. *Kiddushin* 30b.

16. Deuteronomy 6:5.

17. Leviticus 19:18. Rashi, B. *Kiddushin* 32a, s.v. *podin u-ma'akhilin*; R. Elazar Askari, *Sefer Haredim* (1879), 31; R. Abraham Danzig, *Hayyei Adam* (1810), 67:1. These are all cited in Blidstein (1975), 56–57.

18. Maimonides, *Responsa* (ed. J. Blau), 2:728, #448. Cited in Blidstein (1975), 55.

19. *Sifra* Kedoshim 1:10 and B. *Yevamot* 6a. The Talmudic passage then raises the possibility that God's commandments trump the parent's only when the occasion for fulfilling the commandment chronologically antedates the parent's wish, leaving open the possibility that the parent's wish takes precedence when it comes before the time the commandment is incumbent or simultaneous with it. The Tosafot on that talmudic page, however, maintain that the parent's wishes never supersede God's commandments, even when there would be some concrete benefit to the parent.

20. *Responsa Rosh* (1881), 15:5, cited in Herring (1984), 208. The verses cited are Leviticus 19:17 and Psalms 34:15, the latter of which the Rabbis understood to be a positive command to seek peace; see J. *Pe'ah* 1:1.

21. See, for example, Rabbi Israel Isserlien (1390–1460), *Responsa Terumat ha-Deshen*, no. 40 and S.A. *Yoreh De'ah* 240:25.

22. *Responsa of Rabbi Meir of Rothenburg* 79 and *Responsa Mabit* 139. For some modern treatments of this issue, after the State of Israel was founded, see Israeli (1965), 143–146 and Bleich (1977b), 9–13. The commandment to move to Israel is itself a matter of dispute in terms of its source of authority and its scope; see, for example, M. T. *Laws of Kings* 5:7–12, and the comments of Rabbi David ben Zimri (Ridbaz) there, especially on 5:7. See also Segal (1987), 127–138. In the

Middle Ages, only Nahmanides held that emigration to Israel was a command-ment for his time.

In the modern period, Zionism was a matter of heated debate, especially in the nineteenth and early twentieth centuries. Many Orthodox Jews rejected Zionism, because Judaism as they understood it required us to wait until God brings the Messiah to lead us back to Zion; doing that on our own initiative was rejecting faith in God and an act of hubris on our part. Reform theorists rejected Zionism because it would isolate Jews in one corner of the earth, whereas the prophet Micah had proclaimed that our mission was to spread Judaism world-wide: "The remnant of Jacob shall be in the midst of many peoples, like the dew from the Lord, like droplets on grass" (Micah 5:6). Moreover, influenced by the universalist utopianism popular in the late nineteenth century, which saw na-tionalism as retrograde, Reform theorists explicitly rejected this Jewish form of nationalism in its Pittsburgh Platform of 1885; see Segal (1987), 215–222.

Although some Conservative leaders, such as Cyrus Adler and Louis Finkel-stein, were non-Zionist, none was anti-Zionist. On the contrary, Solomon Schechter, leader of Conservative Judaism from 1903 to 1915, wrote a staunch defense of Zionism in 1906, just eight years after the first Zionist Congress; and Mordecai Kaplan and Simon Greenberg, two of Conservative Judaism's ideologi-cal leaders in the first eight decades of the twentieth century, were also strongly Zionist.

23. *Responsa Rashba attributed to Ramban* (1883), 272, cited in Herring (1984), 209. Rashba used B. *Sotah* 2b, "Forty days prior to the formation of the fetus, a heavenly voice says, 'So-and-so will marry So-and-so,' " to justify his claim that the parents do not have the right to interfere in the natural attraction that God has implanted in a particular man and woman for each other. Rabbi Joseph Colon (Maharik, 1420–1480) took the same position on the grounds that the Talmud (B. *Kiddushin* 41a) urges a man to marry a woman to whom he is attracted; see *Responsa Maharik* (1884), 177–178, #164:3, cited in Herring (1984), 209; see also note 27.

24. For example, Rabbi Naftali Zvi Judah Berlin (Netziv, 1817–1893) saw a marriage contrary to parents' wishes as a disgrace to the parents, thus falling under Deuteronomy 27:16, "Cursed be he that dishonors his father and mother"; see *Responsa Meshiv Davar* 50. Similarly, Rabbi Abraham Isaiah Karelitz (Hazon Ish, d. 1953) maintained that a man may marry his beloved only if his parents are not totally opposed; see *Novellae of Hazon Ish* to B. *Kiddushin* 30a, 287.

25. S.A. *Yoreh De'ah* 240:25, gloss. The age-old practice among Jews of arranged marriages thus assumed that the bride and groom agreed to their par-ents' choice.

26. B. *Kiddushin* 32a.

27. B. *Yevamot* 6a; see Tosafot there. Rabbi Solomon ben Adret (Rashba, d. 1310, Spain) maintained that "honor" occurs only when the parent enjoys some benefit from the act of the son, as in the examples given to define "honor" in *Kiddushin* 31b, but if the parent will not benefit, he should do other biblical commandments that he is required to do at that time first; see Rashba on B. *Yevamot* 6a.

Rabbenu Yitzhak of the French Tosafot and Rabbi Moses bar Nahman (Nahmanides d. 1270, Spain) maintained that one may even disregard any parental directive that does not lead to some constructive purpose, similar to those listed in B. *Kiddushin* 31b. And along these lines Rabbenu Yitzhak maintained that one should defer parental honor as well as the return of a lost object to someone else in order to recover one's own lost object, because the father does not have benefit from the son losing something; see Tosafot B. *Kiddushin* 32a and *Novellae* of Ramban to B. *Yevamot* 6a; Rabbi Yomtov ben Abraham Ashbili (Ritva, d. 1340) in *Novellae* of the Ritva to B. *Yevamot* 6a; and Rabbi Joseph Colon (1420–1480, Maharik), *Responsa Maharik* (1884), 177–178, #164:3, cited in Herring (1984), 209.

Others, however, asserted that children may ignore their parents' commands only when asked to do something that violates Jewish law; see, for example, Rabbi Menahem ben Solomon ha-Meiri (d. 1306), *Beit ha-Behirah* to B. *Yevamot* 6a, 27; Rabbi Elijah of Vilna Gaon (d. 1797) in *Be'ur ha-GRA* on S.A. *Yoreh De'ah* 240:36; and the early statement of the Jerusalem Talmud that "a mother's desire is also her honor" (J. *Kiddushin* 1:7).

On another matter, the normative position is that children need not expend their own financial resources to fulfill the commandments of honor and respect, unless the parents are destitute and the children can afford to support them; see B. *Kiddushin* 32a and Blidstein (1975), 60–75. But it is preferable for the children to use their own resources; see note 35.

28. The verse is Leviticus 19:14. In addition to its literal reference to the physically blind, the Rabbis interpreted it to demand also that we not mislead those who lack information or who are morally blind by tempting them to do what is a violation of the law. See *Sifra* Kedoshim on Leviticus 19:14; B. *Pesachim* 22b; B. *Mo'ed Katan* 17a; B. *Kiddushin* 32a; and B. *Bava Metz'ia* 75b.

29. B. *Mo'ed Katan* 17a. See also B. *Kiddushin* 32a.

30. M.T. *Laws of Rebels* (*Mamrim*) 6:8.

31. Attributed to Rabbi Judah ben Samuel He-Hasid, *Sefer Hasidim* (ed. Margoliot, 1957), 513, #954.

32. M. *Ketubbot* 5:8 (64b) and M.T. *Laws of Marriage* 13:3. Maimonides' addition of a yard outside is based on the privileges of a widow enumerated in B. *Ketubbot* 103a. Compare S.A. *Even Ha'ezer* 73:1–2,7.

33. M.T. *Laws of Marriage* 13:3 and S.A. *Even Ha'ezer* 73:4.

34. B. *Kiddushin* 32a; M.T. *Laws of Rebels* (*Mamrim*) 6:7; and S.A. *Yoreh De'ah* 240:3,8.

35. For the law permitting the use of parents' resources, see B. *Kiddushin* 31b–32a; M. T. *Laws of Rebels* (*Mamrim*) 6:7; and S.A. *Yoreh De'ah* 240:5. For the preference for using one's own assets, see *Kesef Mishneh* to M.T. there.

36. M.T. *Laws of Rebels* (*Mamrim*) 6:3.

37. *Menorat Ha-Ma'or* (ed. Enelow), 4:15–16, cited in Blidstein (1975), 53.

38. Genesis 12:1.

39. *Genesis Rabbah* 39:7.

40. Blidstein (1975), 111. For the story to which he is referring, in which Elisha leaves home to join Elijah, see 1 Kings 19:15–21. For rabbinic sources on people

leaving home to study, see B. *Megillah* 16b; M.T. *Laws of Rebels (Mamrim)* 6:13; and S.A. *Yoreh De'ah* 240:13.

41. *Exodus Rabbah* 34:3. The midrash is commenting on Exodus 25:8, "and make for Me a sanctuary, and I will dwell among them."

42. See Blidstein (1975), 113–115.

43. M.T. *Laws of Rebels (Mamrim)* 6:10 and S. A. *Yoreh De'ah* 240:10. This ruling is probably based on the story of Rabbi Assi in B. *Kiddushin* 31b, even though the Talmud records the case of Rabbi Assi without indicating that it is a normative standard for others. Moreover, Rabbi Assi specifically emigrated to Israel to escape his mother; would other destinations—or moving the mother to other destinations—be equally as acceptable? Because of these issues, and because of the worry that the child will not find someone to take care of the parent properly, Rabbi Abraham ben David of Posquieres (Ravad, d. 1198) and some others (*Taz* and *Derishah* on the Shulchan Arukh there; Rabbi Shelomo Luria [Maharshal], *Yam Shel Shelomo* to B. *Kiddushin* 32a, p. 17) maintain that a child must continue to take care of an emotionally or mentally dysfunctional parent; but most agree with Maimonides and Karo that the child may delegate that responsibility to others as long as the child ensures that the delegates are indeed doing their job.

44. See B. *Kiddushin* 31a (the case of Dama), 32a (Rabbi Eliezer's ruling), and 31b (Rabbi Assi) for the two cases of caring for such a parent and the case of abandoning such a parent, respectively.

45. That is the interpretation of Meier (1977).

46. Leviticus 19:14. See B. *Mo'ed Katan* 17a; B. *Kiddushin* 32a; M.T. *Laws of Rebels (Mamrim)* 6:8,9; and S.A. *Yoreh De'ah* 240:19,20.

47. Attributed to Rabbi Judah ben Samuel He-Hasid, *Sefer Hasidim* (ed. Margoliot, 1957), 371, #564; see also 257, #343.

48. *Pele Yo'etz*, part I, *Kaph*, 170–172; cited in Blidstein (1975), 115.

49. *Hasagot Ha-Ra'avad* on M.T. *Laws of Rebels (Mamrim)* 6:10.

50. J. *Pe'ah* 1:1 (15c); compare B. *Kiddushin* 31a–31b and S.A. *Yoreh De'ah* 240:4. The text in the Jerusalem Talmud does not make it completely clear that the king specifically demanded that the father come to work for him, but that is the only way that the story works, as the commentators say there and as Rashi says with reference to the abbreviated version of the story in the Babylonian Talmud.

51. For more on how parents and children should handle the strictly medical aspects of dying within the parameters of Jewish law and values, see Dorff (1998), chaps. 7–9.

52. B. *Kiddushin* 29a. Exodus 13:2 says that every firstborn male is to be consecrated to Temple service. Numbers 3:12–13, however, says that the Levites were to serve in the Temple in place of every firstborn male, and Numbers 18:15–16 requires that after the firstborn is one month old he be redeemed from Temple service with five shekels. This is the origin of the *pidyon ha-ben* ceremony, in which, on the infant's thirty-first day of life, the father gives a *kohen* five silver dollars to redeem his son from Temple service.

53. Deuteronomy 6:7 (part of the first paragraph of the *Shema*, Deuteronomy 6:4–9) and Deuteronomy 11:19 (part of the second paragraph of the *Shema*, Deuteronomy 11:13–21).

54. B. *Sanhedrin* 91b.

55. *Song of Songs Rabbah* on Song of Songs 1:4.

56. B. *Shabbat* 119b. Compare B. *Shabbat* 88a, according to which "The Holy One, blessed be He, stipulated with the works of creation: 'If Israel accepts the Torah, you shall exist; but if not, I will turn you back into emptiness and formlessness.' " Thus the Rabbis believed that world was created and continues to exist only as long as Israel accepts the Torah, but God offered the Torah to Israel in the first place only because children gave God hope that the Torah would be learned and followed. Thus the whole world's existence depends on children learning the Torah.

57. B. *Kiddushin* 30a.

58. M. *Avot* (*Ethics of the Fathers*) 5:23 (5:24 in some editions).

59. B. *Bava Batra* 21a.

60. See, for example, Friedenwald (1967) and Nevins (1996).

61. Simon and Cannon (2001), 17.

62. See note 76 to Chapter Three for the percentages.

63. Bubis (2002), 14–15, 18, and Wertheimer (1999).

64. Herman (1997).

65. Bubis (2002), 16.

66. Ibid., 15–16.

67. Ibid., 17.

68. Phillips (1997), 77.

69. Bubis (2002), 17.

70. B. *Kiddushin* 30a.

71. All of the quotations in this paragraph are from St. John (2002), 1–2.

72. Gibbs (2002). For more about this article, see Chapter Three.

73. For the sources of these statistics and much more on how the Jewish tradition applies to issues of infertility, see Dorff (1998), chaps. 3, 4, and 6.

NOTES TO CHAPTER FIVE

1. I would like to express my sincere thanks to the members of the Conservative movement's Committee on Jewish Law and Standards (CJLS) for their helpful suggestions for improving an earlier draft of the responsum on which this chapter is based. In addition, I would like to thank Rabbi Debra Orenstein, for her extensive comments on an earlier draft; Judith Hauptman, for sharing her work on wife beating with me and for pointing me to the article by Grossman on that subject; Naomi Graetz, who shared with me her book-length manuscript on wife beating before it was published and who was kind enough to offer constructive criticism of an earlier draft of this chapter; Rabbi Benay Lappe, for giving me some materials on the definitions of the various forms of abuse from the psychological literature; Dr. Ian Russ, for supplying me with a bibliography on sexual abuse of children and for giving me important suggestions regarding the

psychological aspects of this chapter; and Mark Rotenberg, for sending me information on false reports of abuse.

This chapter is based, first, on an essay I wrote for a joint project of the University of Judaism and the Jewish Family Service of Los Angeles: Russ et al. (1993), 48–57, 64–66. Subsequently I wrote a much longer essay on family violence in the form of a responsum for the CJLS, and this chapter contains much of that research. For the original version, see Abelson and Fine (2002), 773–816.

2. Genesis 1:26–27, 9:6.

3. M. *Bava Kamma* 8:1 and the Talmud thereon.

4. For the Torah's restriction on the number of lashes, see Deuteronomy 25:3. The Torah (at Deuteronomy 21:22–23) furthermore demands that even someone executed on court order for cause be buried the same day to preserve a degree of respect for God's creation ("for an impaled body is an affront to God"). On these grounds, in fact, the Rabbis further diminished the number of lashes the Torah permitted to impose on a violator of a prohibition; compare M. *Makkot* 3:10–11; B. *Makkot* 22a; and M.T. *Sanhedrin*, chap. 17. For a summary of the use and restrictions of flogging as a penalty, see *Encyclopedia Judaica* 6:1348–1351 at *Flogging*. Such flogging, though, was restricted to courts; individuals acting on their own did not have the authority to whip others. Since the Enlightenment, Jewish courts in the Diaspora no longer have had the authority to inflict lashes, and the Israeli system of justice does not include such a penalty either.

5. J. *Pe'ah* 1:1.

6. M. *Avot* 2:15.

7. One might argue that Jews must avoid family violence because we are bound by civil law under the dictum "the law of the land is the law" (*dina de'malkhuta dina*). That may well be true, but it is not as clear as one might think, for that dictum was usually restricted to commercial matters. Even during the Middle Ages, though, Jews were forced by the government under which they lived to abide by its laws, and rabbis generally saw that as a Jewish obligation as well—at least to protect the Jewish community from expulsion or governmental interference. Certainly, when Jews began living as full citizens under governments shaped by the philosophy of the Enlightenment, they saw themselves both legally and morally bound to abide by the government's laws, and that continues to this day. The operative principle, then, is not so much "the law of the land is the law" as it is (1) the need to avoid the *hillul hashem* (desecration of God's name) involved when Jews break just civil law and (2) the requirement in Jewish law that Jews see themselves bound by moral standards beyond those of other nations.

For a discussion of the scope and rationales of "the law of the land is the law," see Dorff and Rosett (1988), 515–523. For a discussion of sanctification of God's name (and avoiding desecration of God's name) and holiness as reasons to obey Jewish law, see Dorff (1989), 113–134. For the demand that Jews be at least as moral as non-Jews, see, for example, Novak (1983), 90–93 and *Encyclopedia Judaica* 10:979–80 at *Kiddush Ha-Shem*.

8. Heise et al. (1999), described in Hotchkin (2000), 4A.

9. For reports of assaults, see Gorman (1995), 55. For sexual abuse statistics, see Crewdson (1988).

10. "Parents Who Kill Their Children" (1995), 14.

11. Ibid., 14, based on statistics from the U.S. Advisory Board on Child Abuse and Neglect (1995).

12. I would like to thank Rabbis Vernon Kurtz and Gerald Skolnik for alerting me to the current efforts and plans of the Chicago and New York Jewish communities, respectively, on these matters, and Anita Altman, director of resource development for the New York United Jewish Association Federation, for sending me a fact sheet on the services currently provided by New York–area Jewish agencies to counteract family violence and the grant proposal that was funded in 1995 to coordinate their efforts. For a summary of some Conservative movement efforts on this, see Fried (1995). In the last several years, I have co-chaired a special task force on family violence of the Los Angeles–Tel Aviv Partnership between the Los Angeles Jewish Federation Council and the municipality of Tel Aviv. Family violence happens among Jews in Israel as well as among those in North America. See also Jasinski and Williams (1998).

13. Graetz (1998). I want to thank her for sharing her manuscript with me before it was published. I also want to thank Judith Hauptman for sharing with me her article in progress on this subject; it is now tentatively titled "Financial Arrangements of Jewish Marriage." Graetz (1992) argued the same thesis—namely, that wife beating stems at least in part from the inherent inequality in Jewish marriage—but from a metaphoric rather than a legal ground.

14. M.T. *Laws of Marriage* 21:10; compare 21:3. The Mishnah (M. *Ketubbot* 5:5) requires a wife to "grind [flour], bake [bread], wash [clothes], cook food, nurse her child, make his [her husband's] bed, and work in wool." In M.T. *Laws of Injury and Damage* 4:16, however, Maimonides makes the husband who beats his wife liable for the usual remedies of assault, and in M.T. *Laws of Marriage* 15:19, he says that a man should honor his wife more than his body and love her as much as his own body. For Rabbi Yehudai Gaon's position, see *Otzar Ha-Geonim* to B. *Ketubbot*, 169–170. Rabbenu Nissim refers to "the Gaon of blessed memory," who allowed a husband to whip (or to refuse to sustain) his wife if she refused to do the chores delineated for her by law; see Rabbenu Nissim on B. *Ketubbot* 63b. For Rabbi Shmuel Hanaggid's position, see his *Ben Mishlei* (ed. Abramson, 1948), 117, sec. 419.

15. *Terumat Hadeshen*, sec. 218.

16. Rashba, *Responsa*, part 4, sec. 113; part 5, sec. 264; and part 7, sec. 477.

17. S. A. *Even Ha'ezer* 154:3 (gloss).

18. S.A. *Even Ha'ezer* 154:3 (gloss). See also Moses Isserles, *Darkhei Moshe* to the *Tur, Even Ha'ezer* 154:15.

19. A note found in Isserles at S.A. *Even Ha'ezer* 154:3 says that this was said several centuries earlier by R. Mordecai ben Hillel in his commentary on the fourth chapter (*Na'ara*) of B. *Ketubbot*, but I was not able to find it there.

20. See note 14.

21. Hertz (1938), 935.

22. Rabbi Simha in *Or Zarua, Piskei Bava Kamma*, sec. 161.

23. Joseph Karo, *Beit Yosef* to the *Tur, Even Ha'ezer* 154:15. In traditional Jewish law, only a man can initiate a divorce, but under specific circumstances a court will coerce him to grant his wife a writ of divorce (a *get*) "until he says, 'I want to!' " (B. *Kiddushin* 50a and B. *Yevamot* 106a). Such coercion has historically included everything from gentle persuasion to defaming him to his friends and employer to lashes, depending on the degree of the husband's recalcitrance and the remedies available to the Jewish court. In modern times, the State of Israel has gone as far as imprisoning men who have refused to grant their wives a writ of divorce at the command of the court, but Jewish courts in the Diaspora lack that power and have instead used other tactics up to, and including, dissolution of the marriage through annulment. For a discussion of how the Conservative, Orthodox, and Reform movements have dealt with this issue, and the legal theory behind each approach, see Dorff and Rosett (1988), 523–545.

24. Quoted in Moses Isserles' commentary on the *Tur: Darkhei Moshe, Even Ha'ezer* 154:11. However, another source—*Responsa* of Binyamin Ze'ev (early sixteenth century, Greece), #88—cites Rabbi Meir of Rothenburg as one of those who permit physical punishment to chastise a wife. On this entire subject, see Morell (1982) and Biale (1984), 92–96.

25. Maharam, *Responsa of the Maharam* (Prague ed.), sec. 81. See also what he wrote in the Cremona edition, sec. 291, which is a later answer.

26. Finkelstein (1924), 216–217. On the topic of those who reject wife beating altogether, see Graetz (1998).

27. Rashba, *Responsa,* part 7, #477.

28. Radbaz, *Responsa,* part 3, #447; part 4, #157.

29. At 4:38. See Schacht (1964), 161–168.

30. Grossman (1991), 57; see also 53–62, esp. 57 and 59–60. I want to thank Judith Hauptman for calling my attention to this article.

31. Ibid.

32. M. *Kiddushin* 1:1.

33. As I was writing this, I happened to come across a "Dear Abby" column on just this topic. Abigail Van Buren (1995), E2, stated that "the number of men who have been battered by women would shock most people. This crime is underreported because many men are too embarrassed to admit that they have been battered by a woman." She then cited a letter from a man who "was raised never to hit a woman—even in self-defense" (another contributing factor to this phenomenon), but "many times my ex-wife would throw things at me and come at me with her fingernails, drawing blood from the scratches she would inflict on my face and neck. She even broke my arm and ribs when she threw a heavy chair at me." When he finally sued for divorce, she retaliated by filing charges that he had sexually molested their child. He had to "endure humiliating questions," and it cost him ten thousand dollars in legal fees to prove his innocence, and that his ex-wife was clinically psychotic and paranoid with multiple personality disorders. "Meanwhile, the accusations were devastating." Aside from documenting one case of husband abuse, this illustrates another point that I discuss later on in this chapter—namely, the need to take careful steps in determining just who is at fault when there is alleged abuse.

34. Valby (2002), 12.

35. Johnson (1996).

36. M.T. *Laws of Injury and Damage* 4:18 and S.A. *Hoshen Mishpat* 424:10. After my original responsum was submitted and approved by the CJLS, Graetz pointed out to me that it should take note as well of the fact that some gay and lesbian partners abuse each other in patterns similar to wife beating. While it would not be fair to the committee to include this in what they approved after their vote, let me at least mention what is clearly in the spirit, if not the letter, of the responsum that the committee approved—namely, that the same condemnation of abuse would apply to gay or lesbian partners, and the same aid to abused parties to extricate themselves from the abusive situation must be extended.

37. Wingert and Salholz (1992), 84.

38. Proverbs 23:13–14; compare 3:11–12, 13:24, 19:18, 20:30, and 29:17.

39. Proverbs 29:15.

40. M. *Makkot* 2:2; B. *Makkot* 8a–b. For a collection of rabbinic statements concerning corporal punishment, see Blum (1981); see also Blidstein (1975), 123–126, 208–209.

41. Deuteronomy 21:18–21. "Wayward and defiant" is the translation of the new translation published by the Jewish Publication Society of America; other translations render "stubborn and rebellious." Verse 20 adds that "He is a glutton and a drunkard."

42. Briere (1992), 7–8. I would like to thank Rabbi Benay Lappe for calling my attention to this book and for lending it to me. Others, however, maintain that the degree of physical injury is not what makes an action abusive; it is rather the use of physical force in an unwanted and intimidating way. "Unwanted" must be part of that definition because, for example, people who voluntarily play football are certainly expecting to be subjected to physical force and even intimidating force, but since they see that as part of the fun of the game and since they voluntarily play, football in and of itself does not constitute abuse. See also Foote (2000).

Despite the increased awareness of child sexual abuse occasioned by the spate of lawsuits against the Catholic Church in recent years, a federal government study reports that between 1990 and 1998 there was a marked decline in substantiated cases of child sexual abuse. "Although cases of other types of child maltreatment have also declined in recent years, the decrease in child sexual abuse cases has been more marked. Substantiated cases of physical abuse declined 16 percent from a 1995 peak, compared with a 31-percent decline in child sexual abuse cases" and a 26-percent decline in sexual abuse reports in that period; see Jones and Finkelhor (2001), 2. "Possible explanations for the decline include a real underlying decline in the incidence of child sexual abuse or changes in attitudes, policies, and standards that have reduced the amount of child sexual abuse being reported and substantiated. It is possible that both of these processes are affecting trends in child sexual abuse" (ibid.).

43. The CJLS made these declarations through unanimously adopting my original rabbinic responsum on this subject in 1995; see Abelson and Fine (2002),

773–816. For legal sources supporting these bans, see M.T. *Laws of Assault and Injury* 5:1; *Laws of Study* (*Talmud Torah*) 2:2; S.A. *Yoreh De'ah* 240:10; and *Kitzur* Shulchan Arukh 165:7. Compare M. *Semahot*, 2:4–6; B. *Sotah* 47a; and B. *Sanhedrin* 85a, 107b.

44. Proverbs 22:6. The context of the verse—especially the second line of the couplet—requires that the first part of the verse be rendered as the new translation of The Jewish Publication Society of America does: "Train a lad in the way he ought to go; he will not swerve from it even in old age." The Hebrew of the first part of the verse, however, is hard to read that way, and the Rabbis understood its words according to their usual meaning, as translated and developed here.

45. B. *Kiddushin* 30a, and see Rashi there. Compare also B. *Mo'ed Katan* 17a. Maimonides, following the Talmud, spoke of this restriction as applying to a "big child," which presumably means an older child (twenty-two or twenty-four years old, according to Rashi on B. *Kiddushin* 30a, s.v. *mi'shitsar*; see also S.A. *Yoreh De'ah* 240:20) or a married child (even at a younger age), and perhaps even a financially independent child, whatever his or her age. Maimonides, though, in the law immediately previous to this one, stated that even though inordinate demands are included in the commandments of honoring and respecting one's parents, parents (presumably of younger children too) should not make harsh demands on their children lest they thereby create an obstacle to the child's ability to fulfill the commandments demanding their honor and respect; indeed, one who does so is to be excommunicated for violating the commandment in Leviticus 19:14 of not producing such an obstacle! See M.T. *Laws of Rebels* 6:8–9.

As noted in Chapter Four, Leviticus 19:14 is interpreted by the Rabbis to prohibit putting a stumbling block not only before the physically blind, but also before those who are intellectually or morally blind; see *Sifra* on that passage; B. *Pesahim* 22b; and B. *Mo'ed Katan* 17a, which explicitly uses that verse to prohibit striking one's grown child. See also note 112.

46. B. *Sanhedrin* 71a.

47. I want to thank Naomi Graetz for pointing out to me the importance of noting this special class of cases of child abuse.

48. Gershoff (2002).

49. Gershoff (2002), 609. Gershoff notes that eleven countries, including Israel, have legally banned spanking of children, but she says that "a ban in the United States is unlikely to be successful because its use in our culture is supported by a constellation of beliefs about family and childbearing, namely, that children are property, that children do not have the right to negotiate their treatment by parents, and that behaviors within families are private" (p. 610). She calls instead for educational campaigns to teach alternatives to physical blows, like sending the child to his or her room or removing privileges.

50. "A New Look at Effects of Spanking," The New York Times, July 9, 2002, F8.

51. Baumrind et al. (2002); Holden (2002); and Parke (2002).

52. Springen (2000), 64.

53. Cardenas (1995), B1, B6, pointed out the other side of this. He described the efforts of some Latino parents to save their children from America's world of

drugs, sex, and violent gangs by returning them to live with relatives in Latin America, which "offers more rigid school discipline and law enforcement, and encourages stiff corporal punishment—a welcome contrast, they say, to America's softer legal and social systems." The article depicted a mother who

> is still bothered by the fact that when school officials here saw the bruises from the beating she had given Maria, they warned her that she could go to prison. . . . It galled her when Maria began to threaten to call 911 to avoid physical punishment, while [the mother] was required to enroll in parenting classes to avoid criminal charges for beating the girl. When she sent Maria to live for seven months with an aunt in Guadalajara, [the mother] told the aunt to beat Maria if necessary. . . . Maria, afraid that her aunt would hit her, did not misbehave. She said she found out that "in Mexico, that's your child and no one else's business. The police don't care." In Los Angeles, [the mother] had wanted to make her daughter get a full-time job after school to keep her off the streets. That was something else American law did not allow children to do. . . . Today, Maria has replaced gang parties with the LAPD [Los Angeles Police Department] Explorer Academy. A ninth-grader, she has made finishing high school her highest priority.

I do not cite this article to justify child abuse but simply to indicate the other side of the story that we so often, and rightly, hear—namely, while corporal punishment should in most cases be avoided, as I maintain here, discipline of children is definitely necessary, and in some circumstances even corporal punishment short of child abuse may be appropriate.

54. Exodus 21:15. Compare B. *Sanhedrin* 84b. If the child did not cause a bruise while striking his or her parents, however, the child is liable for the damages of assault rather than for the death penalty; see M. *Bava Kamma* 8:3.

55. For the biblical command to honor parents, see Exodus 20:12 and Deuteronomy 5:16. For the command to respect parents, see Leviticus 19:3. That daughters as well as sons are commanded to honor and respect their parents, see M. *Kiddushin* 1:7 and B. *Kiddushin* 29a.

56. *Kiddushin* 31b; see also M.T. *Laws of Rebels (Mamrim)* 6:3 and S.A. *Yoreh De'ah* 240:2,4, 228:11.

57. *Tanna d'bei Eliyahu* 26. See M.T. *Laws of Rebels* 6:3 and S.A. *Yoreh De'ah* 240:5 in regard to forcing the child to provide food.

58. B. *Kiddushin* 31b–32a; M.T. *Laws of Rebels* 6:3; and S.A. *Yoreh De'ah* 240:5. Using one's own resources is, however, preferred; see *Kesef Mishneh* to M.T. *Laws of Rebels* 6:7.

59. B. *Kiddushin* 31b–32a; J. *Kiddushin* 1:7 (61b); J. *Pe'ah* 1:1 (15c-d); and *Deuteronomy Rabbah* 1:15.

60. B. *Kiddushin* 30b.

61. Philo, *Treatise on the Decalogue* (ed. and trans. Colson; Loeb Classical Library, 1929), 7:61, 67, 69.

62. This does *not* mean that one must continue to administer life-support systems to parents in failing health beyond all hope of cure. Quite the contrary,

doing so might arguably be construed as abuse! On such medical issues at the end of life, see Dorff (1991b), which was reprinted with modifications and additions in Dorff (1998), esp. 198–220, and Reisner (1991).

63. For Rashi, see B. *Sanhedrin* 47a, s.v. *'al* and B. *Berakhot* 10b, s.v. *girer*. For Tosafot, see B. *Yevamot* 22b, s.v. *ke-she-asah*. For Rabbenu Tam, see *Mordekhai* to *Yevamot*, sec. 13. For Rabbi Alfas, see B. *Yevamot* 22b. For Maimonides, see M.T. *Laws of Rebels (Mamrim)* 5:12, 6:11. For Karo and Isserles, see S.A. *Yoreh De'ah* 240:18 (with gloss). On this generally, see Blidstein (1975), 130–136 and Lappe (1993).

64. Finkelhor (1994), 31-53. Briere (1992), 4, reported higher figures (20 to 30 percent for females and 10 to 20 percent for males), but they undoubtedly include acts short of physical contact, such as voyeurism and being the subject of unwelcome sexual advances. A classic study of one aspect of this subject is Herman (1981). See also Jasinski and Williams (1998).

65. Leviticus 18:6.

66. Leviticus 18:29–30.

67. The Torah's words "abomination" and "defilement" aptly apply to the kind of sexual abuse of which we are speaking. Whether this biblical language applies as aptly—or, for that matter, at all—in regard to its prohibition against homosexuality is, to put it mildly, a matter of dispute. Even those who would permit homosexual relations, though, would definitely apply that language to coercive sex (be it homosexual or heterosexual), and that is the subject here.

68. Deuteronomy 25:11–12.

69. *Sifre* on Deuteronomy 25:12; compare M. *Bava Kamma* 8:1 and B. *Bava Kamma* 83a, 86a–b, 28a, etc.

70. B. *Shabbat* 13a; M.T. *Laws of Forbidden Intercourse* 21:1; Maimonides, *Sefer Ha-Mitzvot*, prohibition #353; *Sefer Ha-Hinukh* #188; and S.A. *Even Ha'ezer* 20:1. Some scholars maintain that intimacy without penetration, while not biblically forbidden, is rabbinically prohibited. See, for example, Nahmanides on B. *Shabbat* 13a and on *Sefer Ha-Mitzvot*, #188 and the Gaon of Vilna, *Biur ha-Gra* on S.A. *Even Ha'ezer* 20:1.

71. Dr. Ian Russ, a child psychologist active in the Conservative movement and a good friend, has suggested the following as the best literature on the long-term, serious effects of the sexual abuse of children: Briere (1989), Briere and Elliott (1994), Courtois (1988), and Everstine and Everstine (1989). I would like to thank Russ for supplying this bibliography for my use.

72. See Briere (1992), 8–12.

73. Leviticus 25:17. See *Me'irat Einayim* to S.A. *Hoshen Mishpat* 420:49.

74. B. *Bava Kamma* 90a; M.T. *Laws of Assault and Injury* 3:5; and S.A. *Hoshen Mishpat* 420:38.

75. B. *Bava Metz'ia* 59a. Literally, "for since her tears are common, her oppression is near." Rav, whose comment this is, did not limit his remark to verbal abuse; the context is discussing the prohibition of oppressing people by means of words.

76. B. *Ketubbot* 61a.

77. B. *Yevamot* 62b; the biblical verse quoted is Job 5:24.

78. Robert Bly is perhaps most well known for making this point in a number of his books, from *Iron John* (1992) on. Whether due to nature or nurture or both, boys and men are, in his analysis, particularly sensitive to shaming, especially when it is done by someone close to the particular male involved and even more when it is done in public.

79. The two verses are Leviticus 25:14 and 25:17. The Rabbis, in *Bava Metz'ia* 58b, apply verse 14 to monetary oppression and verse 17 to verbal oppression.

80. J. *Pe'ah* 1:1 (15c); see B. *Kiddushin* 31a–31b; S.A. *Yoreh De'ah* 240:4.

81. Exodus 21:17 and Leviticus 20:9; see also Deuteronomy 27:16.

82. Leviticus 19:16.

83. Leviticus 5:1–6.

84. B. *Bava Kamma* 56a and S.A. *Hoshen Mishpat* 28:1, gloss. In B. *Pesahim* 113b, Rav Papa has a man named Zigud punished for testifying alone against another man named Tuvya on the grounds that the testimony of a single witness is inadmissible, and so Zigud, knowing that he was the only witness, was effectively spreading defamatory information (*motzi shem ra*) about Tuvya. That, however, was when the act had already occurred; the requirement in B. *Bava Kamma* and in the comment of Isserles to testify even singly in all cases in which there is a benefit, including preventing another person from sinning, refers to a future gain.

85. M.T. *Laws of Murder* 1:14. In 1:15, Maimonides added both affirmative and negative injunctions to this obligation based on Deuteronomy 25:12, "And you shall cut off her hand [being applied here to the abuser]; your eye shall have no pity." See also Rashi, B. *Sanhedrin* 73a, s.v. *lo ta'amod.*

86. M. *Sanhedrin* 8:7 and B. *Sanhedrin* 73a.

87. Tosafot, B. *Sanhedrin* 72b, s.v. *kan be-av al ha-ben*, makes this explicit in regard to children's right (or perhaps obligation) to defend themselves against abusive parents.

88. Leviticus 18:5.

89. B. *Yoma* 85a–b and B. *Sanhedrin* 72a–74a. The derivation from Leviticus 18:5 appears at B. *Sanhedrin* 74a. The laws of *rodef* appear in the Mishnah *Sanhedrin* 8:7(73a), and the Talmud's discussion takes place there on 73a ff. (primarily on 74a). The talmudic phrase demanding self-defense, *hashkem l'hargo* (at B. *Berakhot* 58b and B. *Sanhedrin* 72a, 62b) may also be translated, "rise up early in the morning to kill him [first]." On these principles generally, see Jakobovits (1975), chaps. 3–7.

90. Leviticus 19:16. The new translation of The Jewish Publication Society reads, "Do not profit by the blood of your fellow." The meaning of this phrase is uncertain. As the note to the verse says, the new translation interprets the verse in the context of the civil legislation in the verse immediately before it. The rabbinic tradition, however, interpreted and applied Leviticus 19:16 to establish a positive obligation to come to the aid of those in danger; see M. *Sanhedrin* 8:7 and B. *Sanhedrin* 73a.

91. M.T *Laws of Testimony* 1:1.

92. *Kesef Mishneh* to M.T. *Laws of Testimony* 1:1 and *Rosh* to *Makkot*, chap. 1, #11. "Destroy the evil from your midst" occurs a number of times in the

Torah as a general purpose of the law: Deuteronomy 13:6, 17:7, 19:19, 21:21, 22:21, 24:7; see also 17:12 and 22:22.

93. M. *Yoma* 8:6; B. *Yoma* 83a; M.T. *Laws of the Sabbath* 2:1; and S.A. *Orah Hayyim* 328:10.

94. Hafez Hayyim, *Be'er Mayyim Hayyim, Laws of Slander* 9:20.

95. M.T. *Laws of Testimony* 9:1 and S.A. *Hoshen Mishpat* 35:1.

96. S.A. *Hoshen Mishpat* 35:14, gloss. Isserles there accepted children as *eidei beirur* (witnesses of clarification) based on the enactments (*takkanot*) of either Rabbenu Tam or Rabbenu Gershom.

97. B. *Bava Metz'ia* 58b. The legal remedy in personal injury cases for embarrassment is discussed in the Mishnah *Bava Kamma* 8:1 and 8:6 and in the Talmud at B. *Bava Kamma* 86a–b and 91a, where the discussion of the essence of shame also appears.

98. Genesis 1:27, 5:1. For a discussion of this principle, see Dorff (1998), 18–20.

99. Deuteronomy 21:23.

100. B. *Gittin* 88b and M.T. *Laws of Courts (Sanhedrin)* 26:7. See Dorff and Rosett (1988), 320–324, 515–539. See also Schachter (1981) and Krauss (1982). I am indebted for much of the material of this section to Dratch (1994).

101. Ha-Shulchan Arukh, *Hoshen Mishpat* 388:7.

102. S.A. *Hoshen Mishpat* 388:7, gloss, and see #45 of the *Shakh* on that passage. *Shakh* (at 338:12, in #60) understood Isserles to be saying categorically that "if someone is accustomed to strike others, it is permissible to hand him over [to gentile authorities] for one's protection so that he will not strike people any longer." See also glosses of Isserles to S.A. *Hoshen Mishpat* 388:9 and 26:4 and his commentary *Darkhei Moshe* to the *Tur, Hoshen Mishpat* 338, #14. The earlier sources he cites are the *Teshuvot Maimoniot* of Maimonides (1140–1204, Spain/Egypt), *Nezikin*, responsum #66; Mordekhai ben Hillel Ha-Kohen (the Mordekhai, 1240?–1298, Germany); Rabbi Jacob ben Judah Weil (d. 1456, Germany); and Maharam of Riszburg (possibly Rabbi Menahem of Merseburg, early fourteenth century, Saxony/Germany).

103. S.A. *Hoshen Mishpat* 388:12, according to the text quoted by *Shakh* at that place, #59, and by the Gaon of Vilna (*Gra*), #71.

104. This was openly declared as its ruling in my responsum on family violence, validated unanimously in 1995, on which much of this chapter is based. See Abelson and Fine (2002), 773–816.

105. The exception to the clergy–client privilege was established in the case of *Tarasoff v. Board of Regents of the University of California* 529 P. 2d 553 (Cal. 1974); modified 551 P. 2d 334 (Cal. 1976), which also affirmed the general privilege itself. The California Evidence Code, art. 8, sec. 1033, states: "Subject to Section 912, a penitent, whether or not a party [i.e., litigant in the case before the court], has a privilege to refuse to disclose, and to prevent another from disclosing, a penitential communication if he claims the privilege"; and sec. 1034 states: "Subject to Section 912, a clergyman, whether or not a party, has a privilege to refuse to disclose a penitential communication if he claims the privilege."

The parallel Arkansas statute, as another example, reads: "No minister of the gospel or priest of any denomination shall be compelled to testify in relation to any confession made to him in his professional character, in the course of discipline by the rule of practice of such denomination." New York and Michigan, like California, substitute "allowed" for "compelled," thus giving the penitent the right to prevent the clergyperson from revealing the confession made in his or her capacity as a member of the clergy.

This "seal of the confessional" has been generally recognized by the civil courts even in states that do not have such a privilege written into their evidence codes and even though the old common law did not consider confessions privileged. New York is possibly the first of all English-speaking states from the time of the Reformation to grant this protection, for it is documented in a decision De Witt Clinton made in June 1813. See Louisell et al. (1976), 666–667. I would like to thank Rabbi Ben Zion Bergman for these references.

106. It is important as well to determine whether the clergy member's immunity from the legal responsibility to report abuse is narrowly or broadly construed in the state in which it takes place. Thus, although California has written that privilege into its laws of evidence, Dr. Ian Russ shared with me an official opinion of the state's Office of the Attorney General according to which a clergy member's immunity from being a mandated reporter of child abuse exists only in the priest–penitent relationship and not when the rabbi is serving as a teacher, camp counselor, or educational director. Under this interpretation, the privilege would never apply to professionals or rabbis acting in those capacities; it probably would not even apply to a cantor, for even though cantors are construed as clergypersons in California for the purposes of performing weddings, they are not regularly called on to engage in confidential counseling, and their job description rarely includes that. Moreover, even for rabbis, the privilege may be very narrowly construed, because—as the definition of the priest–penitent privilege in the third and the last paragraphs of the attorney general's opinion indicates—it exists only when the religion itself affirms it, but Judaism prefers saving life and limb to privacy.

The Attorney General's office opinion states the following:

RESPONSIBILITY OF THE CLERGY UNDER THE CHILD ABUSE REPORTING LAW

PENAL CODE SECTIONS 11165–11174

Participation of the clergy in reporting a case of suspected child abuse is entirely voluntary. Priests, ministers, rabbis and other clergy are not included in any of the categories of professionals required to report child abuse. . . . (See Stats. 1980, ch. 1071, #1–4).

It must be remembered, however, that insofar as a member of the clergy is also practicing a profession or vocation which is included in one of the categories of mandated reporters, he or she must report suspected child abuse discovered while acting in that capacity. For instance, clergy who are teachers, school administrators, marriage, family and child counselors, or social workers are required to report. . . . In no event, however, may clergy be required to

reveal "penitential communications," for these communications are protected by the penitent-clergyperson privilege.

A " 'penitential communication' is a communication *made in confidence,*
in the presence of no third person so far as the penitent is aware, to a clergyperson who, in the course of the discipline or practice of his or her church,
denomination, or organization, is authorized or accustomed to hear such communications and, under the discipline or tenets of his or her church, denomination, or organization, has a duty to keep such communications secret."

This penitent-clergy privilege, when coupled with the Right to Privacy
guaranteed by the California Constitution, may serve to limit voluntary reports of child abuse by the clergy. The privilege can be effectively waived only
by the penitent, for even if a clergy member wishes to waive the privilege
and disclose a penitential communication, the penitent may nonetheless invoke the privilege to bar disclosure.

The clergy member and the penitent are *joint* holders of the privilege. That
means that the clergy member has the right to invoke the privilege on his or
her own behalf, or the penitent has the additional right to prevent the clergy
member from disclosing a penitential communication. Thus, the intent of
the law to afford maximum personal privacy to penitents is manifest. Accordingly it appears that a clergy member may not report, even voluntarily,
child abuse learned of in the course of receiving a penitential communication unless the penitent himself or herself waives the privilege afforded that
communication.

Remember, however, that the legal limitations on disclosure of information received in confidence apply only to those communications that in every
aspect meet the definition of a "penitential communication" as noted above.
Thus, it appears that suspected child abuse learned of through other "confidential" communications received by clergy in the course of performing pas-
toral functions may be reported under the Child Abuse Reporting Law.
Whether or not a clergy member should do so is a matter of personal conscience and integrity measured in the light of the moral and religious obligations of the clergy member's own religious affiliate.

Margaret E. Garnand, Deputy Attorney General, Sacramento

107. M. *Avot (Ethics of the Fathers)* 4:5.
108. Deuteronomy 6:7.
109. B. *Eruvin* 82a; B. *Ketubbot* 65b, 122b–123a. For these and other relevant
sources and a discussion about them, see Herring (1989), 177 ff. See also Chapter
Three herein.
110. See, for example, S.A. *Even Ha'ezer* 82:7.
111. See Schochetman (1992) and Broyde (1994).
112. *Sifra* on Leviticus 19:14; B. *Pesachim* 22b; B. *Mo'ed Katan* 17a; B. *Kiddushin* 32a; B. *Nedarim* 62b; and B. *Bava Metz'ia* 75b. Abayae sets a limit to this
issue—namely, that we must concern ourselves with what the person with
whom we are dealing will do and not with others with whom the person will

come into contact (B. *Avodah Zarah* 14a). But Rabbi Barukh Halevi Epstein argued that that only applies to a non-Jew and that in regard to Jews we must be concerned not to mislead even those who may be lead astray by the ones with whom we are now interacting; see his *Torah Temimah* on Leviticus 19:14, #93.

In any case, in the situation here, the concern is that placing children in non-Jewish homes will lead them to be ignorant of Judaism and even to convert out of the faith. As serious a concern as that is, it must be set aside to save the life of the child. As Rabbi Lionel Moses pointed out to me in a conversation, however, it is not clear that *pikkuah nefesh* would justify such action to save a child from verbal abuse. In such cases all involved with the case must take special care to make sure that removing the child from the custody of one or both parents is warranted and that the new home for the child is Jewish, which, we would hope, is the normal procedure in cases of physical and sexual abuse, too.

113. Hotchkin (2000), 4A.

114. See Roan (1996). As she says there, "Health professionals are required to report suspected cases. But the rule may be stopping victims, fearful of revenge, from getting help" (p. A1).

115. B. *Hullin* 10a; see S.A. *Orah Hayyim* 173:2; and *Yoreh De'ah* 116:5 gloss.

116. For the three exceptions, see B. *Sanhedrin* 74a. That saving your own life takes precedence over saving the lives of others is established in B. *Bava Metz'ia* 62a.

117. B. *Kiddushin* 31b and M.T. *Laws of Rebels* 6:10. Radbaz, on that passage, pointed out that this may be best for the parent, because the child is forbidden from striking the parent, but others may do so if that is in the parent's best interests, "for there are incidents every day" in which striking persons can retrieve them from their insanity (or, presumably, at least from the behavioral effects of it).

118. B. *Kiddushin* 31a.

119. See, for example, B. *Kiddushin* 65b and B. *Bava Metz'ia* 3b.

120. B. *Sanhedrin* 9b, 10a, 25a; B. *Ketubbot* 18b; and B. *Yevamot* 25b. See also T. *Sanhedrin* 11:1; B. *Ketubbot* 27a; and B. *Bava Kamma* 72b. Compare Kirschenbaum (1970) and *Encyclopedia Judaica* 5:877–878 at *Confession*.

121. Leviticus 19:16; compare Jeremiah 9:2–4; Psalms 34:13–15.

122. B. *Bava Kamma* 91a.

123. B. *Bava Kamma* 46a.

124. Rabbi Asher ben Jehiel (ROSH), *Responsa* #101.

125. S.A. *Hoshen Mishpat* 420:38.

126. For defamation, see Numbers 12:1–6 and Deuteronomy 22:13–19. For lying, see Leviticus 19:11. For plotting witnesses, see Deuteronomy 19:15–21.

127. Marcus (1994), 1, n. 1 and Katz and Mazure (1979), 205–206. This quotation is discussed in the modern context of our concern for paying more attention to the testimony of women alleging rape (and children alleging abuse) by Brownmiller (1975), 369.

Marcus (1994) cited, among other statistics, the F.B.I. *Uniform Crime Reports*, according to which 8 percent of forcible rape complaints were "unfounded," meaning that they were "determined through investigation to be false." Torrey (1991); Brownmiller (1975), 387; and Katz and Mazur (1979), 209, all reported that about 2 percent of rape accusations prove to be false. On the other end of the spectrum, Kanin (1994), 84, 90, reported that 41 percent of rape allegations were false in one small Midwestern city and exactly half (50 percent) were false in the police records of two large Midwestern state universities.

128. For a good summary of these steps as required by rabbinic sources, see M.T. *Laws of Repentance (Teshuvah)*, esp. 2:1–2.

129. See Olitzky and Copans (1991).

130. B. *Sanhedrin* 99a, and see Rashi's comment there. See Graetz (1998) for further discussion of when and how the safety of the synagogue can be helpful for airing matters of human intimacy, including areas of vulnerability such as being a victim or perpetrator of abuse.

131. One of the specific examples of *ona'at devarim* given in B. *Bava Metz'ia* 58a is reminding a person of past violations of the law.

132. As Rabbi Mayer Rabinowitz pointed out to me in a private conversation, if the process of *teshuvah* works to its fullest extent, abusers should not even be tempted to abuse others when confronted with situations similar to the ones that led them to abuse people in the past. In a similar situation, we do not tell recovering alcoholics to avoid going to a *Kiddush* after worship services altogether; we ask them, instead, to participate in the *Kiddush* and to take grape juice instead of wine. On this model, abusers who have gone through full *teshuvah* might be trusted, at least under supervision, to resume their former tasks with children.

Although I can understand this line of reasoning and can imagine situations in which that may be appropriate, I hesitate to recommend it, because in cases of abuse, more than in cases of alcoholism, the welfare of others is directly affected. Moreover, a significant percentage of alcoholics have managed to achieve and sustain a state of recovery, but pedophiles have much greater difficulty overcoming their addiction. It is, therefore, better for all concerned for these people simply to avoid situations in which they may be tempted. We must trust the process of *teshuvah* while being realistic of its limits—and of the need to protect those who would be victims if it fails.

133. I would like to thank Rabbi Joel Rembaum for pointing out this aspect of the situation and its implications for the process of *teshuvah*.

134. Clergy Advisory Board (1994).

135. Ibid.

136. The entire fall 1994 issue of *Religious Education* was devoted to the topic of religious education and child abuse. That issue includes important articles on how religious educators (and presumably rabbis and cantors among them) can recognize child abuse when it happens, help victims extricate themselves from the abuse, and help prevent child abuse in the first place. Marian Wright Edelman of the Children's Defense Fund, James Fowler, and Nel Noddings are among the authors included.

In addition to keeping the public attention on this issue alive through writing about it in the popular press, thinking about its various dimensions in scholarly articles, and doing research in ways to prevent abuse or, failing that, to stop it and heal its victims, it is important to make this part of the political agenda as well. On October 28, 2000, President Clinton signed into legislation a reauthorization of the 1994 Violence Against Women Act which, among other things, "provides $3.3 billion over five years to expand shelters for battered women and children and to prosecute wife beaters. It reinforces the existing law by helping battered immigrant women and attacking international traffic in human beings." In signing the law, President Clinton stated that "Every twelve seconds another woman [in the United States] is beaten. That is nearly 900,000 victims every year." He also noted that domestic violence is the number one health risk for women between the ages of fifteen and forty-five; see "New Law Cracks Down" (2000), A16. In addition, of course, other federal and state laws prohibiting and punishing assault and child abuse apply.

137. The Jewish Theological Seminary of America (1992). Emphasis per the original.

NOTES TO CHAPTER SIX

1. I am tempted to use the word "repentance" here, as the English language would have me do. but, as I note later, that would invoke Christian understandings of the process, and I want to adhere carefully to both the words and the substance that Judaism uses in describing a return to God.

2. Leviticus 19:18.

3. M. *Bava Kamma* 8:1 and B. *Bava Kamma* 83b–84a. For a translation and discussion of those passages, see Dorff and Rosett (1988), 152–179.

4. M. *Bava Metz'ia* 4:10; B. *Bava Metz'ia* 58b, where the Rabbis deduce this prohibition from Leviticus 25:17 (since the prohibition against oppressing another in monetary matters was stated earlier in Leviticus 25:14).

5. Milgrom (1991), 245. Milgrom continues to translate the Hebrew *salah* as "forgive" on the grounds that he cannot think of a better substitute, but I think that my discussion here would suggest "pardon."

6. M. *Berakhot* 9:5; M. *Avot* 4:1; B. *Berakhot* 61a–b; B. *Shabbat* 105b; B. *Sotah* 47a; and B. *Avodah Zarah* 5b. The "evil" impulse, though, is not evil in the normal sense, as this rabbinic statement attests: " 'And God saw everything that He had made and, behold, it was very good' (Genesis 1:31). 'Very good' indicates both the good impulse and the evil impulse. But is the evil impulse very good? [Yes, for] were it not for that impulse, a man would not build a house, marry a wife, beget children, or conduct business affairs" (*Genesis Rabbah* 9:7). Thus the "evil impulse" does not denote our penchant to do immoral things; it is rather the self-directed inclination in us, in contrast to the other-directed impulse in us, which is termed the "good impulse." It may indeed be the case that self-directed actions are more likely to result in immorality than other-directed actions are, but they surely do not always do so, as the examples in *Genesis Rabbah* make clear. The "evil impulse," therefore, makes human free will possible (and thus "There is no evil impulse in animals," according to *Avot de-Rabbi Natan* 16) and indeed, since it includes our sexual urges, life itself depends on it (compare B. *Avodah Zarah* 5a). Because the evil impulse, so defined, was created by God for the preservation of the

human species, in the life to come, when there is no further need for it, God will slay it (B. *Sukkah* 52a).

In the meantime, though, the Rabbis interpret "You should love the Lord your God with all your heart" (Deuteronomy 6:5) along these lines. Because the Hebrew word for "heart" in that verse is spelled unusually with two, rather than one, letter *bets*, the Rabbis take the verse to meant that we should love God "With two impulses—the good and the evil" (*Sifrei Devarim* on Deuteronomy 6:5). In general on this, see Cohen (1949), 88–93, and 54–55.

7. I discuss the differences between right and good, on the one hand, and wrong and bad, on the other, in Dorff (2002), 241–261.

8. M. *Avot* (*Ethics of the Fathers*) 2:21.

9. The four modes of return delineated as a, b, d, and e are based on the remark of Rabbi Yitzhak in B. *Rosh Hashanah* 16b. That exile wipes away sin (f) is found in B. *Sanhedrin* 37b.

10. A contemporary of Maimonides, Rabbi Abraham ben David of Posquieres, maintained instead that if a person's sin against God is well known, his process of return should be public as well. Maimonides, though, worried that even if many people knew of the sin, others might not, and so it is better for God's reputation to keep both the sin and the process of return quiet.

11. This exception to enabling people to effect full return was specifically written into my rabbinic ruling "Family Violence," which was the basis for Chapter Five. See also Abelson and Fine (2002), 773–816. That ruling, approved unanimously by the Conservative movement's Committee on Jewish Law and Standards (CJLS), notes the strong evidentiary burden Jewish law requires to prove that a person violated someone because Jewish law, even more than American law, presumes people to be innocent until proven guilty. Once guilt has been established, however, society is under no obligation to restore the person to a former position that would endanger the safety of children just to afford the wrongdoer the possibility of achieving full return.

12. See for example, B. *Pesachim* 50b. I would like to thank Lewis Smedes for calling my attention to the tension that I am discussing in this section.

13. There is an interesting discussion in Jewish sources—and in Kant as well—about whether an act is more or less morally worthy when done out of a sense of duty or out of one's own desire. Both the Talmud and Kant maintain that the act is more morally worthy if done out of a sense of duty. For Kant it has moral character *only* if it is done out of a sense of duty contrary to desire. The Rabbis do not go that far: An act can have moral worth if it conforms to duty even if one acts out of one's desire to do the right or good thing. It is just that acting out of a sense of duty recognizes the authority of God more fully. Moreover, pragmatically, the chances that the good will be done are greater if people recognize a duty to do so, whether or not they want to act that way. Therefore "The one who is commanded [to do a good act] and does it is greater [better] than the one who is not commanded [to do the good act] and does it." See B. *Kiddushin* 31a.

14. *Sifrei Devarim*, 'Ekev, on Deuteronomy 11:22.

15. Deuteronomy 23:4–7; 25:17–19. See Exodus 17:8–16.

16. Deuteronomy 23:8-9.

17. Dorff (2002), 184–211.

18. I would like to thank Robert Enright for emphasizing to me that forgiveness is always within the power of the victim, in contrast to reconciliation. This is true, of course, only if the victim survives the offense. If not, the question of whether family and friends have the standing to forgive arises, similar to the case of communal sins described in the last section. Even if a victim's family does have that right, the question remains as to whether they *should* forgive anyone who caused the death of their loved one. Assuming that the victim does survive, though, Enright's insight led me to recast this section from an earlier draft: The question in these sources is not whether there *can* be forgiveness for egregious sins, but whether there *should* be.

19. M.T. *Laws of Return (Teshuvah)* 3:6. Most of the talmudic passages on which he relied come from *Sanhedrin* chap. 11.

20. M. T. *Laws of Return (Teshuvah)* 3:14.

21. M.T. *Laws of Return (Teshuvah)* 5:4. He called those who deny free will "stupid" and "mentally incompetent" (actually, he used the word *golem*—that is, a human mass totally directed by the will of its master) in 5:2.

22. Wiesenthal (1976).

NOTES TO CHAPTER SEVEN

1. Exodus 34:6–7; compare Numbers 14:18–19.

2. Exodus 15:26; Deuteronomy 32:39; Isaiah 19:22, 57:18–19; Jeremiah 30:17, 33:6; Hosea 6:1; Psalms 103:2–3, 107:20; and Job 5:18. Similarly, the daily liturgy proclaims, "Heal us, Lord, and we shall be healed"; ultimately all health and healing rests with God.

3. Exodus 15:26; see also Deuteronomy 7:15 and compare 28:60.

4. Leviticus 26:14–16 and Deuteronomy 28:22,27,58–61.

5. Job 2:9.

6. Job 1:21.

7. Job 3:1,11.

8. Probably the most famous contemporary articulation of this is Kushner (1981), written in response to his young son's illness and death. This mode of responding to morally unjustified illness and to other aspects of "the problem of evil" through revisions in one's concept of God has been the approach adopted by a number of Jewish theologians in addition to Kushner, especially since the Holocaust. For two other famous examples, see Schulweis (1994) and Rubenstein (1996). One must be careful, though, not to equate evils that occur because of the bad exercise of our free will, such as the Holocaust, with those illnesses where no direct human complicity is involved. Similarly, in medical matters, lung cancer in someone who has smoked heavily can be attributed to a bad use of one's free will, especially since now everyone in the United States and Canada should know better; leukemia in a small child, though, does not lend itself to any neat theodicy.

9. I am among this latter group; see Dorff (1992), 129–148. Others include Birnbaum (1989), who notes that God's knowledge is limited temporally to jus-

tify belief in God's justice; Berkovits (1973); and Borowitz (1991), esp. 148–149. These theologians span the spectrum in contemporary Jewish life, including thinkers in the Orthodox (Birnbaum, Berkovits), Conservative (Dorff), and Reform (Borowitz) movements.

10. See, for example, Exodus 19:5; Deuteronomy 10:14; and Psalms 24:1. See also Genesis 14:19,22—where the Hebrew word for "Creator" (*koneh*) also means "Possessor" and where "heaven and earth" is a merism for those and everything in between—and Psalms 104:24—where the same word is used with the same meaning. The following verses have the same theme, although not quite as explicitly or as expansively: Exodus 20:11; Leviticus 25:23,42,55; and Deuteronomy 4:35,39, 32:6.

11. B. *Shabbat* 32a; B. *Bava Kamma* 15b, 80a, 91b; M.T. *Laws of Murder* 11:4–5; S.A. *Yoreh De'ah* 116:5 gloss; and S.A. *Hoshen Mishpat* 427:8–10. Indeed, Jewish law views endangering one's health as worse than violating a ritual prohibition; see B. *Hullin* 10a; S.A. *Orah Hayyim* 173:2; and S.A. *Yoreh De'ah* 116:5 gloss. So, for example, anyone who cannot subsist except by taking charity but refuses to do so out of pride is shedding blood and is guilty of a mortal offense; see S.A. *Yoreh De'ah* 255:2. Similarly, Conservative, Reform, and some Orthodox authorities have prohibited smoking as an unacceptable risk to our God-owned bodies; see Dorff and Rosett (1988), 337–362.

12. Bathing, for example, is a commandment according to Hillel; see *Leviticus Rabbah* 34:3. Maimonides summarized and codified the rules requiring proper care of the body in M.T. *Laws of Ethics* (*De'ot*), chaps. 3–5. He spelled out there in remarkable clarity that the purpose of these positive duties to maintain health is not to feel good and live a long life, but rather to have a healthy body so that one can then serve God.

13. *Sifra* on Leviticus 19:16; B. *Sanhedrin* 73a; M.T. *Laws of Murder* 1:14; and S.A. *Hoshen Mishpat* 426.

14. S.A. *Yoreh De'ah* 336:1. See B. *Bava Kamma* 85a and B. *Sanhedrin* 73a, where Exodus 21:19–20 and Deuteronomy 22:2 are used to ground, respectively, the permission and the duty to heal.

15. Leviticus 19:18. B. *Bava Kamma* 85a, 81b; B. *Sanhedrin* 73a, 84b (with Rashi's commentary there). See also *Sifrei Devarim* on Deuteronomy 22:2 and *Leviticus Rabbah* 34:3. See also Nahmanides (Rabbi Moses ben Nahman, or Ramban, fourteenth century), *Kitvei Haramban* (ed. Chavel, 1963), 2:43 (Hebrew). This passage comes from Nahmanides' *Torat Ha'adam* (*The Instruction of Man*), Sh'ar Sakkanah (*Section on Danger*) on B. *Bava Kamma*, chap. 8, and is cited by Joseph Karo in his commentary to the *Tur*, *Bet Yosef, Yoreh De'ah* 336. Nahmanides bases himself on similar reasoning in B. *Sanhedrin* 84b.

16. J. *Kiddushin* 66d and compare B. *Sanhedrin* 17b.

17. See, for example, B. *Sanhedrin* 91a–91b and its alternate versions in *Mekhilta*, Be-shallah, Shirah (ed. Horowitz-Rabin, 1960), 125; *Leviticus Rabbah* 4:5; *Yalkut Shimoni* on Leviticus 4:2, #464; *Tanhuma*, Va-yikra' 6. The very development of the term "*neshamah*" from meaning "physical breath" to "one's inner being" clearly bespeaks Judaism's view that the physical and the spiritual are integrated.

18. M. *Avot* 2:1. See B. *Berakhot* 35b, esp. the comment of Abayae there in responding to the earlier theories of Rabbi Ishmael and Rabbi Shimon bar Yoḥai.

19. B. *Sotah* 14a.

20. B. *Shabbat* 127a and cf. M. *Pe'ah* 1:1.

21. S.A. *Yoreh De'ah* 335:3, gloss. Joseph Karo, in the Shulchan Arukh here, assumed that the ill person is lying on the ground; therefore, he said that visitors must lie on the ground next to the sick person. Moses Isserles, in his comment in the gloss on this passage, though, added that if the ill person is lying in a bed, it is permissible to sit near the patient on a bench or chair.

22. Lamm (1995), 132–133.

23. See Dorff (1998), 176–198, esp. 197–198.

24. For some poignant examples of ethical wills, including many modern ones, see Riemer and Stampfer (1983). For some suggestions for preparing an ethical will, see Riemer and Stampfer (1991).

25. Rabbi Lamm (1995), 25–38, 163–172, described the importance of hope for him and his family in helping his daughter overcome Hodgkin disease, and he articulated a ten-point program to bolster hope.

26. M. *Hullin* 3:1; B. *Hullin* 42a; and M.T. *Laws of Slaughter* 10:9.

27. B. *Hullin* 58a; M.T. *Laws of Slaughter* 11:1; and S.A. *Yoreh De'ah* 57:18.

28. M.T. *Laws of Murder* 2:8.

29. M. *Yevamot* 16:4; commentary of Ramban (Nahmanides) to B. *Yevamot* 120b, s.v. *umi matsit*; commentary of Rashba to B. *Yevamot*, #230, s.v. *umi matsit*; commentaries of *Maggid Mishneh* and *Kesef Mishneh* to M.T. *Laws of Divorce* 13:16; and S.A. *Even Ha'ezer* 17:32.

30. *Tosafot* to B. *Gittin* 57b, s.v. *venikar bemokho* and *Tosafot* to B. *Eruvin* 7a, s.v. *kegaon shidra*. See also *Kesef Mishneh* to M.T. *Laws of Divorce* 13:16, and *Tosafot Yom Tov* to M. *Yevamot* 16:4.

31. This is one instance of Maimonides' more general rule that all people guilty of bloodshed who, for some reason, cannot be convicted of a capital crime under the usual evidentiary rules may be executed by the king on his own authority if he deems that necessary to reenforce the moral standards of the society. If the king chooses not to execute such people, he should, said Maimonides, "flog them almost to the point of death, imprison them in a fortress or a prison for many years, or inflict [some other] severe punishment on them in order to frighten and terrify other wicked persons" who specifically plot to commit bloodshed in a way not subject to court action. See M.T. *Hilkhot Rozeah U'Shmirat Haguf* (*Laws of Murder and Care of the Body*) 2:8 and 2:2–5; see also *Hilkhot Melakhim* (*Laws of Kings*) 9:4. As Maimonides explained, homicides that cannot be classified as murder for some reason (specifically, the evidentiary rules are not satisfied, the perpetrator committed the act through an agent, the victim is the killer himself [suicide], or the victim is a *terefah*) are nevertheless prohibited as acts of bloodshed under Genesis 9:6.

The extralegal penalties specified by Maimonides are not mandated by the law for all such cases; rather, God, the human court, and the king, in applying such punishments, have considerable latitude in deciding whether to punish at all and, if so, how. Moreover, the human court and king must consider how this one act affects the general moral standing of the society.

As Rabbi Solomon Duran, a fifteenth-century Algerian authority, noted in a polemic in defense of Jewish law, this is preferable to the usual method by which legal systems deal with such cases—that is, by making the perpetrator liable under the law but eligible for judicial or executive pardon—because the latter approach obscures the true grounds for not administering capital punishment and leaves the public believing that justice simply was not done. Jewish law's approach, on the other hand, excludes the death penalty in this type of case from the very outset, so that the public can know that the law has been upheld in court, but it affords society the ability to rid itself of such behavior if it needs to. See Rabbi Solomon Duran, *Milkhemet Mitzvah* 32b, s.v. *od heshiv* (Hebrew). Sinclair (1989), 57–59, makes a similar point by comparing Jewish law to Anglo-American law.

32. B. *Sanhedrin* 74a.

33. *Minhat Hinukh* #296, s.v. *vehinei beguf hadin*. See also my discussion of the ruling of Rabbi Menahem Meiri along these lines in a case of siege (in his commentary on B. *Sanhedrin* 74a) in Dorff (1991a), 22–24; see also Dorff (1998), 198–217.

This is not, of course, to say that an incurably ill person is totally equivalent to a dead person. On the same page of the Talmud on which Rava said that "all admit" that the killer of a *terefah* is exempt from human legal proceedings, he also asserted that one who has illicit sex with a terminally ill person is liable. As the Talmud goes on to explain, the liability derives from the fact that the sexual act performed with an incurably ill person will still produce pleasure, while the same act with a dead person would not do so since, as Rashi says, all of a dead person's warmth and moisture (humors) have been lost. See B. *Sanhedrin* 78a. See Rashi there, s.v. *hayyav* and *v'ha eit lei hanaah*.

34. Rabbi Simon Efrati, *Responsa Migei Haharigah*, #1 (where he permits taking the infant's life but says that one who chooses martyrdom instead is a "holy person"); Ben-Zimra (1977), 151.

These heart-rending cases are instances of broader precedents within Jewish law. The questionable viability of newly born infants, due, at least in part, to doubts as to whether they were premature or full-term, led Jewish law to exempt one who kills a child who is younger than thirty days old from human prosecution, just as it treats the person who kills the *terefah;* see T. *Shabbat* 15:7; B. *Shabbat* 135b; B. *Niddah* 44b; and *Tosafot, Shabbat* 136a, s.v. *mimhal*. The Mishnah, which subjects the killer of a day-old baby to the death penalty, was taken by later rabbis as only a theoretical rule, since whether the child was premature or full-term could never be conclusively known; see M. *Niddah* 5:3; and *Responsa Noda Beyehudah* 2 *Hoshen Mishpat* #59. According to Rabbi David Zvi Hoffman (in *Responsa Melamed Leho'il* #69), one may even intentionally sacrifice a newly born infant to preserve the life of its mother. Here again, then, the infant younger than thirty days old is a category of human being whose questionable viability makes it subject to bloodshed if—but only if—another person's life could be saved by doing so.

Sinclair also points out that Jewish law treats both the fetus and the *terefah* in a parallel manner in regard to the Sabbath laws: In both cases, whether to save the life of the fetus or the *terefah* at the cost of violating the Sabbath is a debated point, with opinions going in both directions. Since this is never a question in regard to other stages in human life, these Sabbath laws further demonstrate that the blood of both the fetus and the *terefah* is "less red" than that of viable people. On all of this, see Sinclair (1989), 53–57.

35. B. *Sanhedrin* 78a and M.T. *Hilkhot Rozeah* 2:8. See also B. *Bava Kamma* 41a, according to which the owner of an ox that kills a person who has a fatal organic disease is not considered forewarned (*mu'ad*) in regard to the animal's likelihood to kill healthy persons and need not be put to death; and B. *Shevu'ot* 34a, which repeats that a person who kills a *terefah* is exempt from human penalties.

The term *"gavra ketilla"* occurs four times in the Babylonian Talmud. According to *Sanhedrin* 71a, once a person has been sentenced to death, he is immediately a *gavra ketilla*, a "killed man." Because of that, *Sanhedrin* 81a deals with the possibility that one might think that a person sentenced to one of the more lenient forms of execution, since immediately presumed dead, could not subsequently be sentenced to a harsher form of execution for another crime. It rejects that conclusion, but in the meantime reaffirms the description of a doomed person as a dead one. *Sanhedrin* 85a adds the consideration that one sentenced to death, since considered an already killed person, is no longer "abiding among your people" in the terms of Exodus 22:27. And, perhaps most relevant to our purposes, *Pesachim* 110b says that a person who drinks more than sixteen cups of wine is a *gavra ketilla*. There it is medical, rather than judicial, factors that make the person thought of as dead.

Rabbis who explicitly call a *terefah* person a *gavra ketilla* (or the Hebrew equivalent *"k'met"*) include Rashi, B. *Sanhedrin* 78a, s.v., *she'hu patur*; *Hokhmat Shelomoh* on B. *Sanhedrin* 78a, s.v., *mai ta'ama hayyav*; *Minhat Hinnukh* #34 and #296; and *Mitzpeh Eitan* on *Sanhedrin* 78a. In addition, the Midrash, in *Canticles Rabbah* 4:1, translates *"taraf"* in Genesis 8:11 as *"katil,"* comparing it to Genesis 37:33, Jacob's shriek that "Joseph has surely been mangled [torn up]."

36. M. *Berakhot* 9:3.

37. S.A. *Even Ha'ezer* 121:7, gloss, and S.A. *Hoshen Mishpat* 211:2, gloss.

38. On the category of *goses*, including its definition, the requirement to treat a *goses* as a fully living person, and the permission (and, according to the first of these sources, the requirement) to stop medical interventions once this state has occurred, see *Sefer Hasidim* (attributed to Rabbi Judah the Pious, thirteenth century) #723, #234 and S.A. *Yoreh De'ah* 339:1, gloss. That a *goses* is like a flickering candle, see M. *Semahot* 1:4, cited in many later sources, including B. *Shabbat* 151b and the commentaries *Siftei Kohen* and *Be'er Hetev* to S.A. *Yoreh De'ah* 339:1.

39. See Bleich (1979), 34 and the contemporary rabbis he cites in n. 120. See also Bleich (1981), 141–142. The main classical sources Bleich cites for this ruling are *Perishah*, *Tur Yoreh De'ah* 339:5 and the ruling in S.A. *Yoreh De'ah*

339:2 that one must begin observing the laws of mourning three days after the onset of *gesisah.*

40. For example, among Orthodox rabbis, see Eliezer Waldenberg, *Responsa Tzitz Eliezer* 13, #89 and 14, #80, and Jakobovits (1975), 124, n. 46. Among Conservative rabbis, see Goldfarb (1976) and Siegel (1976). I also originally suggested this approach in Dorff (1985), 19–21.

41. I argued this first in Dorff (1991b). A more extensive explanation of the justifications and ramifications of this view appears in Dorff (1998), 199–200.

42. For modern responsa accepting brain death as the modern criterion of death, see Goldman (1978), 229–230. Goldman, 211–237, also presented a good overview of the positions on the criteria of death and the related question of organ transplantation as discussed in all three contemporary American Jewish movements up to 1978. For later Conservative responsa on this, see Dorff (1991a) and Reisner (1991), both of whom assume and explicitly invoke the new medical definition. For the official Reform position on this matter, see Jacob et al. (1983), 273–274.

Some Orthodox rabbis have not accepted the new criterion of brain death, most articulately Bleich (1981), 146–157. The Orthodox chief rabbinate of the State of Israel has accepted the legitimacy of heart transplants, however, and, along with that, the permissibility of using the brain death criteria; see Jakobovits (1989).

43. *Genesis Rabbah* 100:7; *Leviticus Rabbah* 18:1; *Ecclesiastes Rabbah* on Ecclesiastes 12:6; and J. *Mo'ed Katan* 3:5.

44. For example, Numbers 16:33; Isaiah 38:18; and Psalms 6:6, 116:3.

45. 1 Samuel 28. Because of that story, some later rabbinic sources maintain that for the first twelve months after death the soul retains a temporary relationship to the body, coming and going until the body has disintegrated. This explains, for the Rabbis, why the prophet Samuel could be raised from the dead within the first year of his demise in the story of the witch of En-dor. See B. *Shabbat* 152b–153a; *Tanḥuma*, Va-yikra', 8.

46. Isaiah 38:18–19 and Psalms 6:6, 115:17.

47. For example, Job 7:7–10, 9:20–22, 14:7–22, and Ecclesiastes 9:4–5; compare Ecclesiastes 3:19–21.

There is one mention of resurrection of the dead in a much earlier source—Isaiah 26:19—but that would place the doctrine in the eighth century B.C.E., when First Isaiah lived. Because belief in resurrection is not attested in any biblical source even near that time and explicitly denied as late as Ecclesiastes, most biblical scholars presume that Isaiah 26:19 is a verse that was added long after Isaiah gave his sermons; see, for example, *Encyclopedia Judaica* 14:97–98 at *Resurrection—In the Bible.*

48. For Abraham's blessing, see Genesis 18:18. For the levirate marriage, see Deuteronomy 25:6. For children as great blessings, see Genesis 15:5, 17:3–6,15-21, 18:18, 22:17, 28:14, 32:13; Deuteronomy 7:13–14, 28:4,11; and Psalms 128:3,6. For childlessness as a source of frustration, see Genesis 15:2–4, 17:15–22, 18:9–15, 25:21, 30:1–8,22–24, 35:16–20; and 1 Samuel 1:10–20. For the definition of *karet* (being cut off) as seeing one's children die, see B. *Yevamot* 55a.

49. Daniel 12:2–3.

50. 4 Maccabees 9:8, 17:5,18 and 2 Maccabees 7:14,23.

51. B. *Berakhot* 7a.

52. M. *Sanhedrin* 10:1. See B. *Sanhedrin* 90b–91a for the talmudic Rabbis' attempts to identify the biblical verses that promise a life after death.

53. B. *Berakhot* 34b and *Sifrei Devarim* par. 336 (148b).

54. Maimonides, *Commentary on the Mishnah, Sanhedrin*, chap. 10, *Perek Ha-Helek* (trans. Twersky, 1972), 403–404.

55. For God teaching the poor, see *Yalkut Shimoni*, Genesis, chap. 20. For God resolving the scholars' puzzles, see B. *Hagigah* 14a.

56. B. *Berakhot* 17a. For more on rabbinic doctrines of the world to come, see Cohen (1949), 346–389.

57. This is illustrated by a surprising result in a *Los Angeles Times* poll. The poll, taken on December 14 and 15, 1991, in the San Fernando Valley section of Los Angeles, revealed the extent of Jewish belief in reincarnation: 23 percent of Jews believed in the birth of the soul in a new body after death, compared to 20 percent of Christians and 33 percent of the nonreligious. This is especially remarkable because most forms of Judaism do *not* profess belief in reincarnation. See Maller (1992).

Jewish mysticism, though, does affirm reincarnation (*gilgul neshamot*), as do a number of Asian religions, to which some Jews have been attracted in recent times. My guess, though, is that it is the vast numbers of Jewish secularists behind this statistic. Since reincarnation does not involve the outright denial of the disintegration of the body, it is more defensible than resurrection in a secular framework—although certainly not provable within one. There may be no evidence against reincarnation in our experience, but there is also no clear verification of it. Nevertheless, that as many as 23 percent of Jews asserted faith in reincarnation indicates that there are clearly afterlife beliefs beneath the skin of many avowed Jewish secularists, undoubtedly an expression of their hope for continued meaning in life after death.

58. See Goldberg (1985).

59. The *Los Angeles Times* poll cited in note 57 also found that 67 percent of Christians and 45 percent of those with no religious identity believed in life after death, but only 30 percent of Jews said that they did; see Maller (1992). In explaining their position, most Jews claim that we just do not know enough, or that people live on in the influence they have had on the lives of others, especially their children, or that there is nothing after death. Even fewer Jews believe in a devil or a hell to which sinners are condemned: 58 percent of Christians polled believed in those doctrines, but only 4 percent of Jews did. While Maller's study accurately reflects the vast majority of Jews, one notable exception to this is Chabad, with its slogan, "We want Maschiach [Messiah] now!"

60. For a clear discussion of how a number of modern writers have pretended that Judaism has no beliefs in an afterlife whatsoever but that Judaism in fact believes in both an emphasis on improving this world and a life in the hereafter, see Schulweis (1982).

61. See Bleich (1990). Although he does not mention hospice care specifically there, the whole drift of his argument would make it suspect. I also have a private letter from Rabbi Immanuel Jakobovits, from some fifteen years ago, in which he raised this question of whether the halakhically required degree of hope is maintained in hospice care.

62. See, for example, Isaiah 2:1–4, 11:1–12, and Micah 4:1–6.

63. Deuteronomy 7:15.

64. See for example, Isaiah 13–14; Ezekiel 38–39; Amos 5; Joel 2–3; B. *Megillah* 11a; and B. *s* 97b.

65. For a discussion about Jewish views of poverty and Jewish programs to overcome it, see Dorff (2002), 126–160.

The Interaction of Judaism with Morality: Defining, Motivating, and Educating a Moral Person and Society

OR JUDAISM AND MANY OTHER RELIGIONS OF THE WORLD, religion is closely intertwined with morality. There is not, however, a one-to-one relationship between religion and morality, for clearly moral people may deny belief in or affiliation with any religion, and, conversely, some people who see themselves as religious (and whom others see as such too) nevertheless do immoral things. Worse, some of history's greatest moral atrocities have been done in the very name of religion.

In recognition of this complex relationship between religion and morality, here I first suggest at least some of the elements of Judaism that sometimes breed immorality, together with some suggestions for ways to avoid these ill effects. I then describe a number of aspects of Judaism that contribute to moral sensitivity and behavior.

RELIGIOUS FACTORS MOTIVATING IMMORALITY
Individuals, of course, are perfectly capable of holding immoral beliefs and doing immoral things without the assistance of

religion. Often people use religion as an excuse for doing what they have decided to do on other grounds. At the same time, though, some elements of religions are prone to produce, or at least contribute to, immorality; and I discuss some of these elements next.

GOD'S POWER AND GOODNESS

In the three Western religions, God is the ultimate Person and Power. Whether God is actually omnipotent or something short of that is a matter of dispute among the philosophers of all three Western religions, but there is no doubt that in all three God is at least very powerful. That can lead people to have an appropriately humble sense of their own worth and power. At the same time, those who speak for religion sometimes think that they represent God and, therefore, share in God's power. For that matter, some of their constituents contribute to that mistaken self-image, for religious people sometimes treat their leaders as mini-gods. So, for example, David Berger, a modern Orthodox Jew, has written a scathing book about Chabad, the largest Hasidic sect.[1] Berger maintains— rightly, in my opinion—that their veneration of their deceased leader, Rabbi Menachem Shneierson, as the Messiah is nothing short of idolatry.

Sometimes it is not the power of God that leads to immorality on the part of the faithful, but rather God's goodness. If God is the ultimate fount of value, then some conclude that anything is justified if it is in the name of God. This is an old story, going back to the biblical tale of God telling Abraham to sacrifice his son Isaac. The Protestant theologian Søren Kierkegaard interpreted that story to justify the teleological suspension of the ethical—that is, that God's command can and should override any moral demands, even the most basic of them like refraining from murder. The Rabbis of the Talmud and Midrash interestingly drew the exact opposite conclusion—namely, that God never intended for Abraham to sacrifice Isaac and that the whole episode was intended as a dramatic rejection of the child sacrifice commonly practiced in the ancient Near East. After all, in the biblical account, God stops Abraham in the middle of the event and has him substitute a ram instead.

312

Many people throughout history, though, have adopted Kierkegaard's view, in fact if not in name. Thus the Crusades, the Inquisition, Islamic jihads, and even the Holocaust have been rooted in the belief that God wants people to act in that way (consider the Nazi expression *Gott und mein Recht,* "God and my law"). Some Catholic priests were able to sexually abuse children in their care because the children trusted the priests not only as people but also as the benign voice of God who would not do anything improper. Similar reasoning led several Orthodox Jewish institutions to justify to themselves non-payment of withholding taxes to the government, actions for which they were later prosecuted and convicted. They claimed that they needed the money for their institution and, quoting the Talmud, "Studying Torah takes precedence over all other commandments,"[2] apparently including, in their view, outright theft. They, of course, misinterpreted that talmudic phrase: It simply means that study of Torah can be trusted to *lead* to performance of all other commandments, not that it can substitute for them. Still, a religious text served to justify their wrongdoing. Thus the power and moral authority of God can, by psychological transference, persuade those who speak for God that they have the license and justification to do immoral things.

THE FEARSOME NATURE OF RELIGIOUS TOPICS
The significance for human life and yet the ultimate mystery inherent in many of the topics with which religion deals can also be the source of immorality. Religion, after all, deals with all the liminal aspects of life—birth, adolescence, marriage, illness, death, the goals of life, human limitations, etc. These are critically important in people's lives, but they are also aspects of life over which people have limited control. This makes people fearful. Some soothe their fears by adopting superstitious beliefs and practices that sometimes abuse and even kill people. Consider, for example, the trials and executions of witches throughout the ages and the blood libels that Christians leveled against Jews during the Middle Ages, falsely claiming that Jews slaughtered Christian children to obtain blood for use on Passover (even though Jewish dietary laws forbid the consumption of blood, let

alone killing a human being to procure it). Moreover, the fearsome aspects of things like death and disease sometimes lead people too readily to give up their powers of moral judgment to religious authorities who seem to know about such things. A religiously motivated reticence to question authority, together with superstitious beliefs and practices, can sometimes motivate people to think and act immorally.

RITUALS VERSUS ETHICS

Sometimes this fear of the unknown manifests itself in a focus on rituals over ethics. When rituals become not only symbols but also powerful agents in themselves that can lend order and security to the frightening aspects of life, people are sometimes tempted to concentrate so much on them that they neglect their moral duties. So, for example, newly religious Jews may use their ritual practices as a weapon against their parents, violating Jewish law's requirements to honor and respect one's parents. Ideally, the children can find ways to observe their new religious practices while still maintaining good relationships with their parents; a genuine conflict may exist between the Jewish expressions of the parents and the children, and how they are going to handle that conflict must be negotiated with respect and love. But the dietary laws or the laws of the Sabbath or Passover, for example, do not make the laws requiring honor and respect for parents null and void. Similarly, strict observance of such ritual laws does not excuse a person from the equally mandatory Jewish commandments requiring us to help others in need and to treat them with respect. On the contrary, Jews must devote significant amounts of their time, energy, and resources to fulfilling Judaism's moral demands, for ritual piety must accompany moral piety rather than replace it.

THE SOCIAL PRESSURE OF RELIGIOUS COMMUNITIES

The close communities that religions often foster have multiple advantages for human morality and human flourishing. Like closely knit nonreligious groups, though, social pressure can also be used for immoral purposes. That is, members of a close community might well be willing to go along with all kinds of immoral ideas and actions that they would not normally endorse just to belong. They do not want to break ranks with an accepted, but immoral, communal perspective or practice for fear of formal or informal excommunication. Nazi Germany is a stark, avowedly atheist example of this kind of morally corrupt social pressure, and the Ku Klux Klan, with its burning crosses, illustrates how religion can be used to justify the crimes of the mob. In many areas of the world, religious reasons for the suppression of women have both reflected current social practice and justified it.

Sometimes peer pressure is combined with the idea of God's power and goodness in the form of religious chauvinism. That happens when a group thinks that they may do whatever they want because God has chosen them to be an elite. Leaders of cults have thus gotten their followers to commit felonies in the name of the cult, very much resembling criminal gangs. Some have eventually demanded that their followers commit suicide. What marks these groups is a disdain for anyone outside the group, buttressed by their belief that God hates everyone else too. That conviction is produced by a morally and often physically deadly combination of group identity, hatred of others, and religious fervor.

The Conservative Nature of Religions

Religions are inherently conservative because they are tied to human communities, and people do not like to change. Religions are also conservative because they are built on traditions that always must be taken seriously into account before a person or community can veer from them. As I discuss in the next section, in some respects this conservatism aids moral discernment and action, but sometimes it makes religions stand in the way of needed change. For example, the arguments for slavery in the American Confederacy included some based on biblical texts, and in Sudan to this day Muslims enslave the blacks in the south of their own country and use religious grounds to justify their actions. Similarly, some religious leaders refuse to remove racial or gender discrimination within their own midst based on their reading of their religious tradition.

JUDAISM'S CONTRIBUTIONS TO MORALITY: DEFINITION OF MORAL NORMS, MORAL MOTIVATION, AND MORAL EDUCATION

While the factors discussed above and other elements of religions in general and of Judaism in particular may induce immoral behavior or provide theological cover for it, there are many other aspects of religion that buttress morality. Since this book is about Judaism specifically, and since what is true of Judaism is not necessarily true of other religions, I now describe at least some of the factors *in Judaism* that contribute to morality, leaving it to adherents of other religions to determine whether these elements function in the same way in their own religion or whether they are specifically Jewish in either degree or kind.

Before I turn to the major thrust of this appendix—namely, methodological issues—I do want to invoke here the major elements of the *content* of the Jewish moral vision discussed in Chapter One. Jews, of course, are in many respects human beings like all other human beings, with the same pressures, sorrows, and joys, and, like people all over the world, Jews seek to do the good as they understand it. Thus some of the moral norms of Judaism are identical to those of many other traditions—norms, for example, requiring aid to the needy, endorsing marriage and procreation, and prohibiting murder and theft.

The Jewish vision of the ideal person and society, though, is different from that of Christianity and of most other religions and secular philosophies. Indeed, of the religions of the world, Islam may be the closest to Judaism, given the strong emphasis the two place on family, community, and monotheism. On the other hand, if we can set aside monotheism—admittedly not easy to do in Judaism!—Confucianism strikes me as presenting a moral ideal possibly even closer to that in Judaism, since the two share emphases not only on family and community but also on education and on improving life in this world. The varying perspectives of the world's religions and secular philosophies about what is and what ought to be produce, in turn, a variety of concrete moral norms. Thus an important contribution that Judaism makes to morality is its vision of moral ideals.

The thrust of this appendix, though, focuses on the differing methodologies Judaism employs to discern the good and motivate good behavior. Some of the resources Judaism uses to know and motivate the good are discussed in the following sections.

STORIES

The core Jewish story, the Exodus from Egypt, the Revelation at Mount Sinai, and the trek to the Promised Land, loudly proclaims that we can and must work together with God to redeem ourselves and others from slavery of all sorts. It also says that we must live our lives in accordance with revealed norms and that we must continue to hope and work for the Promised Land of the Messianic age. One way, in fact, to grasp the differences between Judaism and Christianity in moral vision is to compare the messages of their central stories, the Passion–Resurrection for Christianity and Exodus–Sinai for Judaism.[3] That same kind of comparative analysis can yield equally illuminating results when juxtaposing the central stories of other religions and secular philosophies to each other and to Judaism.[4]

Stories not only announce the norms and ideals of a religion or culture but also give those norms and ideals a sense of reality and make them easier to apply to one's life. Moreover, because stories are concrete, they are easier to remember than rules or maxims are, and because they portray moral norms in real-life situations, stories are an effective way to educate people about moral norms (including what happens when they are broken) and to motivate people to be moral.

HISTORY

No nation that has gone through the exile and persecution endured by Jews can possibly have an idealistic picture of human beings; the evil that people have foisted on each other must be part of the Jewish perception of reality. This is, of course, all the more true after the Holocaust, which, among other things, makes Jews very wary of medical research on human subjects.

FAMILY AND COMMUNITY

We first learn what is acceptable behavior and what is not from our parents. They make us aware of the whole realm of moral norms. They also provide the first motivation to act morally as we try to please them. Thus parents and, after them, siblings and other relatives are critical for the moral development of any human being. In fact, children who lack continual moral guidance from parents or some other caring adults from infancy on are in serious danger of never understanding the moral dimension of life or acting morally. Judaism, therefore, takes care to buttress family life with the commands discussed in Chapter Four to honor and respect parents and, conversely, to teach one's children. Beyond these legal boundaries, Jewish family rituals are rich and pervasive, strengthening the family further, and this emphasis on the family has been translated into Jewish consciousness through such media as popular literature and even Jewish jokes about family relationships.

As children mature, they come into contact with the larger community. While tightly knit communities can have the negative effects of squelching independent moral analysis and action, as I noted earlier, such communities can also have morally salutary effects. We learn that we cannot steal Johnnie's marbles on the playground when we see his and other children's reactions to such behavior. Throughout life, in fact, a strong part of our motivation to follow moral rules stems from our desire to have friends and to be part of a larger community. We also aspire to moral ideals, in part, because we crave the esteem of other people, especially those near and dear to us.

Contemporary communities in the United States, including Jewish ones, tend to be much more fractionalized and voluntary than they were in times past, and communities the world over are apt to find themselves in continual interaction with other communities, thus blurring the coherence and authority of any one community's moral message. Nevertheless, communities still function to provide a shared life, including experiences and vocabulary that shape moral vision and behavior.

In our own day, Jewish communities, like many others, are increasingly influenced in these matters by their female members, whose perspectives and voices are for the first time becoming a conscious and public part of how the community understands morality and motivates moral action. People, of course, are unique individuals, and, conversely, we are all human beings with shared experiences as such. Moreover, women do not automatically agree with each other any more than men do. Still, based on research by people like Nel Noddings, Carol Gilligan, and Deborah Tannen,[5] we have come to learn that, even in today's more egalitarian society, men and women as groups approach life generally and morality in particular differently. Indeed, as I noted earlier, imaging of the human mind indicates that men and women even use different parts of their brains when responding to moral and other questions. Thus the increased public involvement of women in communal moral discussions is an important new resource for moral vision and discernment for any community; in Judaism, women as a group add perspectives on Jewish texts, laws, cases, norms, and ideals that significantly expand the ways in which Jews as a whole are understanding what God wants of us in our time.

LEADERS AND OTHER MORAL MODELS

Just as children learn morality first from their parents, so too adults learn to discern what is moral and gain the motivation to work for moral goals by their leaders and by their other moral models. Nobody is perfect, of course, and part of the task in seeking moral leadership is to understand that specific people may be ideal in certain ways and not in others. When some of our political or religious leaders have been shown to have moral faults, that sometimes unfairly and unrealistically undermines our appreciation of their real moral leadership on other matters. Thus the leadership in civil rights shown by Presidents Kennedy and Johnson should not be forgotten just because they were each involved in morally questionable behavior in other aspects of their lives.

Similarly, Judaism uses leaders like the Patriarchs and Matriarchs, Moses, other biblical people, and rabbinic figures throughout the ages as models of ideal behavior and also as models of what happens when you do something morally wrong. In that way, Judaism keeps its leaders from becoming idols while still holding them up as figures to be thought of when deciding on one's own moral course. So, for example, when President Clinton was involved in the Monica Lewinsky affair, many rabbis

invoked the David and Bathsheba story to discuss the implications of sexual impropriety on the part of political leaders.

It is not only people with specific offices in society who influence us morally. Teachers, counselors, friends, and even our children and students can show us how to behave. Although Rabbi
Judah, the president of the Sanhedrin (or, in another version,
Rabbi Hanina) was probably referring to the intellectual knowledge of the Jewish tradition, his famous dictum can equally
apply to the moral lessons we learn from it: "Much have I
learned from my teachers, more from my peers, but most from
my students."[6]

GENERAL VALUES, MAXIMS, AND THEORIES

The Torah announces some general moral values that should inform all our actions—values like formal and substantive justice,
saving lives, caring for the needy, respect for parents and elders,
honesty in business and in personal relations, truth telling, and
education of children and adults. The Torah's laws articulate
some of these general moral values, and others found their way
into books of moral maxims. The biblical Book of Proverbs and
the Mishnah's tractate *Ethics of the Fathers* (*Pirke Avot*) (c. 200
C.E.) are two important ancient reservoirs of Jewish moral precepts, and medieval and modern Jewish writers have produced
some others as, for example, Moses Hayyim Luzzato's *Paths of
the Righteous* (*Mesillat Yesharim*).

Some medieval and modern Jewish thinkers formulated complete theories of morality, depicting a full conception of the
good person and the good community, together with justifications for seeing them in that particular way and modes of edu-
cating people to follow the right path. Several disparate
examples of such theories, each with its own recipe for living a
moral life out of the sources of Judaism, include the following:
Maimonides' twelfth-century rationalist approach, borrowing
heavily from Aristotle, articulated in his code (*Mishneh Torah*)
and his philosophical work (*Guide of the Perplexed*); the mystical views of the thirteenth-century *Zohar* and the sixteenth-
century Lurianic *kabbalah*; the behaviorist approach of the
nineteenth-century figure Israel Salanter; the neo-Kantian ra-
tionalism of Hermann Cohen in the early twentieth century;

320

and the existentialism of Emanuel Levinas in the last half of the twentieth century.

THEOLOGY

As in other Western religions, for Judaism God is central not only to defining the good and the right but also to creating the moral person. God does that in several ways.

First, acting in His judicial and executive functions, God helps ensure that people will do the right thing. God is the infallible Judge, for He knows "the secrets of the world," as the High Holy Day liturgy reminds us. Nothing can be hidden from God, and God cannot be deceived. Moreover, God holds the power of ultimate reward and punishment. To do the right thing just to avoid punishment or to gain reward is clearly not acting out of a high moral motive, but such actions may nevertheless produce good results. Moreover, the Rabbis state many times over that even doing the right thing for the wrong reason has its merit, for eventually correct moral habits may create a moral person who does the right thing for the right reason.[7]

God also contributes to the creation of moral character in serving as a model for us. The underlying conviction of the Bible is that God is good, and God's actions are, as such, paradigms for us. The Bible itself raises questions about God's morality, for there are times when God appears to act arbitrarily and even cruelly; but, for all that, Jewish texts trust that God is good.[8] We, then, should aspire to be like God: "As God clothes the naked, . . . so you should clothe the naked; as God visited the sick, . . . so you should visit the sick; as God comforted those who mourned . . . so you should comfort those who mourn; as God buries the dead, . . . so you should bury the dead."[9]

God's role as covenant partner and as Israel's Lover probably has the greatest effect on creating moral character within us. We should abide by God's commandments, in part, because we were at Sinai, we promised to obey them there, and we should keep our promises. Thus, as the Haggadah of Passover reminds us, "In each and every generation a person is obliged to view himself as if he himself went out of Egypt" on the trek to Sinai, where God made the covenant with all generations to come: "It is not with you alone that I create this Covenant and this oath [of obedience], but with those who are standing with us this day before the Lord, our God, and with those who are not with us today. . . . Secret things belong to the Lord, our God, but that which has been revealed is for us and for our children forever to carry out the words of this Torah."[10]

Ultimately, though, God serves to shape moral character by entering into a loving relationship with us. That is, not only is the covenant a legal document, with provisions for those who abide by it and those who do not, but also the covenant announces formal recognition of a relationship that has existed for a long while and that is intended to last, much as a covenant of marriage does. Relationships, especially intense ones like marriage, create mutual obligations that are fulfilled by the partners sometimes grudgingly but often lovingly, with no thought of a *quid pro quo* return. For God, as for a human marital partner,[11] we should do what the norms of morality require, and then we should go beyond the letter of the law (*lifnim m'shurat ha-din*) to do favors for our beloved. In moral terms, we then become the kind of people who seek to do both the right and the good, not out of hope for reward but simply because that is the kind of people we are and the kind of relationships we have.

PRAYER
Along with theology comes a life of prayer. Jews are commanded to pray three times each day, with four services on Sabbaths, Festivals, and the New Year, and five on the Day of Atonement. Aside from the spiritual nourishment, intellectual stimulation, aesthetic experience, and communal contact that Jewish prayer brings, it also serves several significant moral functions.

One of these is moral education. Until the twentieth century, most Jews could not afford to attend formal schooling beyond ten years of age. Since the printing press was not invented until 1450 or so, Jews could not learn about the Jewish tradition through reading books either. The Rabbis long ago instituted the practice of reading a section of the Torah four times each week, but that would mean it took a year for Jews to be exposed to the entirety of the Torah. As a result, the Rabbis created a framework of three biblical paragraphs constituting the *Shema* and twenty-two one-line blessings surrounding the *Shema* and constituting the *Amidah* so that Jews would have an easily memorized formula to teach them the essence of Jewish belief. In fact, that outline is as close as Judaism ever got to a creed, an official statement of Jewish beliefs. That outline also serves to announce and rehearse some of Judaism's central values, including knowledge, forgiveness, health, justice, hope, and peace.

Moreover, the fixed liturgy reorients us to think about things from God's perspective. Even though the English word "prayer" denotes petition ("Do this, I pray"), and even though Jewish liturgy has room for asking God for things, the vast majority of the fixed liturgy praises and thanks God. This immediately tells Jews that they must get out of their egocentric concerns and think of life from God's vantage point. That alone should help them focus on the important things in life rather than the partial goods to which they may devote too much energy.

Prayer also serves as a way for people to confront what they have done wrong and to muster the courage to go through the process of *teshuvah*, return to the proper path and to the good graces of God and the community. People sometimes are stymied by their sins and by the guilt they feel. Jewish liturgy has Jews asking God to forgive our sins three times each day. Such confessional prayers enable people to relieve the guilt involved in sin so that they can repair whatever harm they have done and take steps to act better in the future.

STUDY
Although family, community, authority figures, and even God and prayer are used by other societies to create moral character, albeit in different ways and degrees than Judaism uses those elements, study is one Jewish method for creating moral people that few other societies use.[12] Moreover, this is an ancient Jewish method, stemming from the Torah itself. The Torah was not given to a group of elders who alone would know it; it was rather given to the entire People Israel assembled at Mount Sinai. In keeping with the public nature of revelation in Judaism, God tells Moses a number of times, "Speak to the people Israel and say to them (or command them)."[13] Moreover, every Jew is responsible to know God's commands and to teach them to their children.[14] To ensure that that would happen, the Torah itself

institutes a public reading of the entire Torah every seven years at which "men, women, and children" were to be present.[15]

By the Second Temple period the Torah was actually read much more often than that, with small sections read on Saturday afternoons and on the mornings of the market days—Mondays and Thursdays—and larger sections read every Sabbath and festival morning. These selections were arranged so that the entire Torah would be read once every year—or, for some communities, every three years. The reading would commonly include a translation into the vernacular and, on the Sabbath and festivals, a lesson or homily based on the section chanted that day. This helped ensure that the reading was not merely a mechanical act but rather a truly educational experience. All of these public readings were part of the regular service, and so Jewish worship is characterized by the combination of prayer and study.

Moreover, the Pharisees made study an end in itself.[16] Thus they say things like this:

> These are the deeds for which there is no prescribed measure: leaving crops at the corner of the field for the poor, . . . doing deeds of lovingkindness, and studying Torah.[17]

> These are the deeds that yield immediate fruit and continue to yield fruit in time to come: honoring parents; doing deeds of lovingkindness; attending the house of study punctually, morning and evening; providing hospitality; visiting the sick; helping the needy bride; attending the dead; probing the meaning of prayer; making peace between one person and another, and between husband and wife. And the study of Torah is the most basic of them all.[18]

As a result, those who teach others have, in the rabbinic view of things, special merit:

> David said: "O Lord, many groups of righteous people shall be admitted into Your presence. Which one of them is most beloved before You?" God answered: "The teachers of the youth, who perform their work in sincerity and with joy, shall sit at My right hand."[19]

> He who teaches his neighbor's child deserves to sit in the Heavenly Academy . . . and he who teaches the child of an ignoramus deserves to have God nullify a decree against him.[20]

> He who teaches his neighbor's child is as if he had created him.[21]

The relationship between study and morality goes in both directions: Study can refine moral sensitivity and buttress the drive to act morally; conversely, morality is a prerequisite for appropriate teaching and study. Maimonides expressed this latter point explicitly:

> We teach Torah only to a student who is morally fit and pleasant in his ways, or to a student who knows nothing [and therefore may become such a person with learning]. But if the student goes in ways that are not good, we bring him back to the good path and lead him to the right way, and then we check him and [if he has corrected his ways] we bring him in to the school and teach him. The Sages said: Anyone who teaches a student who is not morally fit is as if he is throwing a stone to Mercury [i.e., contributing to idolatry]. . . . Similarly, a teacher who does not live a morally good life, even if he knows a great deal and the entire people need him [to teach what he knows because nobody else can], we do not learn from him until he returns to a morally good way of life.[22]

How, though, does study contribute to morality? It does so in at least four distinct ways. To aid in exploring how study functions morally, I shall call on the insights of three disparate modern theologians: Samson Raphael Hirsch, founder of neo-Orthodoxy (or modern Orthodoxy) in nineteenth-century Germany; Mordecai Kaplan, a twentieth-century exponent of philosophical naturalism and the founder of the Reconstructionist movement in the United States; and Martin Buber, an early-twentieth-century existentialist thinker. Their three different approaches to Judaism enable us to highlight the many ways in which texts can be used to contribute to the shaping of the moral person.

CONTENT

The most obvious goal of text study is to inform students about what is right and wrong, good and bad. The classical literature of the tradition announces its norms through maxims, laws, poetry, and stories. Therefore, those who study that literature learn those norms. Even though children and adults learn the content of moral norms in other informal ways as well, this cognitive moral education is necessary, as Kaplan pointed out, to make one's moral knowledge articulate and systematic:

Even if children are not sent to religious schools, they are usually taught worthwhile ideals. But just as parents supplement the child's vernacular with systematic school training in grammar, rhetoric, and literature, so they should supplement this vague, casual and more or less inarticulate imparting of higher ideals with a systematized presentation of them in the religious school.[23]

The texts, though, should not be taught or treated as cookbooks that will render specific answers to moral questions. That kind of mechanical reading of the text undermines its very meaning and purpose. Moreover, Conservative and Reform Jews, and even some Orthodox Jews, would maintain that some texts must be updated, at least in their application and possibly even in the content of the norms themselves.

Thus the point of text study is not so much to inculcate specific moral rules, but rather to impart a general moral outlook. Only a person who has such a framework will be able to discern how to apply traditional norms to contemporary circumstances in a contextually sensitive way, and only those who appreciate the broad perspective of Judaism can deal with new situations not covered by existing laws. Understanding the philosophy of Judaism embedded in its moral rules also motivates Jews to be willing to sacrifice immediate goods for Judaism's long-term ends.

JUDGMENT

In real-life situations, values often clash, and so good judgment in resolving moral conflicts is a necessary asset of a moral person. Those who can only follow orders or rules are not moral agents in the full sense of the term, neither in the way they arrive at decisions nor in the content of the decisions themselves. They are automata, and their blindness to the range of values can lead them to blatantly immoral actions. Consequently, moral education must seek to develop the individual's powers of judgment, including the ability to weigh values and to think creatively of practical ways to reconcile them when they conflict.

Two types of text study aid the development of moral judgment. One is to choose dialectic texts that themselves demonstrate moral argumentation so that those who study them sharpen their own abilities to analyze, criticize, and synthesize moral arguments.

Hirsch strongly recommended the study of Talmud for this purpose:

> The study of these writings is the finest training both in theoretical and practical reasoning, all the more so because their subjects are the circumstances of actual life. In them the rules laid down in the "Scripture" are given precision and made practically applicable. Their form is such that the youthful mind is continually trained to analyze statements presented synthetically in order to find the principles underlying them, to apply such principles, whether given or discovered, to new and analogous cases, and to discern the real disparity between cases that seem analogous and the real analogy between the cases that seem disparate. In a word, . . . in the study of Talmud we have the finest school for forming logical and ethical judgments.[24]

Part of Hirsch's enthusiasm for the Talmud no doubt stems from his traditional approach to Judaism, but it is noteworthy that he stresses the Talmud and not the codes in this context. The codes give the reader clear-cut prescriptions for action. They can stimulate intense debate and judgmental acumen if they are studied comparatively, but their form encourages the reader to accept their dictates passively without asking the basis for the rulings or even how they are to be applied to different cases. The Talmud, on the other hand, cannot possibly be studied that way. Its style requires the student to understand conflicting arguments on the issues it treats, since it records not only differing opinions but also the reasons each side would give for its decision and the ways it would meet the objections raised by the advocates of the other positions. It thus is a more significant aid to the development of moral judgment than the codes are—and, indeed, traditional Jewish education has devoted much more time to the Talmud than to the codes. Similar considerations underlie the case-study method used in most modern law schools and medical schools.

Buber and Kaplan would use classical text study for developing the student's power of judgment in a very different way. Because they do not accept the enduring authority and relevance of Jewish law, they are more interested in teaching students how to approach the texts than in demonstrating how to master the reasoning of the texts' arguments. Thus students should exercise their powers of judgment, not by standing within a text and striving to understand it but, rather, by standing outside it and evaluating it. For Kaplan, the student's assessment should take the form of reinterpreting the text, since that is the way that the Jewish tradition has gained new meaning and relevance throughout history:

> In the course of his Jewish studies, the Jew should nowadays be fully apprised of the causes which have rendered the Torah, in its traditional form, largely irrelevant to his needs. This knowledge would clear the ground for that process of reinterpretation which would make of Jewish tradition a means of stimulating our people to resume its quest for the good life. *It should be the purpose of adult Jewish study to train the Jew in that process of reinterpretation, so that the tradition of his people, even if not infallible, might function as a potent influence in shaping the ethical and spiritual ideals which alone can render life worth living.*[25]

Buber was even less concerned with the traditional texts themselves. For him, they should be used as a stimulant for a dialogue between the teacher and the student in which they can encounter each other as individuals and struggle together over the moral issues that the text raises. The student's powers of judgment would thus be sharpened through the dialogue rather than through an analysis or reinterpretation of the text.[26]

Note, though, two things about the use of text study to hone moral judgment. First, it depends on the assumption that moral education cannot be properly restricted to the formal elements of reasoning or to a clarification of the student's own values; it must convey moral content as well. That is, Judaism asserts that it has something to teach people that they could not learn on their own. Thus students need to be taught to apply their reasoning powers *to the traditional texts* so that they can not only develop their powers of moral judgment but also learn their tradition's system of values.

Second, the goals of using classical texts to teach values and to hone moral judgment can be mutually contradictory. Some teachers, in some settings, can intimidate the student, whether the subject is moral issues or anything else. That would make it impossible for students to judge a matter on their own and to express contrary views. That conflict is not a necessary one, but resolving it requires the teacher to explain the content in a way that respects students and invites them to evaluate, and not just memorize, the materials in front of them. The Rabbis of the Mishnah were keenly aware of the danger that content learning could preclude the acquisition of moral judgment, and so Hillel, one of the earliest and most respected Sages, said: "A shy person [who does not ask questions and participate in class discussion] cannot learn, and an ill-tempered [overbearing, nasty] person cannot teach."[27]

MOTIVATION

Text study can also help motivate people to act morally. Exactly how it can function in that way is a matter of dispute among the three modern theologians we are considering. Hirsch claimed that a person's study of the traditional texts "stirs his passion for the noble and good, for the pure and the virtuous, and inspires in him an antipathy for what is rough and common, vile and bad"; "the refreshing draughts" that he draws from it give him "new strength to meet the troubles of life."[28] He did not explain the specific mechanism by which this happens, but, given what he said in other contexts, one would presume that for Hirsch it is the constant exposure to detailed moral rules, the continual practice in good moral reasoning, and the inspiration of the Jew's ultimate moral mission in life that together move a person to adhere to moral norms and aspire to moral ideals.

Kaplan, like Hirsch, believed that the long-range thinking characteristic of a religious view of life motivates moral behavior because it gives people a reason to sacrifice immediate, immoral gains:

> The sort of education implicit in the Jewish ideal of Talmud Torah [study of the Torah] would give to the democracies the one thing that they have thus far lacked, the long-range view that renders a people willing to make sacrifices for the building of a better world based on reason, righteousness, and peace.[29]

But Kaplan concentrated more on the fact that religion fosters a feeling of peoplehood, which, he stressed, is absolutely indispensable in motivating moral behavior. When people have ties to a group, they gain a sense of responsibility to those beyond the members of their own family, sympathy for them, and loyalty to them. When the group extends over past, present, and future, as the Jewish group does, it also gives people a sense of rootedness and purpose: I should act morally so that I do not frustrate, but rather further, the noble goals of my ancestors and ensure a better world for my children. Group membership, in addition, provides a person with a sense of self-worth since it betokens the fact that there are others who are concerned for your welfare and who need you. Furthermore, the group represents a reservoir of talent, energy, and accomplishment that can give a sense of justifiable pride to all of its members far beyond that which any member could earn individually. A person with such dignity and pride would think twice before compromising them by doing something immoral. And finally, the group creates expectations of its members, and those are among the most powerful stimulants to moral behavior, because few people are willing to disappoint those who are near and dear to them, let alone risk being alienated from them.[30] For these reasons Kaplan claimed that group identity is critical for morality: "We cannot forego that unity without foregoing all that gives us human dignity, self-confidence, and a purpose in life. It thus spells for us the very source of all religious values. Remove that unity and sense of Jewish peoplehood and those values are dried up for us at the very source."[31]

Kaplan was well aware that collective consciousness may lead to nationalistic abuses. That danger is especially great in modern times, when nationhood has acquired religious significance. He said, in fact, that one of the most important functions of religion is precisely to expose such abuses so that the energies generated by national fervor can be used for good purposes. But he recognized that national feeling is both normal and powerful; that indeed "nationality, next to physiological heredity, is the most decisive influence in a person's life";[32] and that, therefore, religion neither can nor should ignore it. Instead, religion should seek to mobilize and direct national feelings toward moral ends.

Text study is an important method for creating group consciousness and gaining its moral benefits: "To be able to affirm our peoplehood in that [moral] spirit, we have to become once again Bible conscious."[33] Studying the group tradition helps any group strengthen its sense of identity, but for the Jews it is especially important, according to Kaplan, because of the negative way in which others have portrayed them:

> A tradition which would present in dignified fashion the case of the Jewish people is absolutely indispensable as a therapeutic to Jewish character. The Jew must regard Jewish life not through the eyes of a hostile civilization, but through the authentic voices of its own heroes, sages, poets, prophets, and leaders. . . . Stifled by the poison gas of antipathy and contempt, the Jew requires the spiritual oxygen of his tradition to infuse his character with the therapy of human dignity.[34]

Thus text study can serve as a stimulus to moral behavior because it fosters the group feelings of love, sympathy, loyalty, rootedness, direction, self-worth, pride, and responsibility that are crucial for an effective moral system.

Group feeling, however, is not the only way to motivate moral behavior; the effect of a respected individual can also be very telling. Text study uses this factor in two ways: It portrays exemplary (and not so exemplary) personalities of the past, and it aids teachers in being a personal model themselves. The biographies of honored leaders of the past have long been used as inspirations for the people of the present and as the basis for the discussion of moral challenges and issues, and this mode of moral teaching has recently been given careful attention by philosophers of ethics.[35]

All three of the thinkers that we have been considering endorsed this approach. Kaplan even complained that we focus too narrowly on the figures of the Torah and the Prophets in this kind of modeling; we should also use Job, Kohelet, and a number of the Rabbis. He also issued a caveat: "The very remoteness of ancestors is conducive to the tendency of idealizing and apotheosizing them into a race of supermen who knew God more truly and more intimately than any other people and who noted down their experiences in the Bible, which is the greatest religious classic of all time."[36] One must be careful that such a tendency does not make our study of the figures of the past an escape from the concrete issues of the present.

Text study can also aid the teacher to function as a model if it is used correctly. Our authors differ, however, as to how to do this according to their varied understandings of the texts themselves. For Hirsch, the Bible, the Talmud, and the codes are the eternal and indisputable word of God. Therefore, teachers become models for their students to the extent that they themselves accept the texts as divine and follow Judaism's precepts unquestioningly. For Buber and Kaplan, that is precisely what the teacher should not do, both because the texts do not embody a fixed corpus of prescriptions and because when presented as such they have no power to motivate. As Buber said, those "who are seriously laboring over the question of good and evil rebel when one dictates to them, as though it were some long established truth, what is good and what is bad; and they rebel just because they have experienced over and over again how hard it is to find the right way."[37] Instead, the text, to be ethically effective, must be used as a springboard for discussion in which teachers reveal how they personally respond to the values of the tradition. That gives the tradition concrete reality so that it can affect the student through the teacher.

Similarly, Kaplan claimed that "we must avoid as far as possible the oracular approach which ignores challenges, questions, and alternative solutions," pretending that all is clear and simple; instead, "we should take the student into our confidence and make him aware that we are all engaged in a common search after a way of Jewish life that shall elicit from us the best we can be and that shall enable us to bear the worst that can befall us."[38] In that way text study can motivate moral conduct by mobilizing the effectiveness of both the teacher and the tradition.

Probably the most straightforward way in which text study motivates moral action, though, is through informing the learner that the tradition imposes *obligations* on all Jews. Hirsch gave a theological explanation for the authority of those obligations (that is, we should obey the Torah's moral rules because God commanded them), Kaplan gave a sociological justification (we should obey Jewish moral rules as an act of identification with the Jewish people and as part of its effort to actualize the divine in human life), and Buber gave a psychological account (we should obey Jewish moral rules in response to the I–Thou encounters we have with God). These different understandings of the power of the text to obligate a person meet with varying degrees of success, according to the student's beliefs and attitudes. The simple fact, though, is that, however their authority is explained, classical Jewish texts do impose responsibilities on the Jewish reader. Jews might be unaware that they are complying with the Torah when they obey at least some of its commandments for other reasons, but text study reveals the entire breadth of God's demands as interpreted by the tradition as well as the theological grounds for obeying them.

The classical Rabbis were keenly aware that the virtues involved in text study would provide no guarantee that the student would ultimately act morally. That depended on the openness of the student to moral education in the first place. Those who studied with no intention of carrying out the moral instruction embedded in the texts were to be cursed, while those who were open to such an influence were to be praised: "Rabbi Hiyya said: If a man learns the Torah without the intention of fulfilling it, it were better for him had he never been born. . . . Rabbi Aka said: He who learns in order to do is worthy to receive the Holy Spirit."[39] In the end, though, the Rabbis, like our three modern thinkers, placed great trust in text study as a stimulus to action: "The question was raised: Is study greater, or action? Rabbi Tarfon said: 'Action is greater.' Akiva said: 'Study is greater.' Then they all said that study is greater because study leads to action."[40]

THE MORAL VALUES ATTACHED TO STUDY ITSELF
Study can teach students the content of moral norms and the skills of moral judgment, and it can motivate people to act morally. In addition, the very act of studying itself might inculcate moral values. Kaplan and Buber were not nearly as much convinced of this as Hirsch was. Thus Kaplan did not even list study in his ninety-five-page chapter titled "Basic Values in Jewish Religion,"[41] and he continually declared that world betterment is the aim of education, to be achieved through making the Jewish heritage relevant to the present moral and spiritual needs of Jews.[42] In line with that, however, he advocated more study and less praying, since "worship and prayer are directed toward the attainment of peace of mind, [while] the study of Torah can set in motion all of the moral influences that go into the

molding of character and the shaping of society."[43] For Buber, also, the aim of education was functional: It is a means to train good character by exposing the student to God as a model to the extent that the instructor can.[44] For Buber, then, the text was only a vehicle for the instructor to reveal his or her own understanding of what it means to be in dialogue with God.

Hirsch, though, saw immense moral value in the act of studying itself. That is not surprising, for Hirsch's Orthodoxy directed him much more intensely to study the traditional texts. Hirsch believed that the process of intensive textual study was the way to inculcate a number of moral values. Specifically, morality is largely a matter of the proper exercise of one's will. The development of mental skills, though, is also a matter of free will, since students will engage in concentration, analysis, memorization, and creative thinking only if they choose to do so. Thus "the entire intellectual schooling of our youth" is, in effect, a "continuous exercise in moral education," since it trains the student to choose to act constructively. Moreover, study engenders specific moral virtues, including "obedience, the readiness to comply with a superior will, the consequent exercise of self-control, the punctual and most perfect possible performance of duties imposed, the pleasure of work and pure joy in work done, self-disciplined serenity, modesty, sociability, friendliness, [and] team-spirit" in addition to "care, caution, exactitude, and circumspection."[45] Hirsch was especially concerned with inculcating obedience and submission to authority, perhaps a function of his Orthodox orientation.[46]

Hirsch's conviction that the process of study in and of itself will engender moral virtues reflects an ancient rabbinic belief, for the Rabbis spell out in great detail how study involves moral virtues and sharpens them:

> Rabbi Meir taught: Whoever engages in the study of Torah for its own sake achieves a host of merits; moreover, it was worth creating the world for his sake alone. He is called: beloved friend, lover of God, lover of humanity, a joy to God, and a joy to humanity. Torah clothes him with humility and reverence; it equips him to be righteous, saintly, upright, and faithful. It keeps him far from sin and draws him near to virtue. People benefit from his counsel and skill, his understanding and strength, as it is written: "Counsel and skill are Mine; I am understanding,

strength is Mine" (Proverbs 8:14). It endows him with sovereignty, with authority, with power of keen judgment. The secrets of Torah are revealed to him; he becomes an effluent fountain, a never-failing stream; he becomes modest and patient, forgiving of insults; it magnifies and exalts him over all creations.[47]

Learning [Torah] is acquired through forty-eight virtues: By study; by attentiveness; by orderly speech; by an understanding heart; by a perceptive heart; by awe; by reverence; by humility; by joy; by ministering to the sages; by engaging in give and take with colleagues; by acute discussion with students; by calmness in study; by study of Scripture and Mishnah; by a minimum of business; by a minimum of sleep; by a minimum of small talk; by a minimum of worldly pleasure; by a minimum of frivolity; by a minimum of worldly pursuits; by patience; by a generous heart; by trust in the sages; by acceptance of suffering; by knowing one's place; by contentment with one's lot; by guarding one's speech; by taking no personal credit; by being beloved; by loving God; by loving all creatures; by loving charitable deeds; by loving rectitude; by loving reproof; by shunning honor; by not boasting of one's learning; by not delighting in rendering legal decisions; by sharing the burden [of rendering legal decisions] with someone else; by influencing one's fellow to act virtuously; by setting him on the path of truth; by setting him on the path of peace; by concentrating on one's studies; by asking and answering questions; by absorbing knowledge and contributing to it; by studying in order to teach and to perform God's commandments; by sharpening the wisdom of one's teacher; by being precise in transmitting what one has learned; by quoting one's source of knowledge. From this verse we learn that one who cites his source of knowledge brings redemption to the world, for it is written, "And Esther spoke to the king, in the name of Mordekhai" (Esther 2:22).[48]

Study of texts can be morally effective, though, only if other factors are present. First, the teacher must be a moral role model. He or she need not know all the moral answers; on the contrary, students gain a great deal in their own moral growth when they see their teachers openly wrestling with moral issues and actively encouraging students to express a variety of views for class consideration. However, teachers must demonstrate a sense of moral integrity and seriousness.

Second, the home and the community need to support what students learn in text study. In modern North America, this often does not happen, resulting in considerable dissonance between what the students learn from texts and what goes on in the rest of their lives. This is true for adults as well as for children. If one thinks that the traditional concepts or values themselves need to be changed, as Kaplan and Buber did, then the way that texts are studied—and the selection of which texts to study in the first place—must be carefully considered in order to attain one's moral goals. In any case, the more the person's home and community live in consonance with how the text's values are taught, the more that text study can morally influence students' lives.

Third, except for the most ultra-Orthodox, Jewish text study does not exist in a vacuum. It is complemented with the study of non-Jewish texts, whether they be in very different fields, like physics or art, or in related fields, like philosophy, law, and religion. Intelligent study of Jewish texts will not reject out of hand what one learns from outside sources; on the contrary, learning about other matters can enrich and deepen one's knowledge of Jewish values. Comparative analyses, like the one presented in Chapter One, can clarify Jewish concepts and values. Outside sources might also indicate to us exactly what we do *not* want to affirm. On the other hand, through the ages Jews have borrowed from the cultures of the peoples among whom they lived, and we in our own time may want to synthesize Jewish values or concepts with others that we learn from elsewhere. Certainly, the value of individual freedom, which is largely a bequest of the Enlightenment, is something that most modern Jews want to integrate into their contemporary expression of Judaism, no matter how difficult that may be. However they are used, non-Jewish materials should be studied not only for their own sake but also to complement how one learns the Jewish tradition and expresses it in one's life.

Fourth, what one derives from Jewish text study depends critically on the methods one uses to study the text and the viewpoint that one brings to that study. Studying the text sheerly on an academic basis for what it can reveal about ancient times will, if done properly, yield such results but little else. On the other hand, studying it only to learn what the tradition says will lead to knowledge of the tradition but not moral judgment; indeed, it is likely to lead to mechanical, behavioristic obedience with no ability to critique the texts themselves or the values they announce. The wisest way to study the texts is to combine all these methods and more.

Finally, text study, for all its importance, should not fill the whole of one's life. Rather, one should combine text study with work, because, as Rabban Gamliel, son of Rabbi Judah, said in *Ethics of the Fathers*, "Study of Torah is beautiful with a worldly occupation, for the effort involved in the two of them makes one forget sin; [on the other hand,] all study of Torah that is not accompanied by work will ultimately fail and lead one to sin."[49]

Study of texts is best done, then, if one brings to classical Jewish texts a respectful but critical religious perspective. Our three thinkers would advocate that for different reasons. Hirsch stressed the authority that religion provides for moral norms, the wealth of experience within the tradition, and the expansive scope of its visions and concerns.[50] Kaplan wrote about the sense of worthwhileness that a person derives from religion, a sense that makes moral effort and sacrifice reasonable and that gives life direction and meaning.[51] Buber was interested in the fact that religion provides absolute moral standards as well as the cosmic but personal framework in which to learn and understand them.[52] However one understands the content and impact of the Jewish religious vision, it undergirds Judaism's effect on morality; and when one approaches text study with a religious perspective, the text study itself can be all the more effective in informing and motivating moral conduct and in creating moral character.

The Jewish tradition thus seeks to form moral character through the commonly used elements of family, community, and authority figures, but it also uses God, prayer, law, and study of Jewish texts in that effort. That Judaism employs all these factors in its effort to produce a moral person demonstrates both its seriousness in succeeding at this task and the rich understanding it has about how to educate a person morally.

LAW

Law is the other methodology employed by Judaism on which I concentrate in this Appendix. I decided to focus on law for two reasons. First, Judaism puts a great deal of emphasis on law as a moral tool—more, I think, than most other traditions, but in this too Islam and Confucianism come close to Judaism in their common emphasis on legal methods to discern moral norms and motivate moral behavior.

Second, classical Christian texts have a very negative view of law. The view of the Pharisees as narrow, legalistic, and downright mean people in the New Testament, especially in Matthew, sets the tone for seeing Jews as concerned only with details of rules and not with the broader aims that they have. Paul's description of law as leading people to sin and as the exact opposite of life lived by the Spirit is another major source of Christians' negative views of the law.[53] Society may need laws as long as we live in Augustine's City of Man, but law is not, for Christian writers, the way to know what is right and good. So both the importance of law within Judaism and the disparaging attitude toward it within Christianity motivated me to focus on the role of law in Jewish morality.

The following, then, are some of the ways Jewish law aids in defining and motivating morality.

DEFINING AND ENFORCING MINIMAL STANDARDS
The most obvious contribution is simply that Jewish law establishes a minimum standard of practice. This is important from a moral standpoint because many moral values can be realized only through the mutual action of a group of people, and a minimum moral standard enforced as law enables the society to secure the cooperation necessary for such moral attainment. Furthermore, there is an objective value to a beneficent act, whether it is done for the right reason or not. Consequently, establishing a minimum standard of moral practice through legislation provides for at least some concrete manifestations of conduct in tune with the dictates of morality, even if that conduct is not moral in the full sense of the word for lack of proper intention.

In spelling out minimal standards of moral conduct, there is always the danger that people will interpret the minimum requirements legalistically as the total extent to which they need to extend themselves for others. That, however, would involve a serious blindness to the realm of morality that would probably not be cured by removing the legal trappings from the minimum standards. Moreover, Judaism guards against such an abuse through its requirements of public and private study of the Bible

338

and other morally enriching literature, through liturgy and sermons, and through making the minimal requirements of action rather demanding in the first place!

ACTUALIZING MORAL IDEALS

But it is not just on a minimal level that law is important for morality; law is crucial at every level of moral aspiration in order to translate moral values into concrete modes of behavior. The Prophets enunciated lofty values, and we rightly feel edified and uplifted when we read their words or those of other great moral teachers in each generation. On the other end of the spectrum, when we hear fire-and-brimstone sermons or go through the painful self-examination of a confessional procedure, such as on Yom Kippur, we come away feeling chastened and purified. But the vast majority of life is lived in between those two extremes of moral awareness as we pursue our daily tasks. Consequently, if that edification or chastening is going to contribute to a better world in any significant way, it must be translated into the realm of day-to-day activities. We ordinarily do not have sufficient time or self-awareness to think seriously about what we are doing, and hence a regimen of concrete laws that articulate what we should do in a variety of circumstances can often enable us to act morally when we would not ordinarily do so. Rabbi Morris Adler articulated this point well:

> Religion is not a matter of living on the "peaks" of experience. That is for the saint and the mystic. More fundamentally, religion must mean transposing to a higher level of spiritual awareness and ethical sensitivity the entire plateau of daily living by the generality of men. Idolatry is defeated not by recognition of its intellectual absurdity alone, but by a life that expresses itself in service to God. Selfishness and greed are overcome not by professions of a larger view but by disciplines that direct our energies, our wills, and our actions outward and upward.[54]

WEIGHING CONFLICTING MORAL VALUES AND SETTING MORAL PRIORITIES

Until now, I have spoken about areas in which the moral norm is more or less clear and the problem is one of realizing those norms. There are many situations, however, where there is a conflict of moral values, and it must be determined which value will take precedence over which, and in what circumstances. Nonlegal moral systems usually offer some mechanism for treating moral conflicts, but they often depend on the sensitivity and analytic ability of an authority figure or each individual. By contrast, the law provides a format for deciding such issues *publicly,* thus ensuring that many minds of a variety of convictions will be brought to bear on the issue. This does not guarantee wisdom, but it does at least provide a greater measure of objectivity and hence a more thorough consideration of the relevant elements.

GIVING MORAL NORMS A SENSE OF THE IMMEDIATE AND THE REAL

Issues are often joined more clearly in court than they are in moral treatises or announcements of policy because the realities with which the decision deals are dramatically evident in the courtroom and a decision must be reached. Moral essayists or theorists, on the other hand, do not face the immediate responsibility of having people act on their decisions, and hence they tend to be somewhat "ivory towerish." Consensus statements on moral issues produced by denominations or other groups of people often suffer from the need to include the opinion of everyone in the group and thus lose sharpness and even sometimes coherence. In contrast, a court ruling is specific and addressed to a real situation. In fact, it seems to me that much of the sheer wisdom of the rabbinic tradition can be attributed to the fact that the Rabbis served as judges as well as scholars and teachers. Of course, how to apply a precedent to a new case is not always clear, but the legal context adds a sense of immediacy and reality to moral deliberation.

PROVIDING A BALANCE OF CONTINUITY AND FLEXIBILITY

Because law operates on the basis of precedent, there is a greater sense of continuity in a moral tradition that is structured legally than in one that is not. After all, one of the things that people seek in creating a legal system in the first place is the security of knowing what they can expect of others and what others can expect of them, and that is achieved in law by the methodology of precedent, of *stare decisis,* "it stands decided." On the other hand, through legal techniques like differentiation of cases, the law preserves a reasonable amount of flexibility and adaptability. By contrast, moral decisions made on the basis of conscience often have little public effect or staying power; and moral decisions made on the basis of natural law or divine law understood in a fundamentalistic way lack sufficient malleability to retain relevance to new situations and to take advantage of new knowledge. A legal tradition, although certainly not without its problems in practice, attains the best balance that human beings can achieve between tradition and change.

SERVING AS AN EDUCATIONAL TOOL FOR MORALITY

Theories of education are obviously many and diverse, but the Jewish tradition has a clear methodology for moral education: "Rab Judah said in Rab's name: A man should always occupy himself with Torah and good deeds, though it is not for their own sake, for out of (doing good) with an ulterior motive he will come to (do good) for its own sake."[55] This largely behavioristic approach to moral education is not totally so: Study of the Tradition is also an integral part of Jewish moral education. But in the end, the emphasis is on action: "An excellent thing is the study of Torah combined with some worldly occupation, for the labor demanded by both of them causes sinful inclinations to be forgotten. All study of the Torah without work must in the end be futile and become the cause of sin."[56]

The same educational theory is applied to moral degeneracy and repentance:

- "Once a man has committed a sin and repeated it, it appears to him as if it were permitted."[57]
- "Run to fulfill even a minor precept and flee from the slightest transgression; for precept draws precept in its train, and transgression draws transgression."[58]
- "If a transgression comes to a man a first and second time without his sinning, he is immune from the sin."[59]

If one accepts this approach to moral education in whole or in part, formulating moral norms in terms of law is very important educationally; for legally *requiring* people to act in accord with moral rules is a step in teaching them how to do the right thing for the right reason.

MAKING AMENDS AND REPAIRING MORAL DAMAGE

One goal of law is social peace. Legal systems, therefore, generally provide ways for dealing with antisocial behavior and for adjudicating disputes. A religious legal system like Jewish law also provides a way for overcoming guilt, making amends, and reconciling with God, with the aggrieved parties, and with the community as a whole. That process is *teshuvah*, "return," according to which, as Chapter Six explains, the assailant must acknowledge that he or she sinned, experience and express remorse, apologize to the victim, compensate the victim in whatever way possible, and take steps to ensure that when a similar occasion arises again, he or she will act differently. In defining that process, Jewish law makes moral repair demanding but possible.

It goes further: It demands that when the process has been completed, the victim must respond in kind. So, for example, according to the Mishnah, if one person injures another, the assailant must pay the victim for five remedies: the injury itself, the time lost from work, pain, medical expenses, and the embarrassment the injury caused. After describing how each of these payments is to be calculated, the Mishnah says, "Even though the assailant pays the victim, God does not forgive him until he asks the victim's forgiveness"; this is the apology required in the process of return. But the Mishnah then states that if the victim refuses to pardon the assailant, the victim becomes the wrongdoer and is regarded as "cruel."[60] There clearly are cases when wrongdoers should not be forgiven; but, by and large, we must forgive those who have fulfilled the requirements of the process of return and have asked for forgiveness. In American law, a felon who has been released from prison is barred from voting and from government jobs the rest of his or her life and must reveal the past felony to any potential employer; in Jewish law, by contrast, it is prohibited even to mention the person's past crime unless it has direct bearing on a practical decision, for once the person has fulfilled the requirements of the process of return, to mention the past sin is, according to the Mishnah, oppressive, slanderous speech.[62] Thus Jewish law aids and abets reconciliation and peace.[63]

PRESERVING THE INTEGRITY OF MORAL INTENTIONS

We usually construe ourselves as having good intentions, but actions test, clarify, and verify our intentions. Rabbi Abraham Joshua Heschel put it this way:

> The dichotomy of faith and works which presented such an important problem in Christian theology was never a problem in Judaism. To us, the basic problem is neither what is the right action nor what is the right intention. The basic problem is: what is right living? And life is indivisible. The inner sphere is never isolated from outward activities. . . .

> It would be a device of conceit, if not presumption, to insist that purity of heart is the exclusive test of piety. Perfect purity is something we rarely know how to obtain or how to retain. No one can claim to have purged all the dross even from his finest desire. The self is finite, but selfishness is infinite. . . . God asks for the heart, but the heart is oppressed with uncertainty in its own twilight. God asks for faith, and the heart is not sure of its own faith. It is good that there is a dawn of decision for the night of the heart; deeds to objectify faith, definite forms to verify belief.[64]

Concretizing moral values in the form of law is thus an important method for testing the nature and seriousness of our intentions so that we may avoid hypocrisy. It also graphically shows us the effects of our intentions, so that hopefully we will alter those that are knowingly or unknowingly destructive. In other words, law brings our intentions out into the arena of action, where we can see them clearly and work on them if necessary.

In all of these ways, then, law contributes to morality. I have taken the trouble to discuss this rather thoroughly to demonstrate that the interaction between law and morality involves contributions in both directions. This is especially important when we are trying to understand Judaism, which went so far in trying to deal with morality in legal terms.

As important as law is in shaping Jewish moral vision and behavior, however, it is not the sole vehicle that Judaism uses to create a moral person and society. All of the other methods discussed above—stories, history, family and community, moral leaders and models, moral maxims and theories, theology, prayer, and study—play critical roles, along with law, in enabling Judaism to contribute mightily to creating moral individuals and communities. These methods do not guarantee moral character or behavior, for life does not come with guarantees, especially for something as difficult to acquire as moral sensitivity and action. Moreover, there are aspects of Judaism and of religions generally that actually function as obstacles to moral vision and behavior, and people of all religions must take steps to ensure that those factors do not lead to morally atrocious results. At the same time, we must recognize and seek to enhance the morally beneficial effects of the multiple ways in which Judaism contributes to morality. On balance, many of us, myself certainly included, are grateful for the moral contributions of Judaism to our lives, as we are for the many other ways it makes our lives richer. Ultimately, we might celebrate those gifts in language much like that of the Psalmist:

The Teaching (Torah) of the Lord is perfect, renewing life.
The decrees of the Lord are enduring, making the simple wise.
The precepts of the Lord are just, giving the heart joy.
The instruction of the Lord is lucid, making the eyes light up.
The fear of the Lord is pure, enduring forever.
The judgments of the Lord are true, completely just.
More precious than gold, than much fine gold,
Sweeter than honey, than drippings of the comb.[65]

NOTES TO APPENDIX

1. Berger (2001).
2. B. *Shabbat* 127a.
3. One of my former students did just this in a book that I recommend; see Goldberg (1985).
4. I summarize the differences between the Jewish, Christian, and American secular visions in Dorff (2002), chap. 1.
5. Gilligan (1982), Noddings (1984), and Tannen (1990).
6. B. *Makkot* 10a, where this is quoted in the name of Rabbi Judah; B. *Ta'anit* 7a, where it is quoted in the name of Rabbi Hanina.
7. B. *Peshachim* 50b; B. *Sanhedrin* 105a; B. *Arakhin* 16b; B. *Sotah* 22b, 47a; B. *Horayot* 10b; and B. *Nazir* 23b.
8. See Dorff and Rosett (1988), 110–123, 249–257.
9. B. *Sotah* 14a.
10. Deuteronomy 29:13,28.
11. God is depicted as Israel's marital partner a number of times in the Bible, whether fondly, as in Jeremiah 2:2, or angrily when Israel proves to be an unfaithful lover, as in Hosea 2.
12. This section is based on part on Dorff (1980).
13. For example, Numbers 15:1–2,17–18,37–38, 19:1–2, 28:1–2, 34:1–2, 35:1–2,9–10.
14. For the duty of Jewish adults to learn the Torah, see Deuteronomy 5:1. For the duty of parents to teach their children, see Deuteronomy 6:7, 11:19.
15. Deuteronomy 31:9–13.
16. The Pharisees may have been influenced in this, as Hadas (1959), 69–71, contends, by the Greeks. I would like to thank Rabbi Neil Gillman for this reference. The Rabbis, though, also stressed action, and so their stance toward whether study or action was more important was deeply ambivalent in a way that the Greek worship of knowledge never was. See B. *Kiddushin* 40b (quoted herein at note 40).
17. M. *Pe'ah* 1:1.
18. B. *Shabbat* 127a.
19. *Pesikta Buber* 180a (a paraphrase of Psalms 16:11).
20. B. *Bava Metz'ia* 85a.
21. B. *Sanhedrin* 19a.
22. M.T. *Laws of Study* 4:1.
23. Kaplan (1970), 180.
24. Hirsch (1956), 1:201–202.
25. Kaplan (1948), 359–360, emphasis in the original.
26. Buber (1947), 105, 107, 115.
27. M. *Avot* (*Ethics of the Fathers*) 2:6.
28. Hirsch (1956), 1:192–193; see also 166.
29. Kaplan (1948), 492.
30. Ibid., 82–83, 94–96; Kaplan (1970), 178–182.
31. Kaplan (1948), 457.
32. Ibid., 519; see generally 516–522.
33. Ibid., 457.
34. Kaplan (1970), 181–182.
35. For example, McClendon (1974).

36. Kaplan (1970), 194–195, 188–189. When Hirsch (1956), 2:59, wrote about "the spiritual and moral halo which surrounds the head of Abraham," he provided a good example of the danger that Kaplan worried about.

37. Buber (1947), 105; compare 107, 114.

38. Kaplan (1948), 471–472.

39. *Leviticus Rabbah* 35:7.

40. B. *Kiddushin* 40b.

41. Kaplan (1948), chap. 15; reprinted in Kaplan (1963).

42. Kaplan (1948), 446, 468 and chap. 25, sec. 1, esp. 488–489; Kaplan (1970), 188–189, 197–198.

43. Kaplan (1970), 175.

44. Buber (1947), 101–104.

45. Hirsch (1956), 1:178.

46. See Hirsch (1956), 1:230, 2:280–281.

47. M. *Avot (Ethics of the Fathers)* 6:1.

48. Ibid., 6:6.

49. Ibid., 2:2; compare M.T. *Laws of Study of the Torah* 3:10.

50. Hirsch (1956), 1:161–168, 2:282–290.

51. Kaplan (1937), chap. 1 and *passim*, and Kaplan (1948), 44–53, 99–105, 343–350, chaps. 10–12.

52. Buber (1952), chap. 6, esp. 95–99, and Buber (1947), 13–18, 101–103.

53. On the New Testament's view of the Pharisees, see, for example, Matthew 3:7, chap. 23, and Luke 18:9 ff., in which they are variously called "hypocrites" and "offspring of vipers." The Rabbis themselves recognized the insincere among their numbers, whom they called "sore spots" or "plagues on the Pharisaic party"; see M. *Sotah* 3:4 and B. *Sotah* 22b. With the exception of the relatively favorable depiction of Rabban Gamliel in the Acts of the Apostles, though, the New Testament paints the Pharisees with quite a broad negative brush, particularly for being legalistic in their approach to Jewish law—and then, to make matters worse, for hypocritically acting in violation of that law (at least as the New Testament writers saw things). For the dispute between Jesus and the Pharisees over the details of Sabbath laws, see Matthew 12:9–14; Mark 3:1–6; Luke 6:6–11, 13:10–17, 14:1–6; and John 5:1–18. For Jesus' dispute with the Pharisees over divorce, see Matthew 19:1–14 and Mark 10:1–14. For the replacement of law with Spirit, see, in particular, Paul's Letter to the Romans 7:1–8:8, 9:30–33, and his Letter to the Galatians 5:16–26.

54. Adler (1963), 64.

55. B. *Pesachim* 50b, and parallel passages elsewhere.

56. M. *Avot (Ethics of the Fathers)* 2:1.

57. B. *Yoma* 86b.

58. M. *Avot* 4:2.

59. B. *Yoma* 38b.

61. M. *Bava Kamma* 8:7.

62. M. *Bava Metzia* 4:10.

63. The Jewish process of return, including a discussion of when forgiveness is not appropriate, is discussed fully in Chapter Six.

64. Heschel (1955), 297–297.

65. Psalms 19:8–11.

Bibliography of Cited Modern Sources

Abelson, Kassel, and David J. Fine, eds. 2002. *Responsa 1991–2000: The Committee on Jewish Law and Standards of the Conservative Movement.* New York: Rabbinical Assembly.

Adler, Morris. 1963. *The World of the Talmud.* New York: Schocken.

Aftergood, Steven. 1999. "How Not to Combat Chinese Espionage." *Los Angeles Times* (July 4): M2, M6.

Allen, Jane E. 1999. "A New Push Is On for Patients' Privacy Law." *Los Angeles Times* (February 8): S1, S4.

"A New Look at Effects of Spanking," *The New York Times,* July 9, 2002, F8.

Aries, Philippe. 1962. *The Centuries of Childhood: A Social History of Family Life.* Trans. Robert Baldick. London: Cape.

Astor, Carl. 1985. *". . . Who Makes People Different": Jewish Perspectives on the Disabled.* New York: United Synagogue of America.

Baron, Salo W. 1942. *The Jewish Community.* 2 vols. Philadelphia: Jewish Publication Society.

Baumrind, Diana, Robert E. Larzelere, and Philip A. Cowan. 2002. "Ordinary Physical Punishment: Is It Harmful? Comment on Gershoff." *Psychological Bulletin* 128, no. 4, (July): 580–589.

Ben-Zimra, Eliyahn. 1977 (5737). "Halakhic Decisions Relating to the Sanctity of Life and Martyrdom in the Holocaust Period" (Hebrew). *Sinai* 80, 151–185.

Berger, David. 2001. *The Rebbe, the Messiah, and the Scandal of Orthodox Indifference.* London: Littman Library of Jewish Civilization.

Berkovits, Eliezer. 1973. *Faith after the Holocaust.* New York: Ktav.

Biale, Rachel. 1984. *Women and Jewish Law.* New York: Schocken.

Birnbaum, David. 1989. *God and Evil: A Jewish Perspective.* Hoboken, NJ: Ktav.

Bleich, J. David. 1977a. "Smoking." *Tradition* 16, no. 4 (summer): 130–133.

Bleich, J. David. 1977 *Contemporary Halakhic Problems*. New York: Ktav.

Bleich, J. David. 1979. "The Quinlan Case: A Jewish Perspective." In *Jewish Bioethics* (266–276). Ed. Fred Rosner and J. David Bleich. New York: Sanhedrin Press.

Bleich, J. David. 1981. *Judaism and Healing*. New York: Ktav.

Bleich, J. David. 1990. "The Jewish Entailments of Valuing Life." *Sh'ma* 21, no. 401 (November 16): 1–3.

Blidstein, Gerald. 1975. *Honor Thy Father and Mother*. New York: Ktav.

Blum, Tsevi Elimelekh. 1981 (5741). *Hanhagot Ha-Hinukh*. Jerusalem: Author.

Bly, Robert. 1992. *Iron John: A Book about Men*. New York: Vintage. [Originally published 1990.]

Borowitz, Eugene B. 1983. *Reform Judaism Today*. New York: Behrman House.

Borowitz, Eugene B. 1991. *Renewing the Covenant*. Philadelphia: Jewish Publication Society.

Borowitz, Eugene B. 1997. "An Open Letter to Elliot Dorff." *Conservative Judaism* 50, no. 1 (fall): 61–65.

Briere, John. 1989. *Therapy for Adults Molested as Children: Beyond Survival*. New York: Springer.

Briere, John. 1992. *Child Abuse Trauma*. Newbury Park, CA: Sage.

Briere, John, and Diana Elliott. 1994. "Immediate and Long-Term Impacts of Child Sexual Abuse." In *The Future of Children* 4, no. 12, 54–69. Los Altos, CA: Center for the Future of Children of the David and Lucille Packard Foundation.

Brownmiller, Susan. 1975. *Against Our Will: Men, Women, and Rape*. New York: Simon & Schuster.

Broyde, Michael J. 1993. "Symposium on Religious Law." *Loyola of Los Angeles International and Comparative Law Journal* 16, no. 1 (November): 95–100.

Broyde, Michael J. 1994. "Child Custody in Jewish Law: A Pure Law Analysis." In *Jewish Law Association Studies VII: The Paris Conference Volume* (1–20). Ed. S. M. Passamaneck and M. Finley. Atlanta: Scholars Press.

Buber, Martin. 1947. *Between Man and Man*. Trans. Ronald Gregor Smith. London: Kegan Paul.

Buber, Martin. 1952. *The Eclipse of God*. New York: Harper.

Buber, Martin. 1961. *Tales of the Hasidim: Later Masters*. 2 vols. New York: Schocken. [Originally published 1948.]

Buber, Martin. 1970. *I And Thou*. Trans. Walter Kaufmann. New York: Charles Scribner's Sons. [Originally published 1934.]

Bubis, Gerald. 2002. *The Costs of Jewish Living: Revisiting Jewish Involvements and Barriers*. New York: American Jewish Committee.

Bulmer, Martin. 1979. *Censuses, Surveys and Privacy*. London: Macmillan.

Cardenas, Jose. 1995. "Unruly Teens Packed Off to Mexico." *Los Angeles Times* (December 12): B1, B6.
Clausing, Jeri. 1999. "Revised Banking Legislation Raises Concerns about Privacy." *New York Times* (October 25): C1, C10.
Clergy Advisory Board of the California Consortium to Prevent Child Abuse, in collaboration with The Office of Child Abuse Prevention of the California Department of Social Services. 1994. *Protecting Our Children: Information for Clergy Members about Child Abuse and Neglect*. Sacramento, CA: Author. [Available from The Office of Child Abuse Prevention of the California Department of Social Services, 1600 Sacramento Inn Way, Suite 123, Sacramento, CA 95815; 800-405-KIDS.]
Cloud, Adam. 1999. "Tracking Down Mom: Should Adopted Children Have the Right to Uncover Their Birth Parents?" *Time* (February 22): 64–65.
Cohen, Abraham. 1949. *Everyman's Talmud*. New York: Schocken.
Cohen, Alfred S. 1984. "Privacy: A Jewish Perspective." In *Halacha and Contemporary Society* (193–242). Ed. Alfred S. Cohen. New York: Ktav.
"Congress Dawdles as Deadline for Guarding Medical Data Nears." 1999. *USA Today* (June 11): A25.
"Court Throws Out State's Sodomy Law." 1999. *Los Angeles Times* (February 13): A26.
Courtois, Christine. 1988. *Healing the Incest Wound*. New York: Norton.
Crewdson, J. 1988. *By Silence Betrayed: Sexual Abuse of Children in America*. New York: Harper & Row.
Crossette, Barbara. 1999. "Testing the Limits of Tolerance as Cultures Mix: Does Freedom Mean Accepting Rituals That Repel the West?" *New York Times* (March 6): A15, A17.

Dorff, Elliot N. 1980. "Study Leads to Action." *Religious Education* 75, no. 2 (March–April): 171–192.
Dorff, Elliot N. 1985. " 'Choose Life': A Jewish Perspective on Medical Ethics" (*University Papers*, 4, no. 1). Los Angeles: University of Judaism.
Dorff, Elliot N. 1987. "Training Rabbis in the Land of the Free." In *The Seminary at 100* (11–28). Ed. Nina Beth Cardin and David Wolf Silverman. New York: Jewish Theological Seminary of America.
Dorff, Elliot N. 1989. *Mitzvah Means Commandment*. New York: United Synagogue of America.
Dorff, Elliot N. 1991a. "A Jewish Approach to End-Stage Medical Care." *Conservative Judaism* 43, no. 3 (spring): 3–51.

Dorff, Elliot N. 1991b. "A Time to Live and A Time to Die." *United Synagogue Review* 44, no. 1 (fall): 21–22.

Dorff, Elliot N. 1992. *Knowing God: Jewish Journeys to the Unknowable*. Northvale, NJ: Jason Aronson.

Dorff, Elliot N. 1996a. "Autonomy vs. Community: The Ongoing Reform/Conservative Difference. *Conservative Judaism* 48, no. 2 (winter): 64–68.

Dorff, Elliot N. 1996b. *"This Is My Beloved, This Is My Friend": A Rabbinic Letter on Intimate Relations*. New York: Rabbinical Assembly.

Dorff, Elliot N. 1996c. "Artificial Insemination, Egg Donation, and Adoption." Conservative Judaism 49, no. 1 (fall): 3–60.

Dorff, Elliot N. 1997. "Matters of Degree and Kind: An Open Response to Eugene Borowitz's Open Letter to Me." *Conservative Judaism* 50, no. 1 (fall): 66–71.

Dorff, Elliot N. 1998. *Matters of Life and Death: A Jewish Approach to Modern Medical Ethics*. Philadelphia: Jewish Publication Society.

Dorff, Elliot N. 2002. *To Do the Right and the Good: A Jewish Approach to Modern Social Ethics*. Philadelphia: Jewish Publication Society.

Dorff, Elliot N., and Louis E. Newman, eds. 1995. *Contemporary Jewish Ethics and Morality: A Reader*. New York: Oxford University Press.

Dorff, Elliot N., and Arthur Rosett. 1988. *A Living Tree: The Roots and Growth of Jewish Law*. Albany: State University of New York Press.

Dratch, Mark. 1994. "The Physical, Sexual and Emotional Abuse of Children." In *Shalom Bayit: A Jewish Response to Child Abuse and Domestic Violence* [Orthodox version] (1–8, 59–62). Ed. Ian Russ, Sally Weber, and Ellen Ledley. Los Angeles: Unversity of Judaism and Jewish Family Service of Los Angeles.

"E-Mail Snooping Is OK in the Eyes of the Law." 1996. *Wall Street Journal* (March 19): A1.

Everstine, D., and L. Everstine. 1989. *Sexual Trauma in Children and Adolescents: Dynamics of Treatment*. New York: Brunner/Mazel.

Feldman, David M. 1973. *Marital Relations, Birth Control, and Abortion in Jewish Law*, New York: Schocken. [Originally published as *Birth Control in Jewish Law*, 1968.]

Finkelhor, David. 1994. "Current Information on the Scope and Nature of Child Abuse." In *The Future of Children* 4, no. 12, 31–53. Los Altos, CA: Center for the Future of Children of the David and Lucille Packard Foundation.

Finkelstein, Louis. 1924. *Jewish Self-Government in the Middle Ages*. New York: Jewish Theological Seminary of America.

Foote, Donna. 2000. "The War of the Wills," *Newsweek* (fall–winter): 66–67. [Special edition.]

Freehof, Solomon. 1960. *Reform Responsa*. Cincinnati: Hebrew Union College Press.

Freehof, Solomon. 1977. *Reform Responsa for Our Time*. Cincinnati: Hebrew Union College Press.

Fried, Bette. 1995. "Responding to Domestic Violence: A Progress Report." *United Synagogue Review* 47, no. 2 (spring): 15–16, 23.

Fried, Charles. 1983. "Privacy." *Yale Law Journal* 77, no. 3 (January): 475–493.

Friedenwald, Harry. 1967. *The Jews and Medicine: Essays*. 2 vols. New York: Ktav. [Originally published 1944.]

Fromm, Eric. 1956. *The Art of Loving*. New York: Harper & Row.

Gaon, Saadia. 1960. "Books of Doctrines and Beliefs." In *Three Jewish Philosophers* (part II, 25–191). Ed. Hans Lewy, Alexander Altman, and Isaak Heinemann. Philadelphia: Jewish Publication Society.

Gavison, Ruth. 1980. "Privacy and the Limits of the Law." *Yale Law Journal* 89, no. 3, 421–471.

Gershoff, Elizabeth Thompson. 2002. "Corporal Punishment by Parents and Associated Child Behaviors and Experiences: A Meta-Analytic and Theoretical Review." *Psychological Bulletin* 128, no. 4 (July): 539–579, 602–611.

Gibbs, Nancy. 2002. "Making Time for a Baby." *Time* (April 15): 48–58.

Gilligan, Carol. 1982. *In a Different Voice*. Cambridge, MA: Harvard University Press.

Gindin, Susan E. 1997. "Lost and Found in Cyberspace: Informational Privacy in the Age of the Internet." *San Diego Law Review* 34, no. 3 (summer): 1153–1223.

Gleick, Elizabeth. 1995. "Should This Marriage Be Saved?" *Time* (February 27): 48–56.

Gold, Michael. 1988. *And Hannah Wept: Infertility, Adoption and the Jewish Couple*. Philadelphia: Jewish Publication Society.

Gold, Michael. 1992. *Does God Belong in the Bedroom?* Philadelphia: Jewish Publication Society.

Goldberg, Michael. 1985. *Jews and Christians Getting Our Stories Straight: The Exodus and the Passion-Resurrection*. Nashville, TN: Abingdon.

Goldfarb, Daniel C. 1976. "The Definition of Death." *Conservative Judaism* 30, no. 2 (winter): 10–22.

Goldman, Alex J. 1978. *Judaism Confronts Contemporary Issues*. New York: Ktav.

Gordis, Robert. 1990. *The Dynamics of Judaism: A Study in Jewish Law*. Bloomington: Indiana University Press.

Gorman, Christine. 1995. "Memory on Trial." *Time* (April 17): 54–55.

Graetz, Naomi. 1992. "The Haftorah Tradition and the Metaphoric Battering of Hosea's Wife." *Conservative Judaism* 45, no. 1 (fall): 29–42.

Graetz, Naomi. 1998. *Silence Is Deadly: Judaism Confronts Wifebeating*. Northvale, NJ: Jason Aronson.

Greenberg, Simon. 1977. *The Ethical in the Jewish and American Heritage*. New York: Jewish Theological Seminary of America.

Grossman, Avraham. 1991. "Medieval Rabbinic Views on Wife-Beating, 800–1300." *Jewish History* 5, no. 1 (spring): 53–62.

Hadas, Moses. 1959. *Hellenistic Culture*. New York: Columbia University Press.

Harlow, Jules. 1985. *Siddur Sim Shalom*. New York: Rabbinical Assembly and United Synagogue of Conservative Judaism.

Hartman, David. 1997. *A Living Covenant: The Innovative Spirit in Traditional Judaism*. Woodstock, VT: Jewish Lights. [Originally published 1985.]

Healy, Melissa. 1999. "Abortion Consent Bill Passes in House." *Los Angeles Times* (July 1): A13.

Heise, Lori, Mary Ellsberg, and Megan Gottemoeller. 1999. "Ending Violence against Women." *Population Reports* ser. L, no. 11 [Special Issue].

Held, Virginia. 2002. "Feminist Transformations of Moral Theory." In *Morality and Moral Controversies* (53–58). 6th ed. Ed. John Arthur. Upper Saddle River, NJ: Prentice-Hall.

Helm, Leslie. 1999. "Productivity Jumps with Help from Net." *Los Angeles Times* (June 30): A1, A12–A13.

Herbert, Wray. 1999. "When Strangers Become Family." *U.S. News and World Report* (November 29): 58–67.

Herman, Judith Lewis, with Lisa Hirschman. 1981. *Father-Daughter Incest*. Cambridge, MA: Harvard University Press.

Herman, Pini. 1997. *Los Angeles Jewish Population Study 1997*. Los Angeles: Jewish Federation of Los Angeles.

Herring, Basil. 1984. *Jewish Ethics and Halakhah for Our Time*. New York: Ktav and Yeshiva University Press.

Herring, Basil. 1989. *Jewish Ethics and Halakhah for Our Time*. Vol. 2. New York: Ktav and Yeshiva University Press.

Hertz, Joseph. 1938. *The Pentateuch and Haftorahs*. London: Soncino.

Heschel, Abraham Joshua. 1955. *God in Search of Man*. New York: Harper & Row.

Heschel, Abraham Joshua. 1962. *The Prophets*. Philadelphia: Jewish Publication Society.

Hirsch, Samson Raphael. 1956. *Judaism Eternal*. 2 vols. Ed. and trans. Isidor Grunfeld. London: Soncino.

Holden, George W. 2002. "Perspectives on the Effects of Corporal Punishment: Comment on Gershoff." *Psychological Bulletin* 128, no. 4 (July): 590–595.

Hotchkin, Sheila. 2000. "Violence against Women Called Global Health Problem." *USA Today* (January 21): A4.

Israeli, Saul. 1965 (5725). "Emigrating to Israel against the Will of Parents" (Hebrew). In *Shanah be'Shanah* (143–146). Ed. Saul Israeli. Jerusalem: Heikhal Shelomoh.

Jacob, Walter, Leonard S. Kravitz, W. Gunther Plaut, Harry A. Roth, A. Soloff, Bernard Zlotowitz. 1983. "Euthanasia." *American Reform Responsa*. New York: Central Conference of American Rabbis.

Jakobovits, Immanuel. 1975. *Jewish Medical Ethics*. New York: Bloch. [Originally published 1959.]

Jakobovits, Yoel. 1989. "[Brain Death and] Heart Transplants: The [Israeli] Chief Rabbinate's Directives." *Tradition* 24, no. 4 (summer): 1–14.

Jasinski, Jana L., and Linda M. Williams, eds. 1998. *Partner Violence: A Comprehensive Review of 20 Years of Research*. Thousand Oaks, CA: Sage.

Jewish Theological Seminary of America. 1992. "High Holy Day Message." *Newsweek* (September 28) and *Wall Street Journal* (September 28). [Also published October 1 in *New York Times* and *Wall Street Journal*.]

Johnson, John. 1996. "A New Side to Domestic Violence." *Los Angeles Times* (April 27): A1, A19.

Jones, Lisa, and David Finkelhor. 2001. "The Decline in Child Sexual Abuse Cases." *Juvenile Justice Bulletin* (January): 1–12.

Junod, Tom. 1994. "Someone Else's Child." *GQ* (December): 258–266.

Kanin, Eugene J. 1994. "False Rape Allegations." *Archives of Sexual Behavior* 23, no. 1 (February): 81–92.

Kant, Immanuel. 1994. *Grounding for the Metaphysics of Morals*. Trans. James W. Ellington. In *Moral Philosophy: A Comprehensive Introduction* (271–285). Ed. Brooke Noel Moore and Robert Michael Stewart. Mountain View: CA: Mayfield. [Originally published 1785.]

Kaplan, Mordecai M. 1937. *The Meaning of God in Modern Jewish Religion*. New York: Behrman House.

Kaplan, Mordecai M. 1948. *The Future of the American Jew*. New York: Macmillan.

Kaplan, Mordecai M. 1957, 1963. *Basic Values in Jewish Religion*. New York: Reconstructionist Press.

Kaplan, Mordecai M. 1970. *The Religion of Ethical Nationhood*. New York: Macmillan.

Katner, David R. 1996. "The Ethical Dilemma Awaiting Counsel Who Represent Adolescents with HIV/AIDS: Criminal Law and Tort Suits Pressure Counsel to Breach the Confidentiality of the Clients' Medical Status." *Tulane Law Review* 70 (June): 2311–2344.

Katz, Sedelle, and Mary Ann Mazur. 1979. *Understanding the Rape Victim: A Synthesis of Research Findings*. New York: Wiley.

Kirn, Walter. 2000. "Divorce: The Debate: Should You Stay Together for the Kids?" *Time*, September 25, pp. 74–88.

Kirschenbaum, Aaron. 1970. *Self-Incrimination in Jewish Law*. New York: Burning Bush Press.

Klein, Isaac. 1979. *A Guide to Jewish Religious Practice*. New York: Jewish Theological Seminary of America.

Konvitz, Milton R. 1978. *Judaism and the American Idea*. New York: Schocken.

Kosmin, Barry, Sidney Goldstein, Joesph Waksberg, Nava Lerer, Ariella Keysar, Jeffrey Scheckner. 1991. *Highlights of the CJF 1990 National Jewish Population Survey*. New York: Council of Jewish Federations.

Krauss, Simcha. 1982. "Litigation in Secular Courts." *Journal of Halacha and Contemporary Society* 3 (?): 35–??. Also available at www.jlaw.com/Articles/litigation_in_secular_courts1.html.

Kushner, Harold. 1981. *When Bad Things Happen to Good People*. New York: Schocken.

Lamm, Maurice. 1995. *The Power of Hope: The One Essential of Life and Love*. New York: Rawson Associates (Scribner's).

Lamm, Norman. 1967. "The Fourth Amendment and Its Equivalent in the Halacha." *Judaism* 16, no. 4 (fall): 300–312.

Lamm, Norman. 1971. *Faith and Doubt: Studies in Traditional Jewish Thought*. New York: Ktav.

Lappe, Benay. 1993. *Does a Child Who Has Been Sexually Abused by a Parent Have the Obligation to Say Kaddish for That Parent: A Teshuvah*. M.H.L. thesis. University of Judaism, Los Angeles.

Levinas, Emanuel. 1985. *Ethics and Infinity*. Trans. Richard A. Cohen. Pittsburgh, PA: University of Pittsburgh Press.

Lewy, Hans, Alexander Altman, and Isaak Heinemann, eds. 1960. *Three Jewish Philosophers*. Philadelphia: Jewish Publication Society.

Louisell, David W., John Kaplan, and Jon R. Waltz. 1976. *Cases and Materials on Evidence*. 3rd. ed. Mineola, NY: Foundation Press.

MacIntyre, Alasdair. 1967. "Egoism and Altruism." In *The Encyclopedia of Philosophy*. Vol. 2 (463–466). Ed. Paul Edwards. New York: Macmillan.

Mackler, Aaron L. 1995. "Cases and Principles in Jewish Bioethics: Toward a Holistic Model." In *Contemporary Jewish Ethics and Morality: A Reader* (177–183). Ed. Elliot N. Dorff and Louis E. Newman. New York: Oxford University Press.

Mackler, Aaron L., ed. 2000. *Life and Death Responsibilities in Jewish Biomedical Ethics*. New York: Jewish Theological Seminary of America.

Maller, Allen S. March 20, 1992. "Gilgul, Dybbuks, and the Afterlife." *Heritage*, 5.

Marcus, David. 1994. "False Rape Reports." Unpublished manuscript.

McClendon, James William Jr. 1974. *Biography as Theology*. Nashville, TN: Abingdon Press.

Meier, Levi. 1977. "Filial Responsibility to the Senile Parent: A Jewish Approach." *Journal of Psychology and Judaism* 2, no. 1 (fall): 45–53.

Michael, Robert T., John H. Gagnon, Edward O. Laumann, and Gina Kolata. 1994. *Sex in America: Definitive Survey.* Boston: Little, Brown.

Milgrom, Jacob. 1991. *Leviticus 1–16: A New Translation with Introduction and Commentary* (The Anchor Bible, vol. 3). New York: Doubleday.

Mill, John Stuart. 1994. *Utilitarianism.* In *Moral Philosophy: A Comprehensive Introduction* (295-328). Ed. Brooke Noel Moore and Robert Michael Stewart. Mountain View: CA: Mayfield. [Originally published 1863.]

Miller, Greg. 1999. "Consumer Privacy May Be More Secure Online Than Off." *Los Angeles Times* (May 13): A1, A8.

Miller, Greg. 2000. "High-Tech Snooping All in Day's Work." *Los Angeles Times* (October 29): A1, A26, A27.

Morell, Samuel. 1982. "An Equal or a Ward: How Independent Is a Married Woman According to Rabbinic Law?" *Jewish Social Studies* 44, nos. 3–4 (summer–fall): 190–201.

Nevins, Michael. 1996. *The Jewish Doctor: A Narrative History.* Northvale, NJ: Jason Aronson.

"New Law Cracks Down on Domestic Abuse, Global Sex Trade." 2000. *San Francisco Examiner* (October 29): A16.

Nietzsche, Friedrich. 1994. *Beyond Good and Evil.* Trans. Helen Zimmern. In *Moral Philosophy: A Comprehensive Introduction* (331–337). Ed. Brooke Noel Moore and Robert Michael Stewart. Mountain View: CA: Mayfield. [Originally published 1885.]

Noddings, Nel. 1984. *Caring: A Feminist Approach to Ethics and Moral Education.* Berkeley: University of California Press.

Novak, David. 1983. *The Image of the Non-Jew in Judaism.* New York: Edwin Mellon.

Novick, Bernard. 1980. *In God's Image: Making Jewish Decisions about the Body.* New York: United Synagogue of America.

Olitzky, Kerry M., and Stuart A. Copans. 1991. *Twelve Jewish Steps to Recovery.* Woodstock, VT: Jewish Lights.

"One Size of Condom Doesn't Fit All." 1994. *Men's Health* (March): 27.

"Parents Who Kill Their Children." 1995. *U.S. News and World Report* (May 8): 14.

Parke, Ross D. 2002. "Punishment Revisited—Science, Values, and the Right Question: Comment on Gershoff." *Psychological Bulletin* 128, no. 4 (2002): 596–601.

Paul, Shalom. 1969. "Exodus 21:10: A Threefold Maintenance Clause." *Journal of Near Eastern Studies* 28, no. 1, 48–51.

Pear, Robert. 1999. "Clinton to Unveil Rules to Protect Medical Privacy." *New York Times* (October 27): A1, A18.

Phillips, Bruce A. 1997. *Re-Examining Intermarriage: Trends, Textures, Strategies*. Brookline, MA: Wilstein Institute of Jewish Policy Studies at Hebrew College and New York: American Jewish Committee.

Phillips, Bruce A. 1998. *Reexamining Intermarriage: Trends, Textures, and Strategies: Report of a New Study*. Boston: Wilstein Institute of Jewish Policy Studies, and New York: American Jewish Committee.

Piller, Charles. 1993. "Bosses with X-Ray Eyes." *MacWorld* (July): 118–123.

Pliskin, Zelig. 1975. *Guard Your Tongue*. Jerusalem: Aish Ha-Torah.

Prosser, William L. 1960. "Privacy." *California Law Review* 48 (August): 383–423.

Rabbinical Assembly. 1983. *Proceedings of the Rabbinical Assembly*. Vol. 44. New York: Author.

Rabbinical Assembly. 1990. *Proceedings of the Rabbinical Assembly Proceedings*. Vol. 52. New York: Author.

Rakover, Nahum. n.d. *The Protection of Individual Modesty* (Hebrew). Jerusalem: Attorney General's Office.

Reisner, Avram. 1991. "A Halakhic Ethic of Care for the Terminally Ill." *Conservative Judaism* 43, no. 3 (spring): 52–89.

Reisner, Avram. 2001. "On the Conversion of Adopted and Patrilineal Children." In *Proceedings of the Committee on Jewish Law and Standards of the Conservative Movement, 1986–1990* (157–183). Ed. Rabbinical Assembly. New York: Editor. [Originally published 1988.]

Religious Education. 1994. Vol. 89, no. 4. [Special issue.]

Riemer, Jack, and Nathaniel Stampfer, eds. 1983. *Ethical Wills: A Modern Jewish Treasury*. New York: Schocken.

Riemer, Jack, and Nathaniel Stampfer, eds. 1991. *So That Your Values Live on—Ethical Wills and How to Prepare Them*. Woodstock, VT: Jewish Lights.

Roan, Shari. 1996. "Law against Domestic Abuse May Be Backfiring." *Los Angeles Times* (December 25): A1.

Rosenzweig, Franz. 1955. "The Builders." In *On Jewish Learning* (72–92). Ed. and trans. Nahum Glatzer. New York: Schocken.

Ross, W. D. 1930. *The Right and the Good*. Oxford: Oxford University Press.

Rubenstein, Richard. 1996. *After Auschwitz*. 2nd ed. Baltimore: Johns Hopkins University Press.

Rubenstein, William B. 1997. *Cases and Materials on Sexual Orientation and the Law*. 2nd ed. St. Paul: West Publishing.

Rubin, Alissa J. 1999. "House Approves Disclosure of Private Medical Records." *Los Angeles Times* (July 2): A1, A15.

Ruffman, Deborah. 2001. *Sex and Sensibility: The Thinking Parent's Guide to Talking Sense about Sex*. Cambridge, MA: Perseus Books.

Russ, Ian, Sally Weber, and Ellen Ledley, eds. 1993. *Shalom Bayit: A Jewish Response to Child Abuse and Domestic Violence*. Los Angeles: Shalom Bayit Committee of Jewish Family Service of Los Angeles and the University of Judaism. [Available from The Family Violence Project, Jewish Family Service of Los Angeles, 22622 Vanowen St., West Hills, CA 91307; 818-587-3333. An edition for the Orthodox community is also available.]

Sarna, Nahum. 1991. *The JPS Torah Commentary: Exodus*. Philadelphia: Jewish Publication Society.
Sauerwein, Kristina. 1994. "The Dating Dilemma." *Los Angeles Times* (December 28): E2, E4.
Savage, David G. 1996. "Supreme Court to Decide Issue of Right to Die." *Los Angeles Times* (October 2): A16.
Schacht, J. 1964. *An Introduction to Islamic Law*. Oxford: Oxford University Press.
Schachter, Herschel. 1981. "*Dina deMalchusa Dina*." *Journal of Halacha and Contemporary Society* 1, no. 1 (spring): 103–132.
Scheer, Robert. 1988. "Jews in U.S. Committed to Equality." *Los Angeles Times* (April 13): I1, I14–I15.
Scheindlin, Raymond P. 1986 *Wine, Woman, and Death. Medieval Hebrew Poems on the Good Life*. Philadelphia: Jewish Publication Society.
Schochetman, Eliav. 1992. "On the Nature of the Rules Governing Custody of Children in Jewish Law." *The Jewish Law Annual*. Vol. 10 (115–158). Philadelphia: Harwood Academic.
Schulman, Michael, and Eva Mckler 1985. *Bringing Up a Moral Child: A New Approach for Teaching Your Child to Be Kind, Just, and Responsible*. Reading, MA: Addison-Wesley.
Schulweis, Harold. 1982. "The Single Mirror of Jewish Images: The Pluralistic Character of Jewish Ethics" (*University Papers*, 1, no. 2). Los Angeles: University of Judaism.
Schulweis, Harold. 1994. *For Those Who Can't Believe: Overcoming the Obstacles to Faith*. New York: HarperCollins.
Segal, Benjamin J. 1987. *Returning: The Land of Israel as Focus in Jewish History*. Jerusalem: Department of Education and Culture of the World Zionist Organization.
Shalala, Donna E. 2002. "A Loss to Medical Privacy." *New York Times* (March 30): A1.
Shils, Edward Albert. 1956. *The Torment of Secrecy: The Background and Consequences of American Security Policies*. Glencoe, IL: Free Press.
Siegel, Seymour. 1976. "Updating the Criteria of Death." *Conservative Judaism* 30, no. 2 (winter): 23–30.
Simon, Roger, and Angie Cannon. 2001. "An Amazing Journey: The Mirror of the Census Reveals the Character of a Nation." *U.S. News and World Report* (August 6): 11–18.

357

Sinclair, Daniel. 1989. *Tradition and the Biological Revolution: The Application of Jewish Law to the Treatment of the Critically Ill.* Edinburgh, UK: Edinburgh University Press.

Singer, David, and Lawrence Grossman, eds. 2001. *American Jewish Year Book.* New York: American Jewish Committee.

Spero, Shubert. 1983. *Morality, Halakha, and the Jewish Tradition.* New York: Ktav and Yeshiva University Press.

Spitz, Elie. 1986. "Jewish and American Law on the Cutting Edge of Privacy: Computers in the Business Sector" (*University Papers*, 6, no. 1). Los Angeles: University of Judaism.

Springen, Karen, 2000. "On Spanking: New Survey Shows Many Parents Think It's OK." *Newsweek* (October 16): 64.

St. John, Warren. 2002. "Young, Single and Dating at Hyperspeed." *New York Times* (April 21): sec. 9, pp. 1–2.

Sturman, Gladys. 1992. "Privacy, Clearly a Goyish Invention." *Sh'ma* 22, no. 430 (March 20): 73.

Tannen, Deborah. 1990. *You Just Don't Understand: Women and Men in Conversation.* New York: Ballantine.

Tavani, Herman. 1996. "Computer and Privacy [A Bibliography]." Available at www.siu.edu/departments/coba/mgmt/iswnet/ isethics/biblio/part8.htm. Accessed: November 10, 2002.

Torrey, Morrison. 1991. "When Will We Be Believed? Rape Myths and the Idea of a Fair Trial in Rape Prosecutions." *University of California at Davis Law Review* 24, no. 4 (summer): 1013–1071.

Tucker, Gordon. 1984. "The Confidentiality Rule: A Philosophical Perspective with Reference to Jewish Law and Ethics." *Fordham Urban Law Journal* 13, no. 1, 99–112.

United Jewish Communities, 2002. "U.S. Jewish Population Fairly Stable Over Decade According to Results of National Jewish Population Survey 2000–01." Press Release (October 8). www.UJC.org/NJPS.

U.S. Advisory Board on Child Abuse and Neglect. 1995. *A Nation's Shame: Fatal Child Abuse and Neglect in the United States,* 5th report. Washington, DC: Author.

U.S. Congress, Office of Technology Assessment. May 1988. *Infertility: Medical and Social Change* [OTA-BA-358]. Washington, DC: U.S. Government Printing Office.

Valby, Karen. 2002. "Monitor." *Entertainment Weekly* (April 19): 12.

Van Buren, Abigail. 1995. "Not All Spouse Abusers Are Men." *Los Angeles Times* (May 28): E2

Wallerstein, Judith, Julia Lewis, and Sandy Blakeslee. 2000a. *The Unexpected Legacy of Divorce: A 25-Year Landmark Sudy.* New York: Hyperion.

358

Wallerstein, Judith, Julia Lewis, and Sandy Blakeslee. 2000b. "Divorce: Book Excerpt: Fear of Falling." *Time* (September 25): 85–88.

Warren, Samuel D., and Louis D. Brandeis. 1890. "The Right to Privacy." *Harvard Law Review* 4, no. 5 (December): 193–220. [Reprinted as "The Right to Privacy in Nineteenth-Century America" in *Harvard Law Review* 94, no. 8 (June 1981): 1892–1910.]

Wasserstrum, Richard A., ed. 1985. *Today's Moral Problems.* 3rd ed. New York: Macmillan.

Weinhouse, Beth. 1994. "Is There a Right Time to Have a Baby? The Yes, No, and Maybe of Pregnancy at 20, 30, 40." *Glamour* (May): 251, 276, 285–287.

Weinstein, Karen, Gina M. Reese, Roger R. Grass, and Arthur Goldberg. 1996. *Confidentiality in Children's Records in California.* Altoona, WI: Medical Educational Services.

Wertheimer, Jack. 1999. "Jewish Education in the United States: Recent Trends and Issues." In *American Jewish Year Book 1999* (3–118). Ed. David Singer and Ruth R. Seldin. New York: American Jewish Committee; Philadelphia: Jewish Publication Society.

Westin, P., and F. Allan. 1967. *Privacy and Freedom.* New York: Atheneum.

Whitman, David. 1997. "The Trouble with Premarital Sex." *U.S. News and World Report* (May 19): 56–64.

Wiesenthal, Simon. 1976. *The Sunflower; with a Symposium.* New York: Schocken.

Williams, Carol J. 1999. "Germans Speak Up to Defend European Union Privacy Laws." *Los Angeles Times* (April 2): A5.

Wingert, Pat, and Eloise Salholz. 1992. "Irreconcilable Differences." *Newsweek* (September 21): 84–90.

Yovich, John, and Gedis Grudzinskas. 1990. *The Management of Infertility.* Oxford, UK: Heinemann Medical.

Zelin, Judy E. 1996. "Annotation: Physician's Tort Liability for Unauthorized Disclosure of Confidential Information about Patient." *American Law Reports* 48, no. 4 (4th ser.): 668–713. [See also the supplement to *American Law Reports* 1997.]

Zoloth-Dorfman, Laurie. 1995. "An Ethics of Encounter: Public Choices and Private Acts." In *Contemporary Jewish Ethics and Morality: A Reader* (219–245). Ed. Elliot N. Dorff and Louis E. Newman, New York: Oxford University Press.

Index